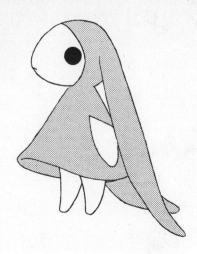

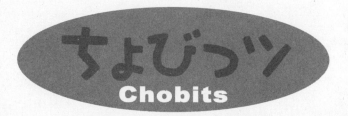
ちょびっツ
Chobits

CLAMP

Satsuki Igarashi
Nanase Ohkawa
Mick Nekoi
Mokona Apapa

ALSO AVAILABLE FROM 🐟 TOKYOPOP®

MANGA

ANGELIC LAYER*
BABY BIRTH* (September 2003)
BATTLE ROYALE*
BRAIN POWERED* (June 2003)
BRIGADOON* (August 2003)
CARDCAPTOR SAKURA
CARDCAPTOR SAKURA: MASTER OF THE CLOW*
CLAMP SCHOOL DETECTIVES*
CHOBITS*
CHRONICLES OF THE CURSED SWORD (July 2003)
CLOVER
CONFIDENTIAL CONFESSIONS* (July 2003)
CORRECTOR YUI
COWBOY BEBOP*
COWBOY BEBOP: SHOOTING STAR* (June 2003)
DEMON DIARY (May 2003)
DIGIMON*
DRAGON HUNTER (June 2003)
DRAGON KNIGHTS*
DUKLYON: CLAMP SCHOOL DEFENDERS* (September 2003)
ERICA SAKURAZAWA* (May 2003)
ESCAFLOWNE* (July 2003)
FAKE*(May 2003)
FLCL* (September 2003)
FORBIDDEN DANCE* (August 2003)
GATEKEEPERS*
G-GUNDAM* (June 2003)
GRAVITATION* (June 2003)
GTO*
GUNDAM WING
GUNDAM WING: ENDLESS WALTZ*
GUNDAM: THE LAST OUTPOST*
HAPPY MANIA*
HARLEM BEAT
INITIAL D*
I.N.V.U.
ISLAND
JING: KING OF BANDITS* (June 2003)
JULINE
KARE KANO*
KINDAICHI CASEFILES* (June 2003)
KING OF HELL (June 2003)

KODOCHA*
LOVE HINA*
LUPIN III*
MAGIC KNIGHT RAYEARTH* (August 2003)
MAN OF MANY FACES* (May 2003)
MARMALADE BOY*
MARS*
MIRACLE GIRLS
MIYUKI-CHAN IN WONDERLAND* (October 2003)
MONSTERS, INC.
NIEA_7* (August 2003)
PLANET LADDER*
PARADISE KISS*
PARASYTE
PEACH GIRL
PEACH GIRL: CHANGE OF HEART*
PET SHOP OF HORRORS* (June 2003)
PLANETS* (October 2003)
PRIEST
RAGNAROK
RAVE MASTER*
REAL BOUT HIGH SCHOOL*
REALITY CHECK
REBIRTH
REBOUND*
SABRE MARIONETTE J* (July 2003)
SAILOR MOON
SAINT TAIL
SAMURAI DEEPER KYO* (June 2003)
SCRYED*
SHAOLIN SISTERS*
SHIRAHIME-SYO* (December 2003)
THE SKULL MAN*
SORCERER HUNTERS
TOKYO MEW MEW*
UNDER A GLASS MOON (June 2003)
VAMPIRE GAME* (June 2003)
WILD ACT* (July 2003)
WISH*
X-DAY* (August 2003)
ZODIAC P.I.* (July 2003)

CINE-MANGA™

AKIRA*
CARDCAPTORS
JIMMY NEUTRON (COMING SOON)
KIM POSSIBLE
LIZZIE McGUIRE
SPONGEBOB SQUAREPANTS (COMING SOON)
SPY KIDS 2

NOVELS

SAILOR MOON
KARMA CLUB (COMING SOON)

TOKYOPOP KIDS

STRAY SHEEP (September 2003)

ART BOOKS

CARDCAPTOR SAKURA*
MAGIC KNIGHT RAYEARTH*

ANIME GUIDES

GUNDAM TECHNICAL MANUALS
COWBOY BEBOP
SAILOR MOON SCOUT GUIDES

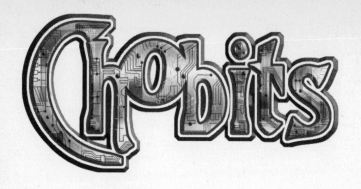

Volume 1 of 8

Story and Art By
CLAMP

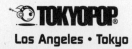
Los Angeles • Tokyo

Translator – Shirley Kubo
English Adaptation – Jake Forbes
Retouch & Lettering – Anna Kernbaum
Production Specialist – Dolly Chan
Associate Editors – Stephanie Donelly and Robert Coyner

Editor – Jake Forbes
Production Coordinator - Antonio DePietro
Production Manager- Jennifer Miller
Art Director – Matt Alford
Editorial Director – Jeremy Ross
VP Production & Manufacturing– Ron Klamert
President & C.O.O. – John Parker
Publisher & C.E.O. - Stuart Levy

Email: editor@TOKYOPOP.com
Come visit us online at www.TOKYOPOP.com

A 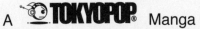 Manga

TOKYOPOP® Manga is an imprint of Mixx Entertainment, Inc.
5900 Wilshire Blvd. Ste 2000, Los Angeles, CA 90036

ISBN: 1-59182-153-3

First TOKYOPOP® printing: April 2003

10 9 8 7 6 5

Manufactured in Canada

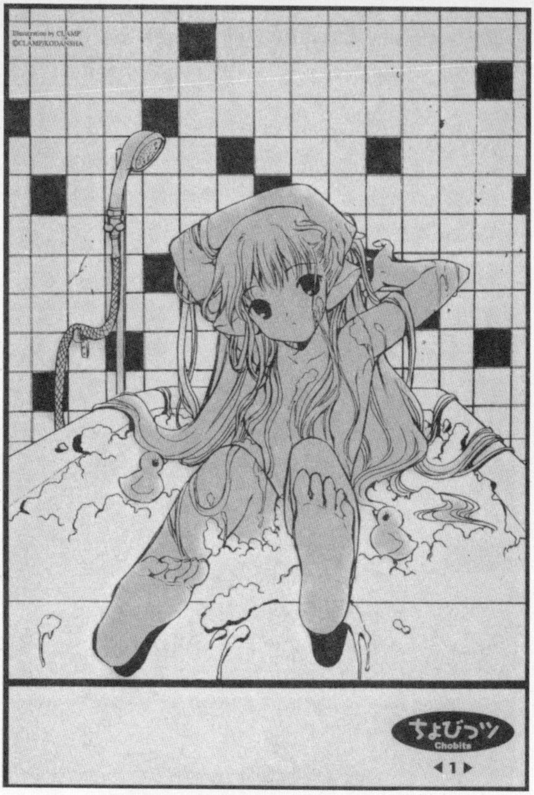
©CLAMP/KODANSHA
ちょびっツ
Chobits
1

www.Contents.com

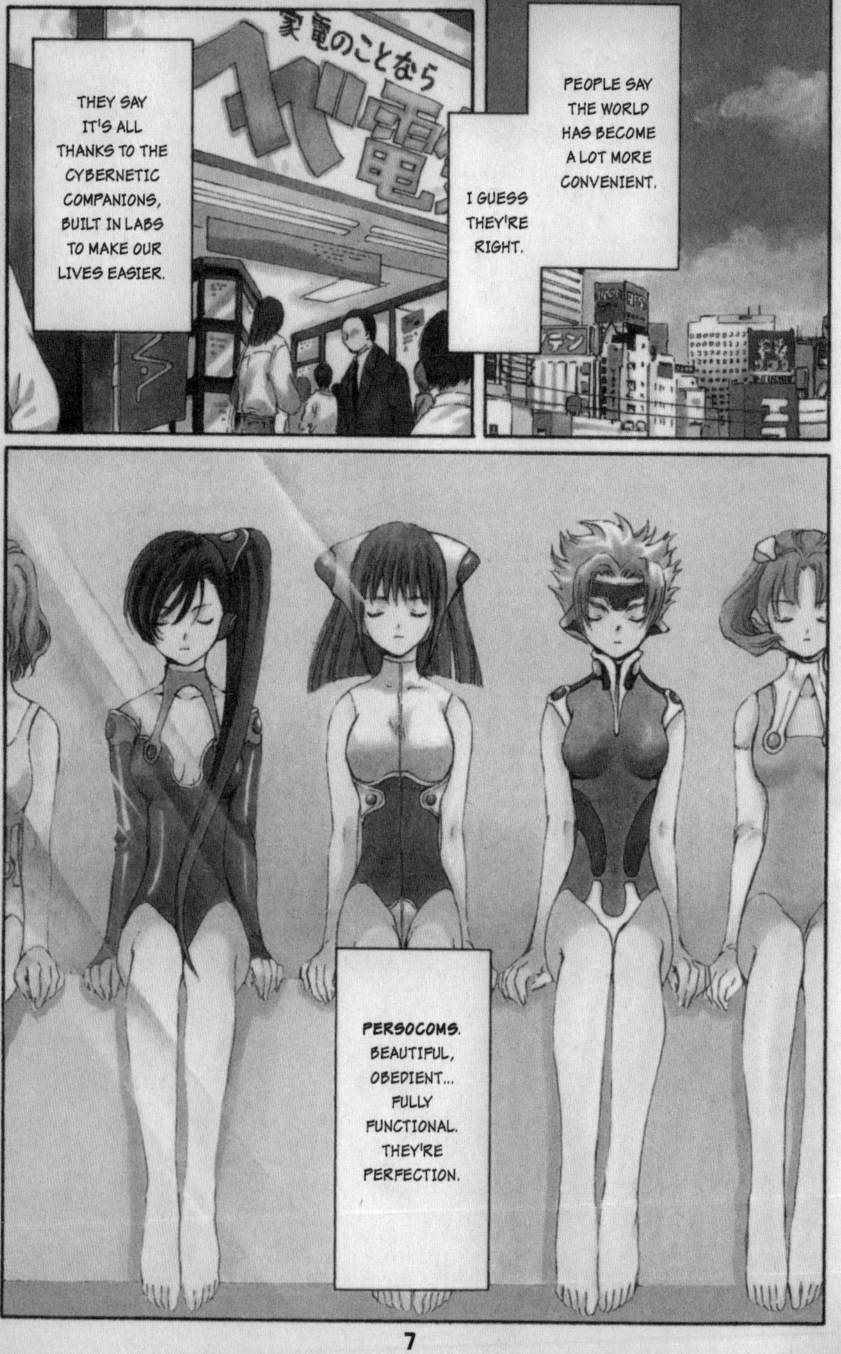
PEOPLE SAY THE WORLD HAS BECOME A LOT MORE CONVENIENT.
I GUESS THEY'RE RIGHT.
家電のことなら
THEY SAY IT'S ALL THANKS TO THE CYBERNETIC COMPANIONS, BUILT IN LABS TO MAKE OUR LIVES EASIER.
PERSOCOMS. BEAUTIFUL, OBEDIENT... FULLY FUNCTIONAL. THEY'RE PERFECTION.

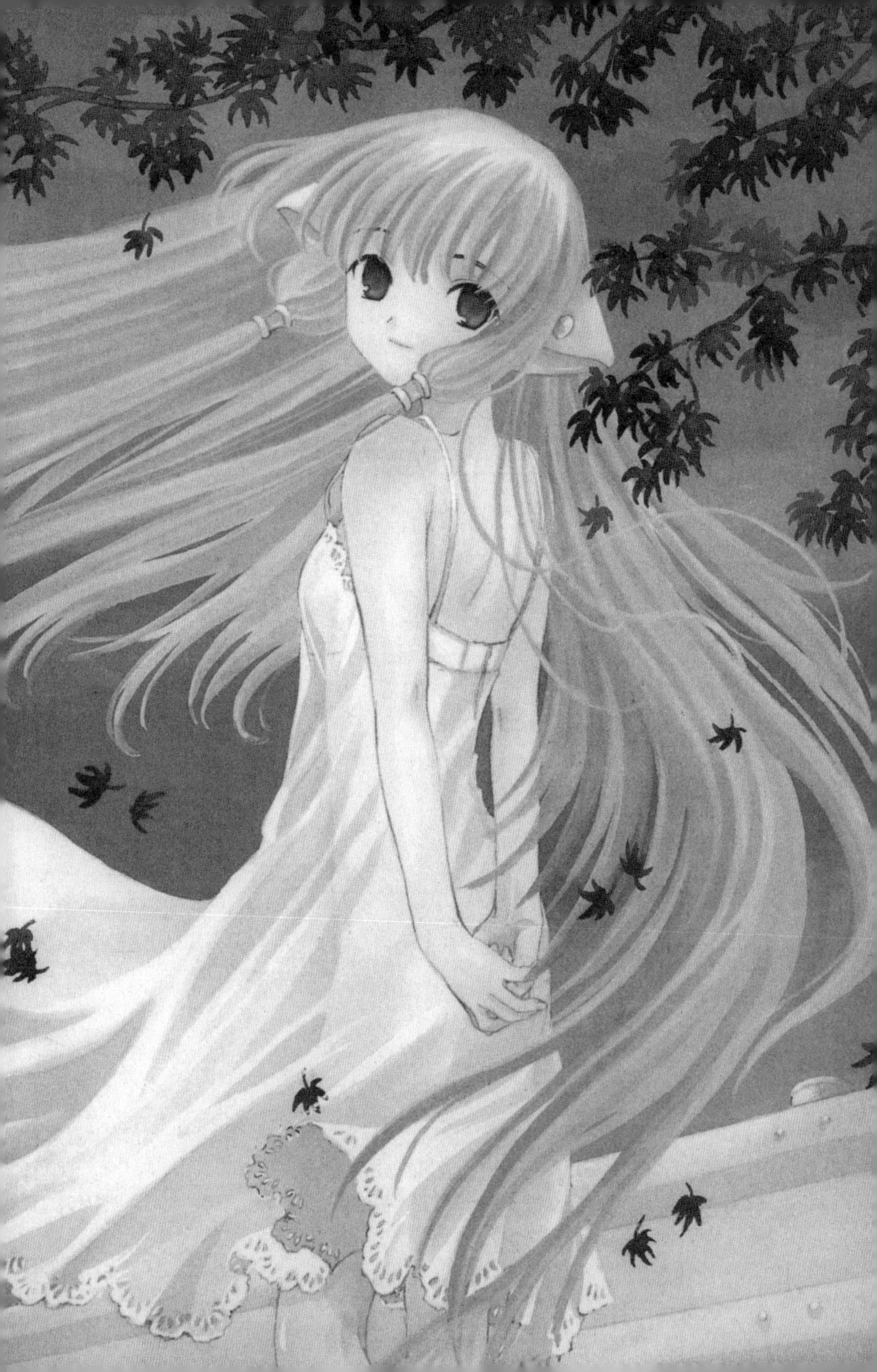

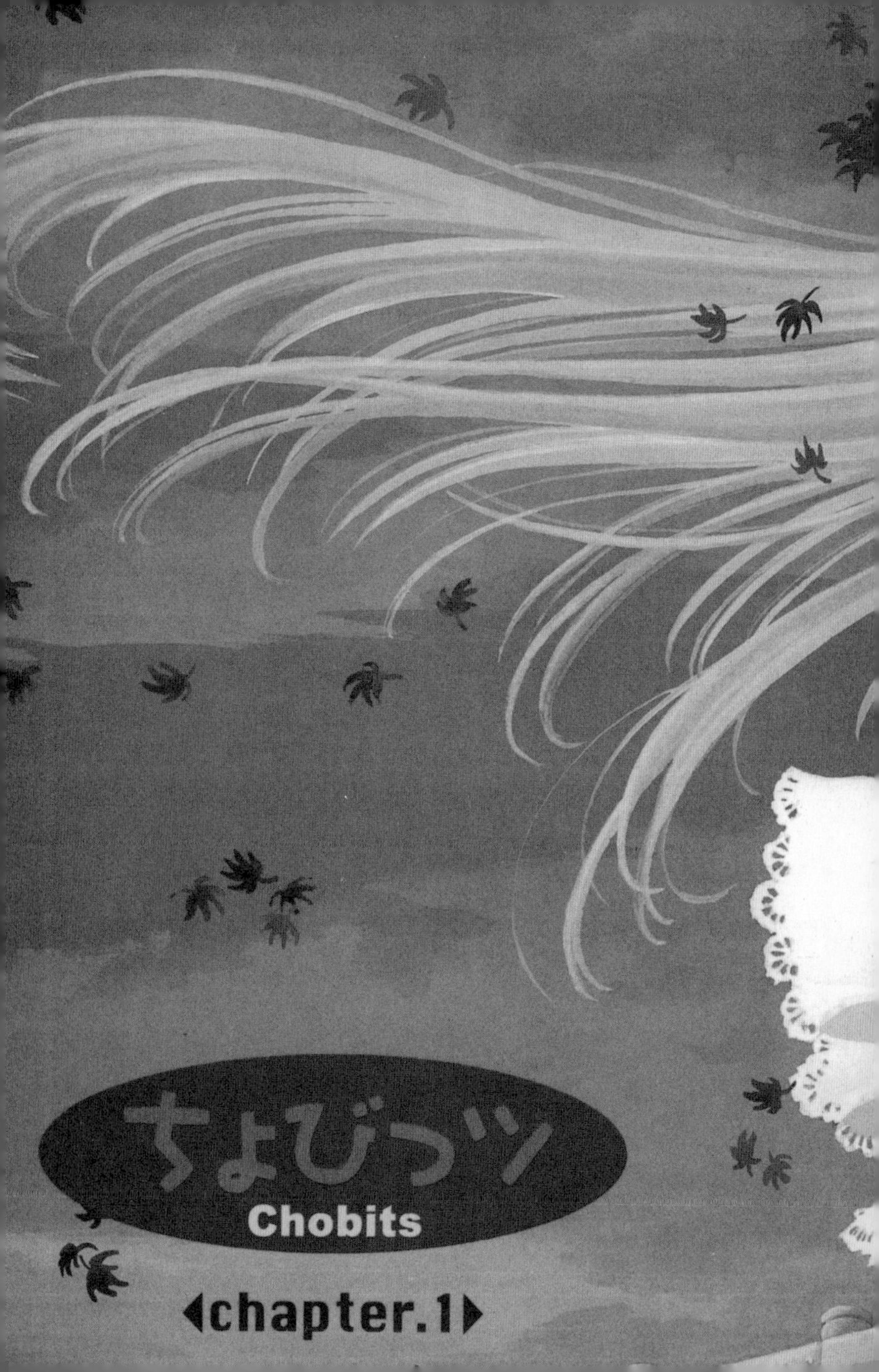
ちょびっツ
Chobits
chapter.1

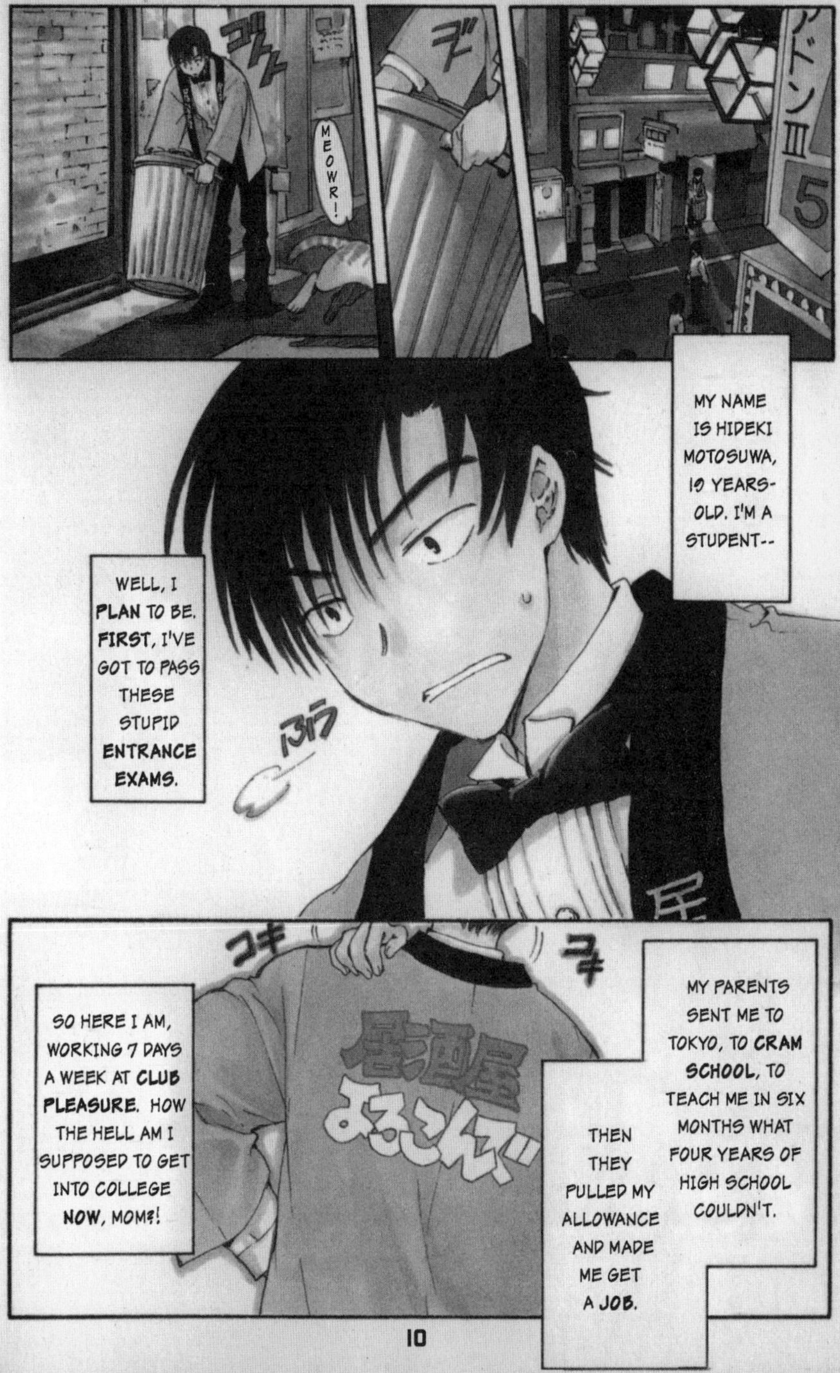
MEOWR!
MY NAME IS HIDEKI MOTOSUWA, 19 YEARS-OLD. I'M A STUDENT--
WELL, I **PLAN** TO BE. **FIRST**, I'VE GOT TO PASS THESE STUPID **ENTRANCE EXAMS**.
MY PARENTS SENT ME TO TOKYO, TO **CRAM SCHOOL**, TO TEACH ME IN SIX MONTHS WHAT FOUR YEARS OF HIGH SCHOOL COULDN'T.
THEN THEY PULLED MY ALLOWANCE AND MADE ME GET A **JOB**.
SO HERE I AM, WORKING 7 DAYS A WEEK AT **CLUB PLEASURE**. HOW THE HELL AM I SUPPOSED TO GET INTO COLLEGE **NOW**, MOM?!

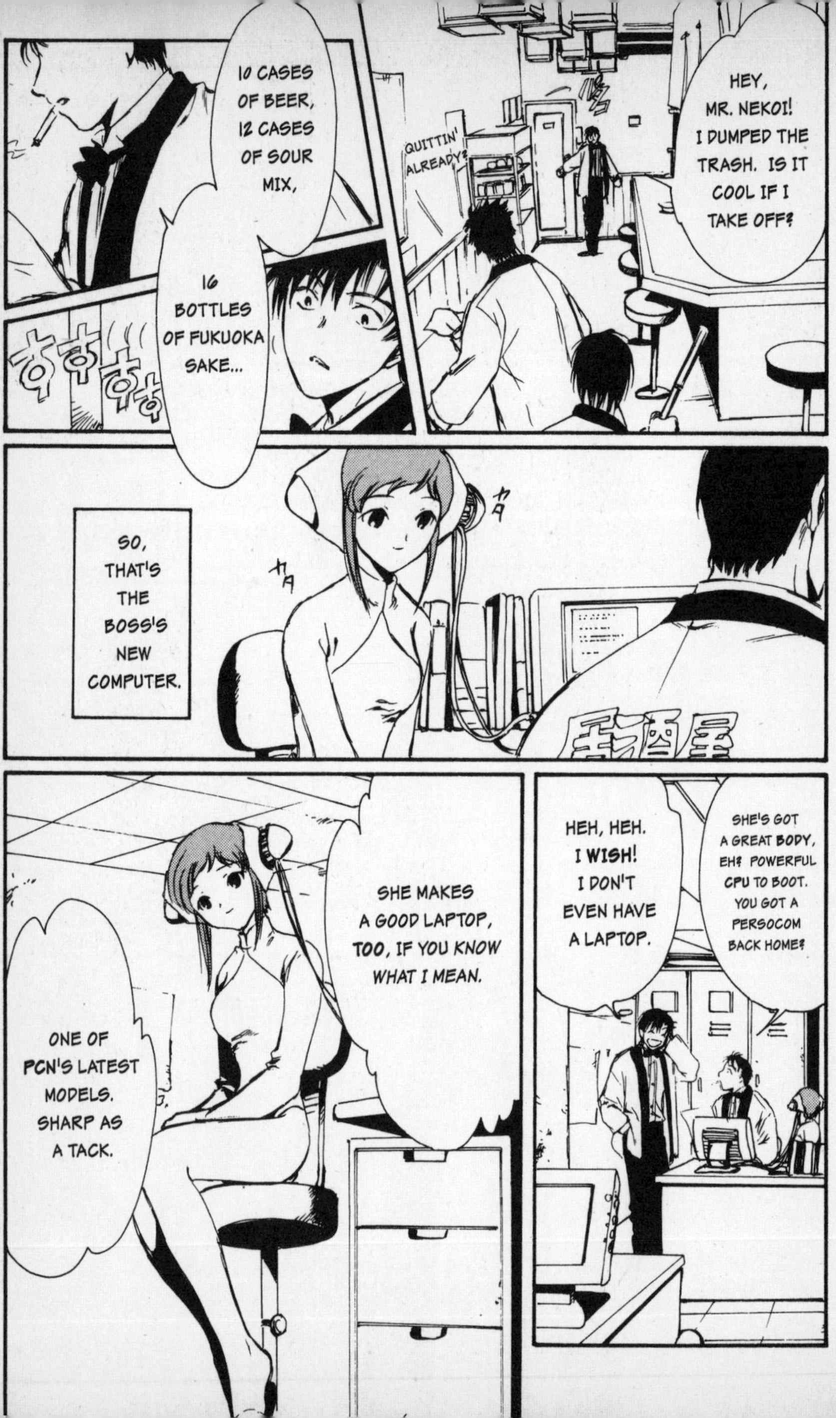
HEY, MR. NEKOI! I DUMPED THE TRASH. IS IT COOL IF I TAKE OFF?
QUITTIN' ALREADY?
10 CASES OF BEER, 12 CASES OF SOUR MIX,
16 BOTTLES OF FUKUOKA SAKE...
SO, THAT'S THE BOSS'S NEW COMPUTER.
SHE'S GOT A GREAT BODY, EH? POWERFUL CPU TO BOOT. YOU GOT A PERSOCOM BACK HOME?
HEH, HEH. I WISH! I DON'T EVEN HAVE A LAPTOP.
SHE MAKES A GOOD LAPTOP, TOO, IF YOU KNOW WHAT I MEAN.
ONE OF PCN'S LATEST MODELS. SHARP AS A TACK.

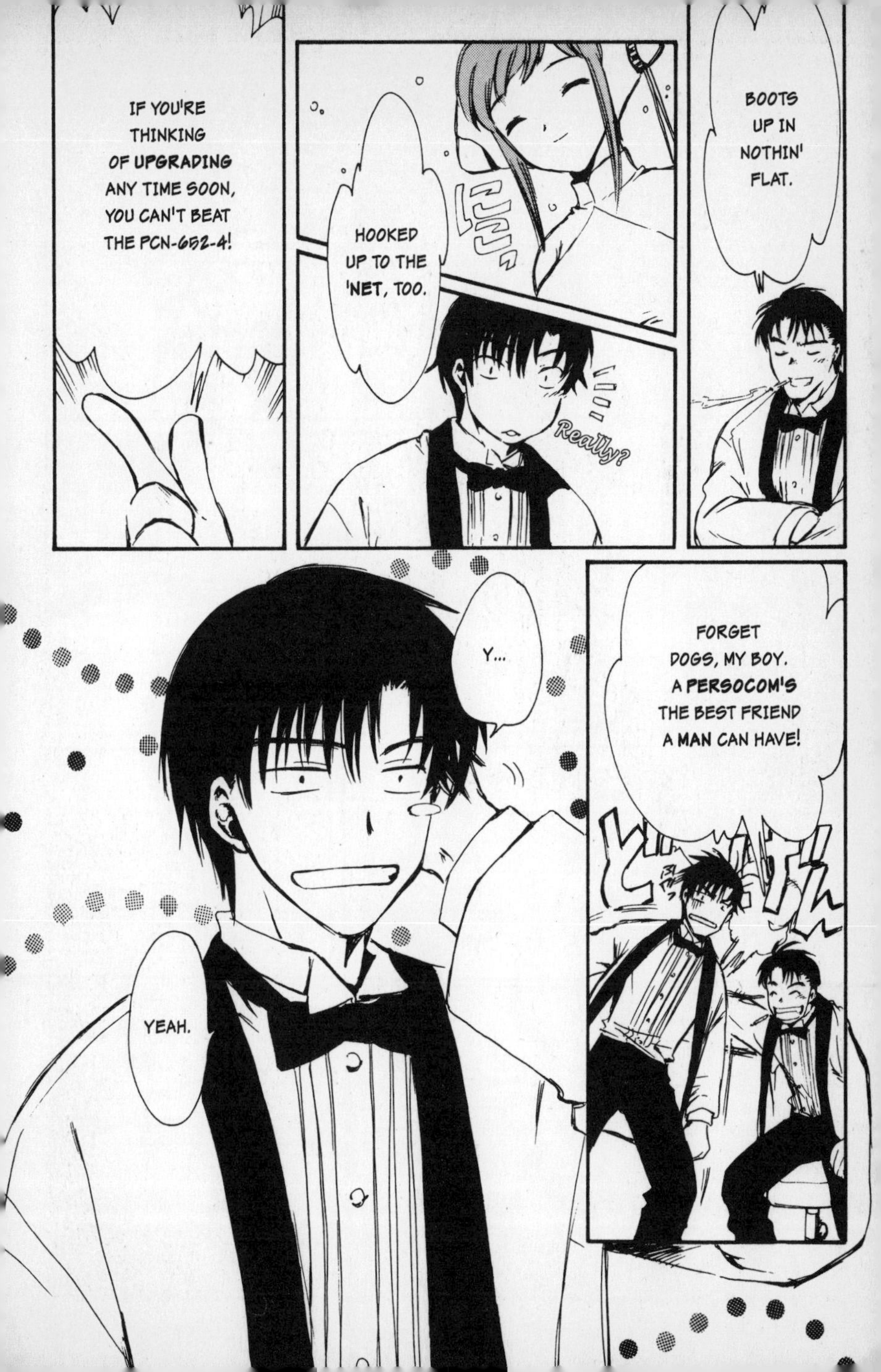
BOOTS UP IN NOTHIN' FLAT.
HOOKED UP TO THE 'NET, TOO.
Really?
IF YOU'RE THINKING OF UPGRADING ANY TIME SOON, YOU CAN'T BEAT THE PCN-652-4!
FORGET DOGS, MY BOY. A PERSOCOM'S THE BEST FRIEND A MAN CAN HAVE!
Y...
YEAH.

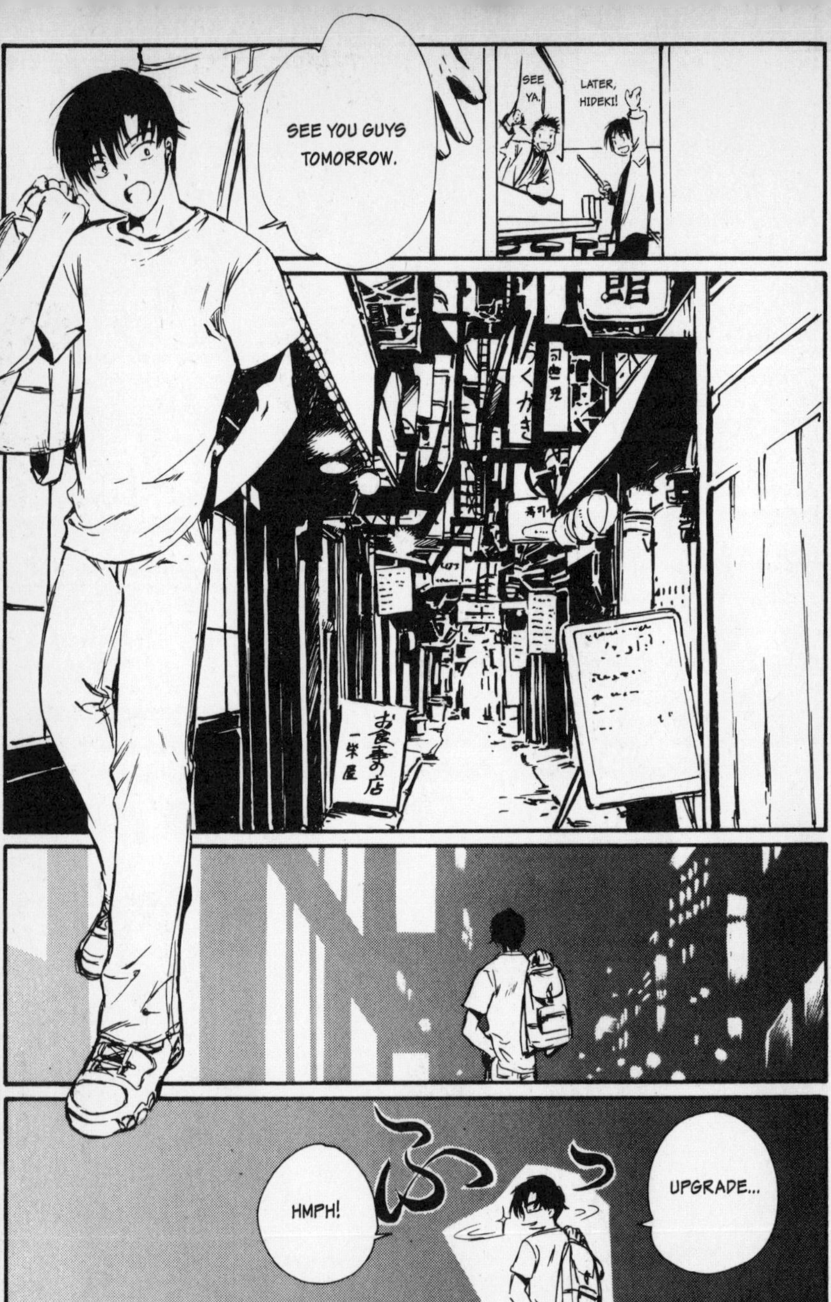
LATER, HIDEKI!
SEE YA.
SEE YOU GUYS TOMORROW.
UPGRADE...
ふっ
HMPH!

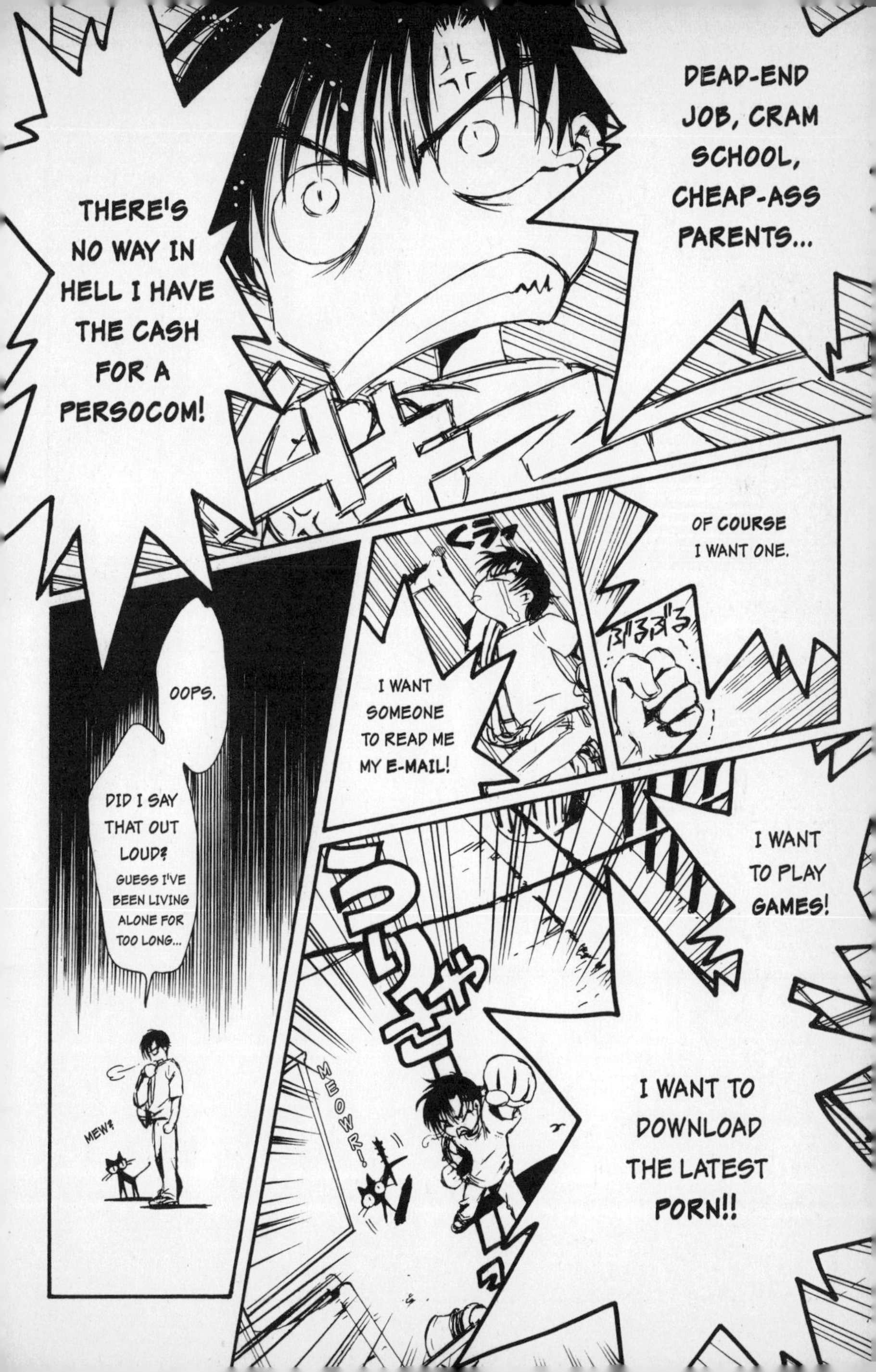
DEAD-END JOB, CRAM SCHOOL, CHEAP-ASS PARENTS...
THERE'S NO WAY IN HELL I HAVE THE CASH FOR A PERSOCOM!
OF COURSE I WANT ONE.
ぶるぶる
I WANT SOMEONE TO READ ME MY E-MAIL!
I WANT TO PLAY GAMES!
うりゃ
I WANT TO DOWNLOAD THE LATEST PORN!!
MEOWR!
OOPS.
DID I SAY THAT OUT LOUD?
GUESS I'VE BEEN LIVING ALONE FOR TOO LONG...
MEW?

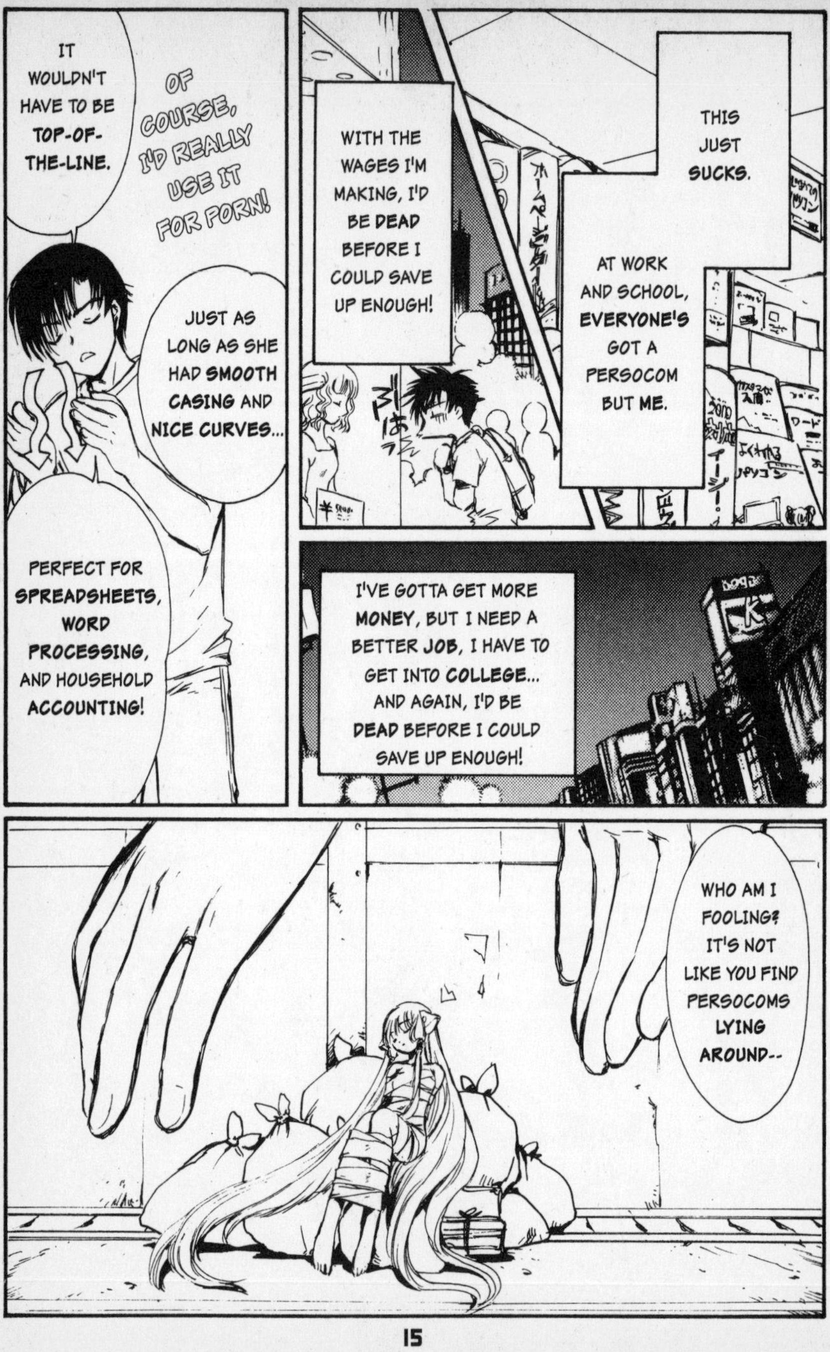
THIS JUST SUCKS.
AT WORK AND SCHOOL, EVERYONE'S GOT A PERSOCOM BUT ME.
WITH THE WAGES I'M MAKING, I'D BE DEAD BEFORE I COULD SAVE UP ENOUGH!
I'VE GOTTA GET MORE MONEY, BUT I NEED A BETTER JOB, I HAVE TO GET INTO COLLEGE... AND AGAIN, I'D BE DEAD BEFORE I COULD SAVE UP ENOUGH!
IT WOULDN'T HAVE TO BE TOP-OF-THE-LINE.
OF COURSE, I'D REALLY USE IT FOR PORN!
JUST AS LONG AS SHE HAD SMOOTH CASING AND NICE CURVES...
PERFECT FOR SPREADSHEETS, WORD PROCESSING, AND HOUSEHOLD ACCOUNTING!
WHO AM I FOOLING? IT'S NOT LIKE YOU FIND PERSOCOMS LYING AROUND--

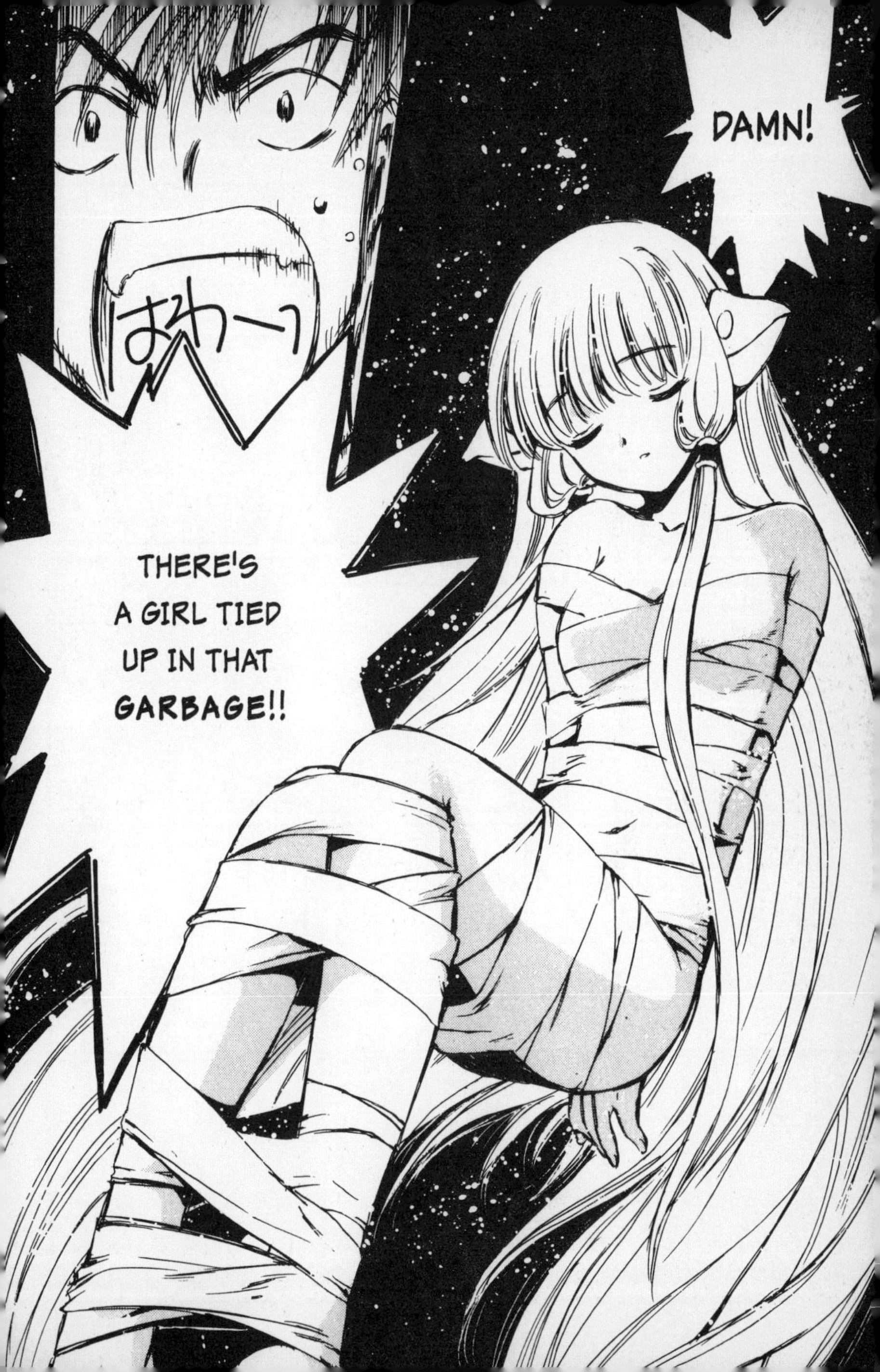
DAMN!
はわ〜っ
THERE'S A GIRL TIED UP IN THAT GARBAGE!!

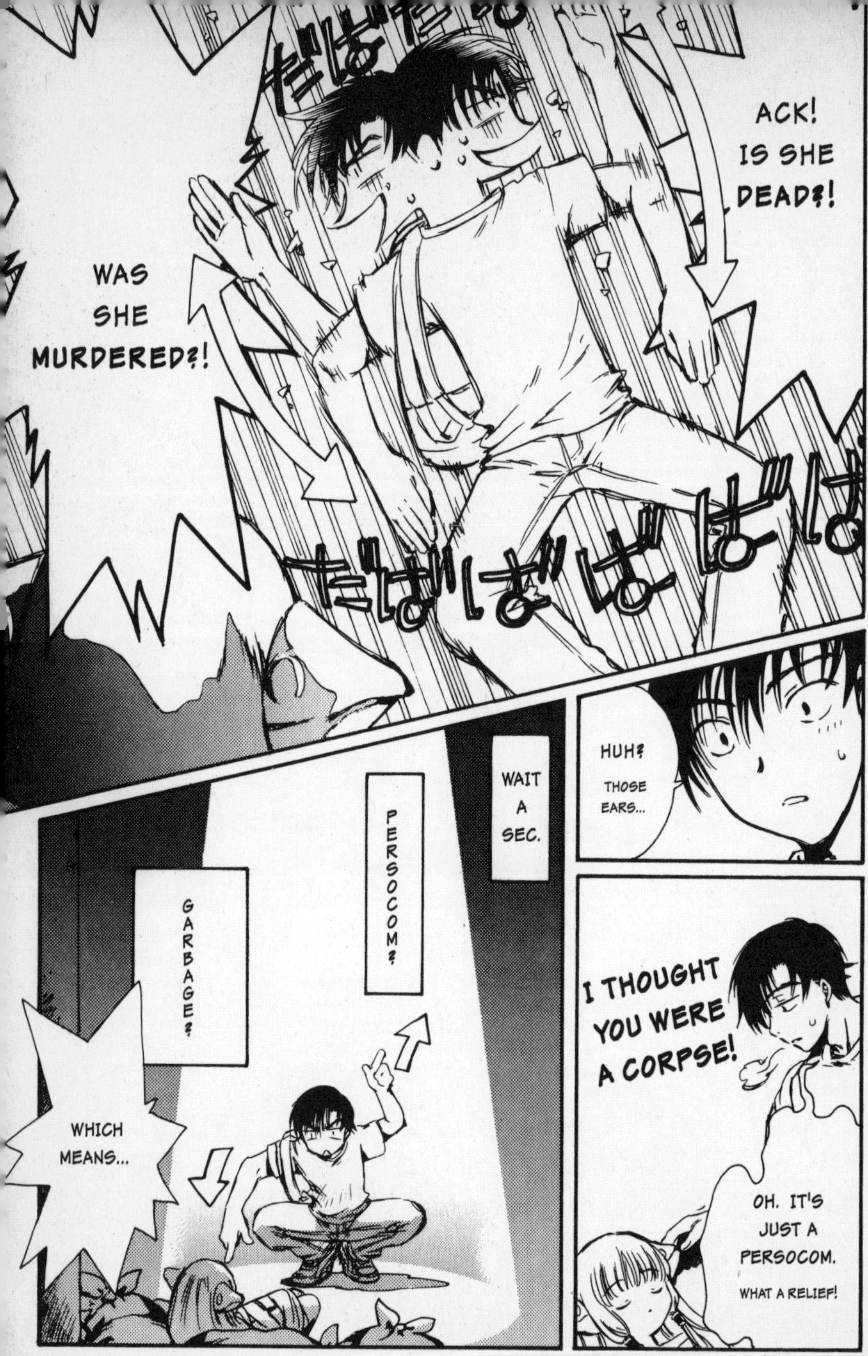
ACK! IS SHE DEAD?!
WAS SHE MURDERED?!
HUH? THOSE EARS...
I THOUGHT YOU WERE A CORPSE!
OH. IT'S JUST A PERSOCOM. WHAT A RELIEF!
WAIT A SEC.
PERSOCOM?
GARBAGE?
WHICH MEANS...

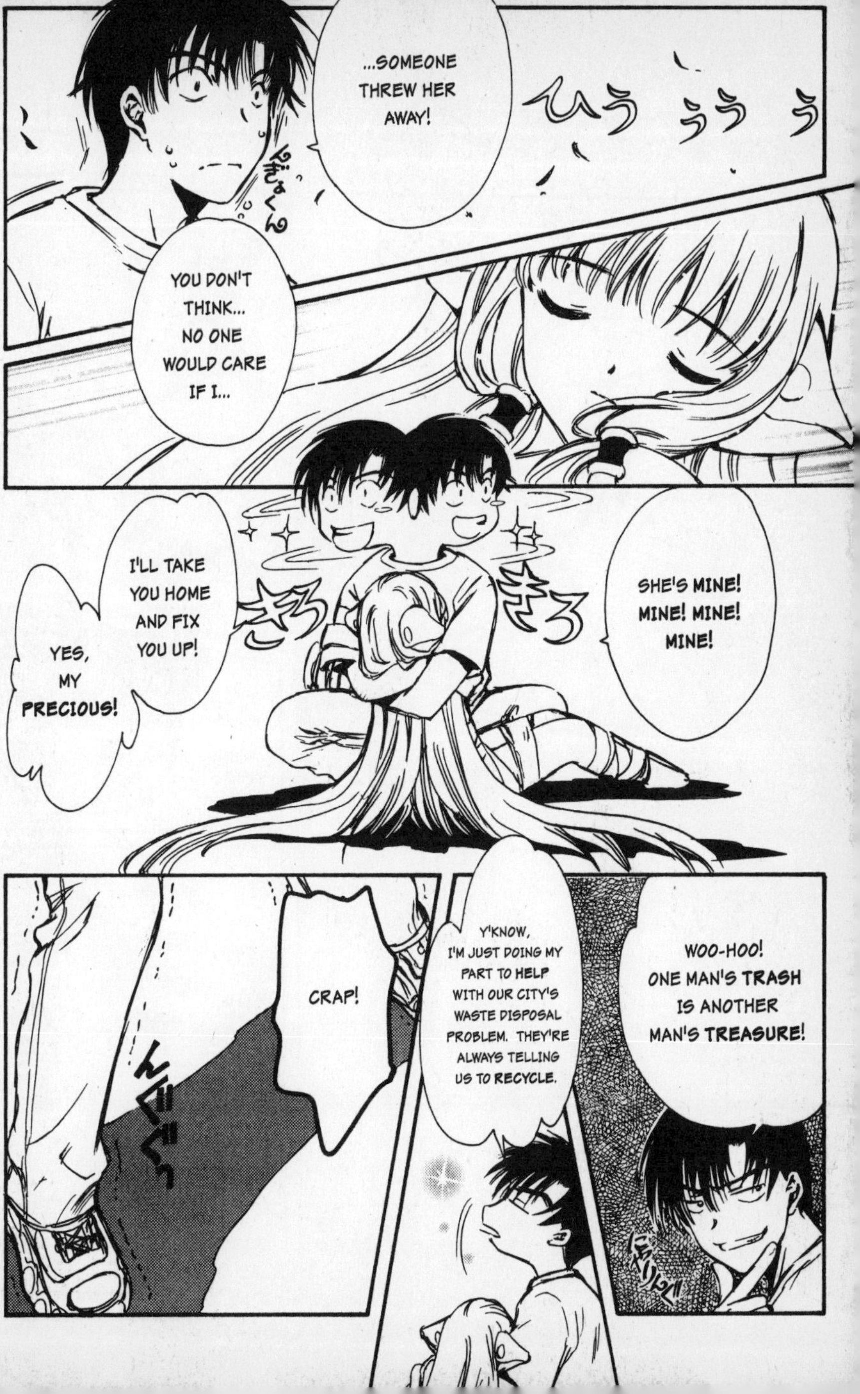

ひう ううう う
...SOMEONE THREW HER AWAY!
YOU DON'T THINK... NO ONE WOULD CARE IF I...
SHE'S MINE! MINE! MINE! MINE!
きろ
きろ
I'LL TAKE YOU HOME AND FIX YOU UP!
YES, MY PRECIOUS!
WOO-HOO! ONE MAN'S TRASH IS ANOTHER MAN'S TREASURE!
Y'KNOW, I'M JUST DOING MY PART TO HELP WITH OUR CITY'S WASTE DISPOSAL PROBLEM. THEY'RE ALWAYS TELLING US TO RECYCLE.
CRAP!

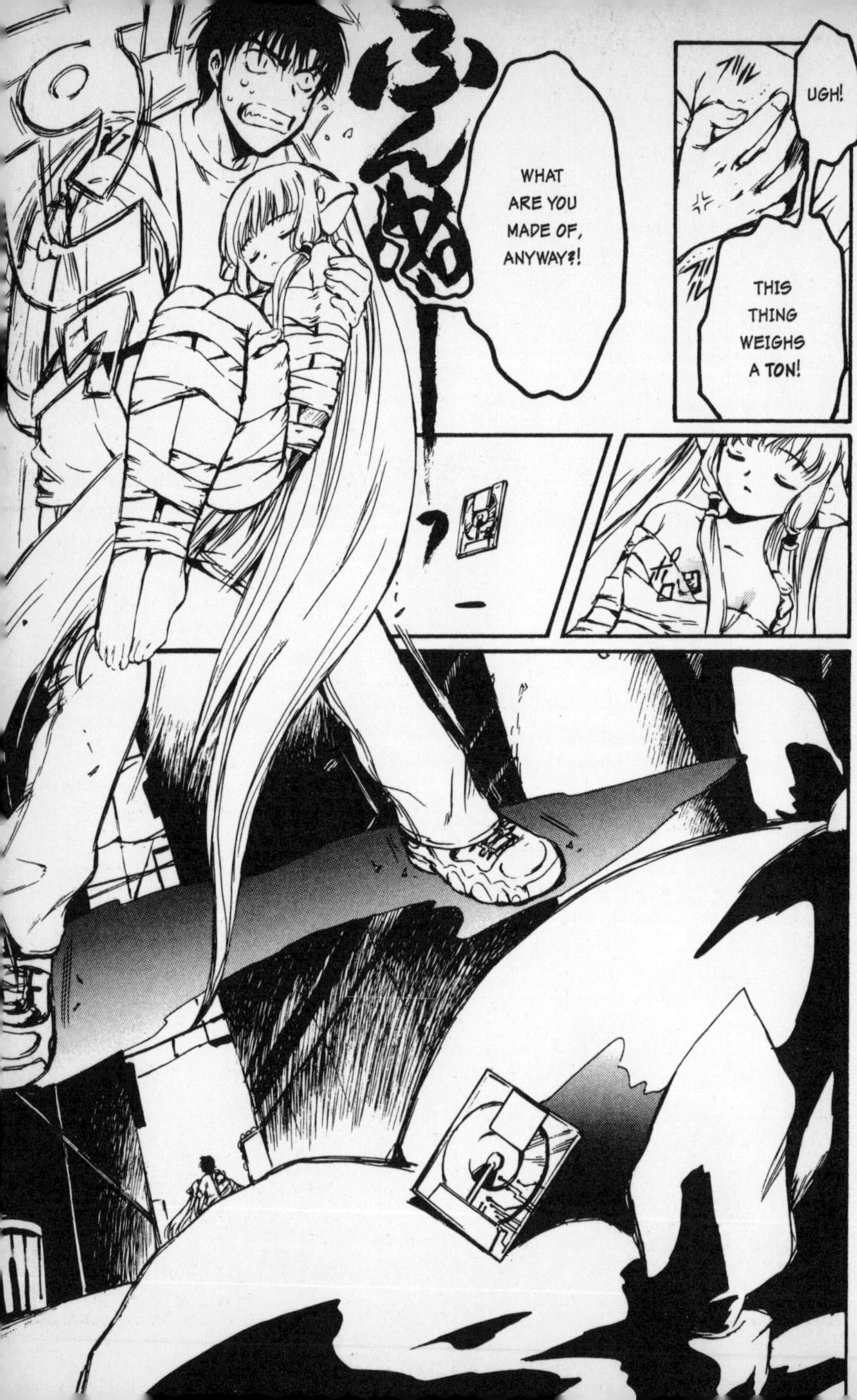
UGH!
THIS THING WEIGHS A TON!
WHAT ARE YOU MADE OF, ANYWAY?!

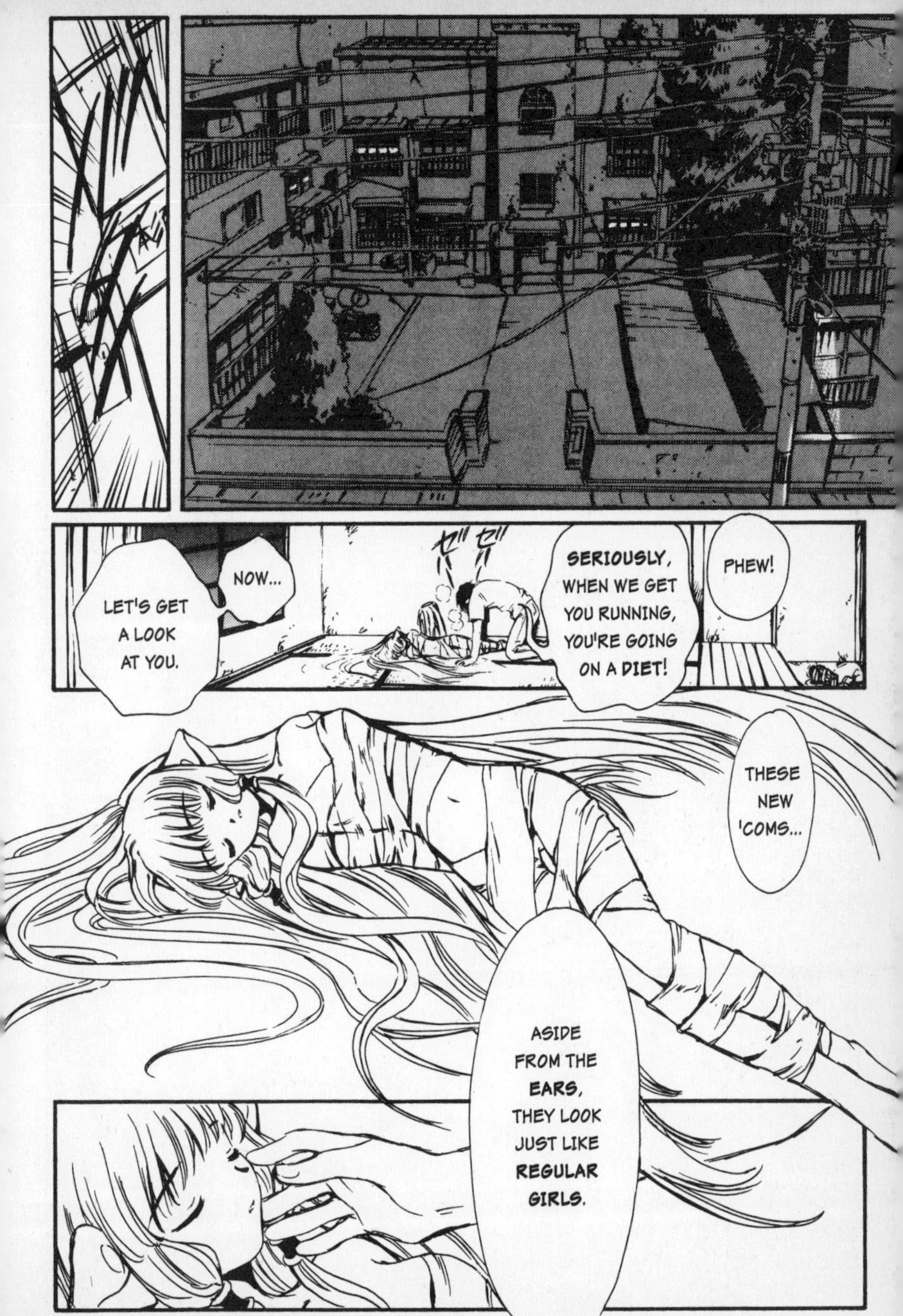
PHEW!
ゼ ゼ
SERIOUSLY, WHEN WE GET YOU RUNNING, YOU'RE GOING ON A DIET!
NOW...
LET'S GET A LOOK AT YOU.
THESE NEW 'COMS...
ASIDE FROM THE EARS, THEY LOOK JUST LIKE REGULAR GIRLS.

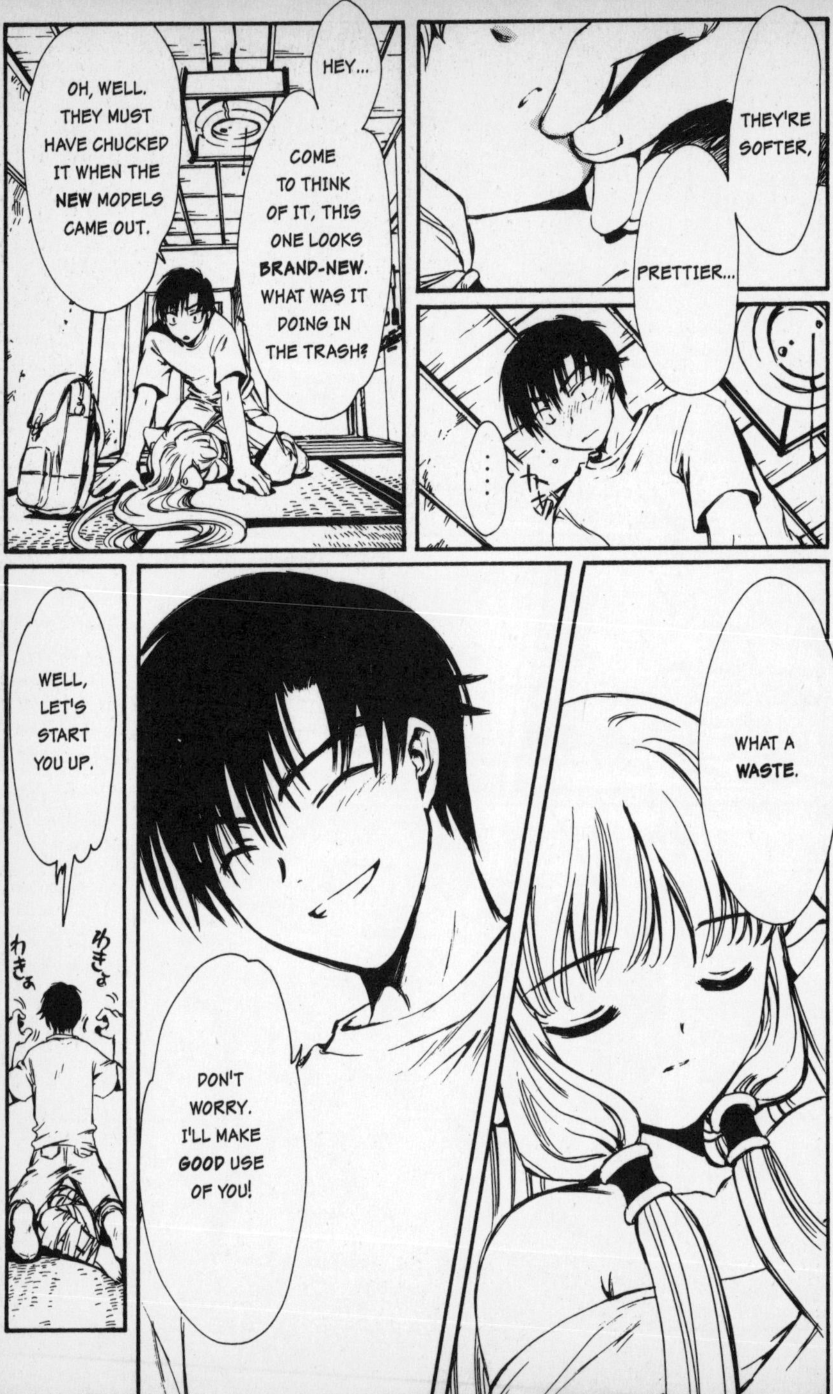
THEY'RE SOFTER,
PRETTIER...
.....
HEY...
COME TO THINK OF IT, THIS ONE LOOKS BRAND-NEW. WHAT WAS IT DOING IN THE TRASH?
OH, WELL. THEY MUST HAVE CHUCKED IT WHEN THE NEW MODELS CAME OUT.
WHAT A WASTE.
DON'T WORRY. I'LL MAKE GOOD USE OF YOU!
WELL, LET'S START YOU UP.
わきょ
わきょ

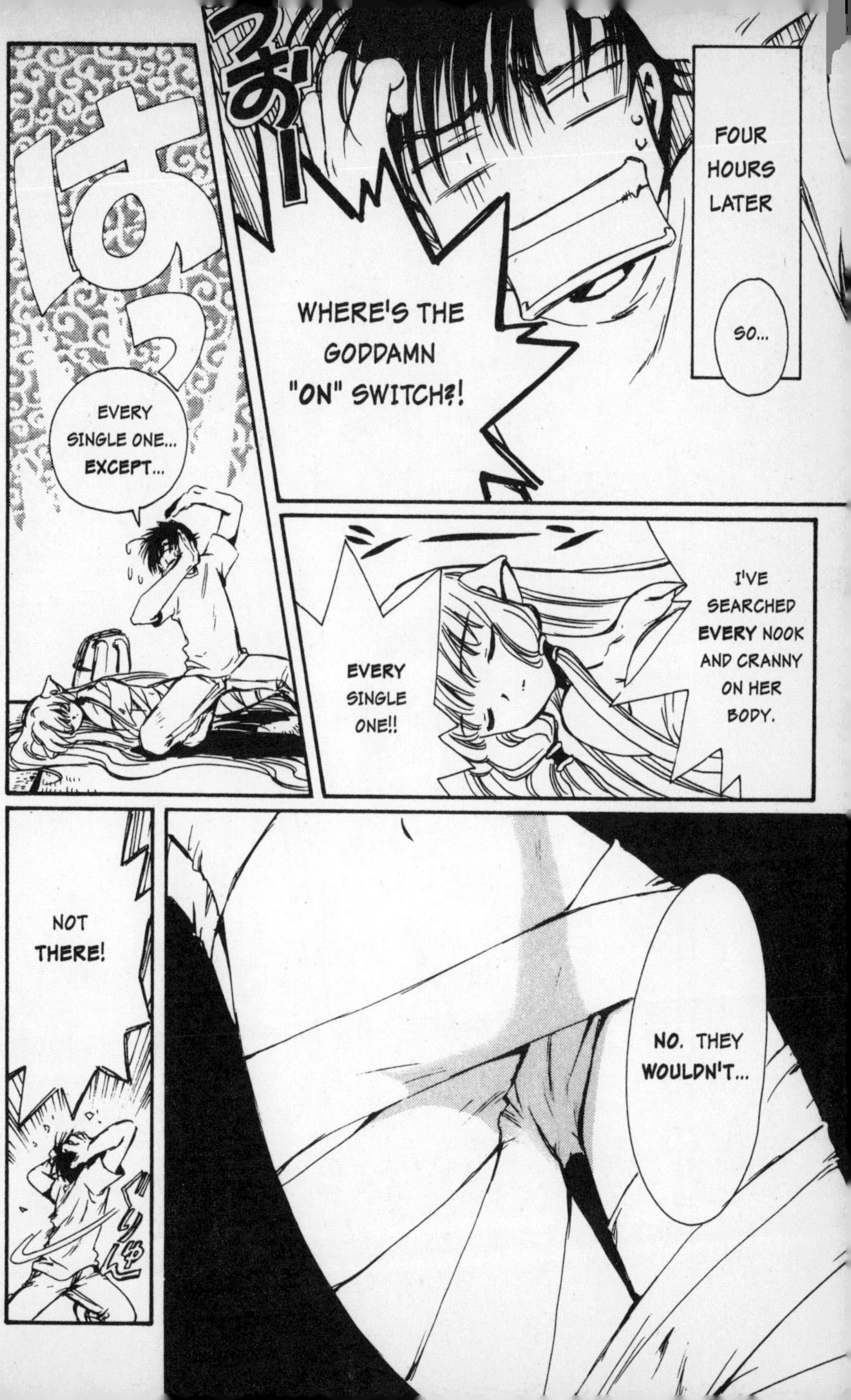
FOUR HOURS LATER
SO...
WHERE'S THE GODDAMN "ON" SWITCH?!
I'VE SEARCHED EVERY NOOK AND CRANNY ON HER BODY.
EVERY SINGLE ONE!!
はっ
EVERY SINGLE ONE... EXCEPT...
NO. THEY WOULDN'T...
NOT THERE!

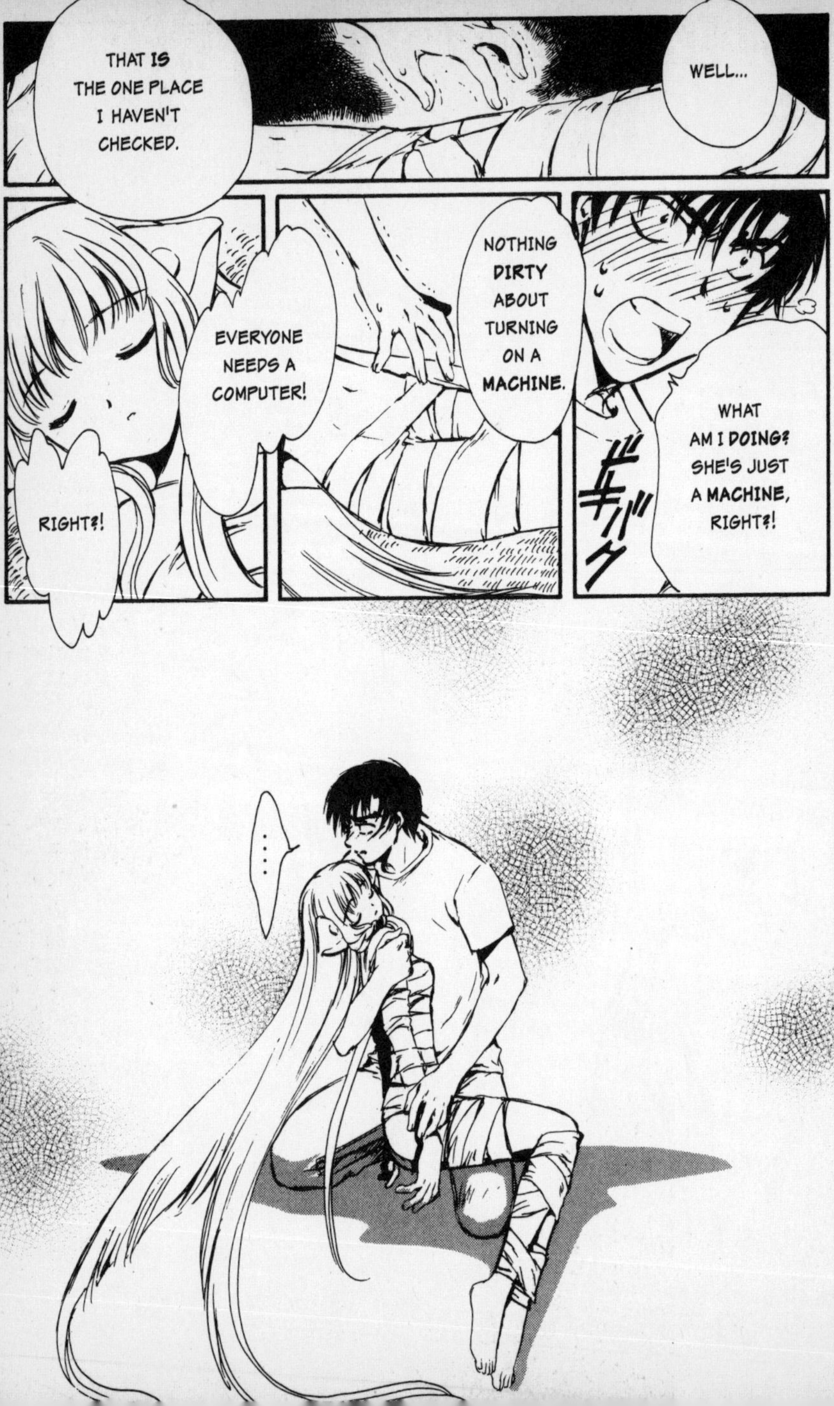
WELL...
THAT IS THE ONE PLACE I HAVEN'T CHECKED.
WHAT AM I DOING? SHE'S JUST A MACHINE, RIGHT?!
NOTHING DIRTY ABOUT TURNING ON A MACHINE.
EVERYONE NEEDS A COMPUTER!
RIGHT?!
.....

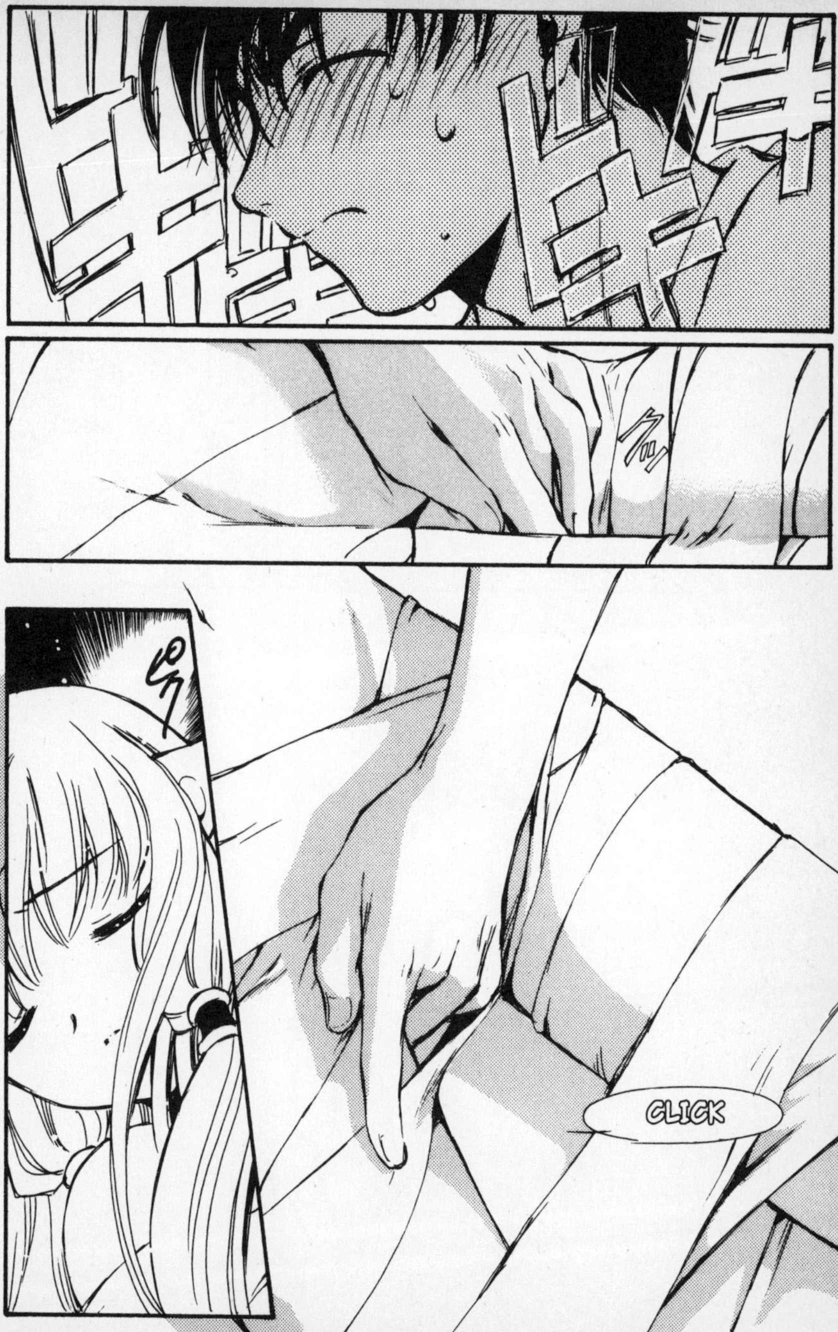
ドキドキ
ドキドキ
CLICK

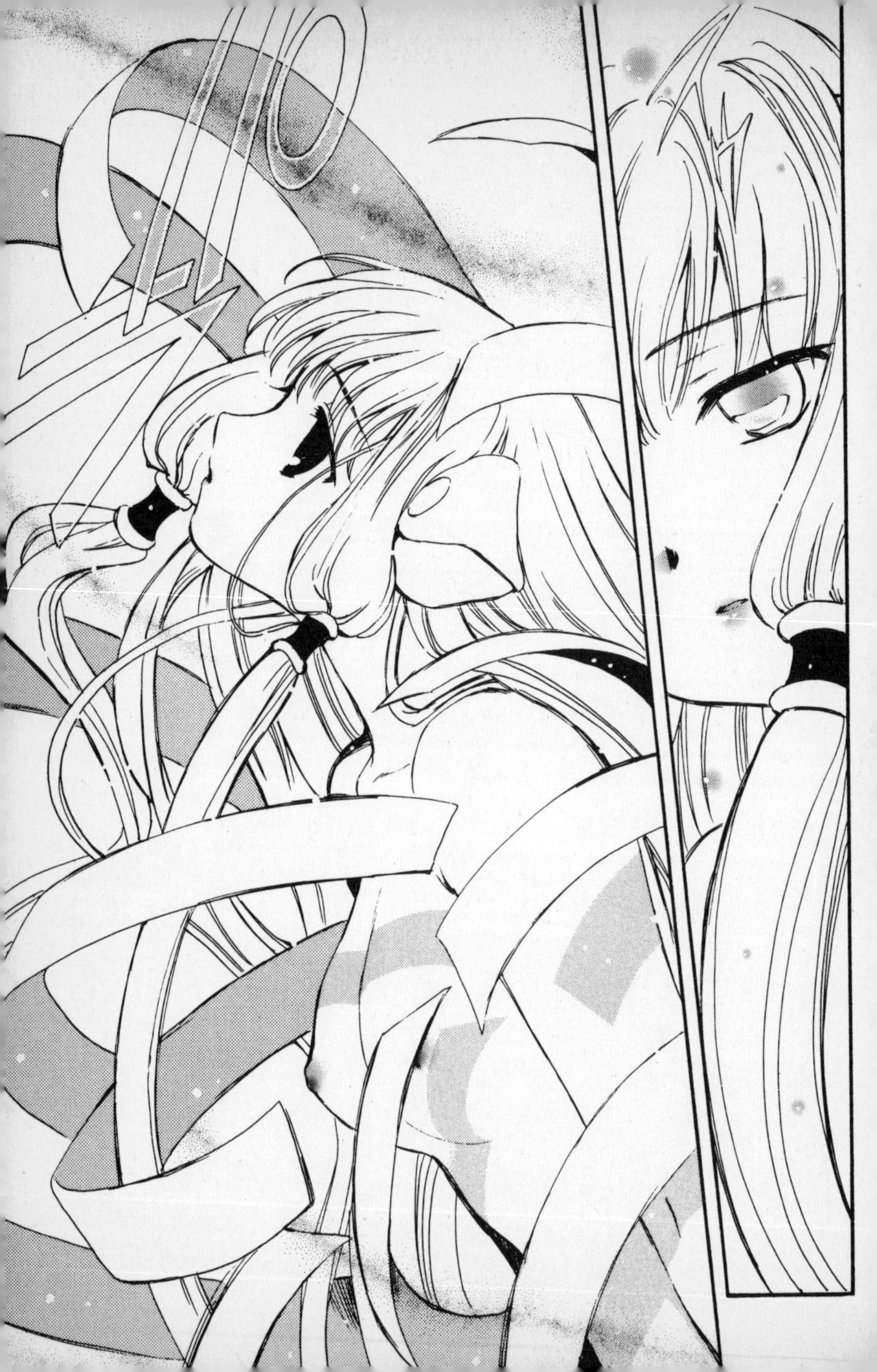

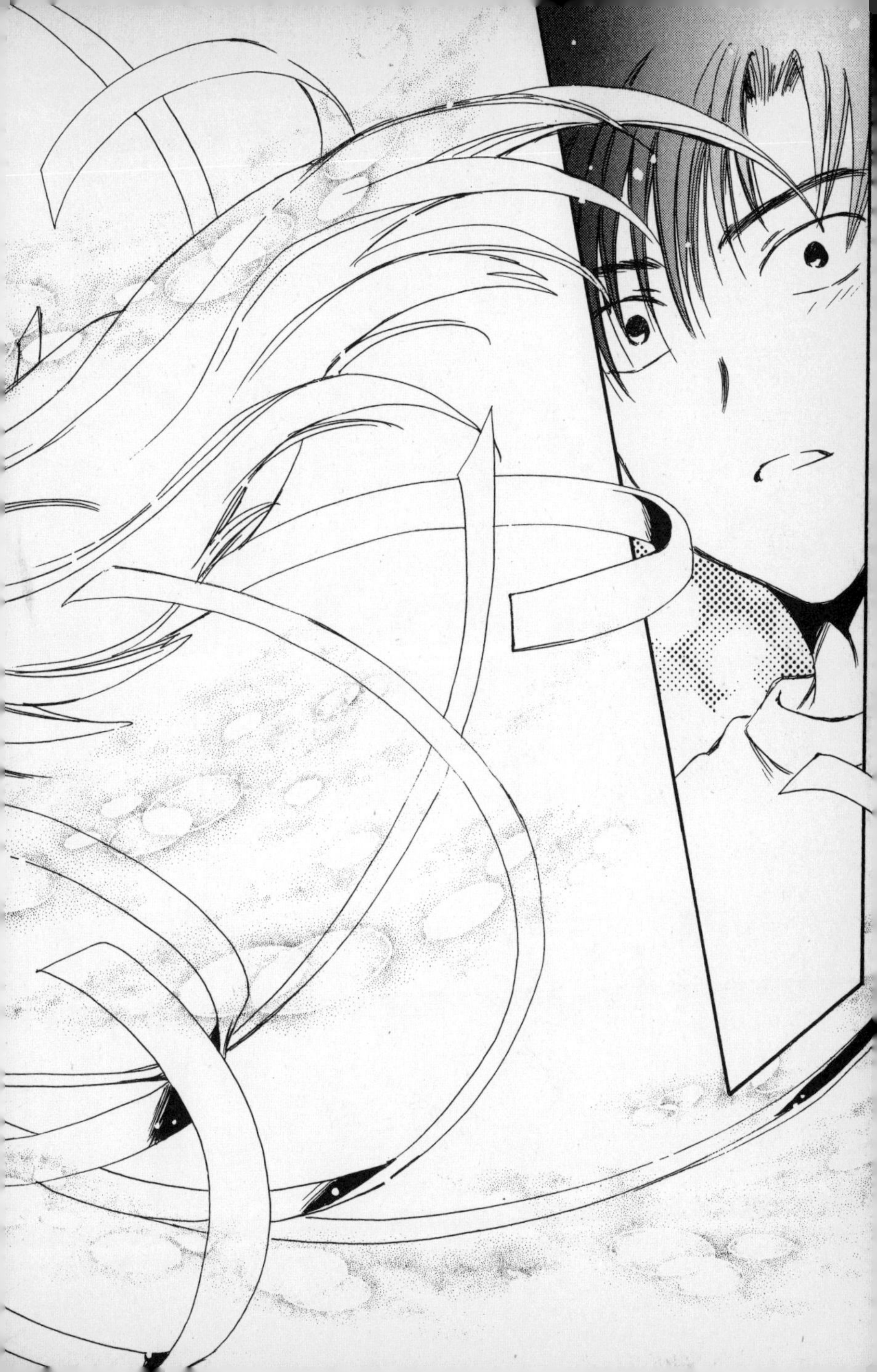

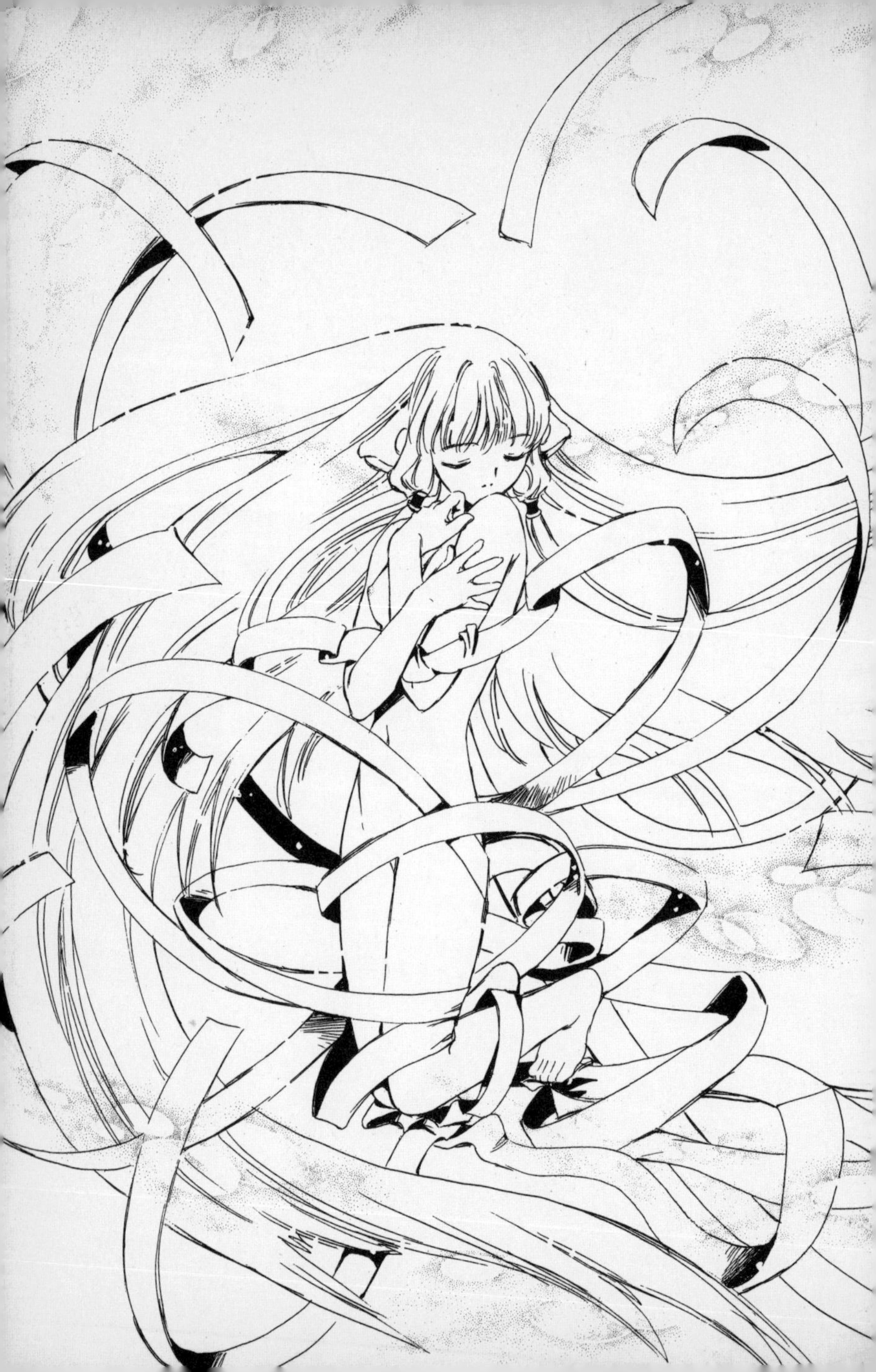

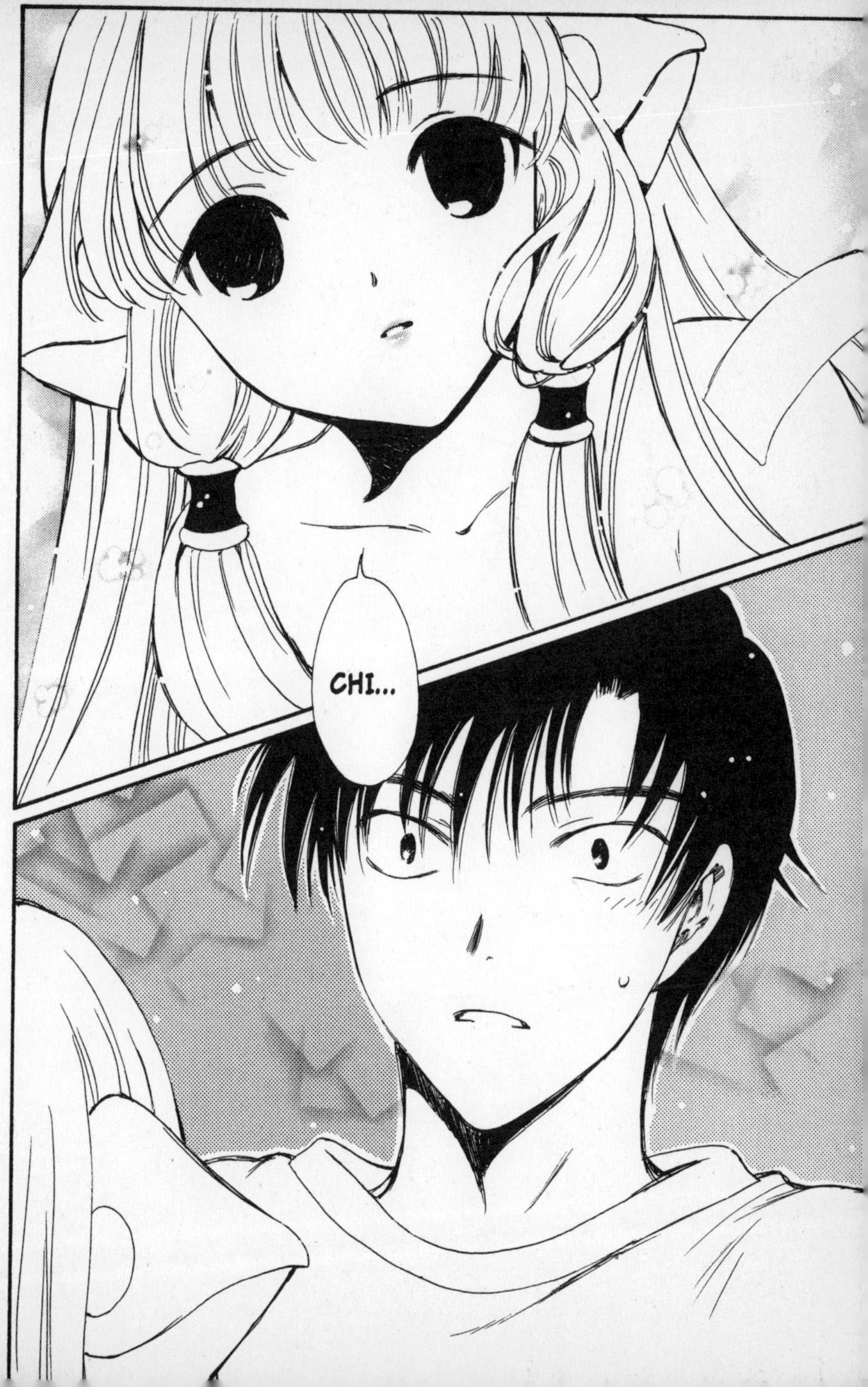
CHI...

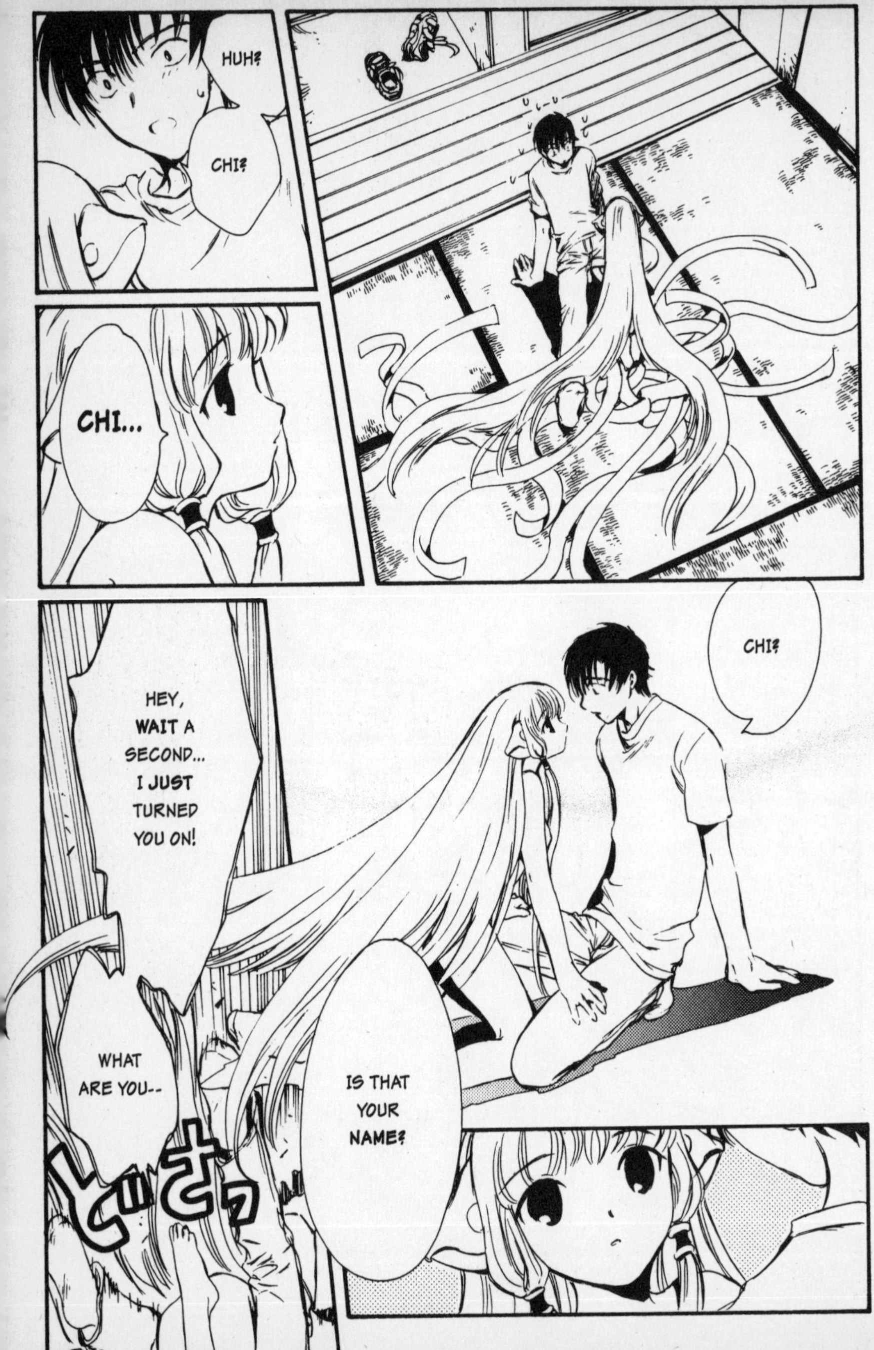
HUH?
CHI?
CHI...
CHI?
IS THAT YOUR NAME?
HEY, WAIT A SECOND... I JUST TURNED YOU ON!
WHAT ARE YOU--
どさっ

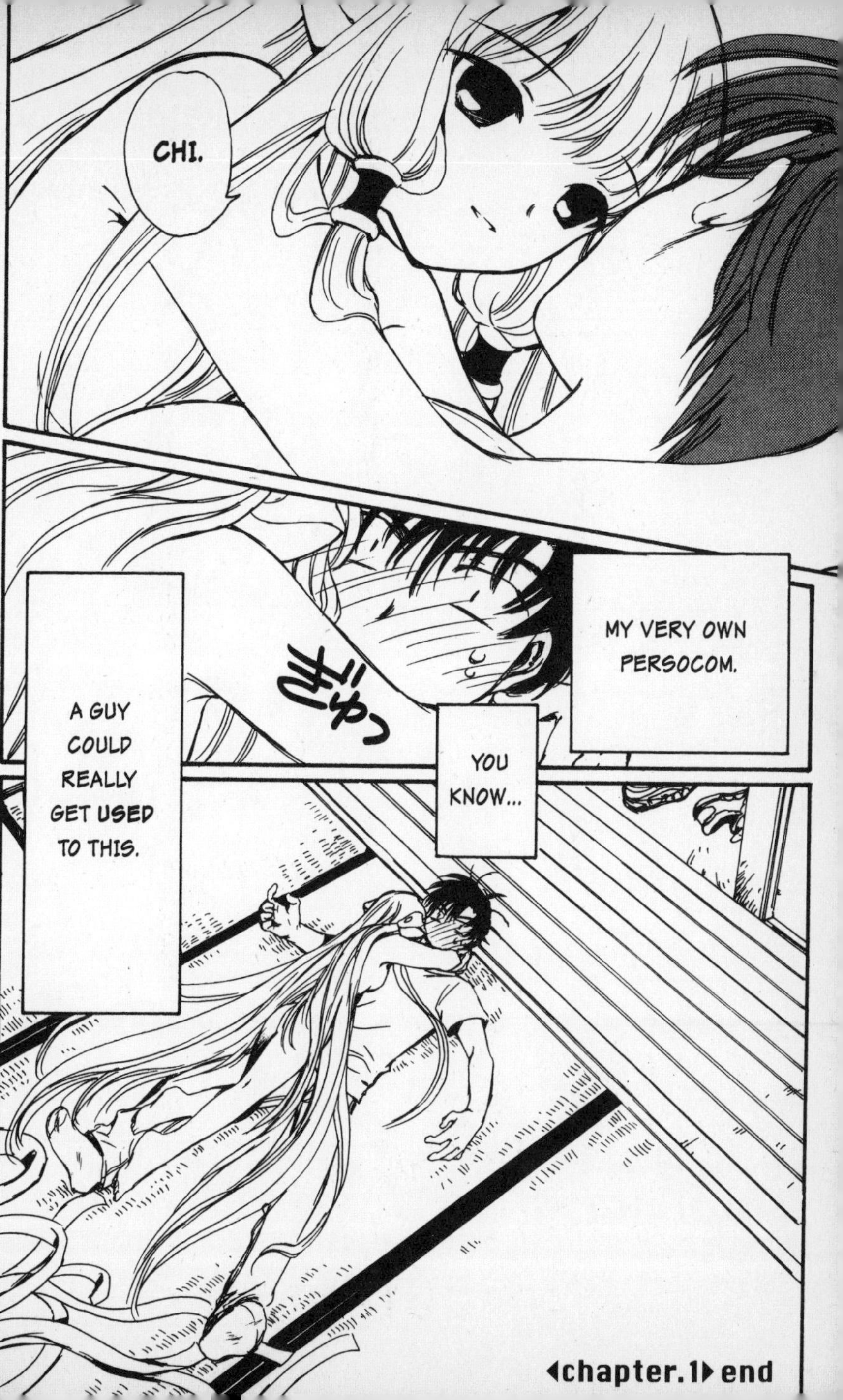
CHI.
MY VERY OWN PERSOCOM.
ぎゅっ
YOU KNOW...
A GUY COULD REALLY GET USED TO THIS.
◀chapter.1▶ end

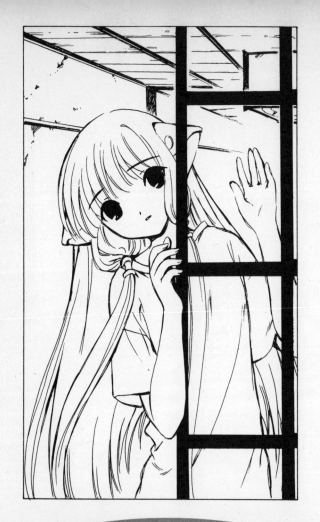

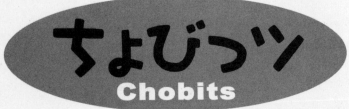

ちょびっツ
Chobits

◀chapter.2▶

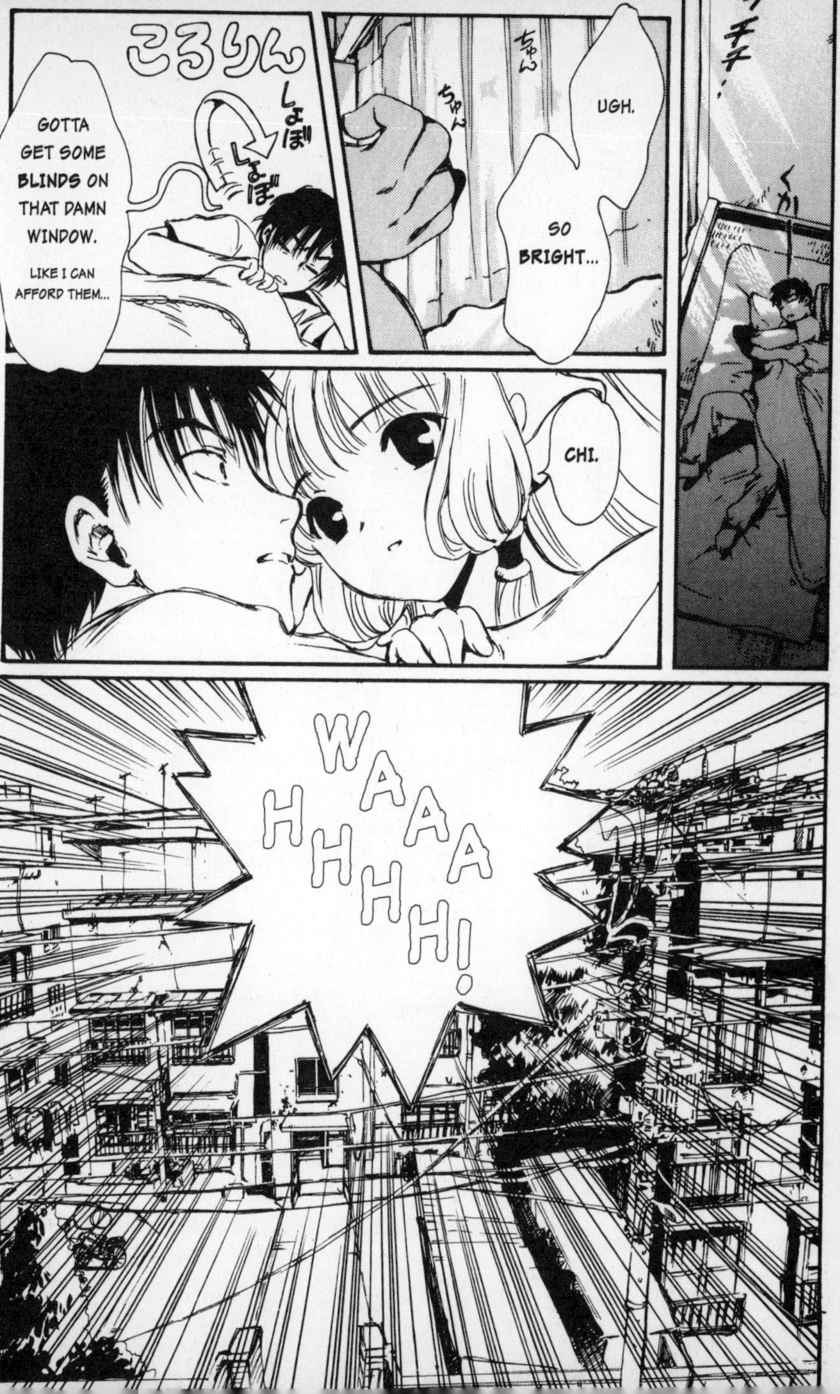
チチチ
ちゅん
ちゅん
UGH.
SO BRIGHT...
ころりん
しょぼ
しょぼ
GOTTA GET SOME BLINDS ON THAT DAMN WINDOW.
LIKE I CAN AFFORD THEM...
CHI.
WAAAHHHHH!

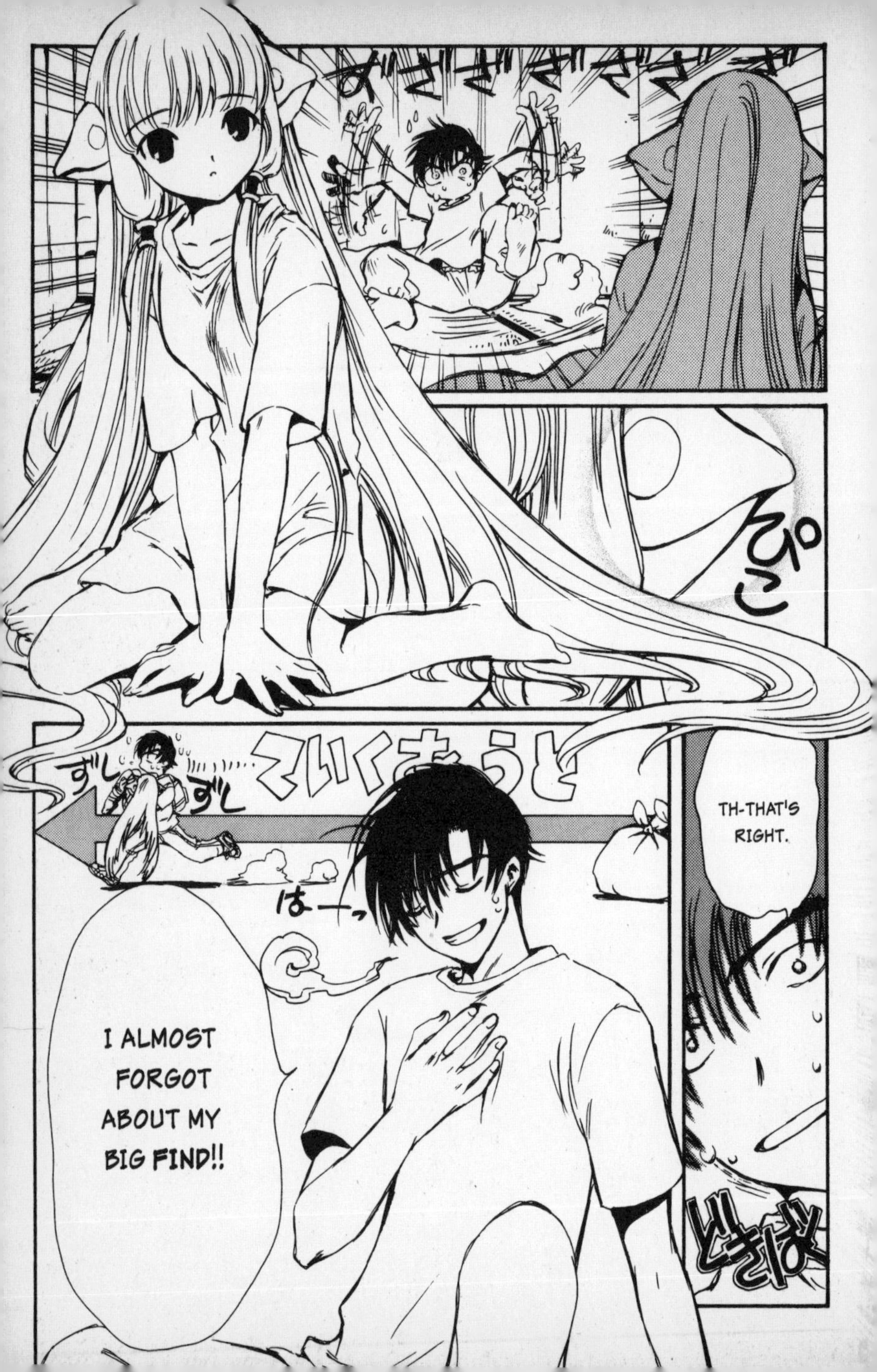
TH-THAT'S RIGHT.
I ALMOST FORGOT ABOUT MY BIG FIND!!

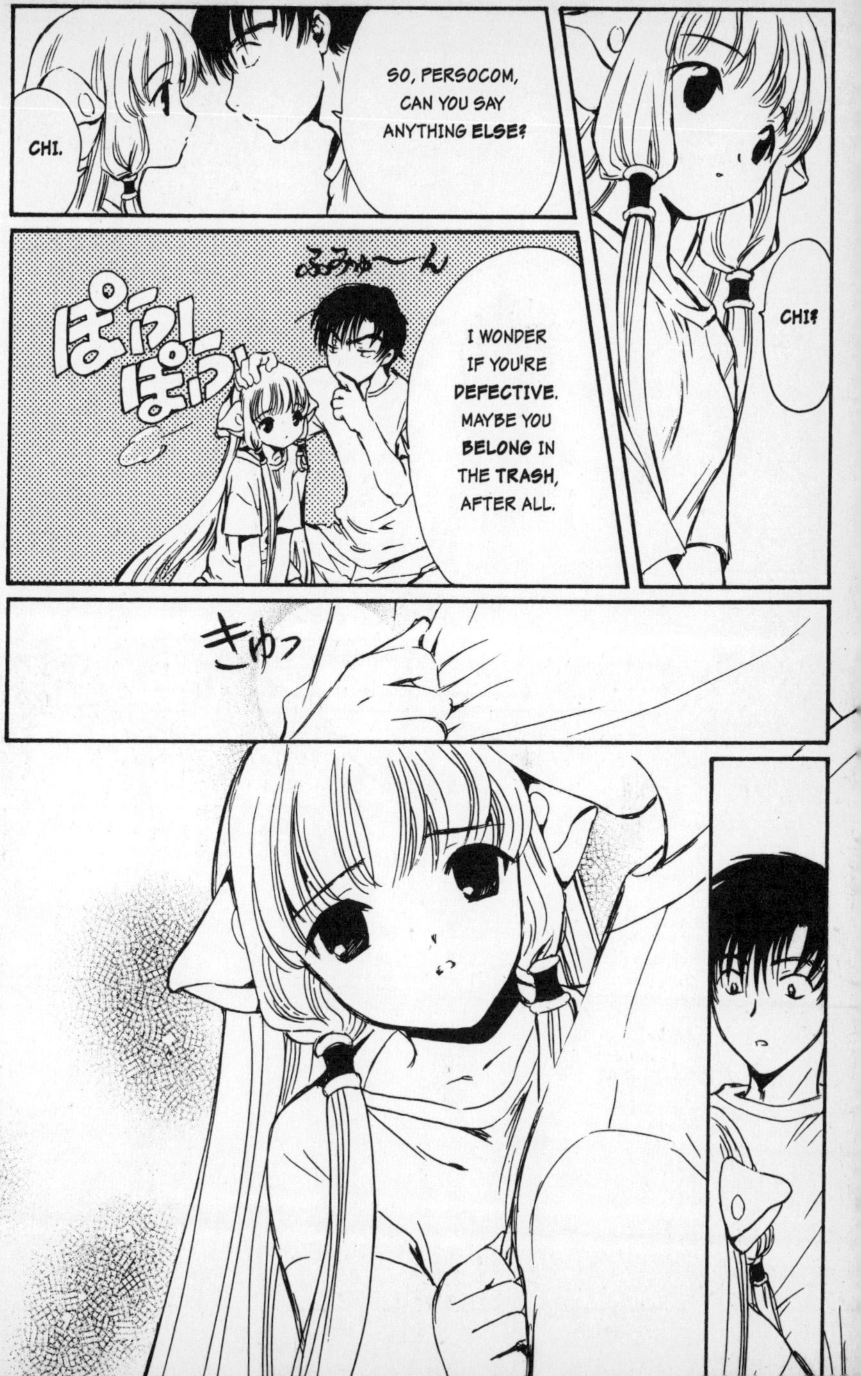
CHI?
CHI.
SO, PERSOCOM, CAN YOU SAY ANYTHING ELSE?
ふみゅ〜ん
I WONDER IF YOU'RE DEFECTIVE. MAYBE YOU BELONG IN THE TRASH, AFTER ALL.
きゅっ

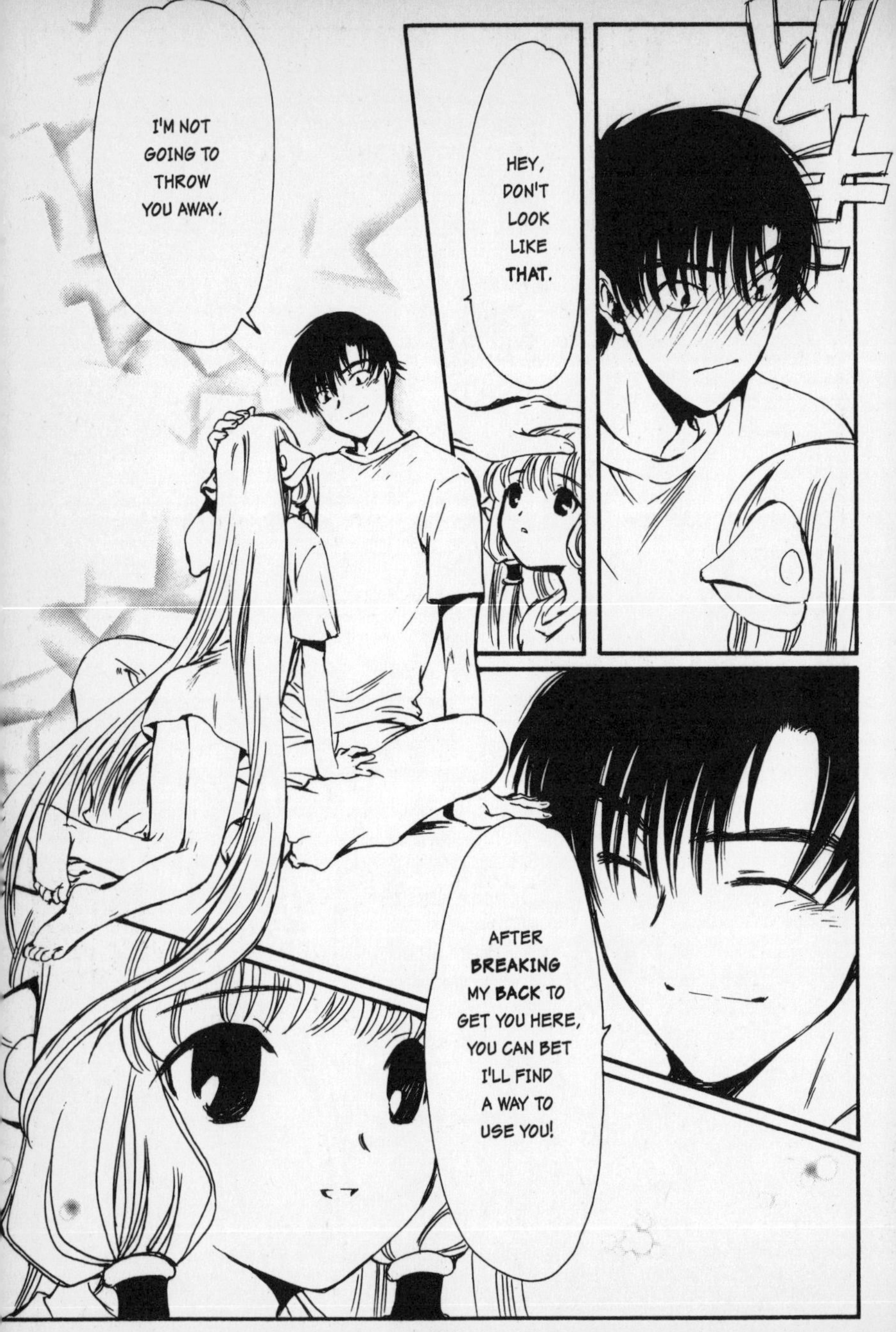
ドキ
HEY, DON'T LOOK LIKE THAT.
I'M NOT GOING TO THROW YOU AWAY.
AFTER BREAKING MY BACK TO GET YOU HERE, YOU CAN BET I'LL FIND A WAY TO USE YOU!

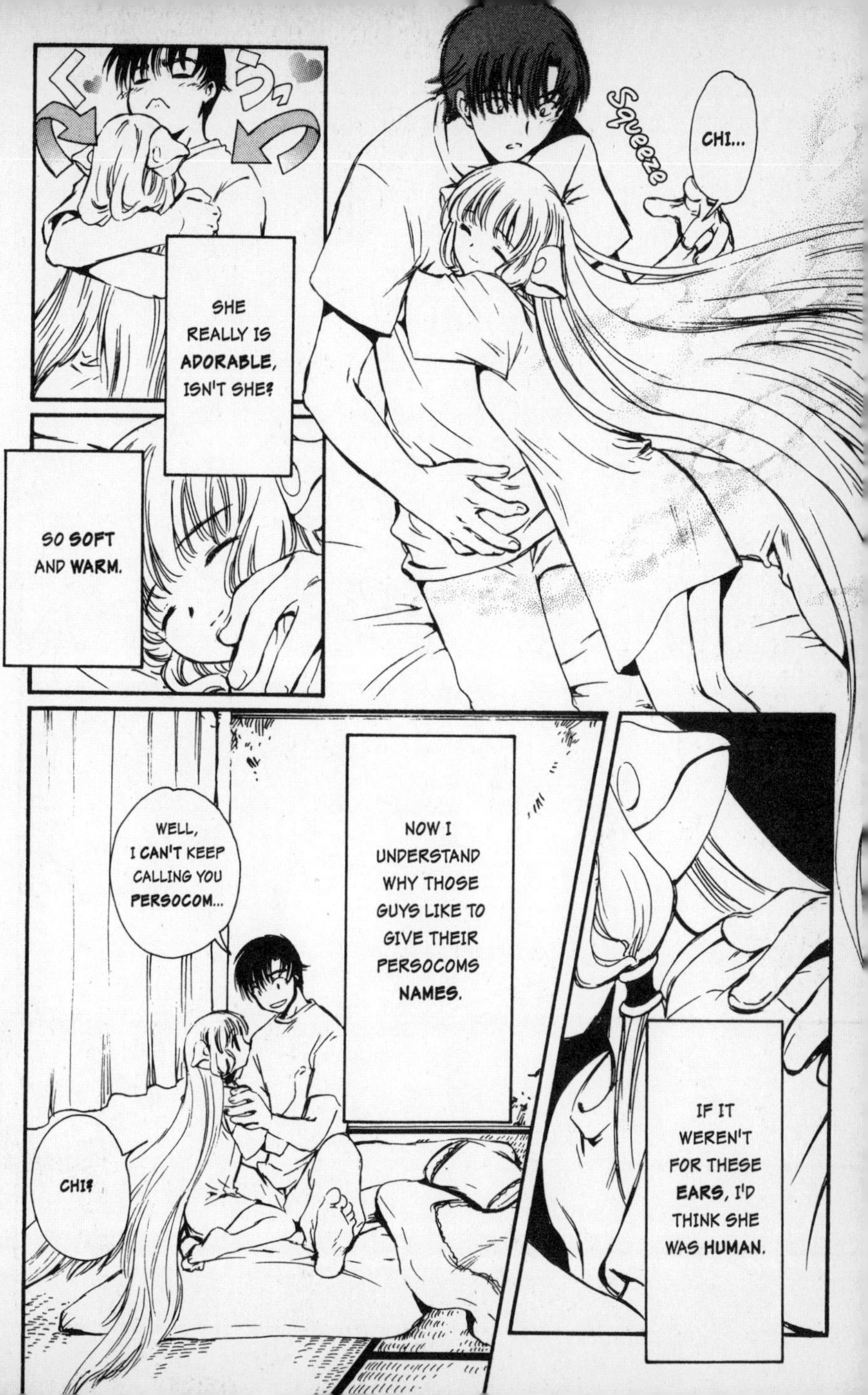
Squeeze
CHI...
く うぅ
SHE REALLY IS ADORABLE, ISN'T SHE?
SO SOFT AND WARM.
IF IT WEREN'T FOR THESE EARS, I'D THINK SHE WAS HUMAN.
NOW I UNDERSTAND WHY THOSE GUYS LIKE TO GIVE THEIR PERSOCOMS NAMES.
WELL, I CAN'T KEEP CALLING YOU PERSOCOM...
CHI?

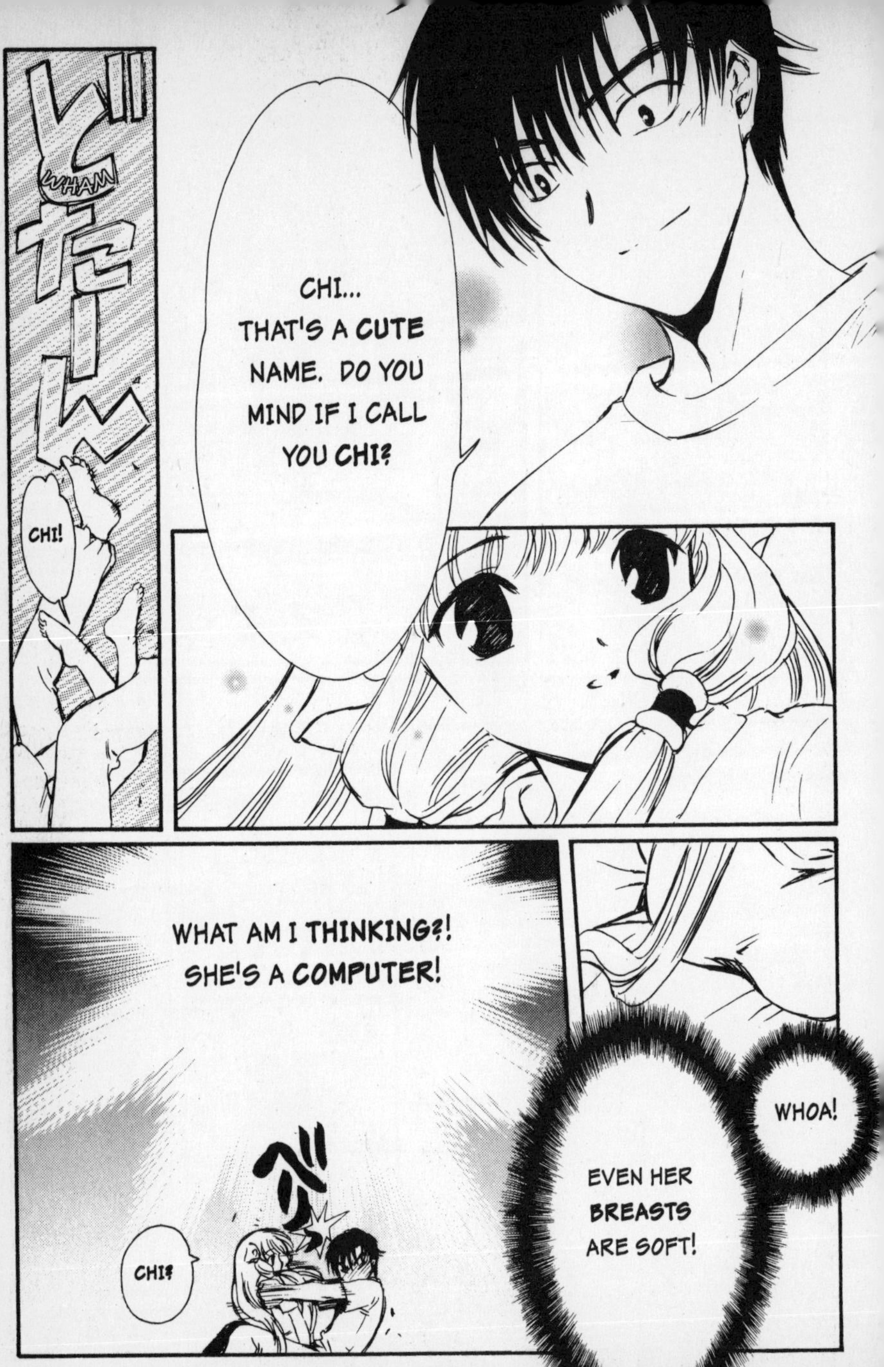

CHI... THAT'S A CUTE NAME. DO YOU MIND IF I CALL YOU CHI?
どたーん
WHAM
CHI!
WHOA!
EVEN HER BREASTS ARE SOFT!
WHAT AM I THINKING?! SHE'S A COMPUTER!
CHI?

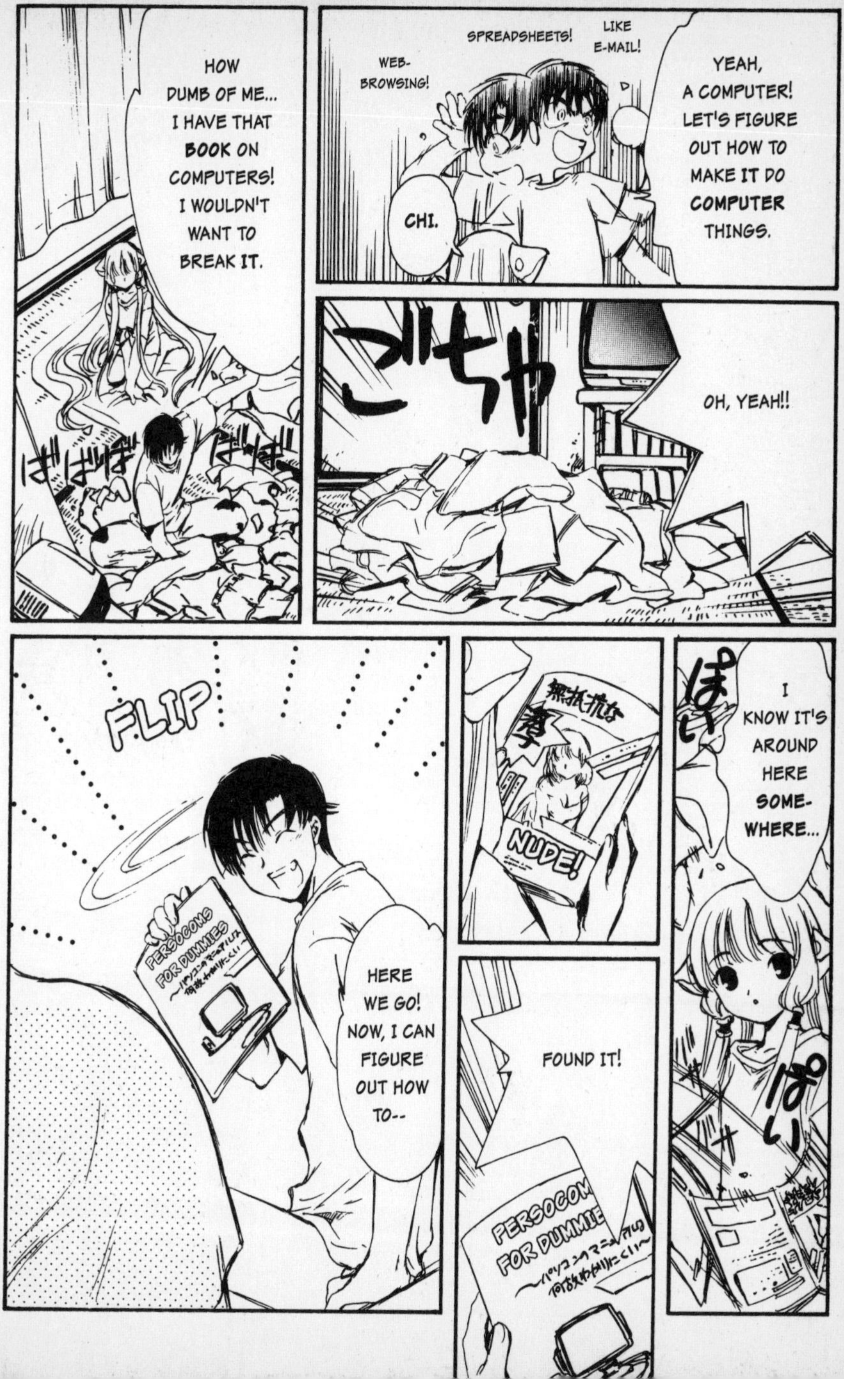
YEAH, A COMPUTER! LET'S FIGURE OUT HOW TO MAKE IT DO COMPUTER THINGS.
LIKE E-MAIL!
SPREADSHEETS!
WEB-BROWSING!
CHI.
ごちゃ
OH, YEAH!!
HOW DUMB OF ME... I HAVE THAT BOOK ON COMPUTERS! I WOULDN'T WANT TO BREAK IT.
ぽい
I KNOW IT'S AROUND HERE SOME-WHERE...
ぽい
NUDE!
FOUND IT!
PERSOCOMS FOR DUMMIES
FLIP
PERSOCOMS FOR DUMMIES
HERE WE GO! NOW, I CAN FIGURE OUT HOW TO--

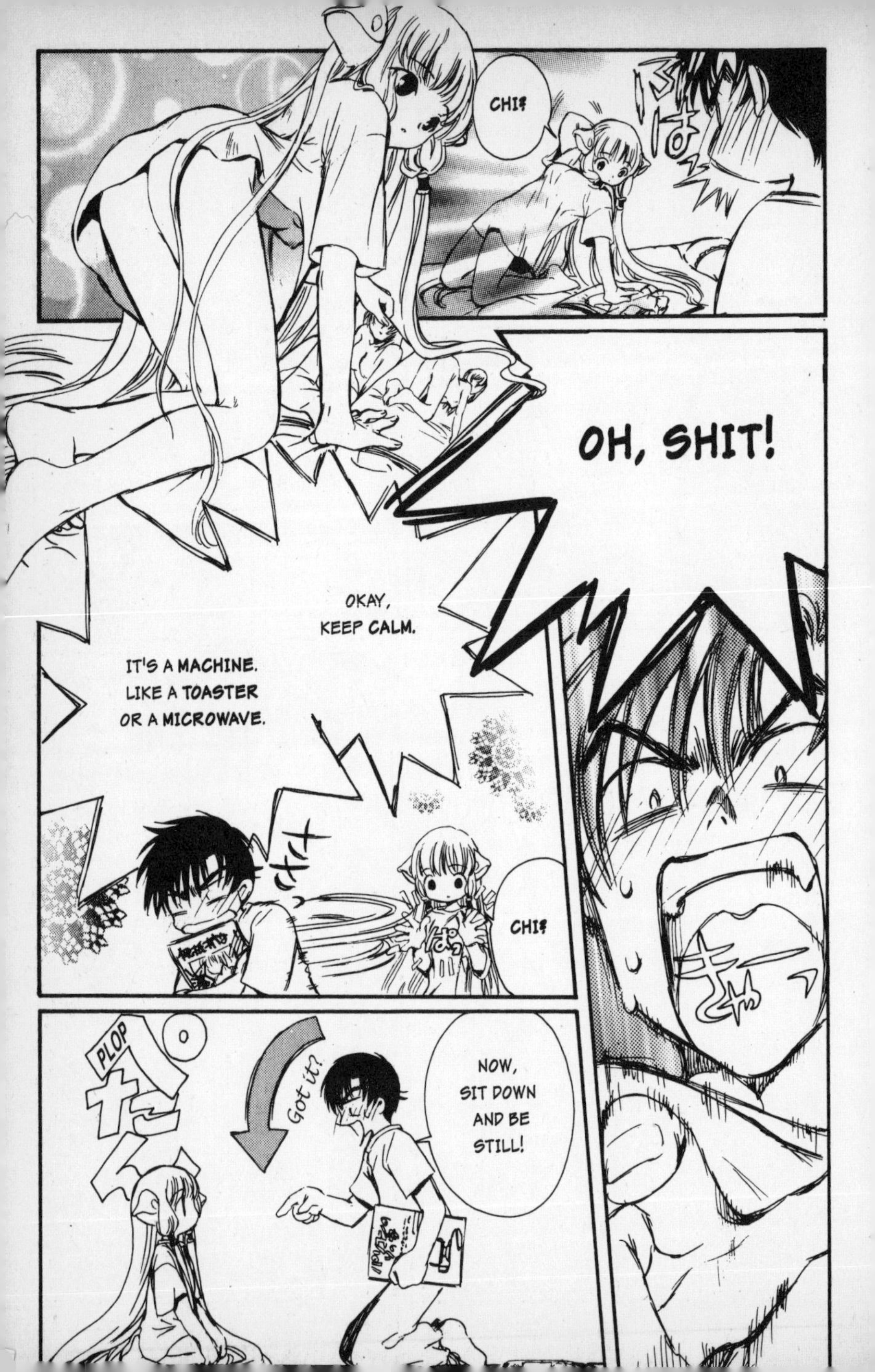
CHI?
OH, SHIT!
OKAY, KEEP CALM.
IT'S A MACHINE. LIKE A TOASTER OR A MICROWAVE.
CHI?
NOW, SIT DOWN AND BE STILL!
Got it?
PLOP

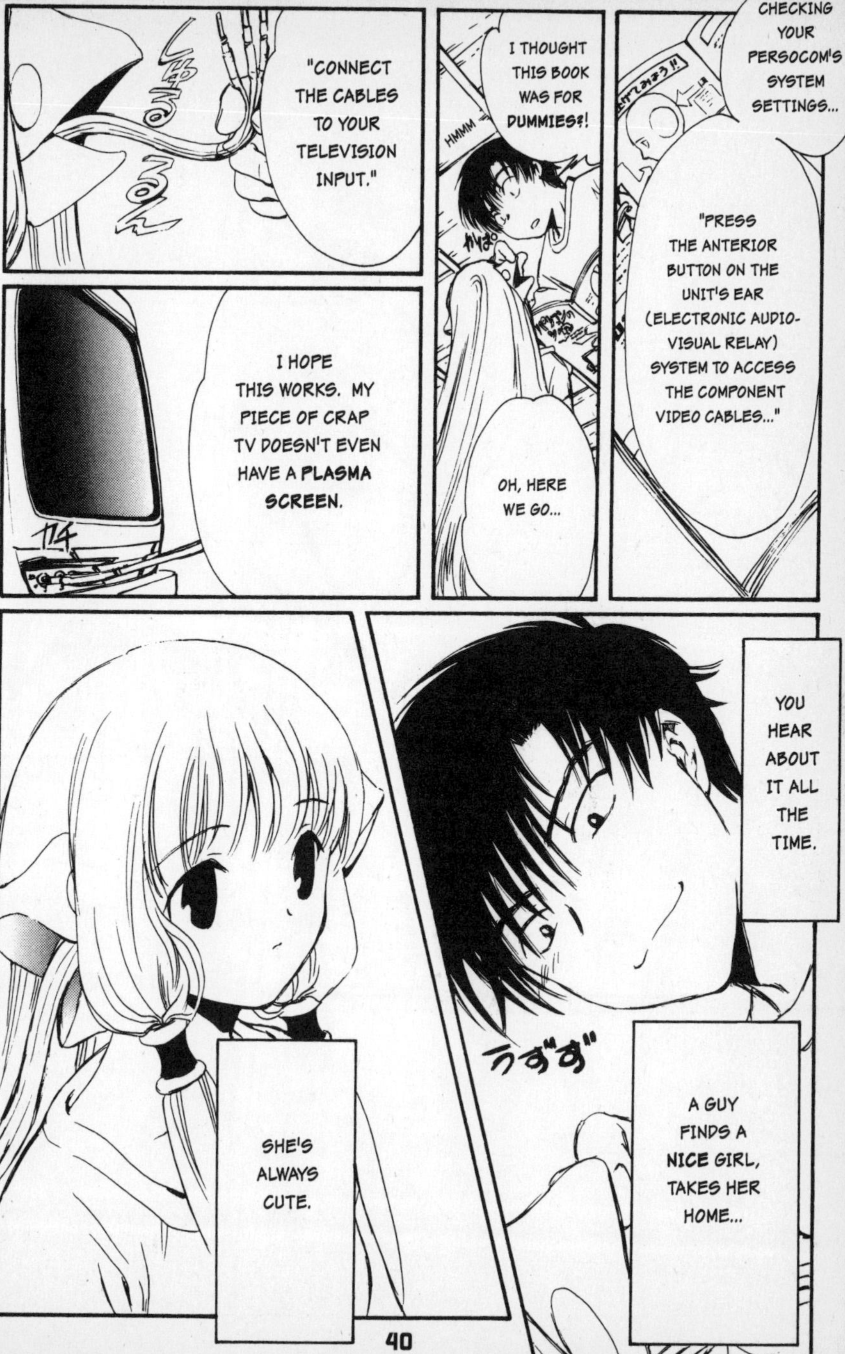
CHECKING YOUR PERSOCOM'S SYSTEM SETTINGS...
"PRESS THE ANTERIOR BUTTON ON THE UNIT'S EAR (ELECTRONIC AUDIO-VISUAL RELAY) SYSTEM TO ACCESS THE COMPONENT VIDEO CABLES..."
I THOUGHT THIS BOOK WAS FOR DUMMIES?!
HMMM
OH, HERE WE GO...
"CONNECT THE CABLES TO YOUR TELEVISION INPUT."
I HOPE THIS WORKS. MY PIECE OF CRAP TV DOESN'T EVEN HAVE A PLASMA SCREEN.
YOU HEAR ABOUT IT ALL THE TIME.
A GUY FINDS A NICE GIRL, TAKES HER HOME...
SHE'S ALWAYS CUTE.

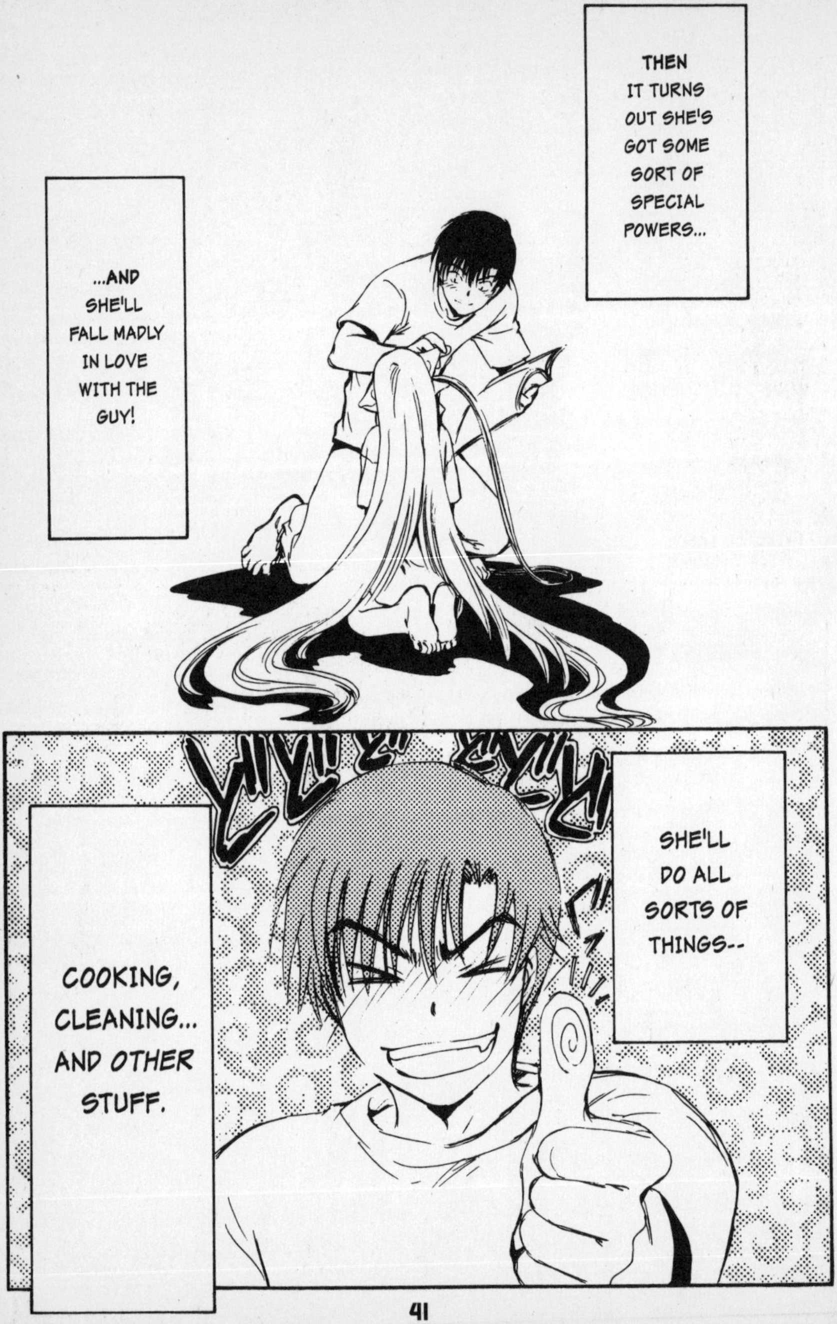
THEN IT TURNS OUT SHE'S GOT SOME SORT OF SPECIAL POWERS...
...AND SHE'LL FALL MADLY IN LOVE WITH THE GUY!
SHE'LL DO ALL SORTS OF THINGS--
COOKING, CLEANING... AND OTHER STUFF.

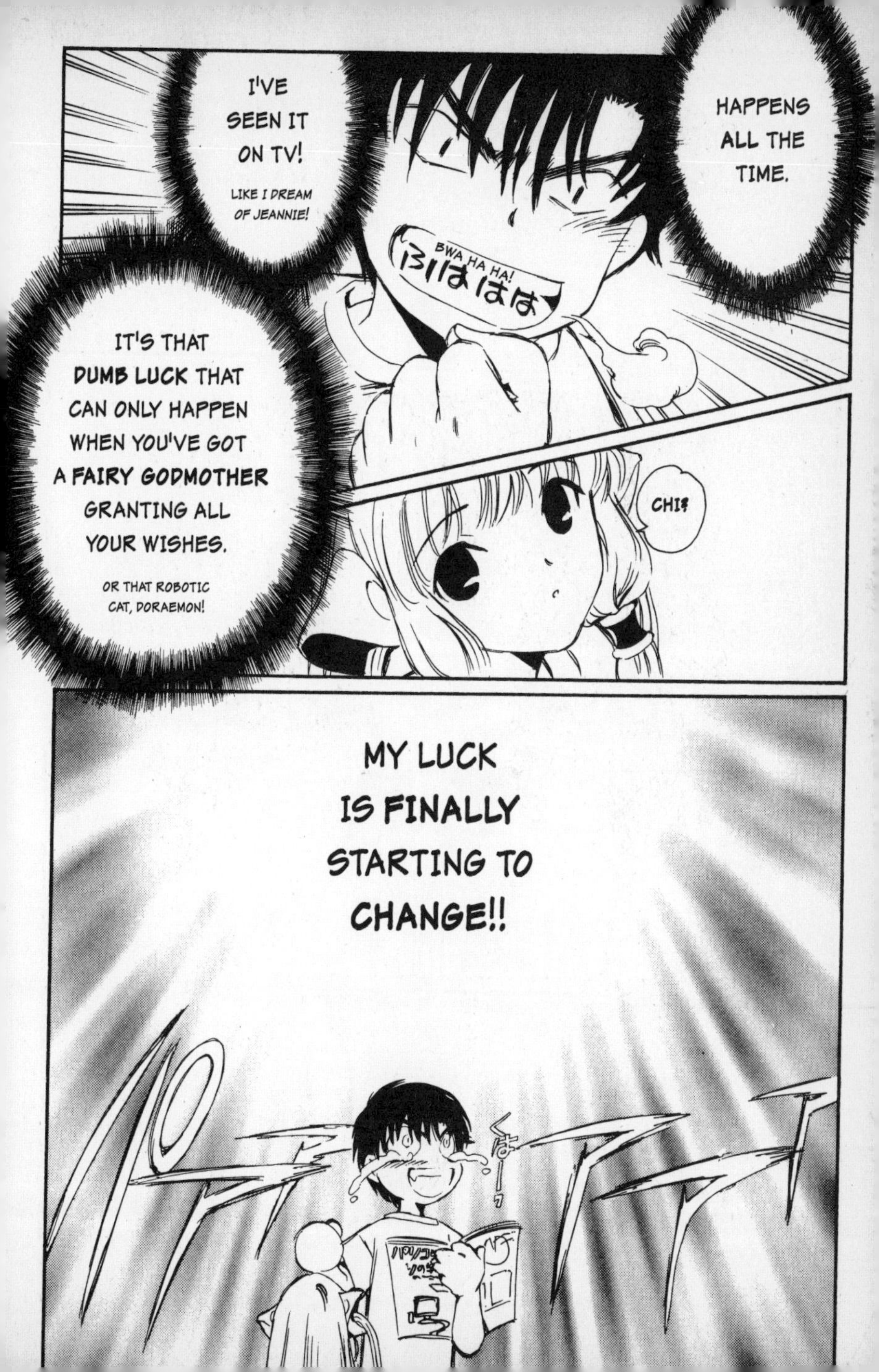
HAPPENS ALL THE TIME.
I'VE SEEN IT ON TV!
LIKE I DREAM OF JEANNIE!
BWA HA HA!
ふははは
IT'S THAT DUMB LUCK THAT CAN ONLY HAPPEN WHEN YOU'VE GOT A FAIRY GODMOTHER GRANTING ALL YOUR WISHES.
OR THAT ROBOTIC CAT, DORAEMON!
CHI?
MY LUCK IS FINALLY STARTING TO CHANGE!!

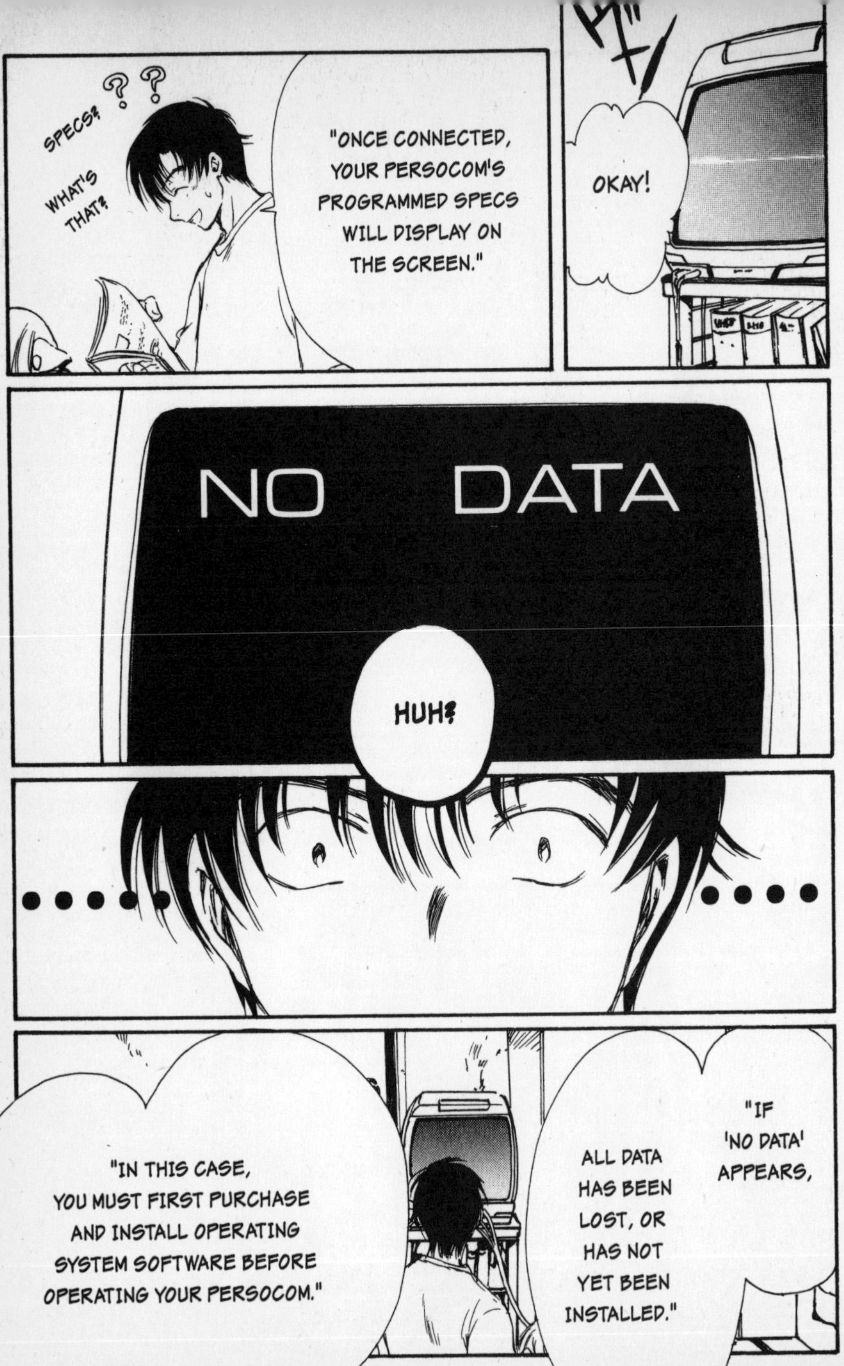
OKAY!
"ONCE CONNECTED, YOUR PERSOCOM'S PROGRAMMED SPECS WILL DISPLAY ON THE SCREEN."
SPECS?
WHAT'S THAT?
NO DATA
HUH?
.....
.....
"IF 'NO DATA' APPEARS,
ALL DATA HAS BEEN LOST, OR HAS NOT YET BEEN INSTALLED."
"IN THIS CASE, YOU MUST FIRST PURCHASE AND INSTALL OPERATING SYSTEM SOFTWARE BEFORE OPERATING YOUR PERSOCOM."

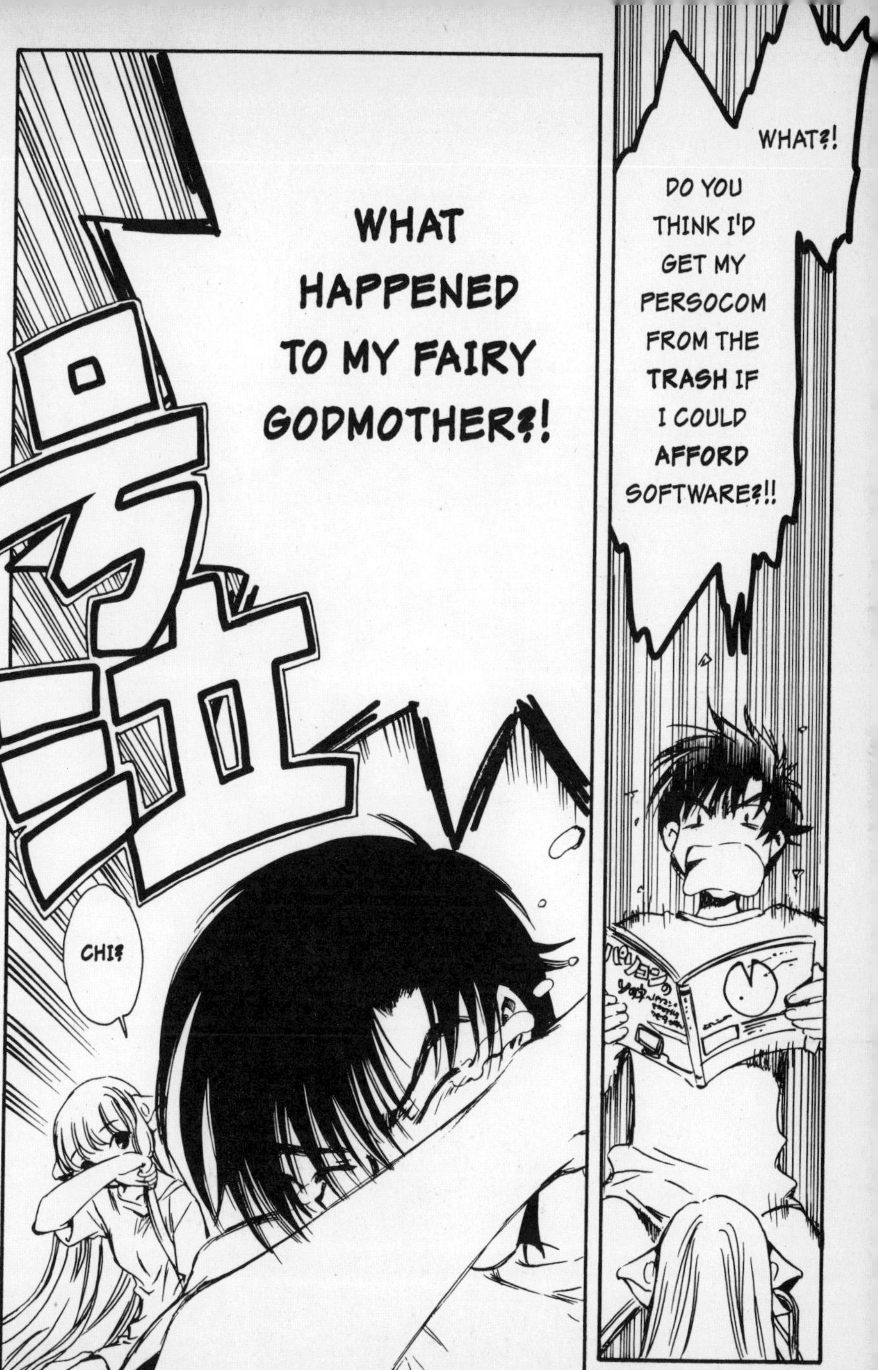
WHAT?!
DO YOU THINK I'D GET MY PERSOCOM FROM THE TRASH IF I COULD AFFORD SOFTWARE?!!
WHAT HAPPENED TO MY FAIRY GODMOTHER?!
CHI?

◂chapter.2▸ end

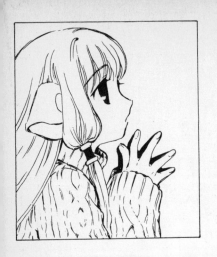
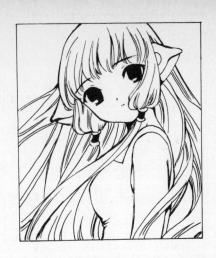
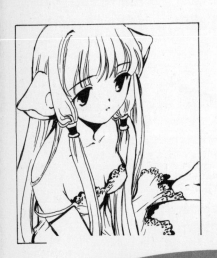
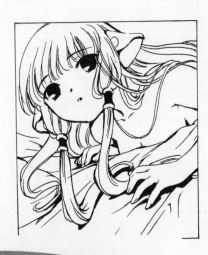

ちょびっツ
Chobits

◄chapter.3►

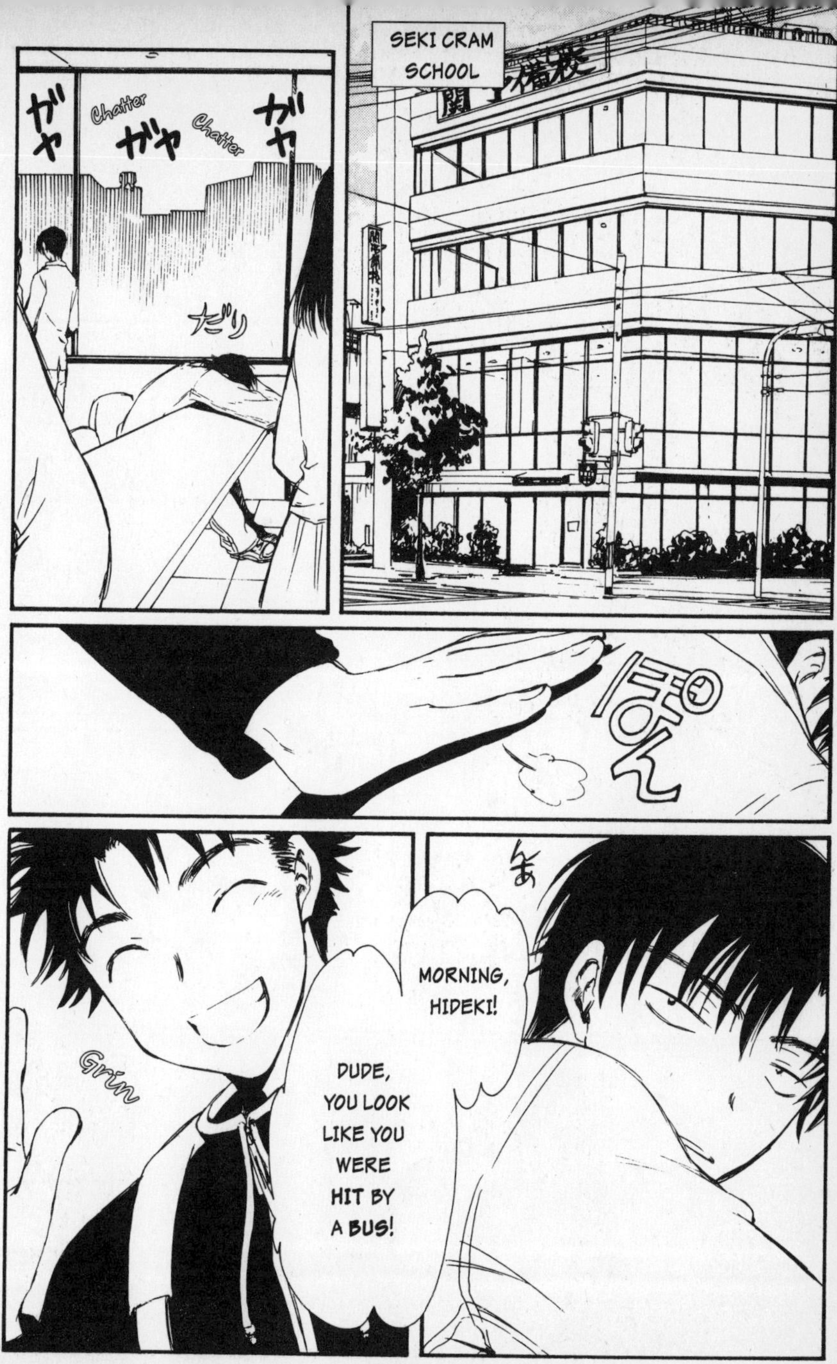
SEKI CRAM SCHOOL
ガヤ
Chatter
ガヤ
Chatter
ガヤ
ぽん
MORNING, HIDEKI!
DUDE, YOU LOOK LIKE YOU WERE HIT BY A BUS!
Grin

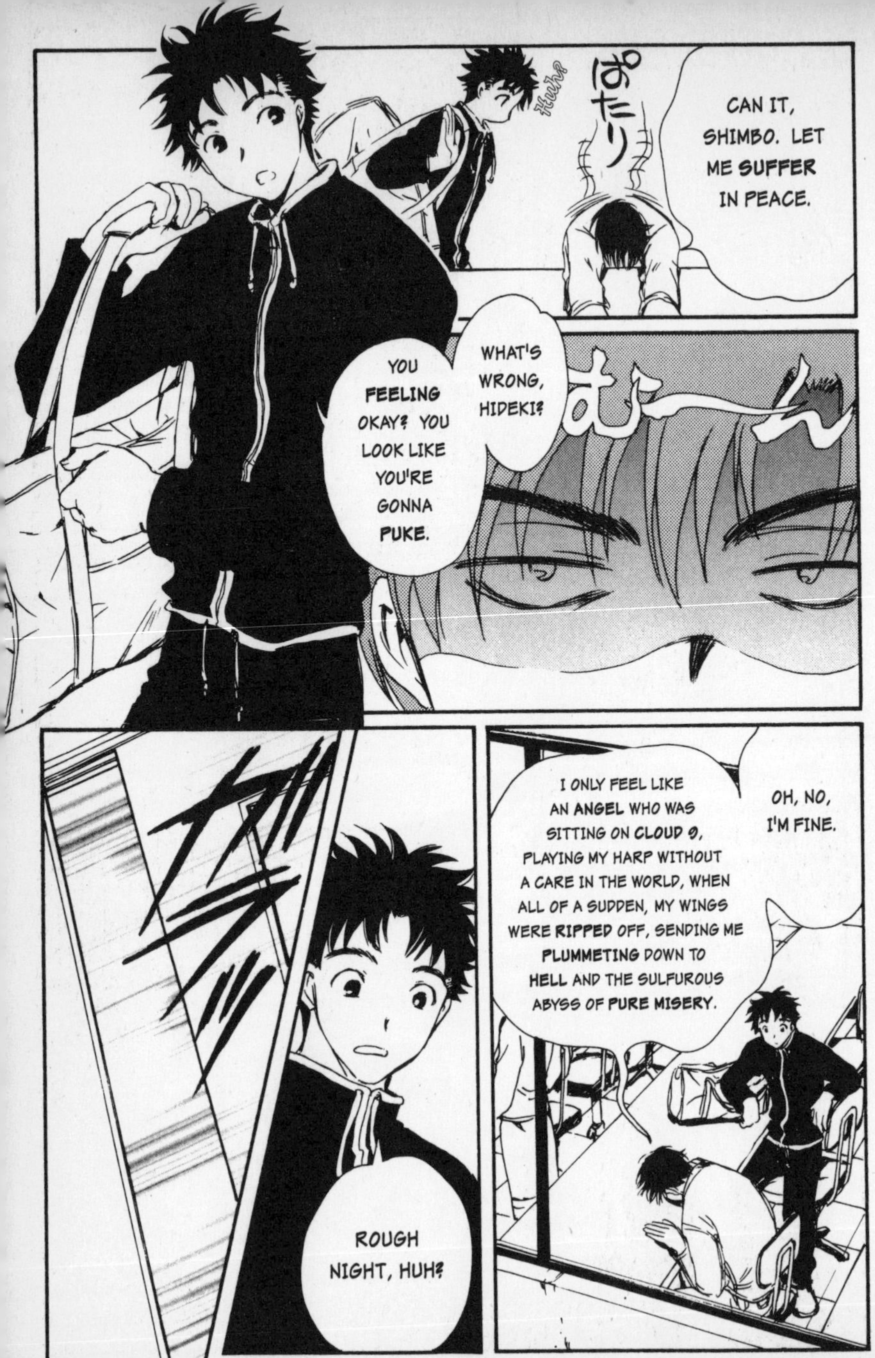
CAN IT, SHIMBO. LET ME SUFFER IN PEACE.
ぱたり
Huh?
むーん
WHAT'S WRONG, HIDEKI?
YOU FEELING OKAY? YOU LOOK LIKE YOU'RE GONNA PUKE.
OH, NO, I'M FINE.
I ONLY FEEL LIKE AN ANGEL WHO WAS SITTING ON CLOUD 9, PLAYING MY HARP WITHOUT A CARE IN THE WORLD, WHEN ALL OF A SUDDEN, MY WINGS WERE RIPPED OFF, SENDING ME PLUMMETING DOWN TO HELL AND THE SULFUROUS ABYSS OF PURE MISERY.
ROUGH NIGHT, HUH?

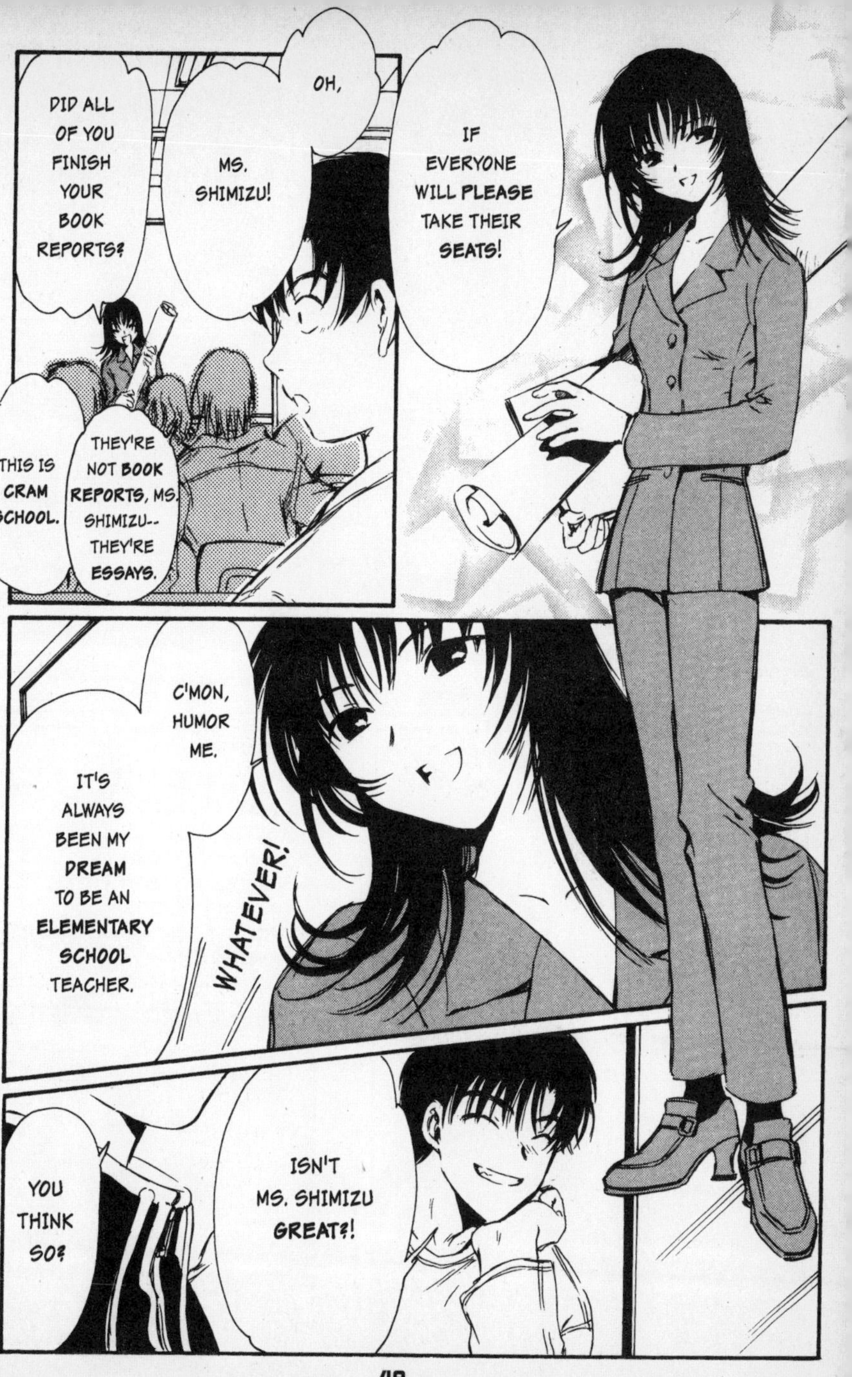
IF EVERYONE WILL PLEASE TAKE THEIR SEATS!
OH,
MS. SHIMIZU!
DID ALL OF YOU FINISH YOUR BOOK REPORTS?
THEY'RE NOT BOOK REPORTS, MS. SHIMIZU-- THEY'RE ESSAYS.
THIS IS CRAM SCHOOL.
C'MON, HUMOR ME.
IT'S ALWAYS BEEN MY DREAM TO BE AN ELEMENTARY SCHOOL TEACHER.
WHATEVER!
ISN'T MS. SHIMIZU GREAT?!
YOU THINK SO?

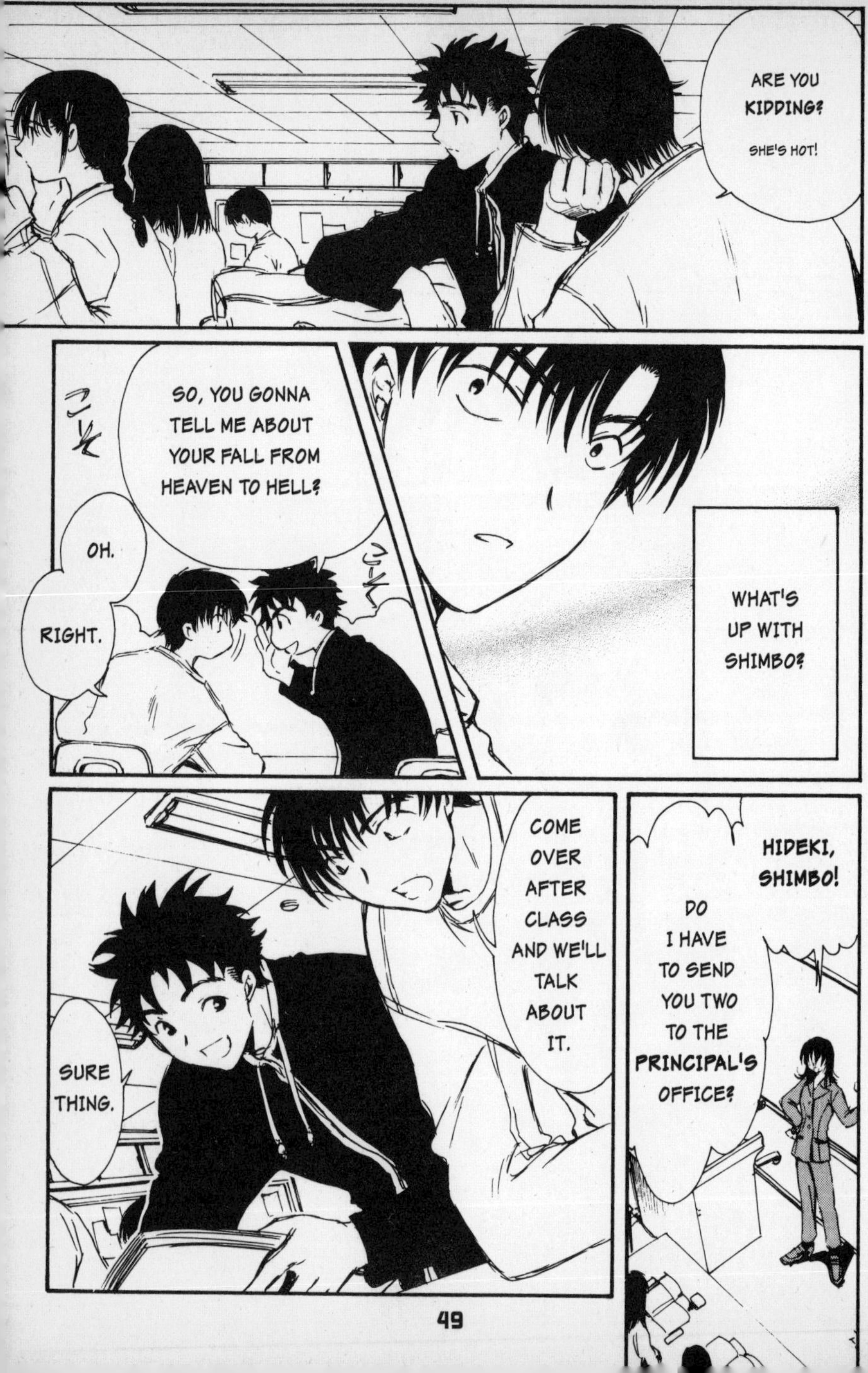
ARE YOU KIDDING?
SHE'S HOT!
WHAT'S UP WITH SHIMBO?
SO, YOU GONNA TELL ME ABOUT YOUR FALL FROM HEAVEN TO HELL?
OH.
RIGHT.
HIDEKI, SHIMBO!
DO I HAVE TO SEND YOU TWO TO THE PRINCIPAL'S OFFICE?
COME OVER AFTER CLASS AND WE'LL TALK ABOUT IT.
SURE THING.

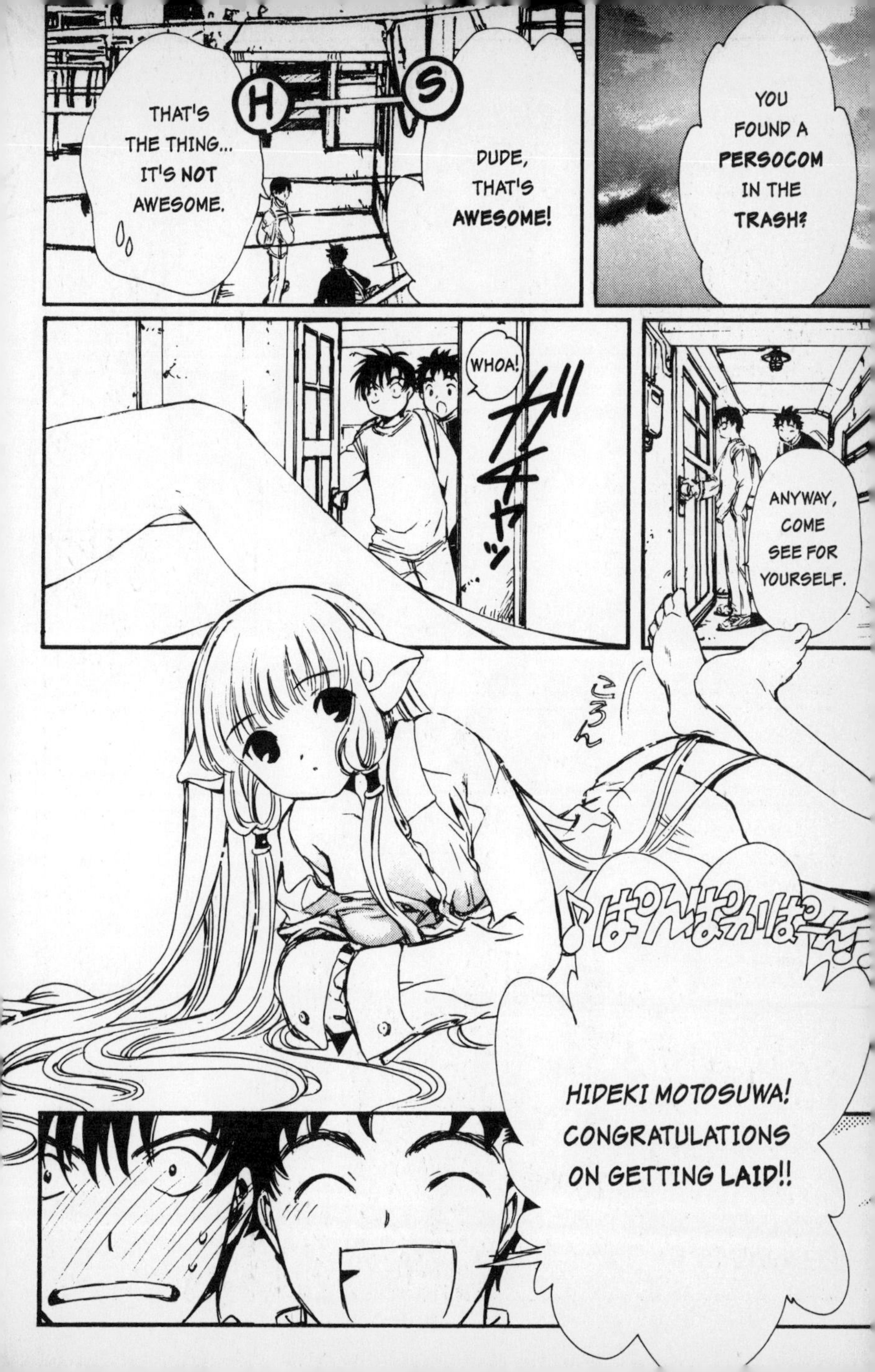
YOU FOUND A PERSOCOM IN THE TRASH?
S
DUDE, THAT'S AWESOME!
H
THAT'S THE THING... IT'S NOT AWESOME.
ANYWAY, COME SEE FOR YOURSELF.
WHOA!
ガチャッ
ごろん
♪ぱんぱかぱーん
HIDEKI MOTOSUWA! CONGRATULATIONS ON GETTING LAID!!

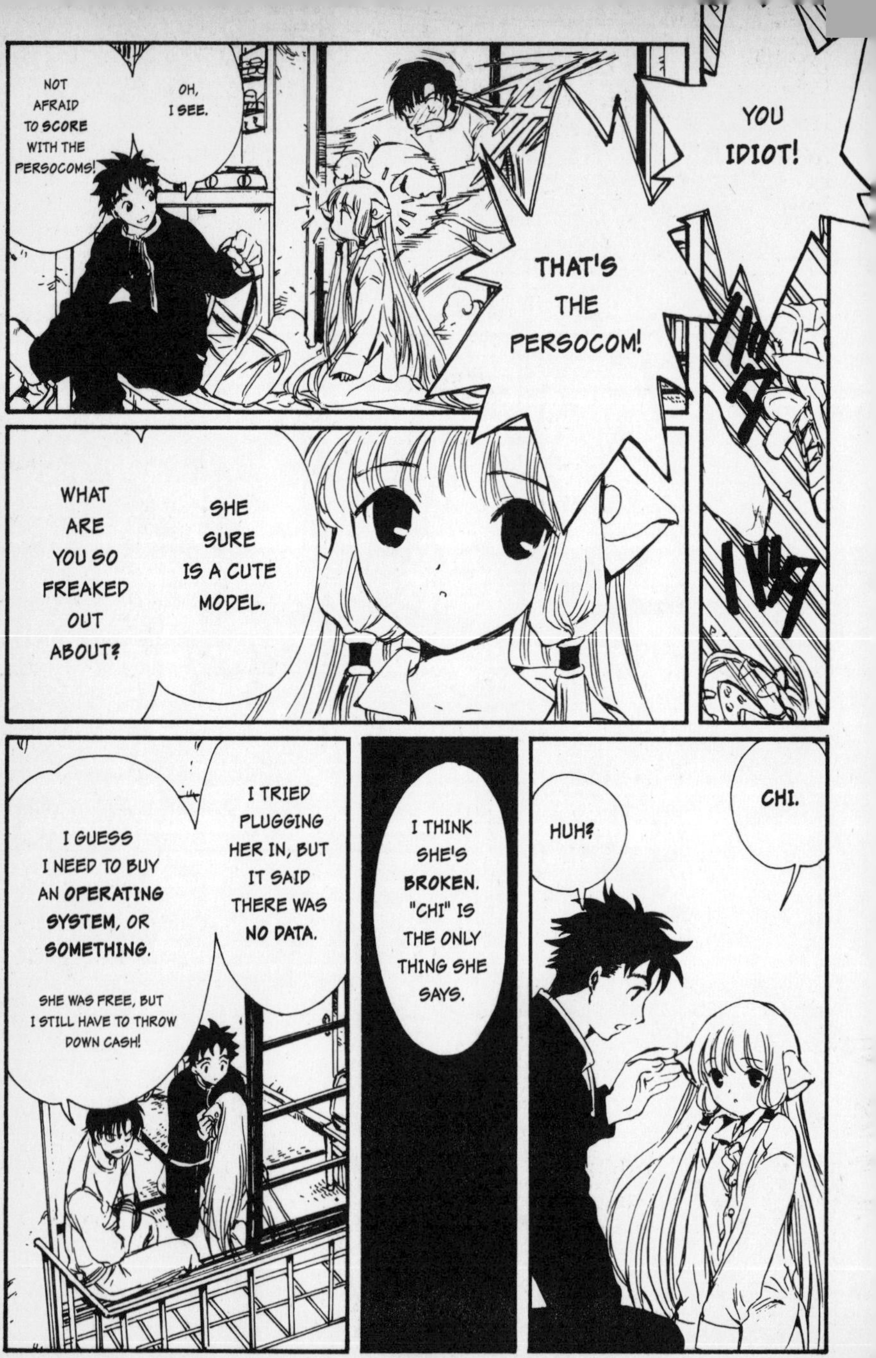
YOU IDIOT!
THAT'S THE PERSOCOM!
OH, I SEE.
NOT AFRAID TO SCORE WITH THE PERSOCOMS!
SHE SURE IS A CUTE MODEL.
WHAT ARE YOU SO FREAKED OUT ABOUT?
CHI.
HUH?
I THINK SHE'S BROKEN. "CHI" IS THE ONLY THING SHE SAYS.
I TRIED PLUGGING HER IN, BUT IT SAID THERE WAS NO DATA.
I GUESS I NEED TO BUY AN OPERATING SYSTEM, OR SOMETHING.
SHE WAS FREE, BUT I STILL HAVE TO THROW DOWN CASH!

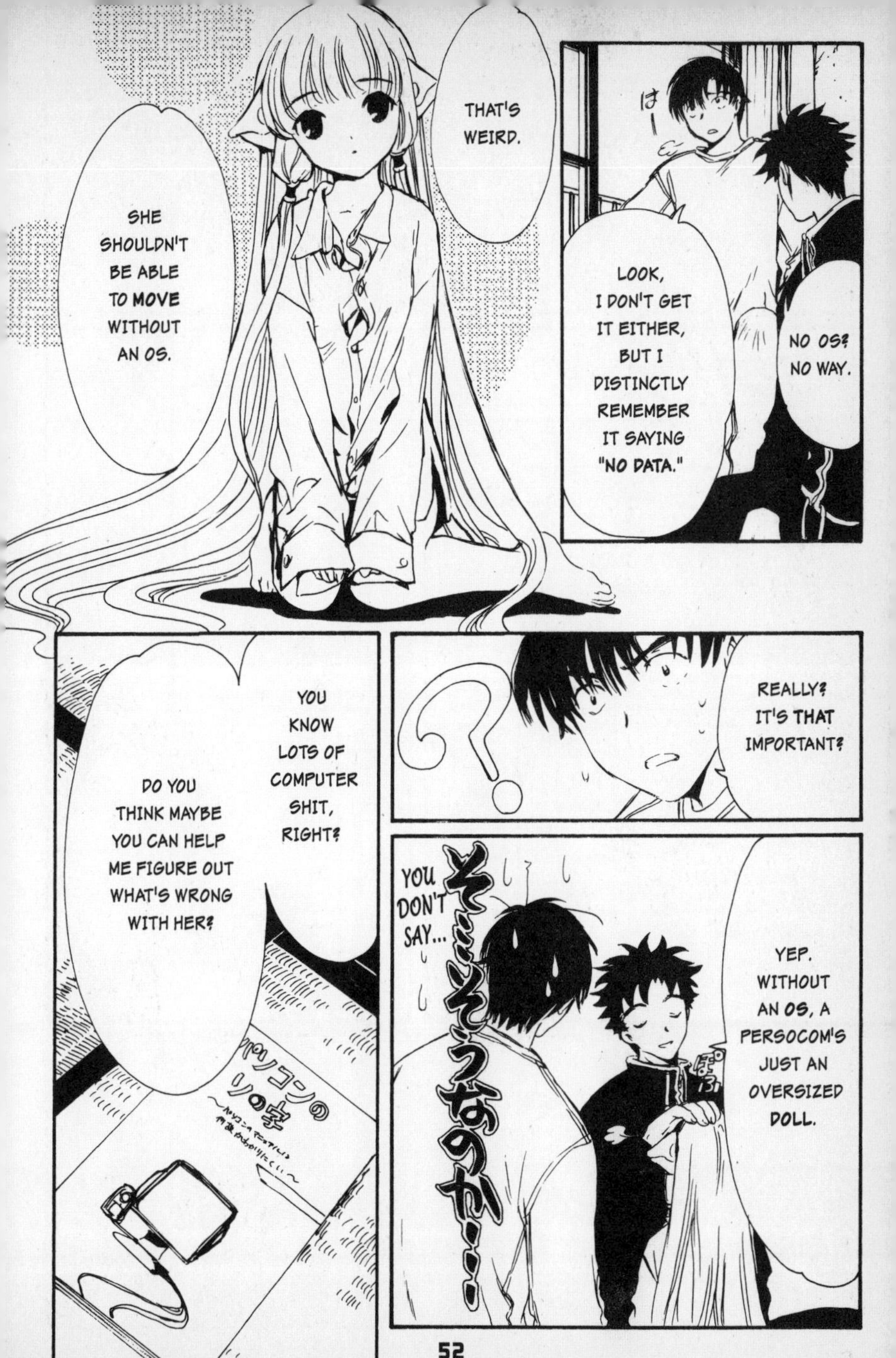

は〜
NO OS? NO WAY.
LOOK, I DON'T GET IT EITHER, BUT I DISTINCTLY REMEMBER IT SAYING "NO DATA."
THAT'S WEIRD.
SHE SHOULDN'T BE ABLE TO MOVE WITHOUT AN OS.
REALLY? IT'S THAT IMPORTANT?
YEP. WITHOUT AN OS, A PERSOCOM'S JUST AN OVERSIZED DOLL.
YOU DON'T SAY...
そ…そうなのか…
YOU KNOW LOTS OF COMPUTER SHIT, RIGHT?
DO YOU THINK MAYBE YOU CAN HELP ME FIGURE OUT WHAT'S WRONG WITH HER?
パソコンのリの字

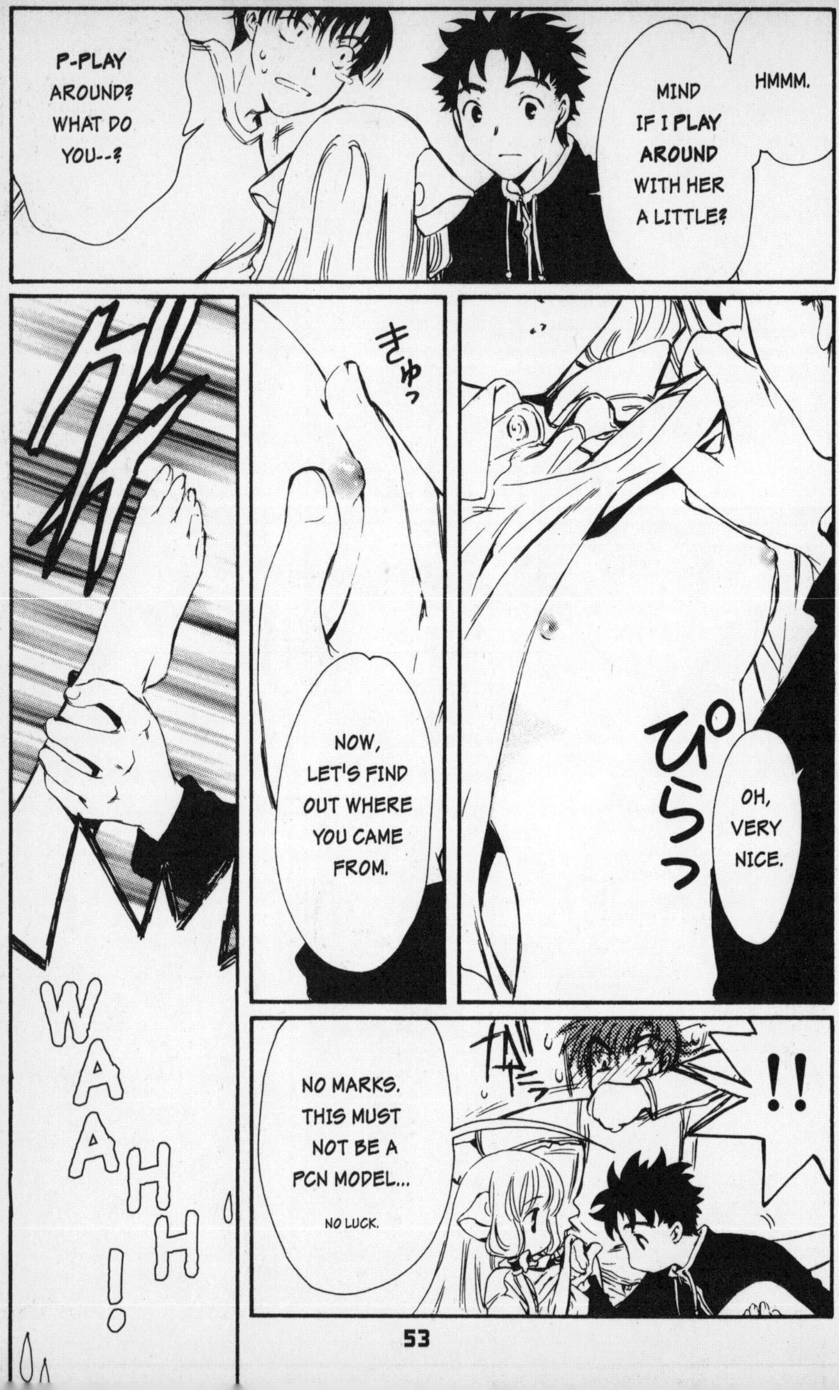
HMMM.
MIND IF I PLAY AROUND WITH HER A LITTLE?
P-PLAY AROUND? WHAT DO YOU--?
ぴらっ
OH, VERY NICE.
きゅっ
NOW, LET'S FIND OUT WHERE YOU CAME FROM.
!!
NO MARKS. THIS MUST NOT BE A PCN MODEL...
NO LUCK.
WAAHHH!

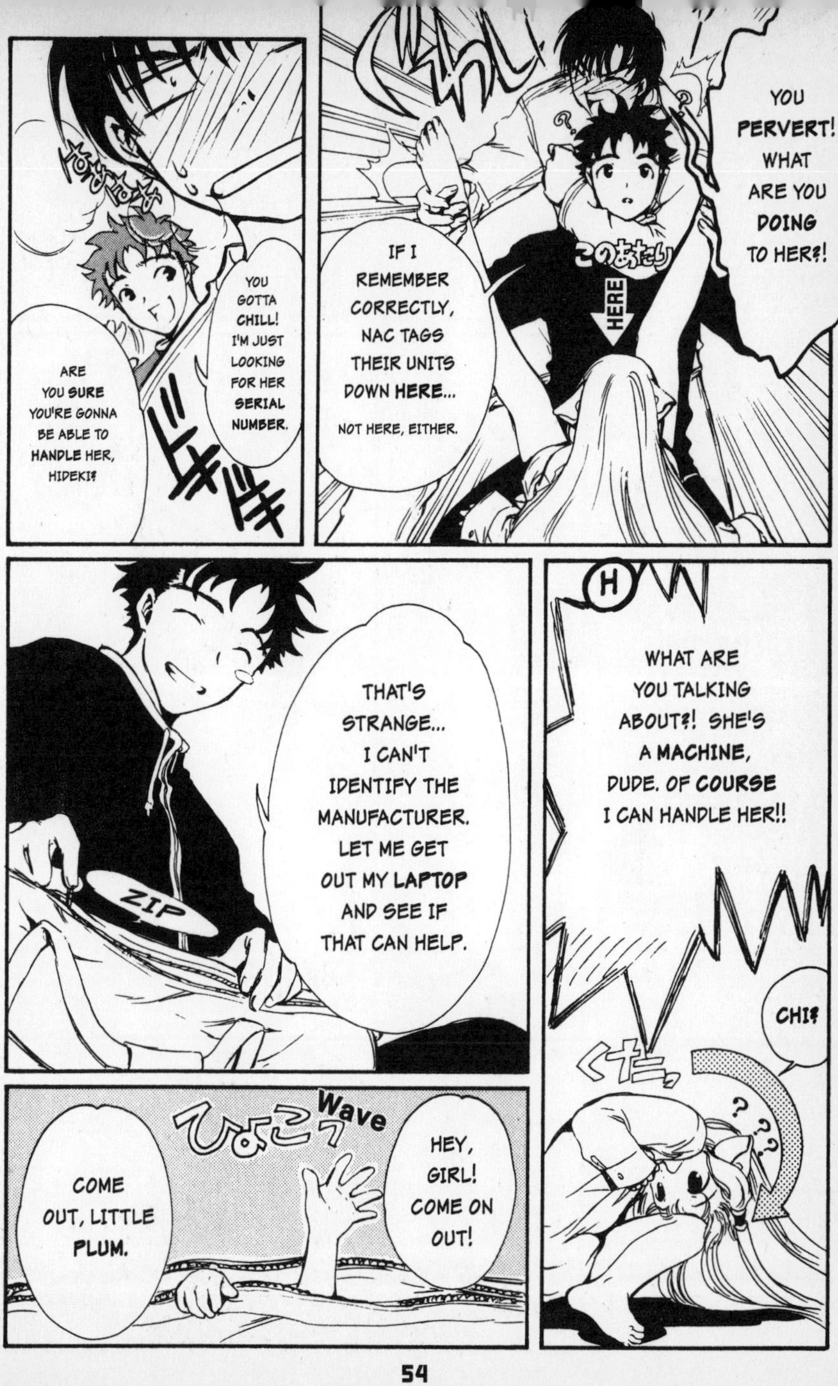

YOU PERVERT! WHAT ARE YOU DOING TO HER?!
このあたり
HERE
IF I REMEMBER CORRECTLY, NAC TAGS THEIR UNITS DOWN HERE...
NOT HERE, EITHER.
YOU GOTTA CHILL! I'M JUST LOOKING FOR HER SERIAL NUMBER.
ドキドキ
ARE YOU SURE YOU'RE GONNA BE ABLE TO HANDLE HER, HIDEKI?
H
WHAT ARE YOU TALKING ABOUT?! SHE'S A MACHINE, DUDE. OF COURSE I CAN HANDLE HER!!
CHI?
THAT'S STRANGE... I CAN'T IDENTIFY THE MANUFACTURER. LET ME GET OUT MY LAPTOP AND SEE IF THAT CAN HELP.
ZIP
Wave
ひょこっ
HEY, GIRL! COME ON OUT!
COME OUT, LITTLE PLUM.

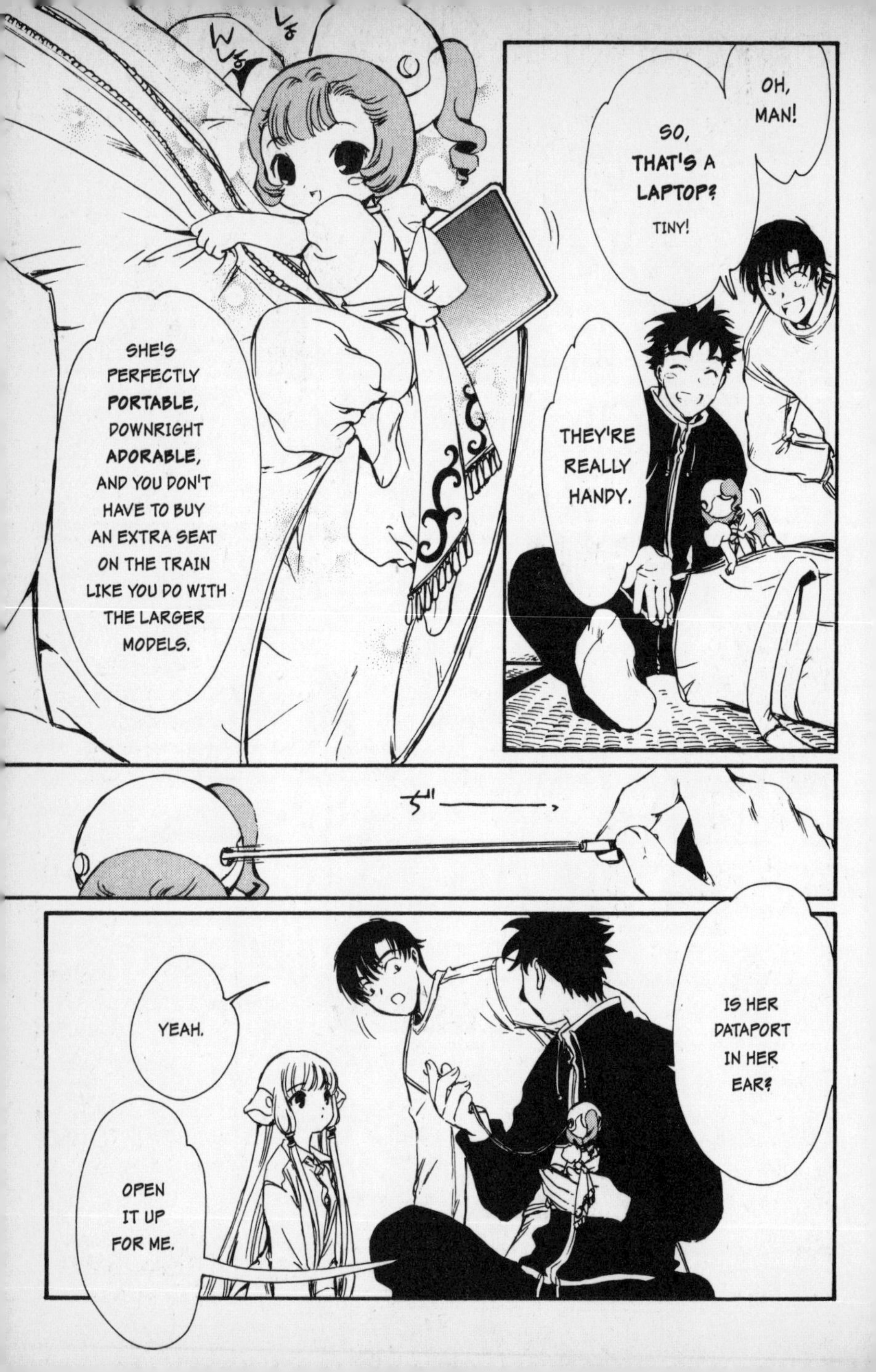
OH, MAN!
SO, THAT'S A LAPTOP?
TINY!
THEY'RE REALLY HANDY.
SHE'S PERFECTLY **PORTABLE**, DOWNRIGHT **ADORABLE**, AND YOU DON'T HAVE TO BUY AN EXTRA SEAT ON THE TRAIN LIKE YOU DO WITH THE LARGER MODELS.
IS HER DATAPORT IN HER EAR?
YEAH.
OPEN IT UP FOR ME.

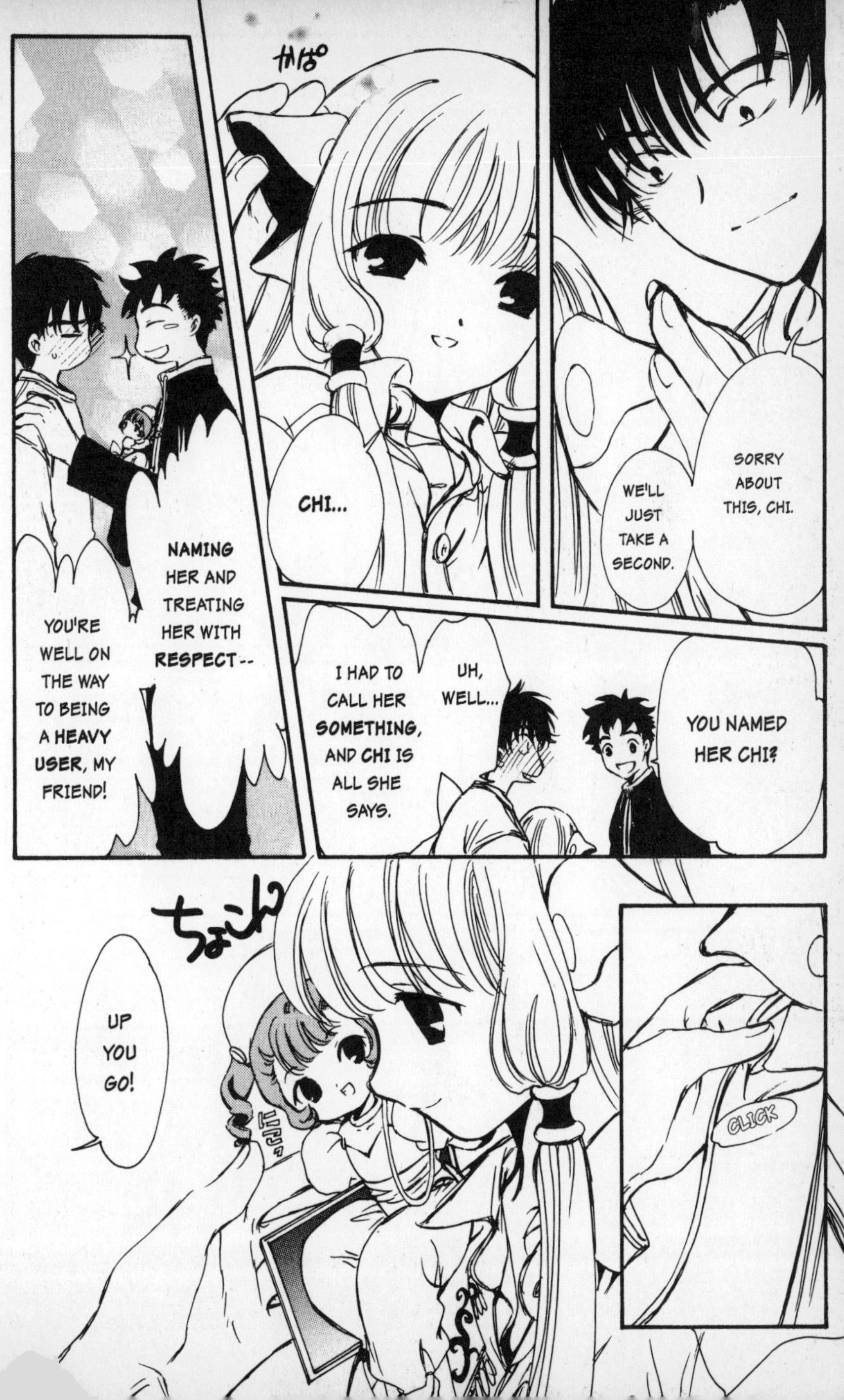
SORRY ABOUT THIS, CHI.
WE'LL JUST TAKE A SECOND.
かぽ
CHI...
YOU NAMED HER CHI?
UH, WELL...
I HAD TO CALL HER SOMETHING, AND CHI IS ALL SHE SAYS.
NAMING HER AND TREATING HER WITH RESPECT--
YOU'RE WELL ON THE WAY TO BEING A HEAVY USER, MY FRIEND!
CLICK
ちょこん
UP YOU GO!

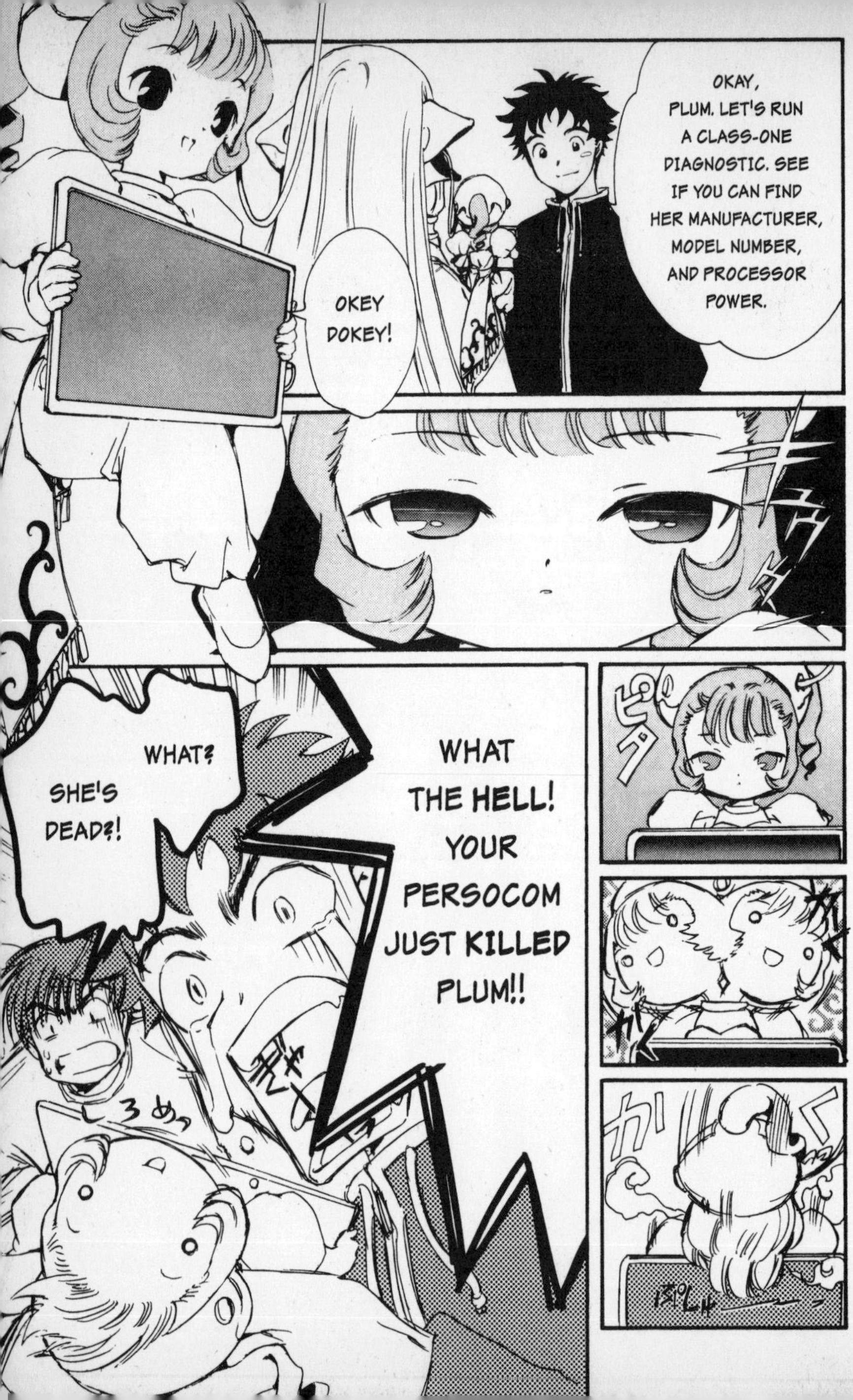
OKAY, PLUM. LET'S RUN A CLASS-ONE DIAGNOSTIC. SEE IF YOU CAN FIND HER MANUFACTURER, MODEL NUMBER, AND PROCESSOR POWER.
OKEY DOKEY!
WHAT THE HELL! YOUR PERSOCOM JUST KILLED PLUM!!
WHAT? SHE'S DEAD?!

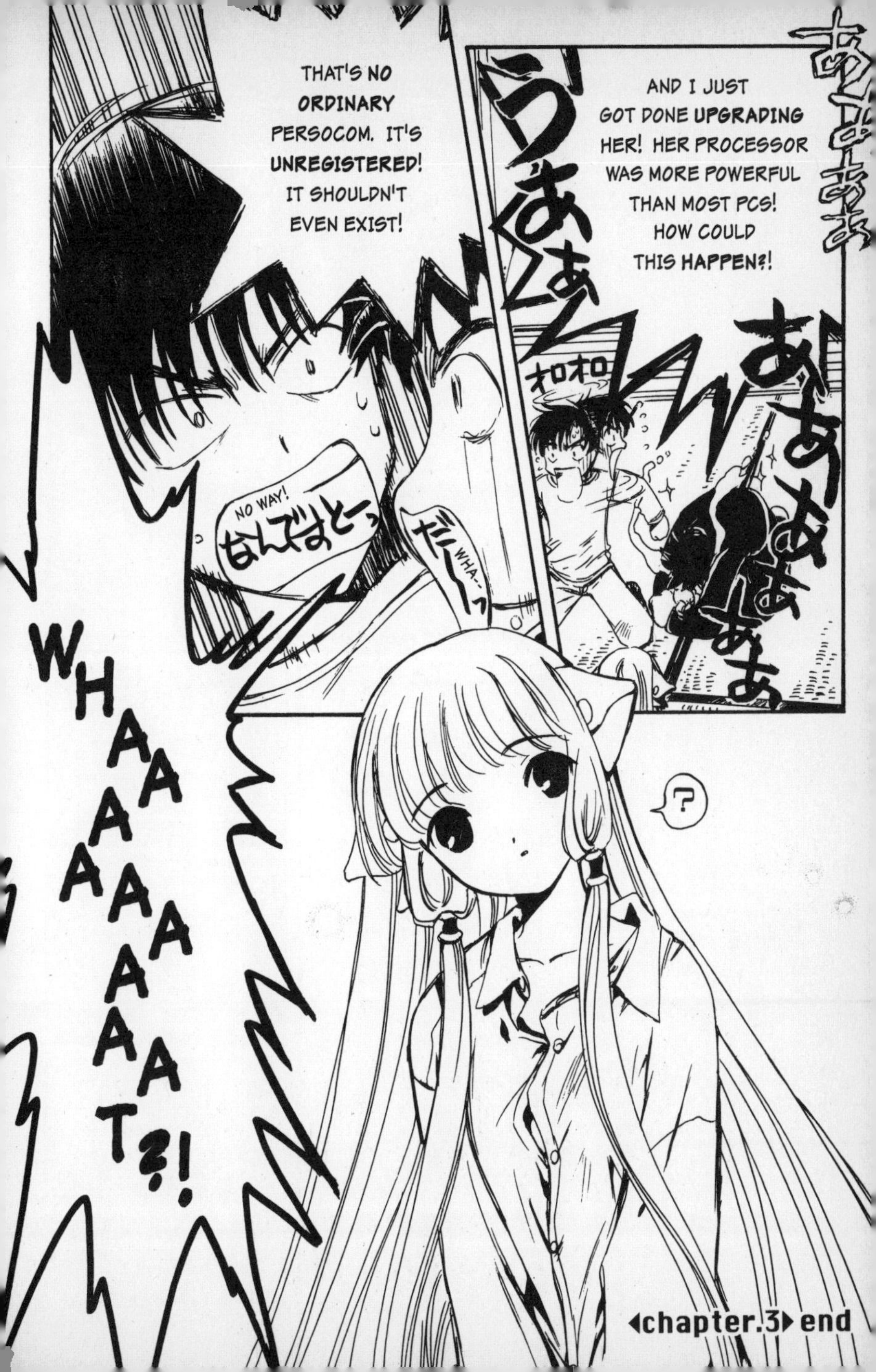
AND I JUST GOT DONE UPGRADING HER! HER PROCESSOR WAS MORE POWERFUL THAN MOST PCS! HOW COULD THIS HAPPEN?!
オロオロ
THAT'S NO ORDINARY PERSOCOM. IT'S UNREGISTERED! IT SHOULDN'T EVEN EXIST!
NO WAY!
なんですとーっ
だーーっ
WHA...
WHAAAAAAAAAAT?!
?
chapter.3 end

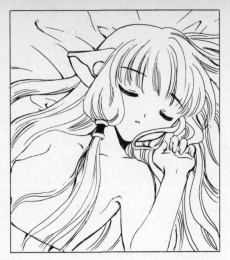

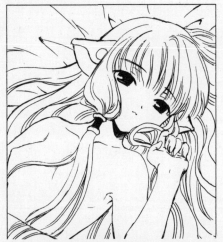

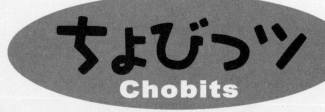

ちょびっツ
Chobits

◀chapter.4▶

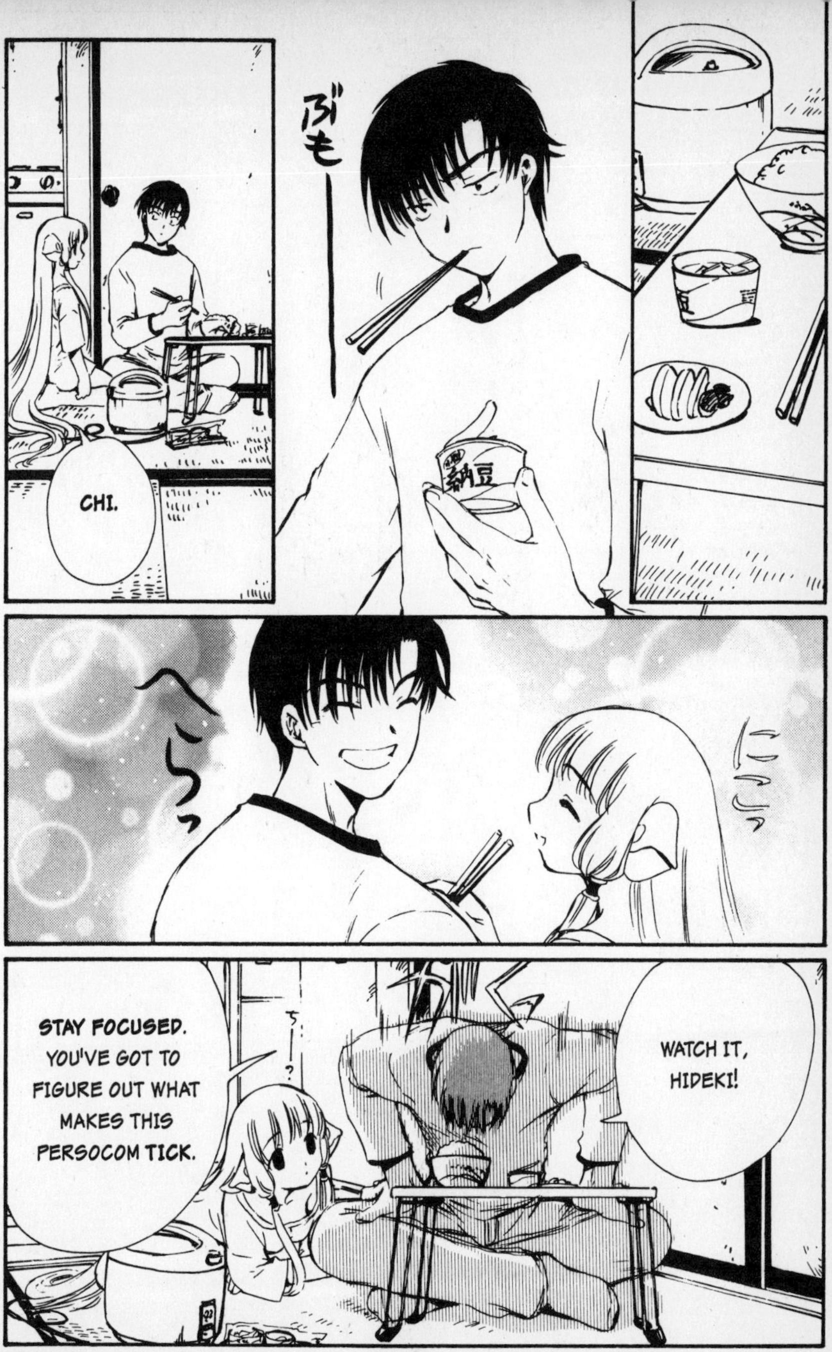
ぶもー
納豆
CHI.
WATCH IT, HIDEKI!
ちー?
STAY FOCUSED. YOU'VE GOT TO FIGURE OUT WHAT MAKES THIS PERSOCOM TICK.

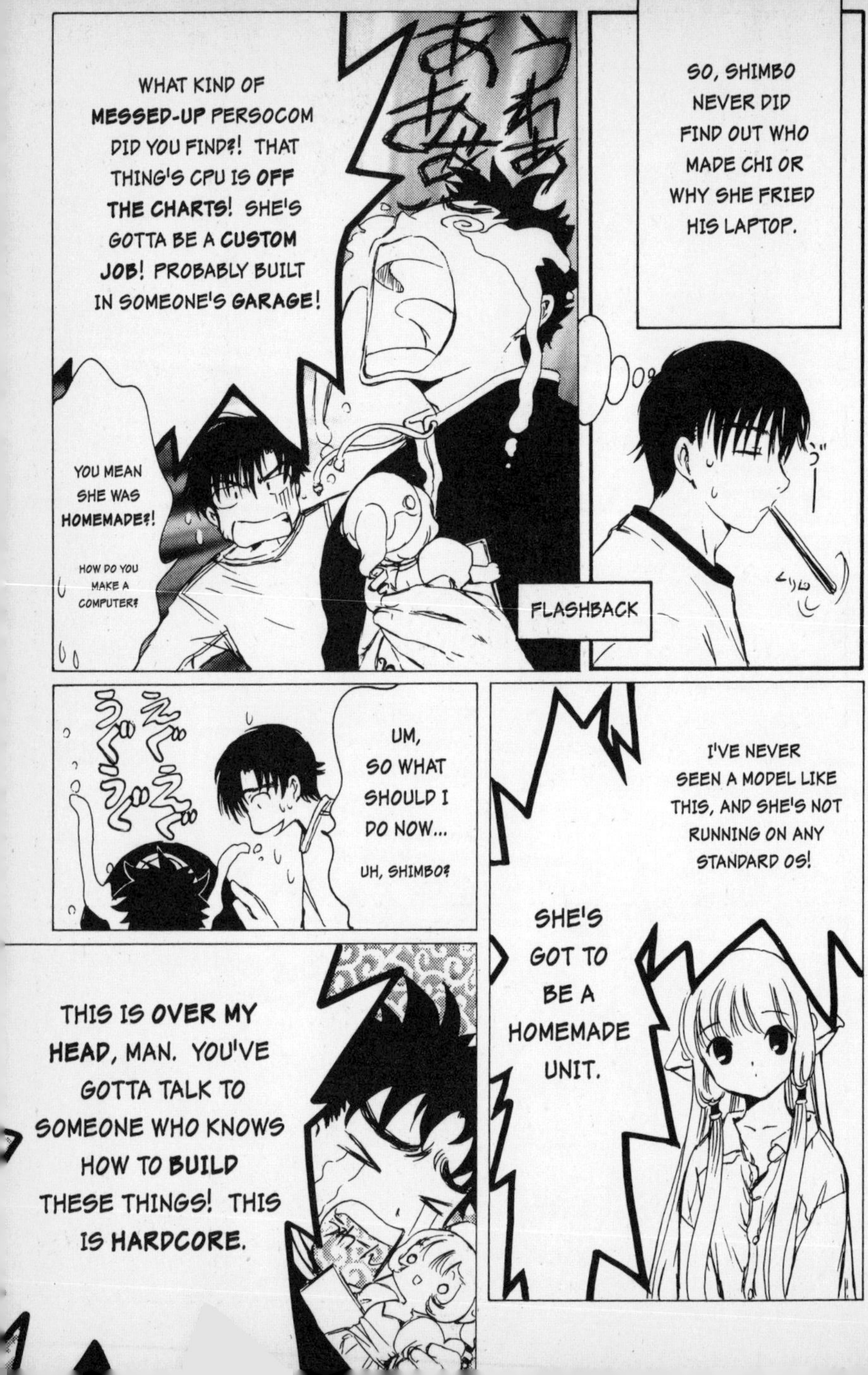
SO, SHIMBO NEVER DID FIND OUT WHO MADE CHI OR WHY SHE FRIED HIS LAPTOP.
FLASHBACK
WHAT KIND OF MESSED-UP PERSOCOM DID YOU FIND?! THAT THING'S CPU IS OFF THE CHARTS! SHE'S GOTTA BE A CUSTOM JOB! PROBABLY BUILT IN SOMEONE'S GARAGE!
YOU MEAN SHE WAS HOMEMADE?!
HOW DO YOU MAKE A COMPUTER?
I'VE NEVER SEEN A MODEL LIKE THIS, AND SHE'S NOT RUNNING ON ANY STANDARD OS!
SHE'S GOT TO BE A HOMEMADE UNIT.
UM, SO WHAT SHOULD I DO NOW...
UH, SHIMBO?
THIS IS OVER MY HEAD, MAN. YOU'VE GOTTA TALK TO SOMEONE WHO KNOWS HOW TO BUILD THESE THINGS! THIS IS HARDCORE.

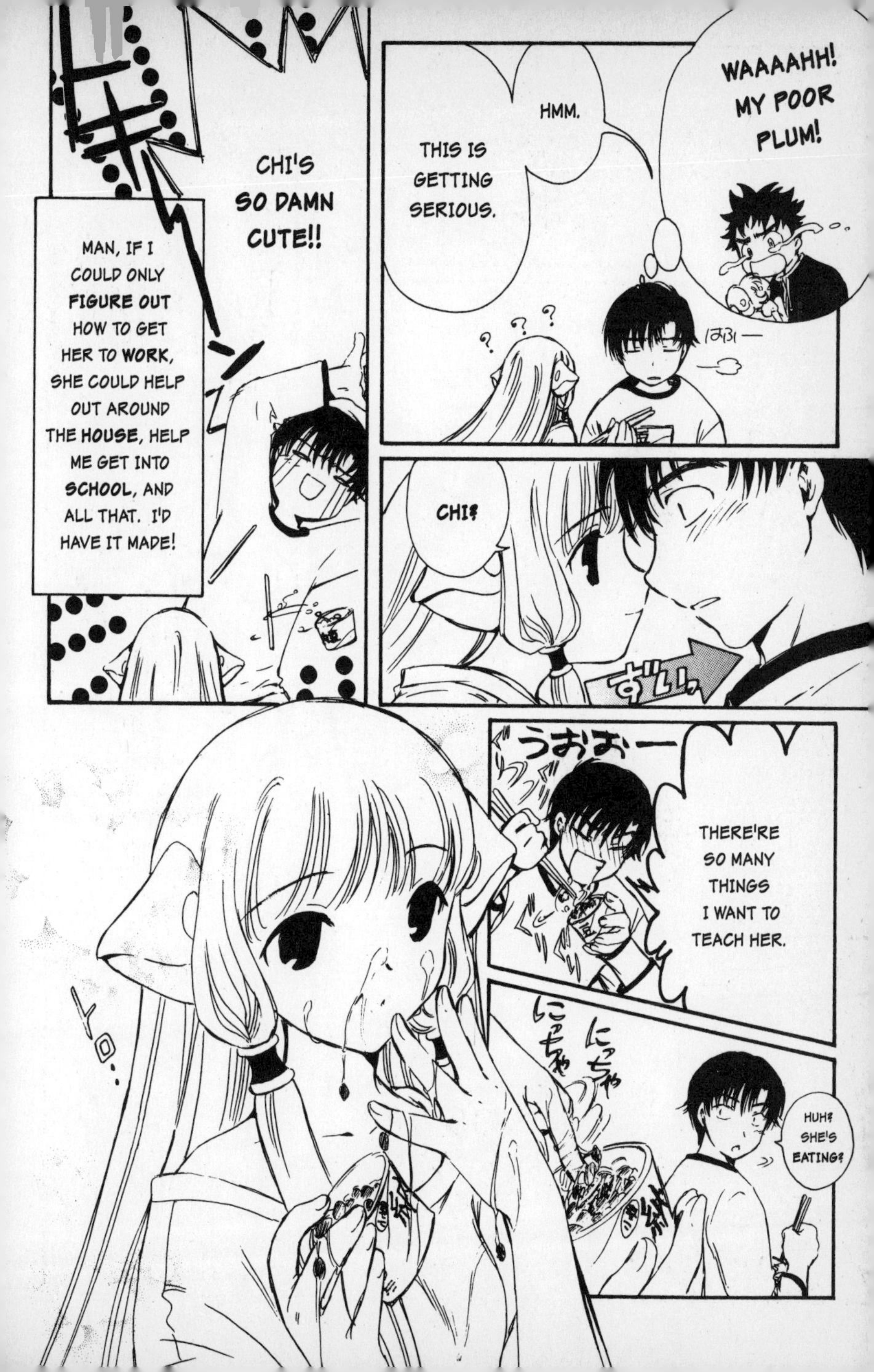
WAAAAHH! MY POOR PLUM!
HMM.
THIS IS GETTING SERIOUS.
はふー
CHI?
ずいっ
CHI'S SO DAMN CUTE!!
MAN, IF I COULD ONLY FIGURE OUT HOW TO GET HER TO WORK, SHE COULD HELP OUT AROUND THE HOUSE, HELP ME GET INTO SCHOOL, AND ALL THAT. I'D HAVE IT MADE!
うおおー
THERE'RE SO MANY THINGS I WANT TO TEACH HER.
HUH? SHE'S EATING?
にっちゃ
にっちゃ

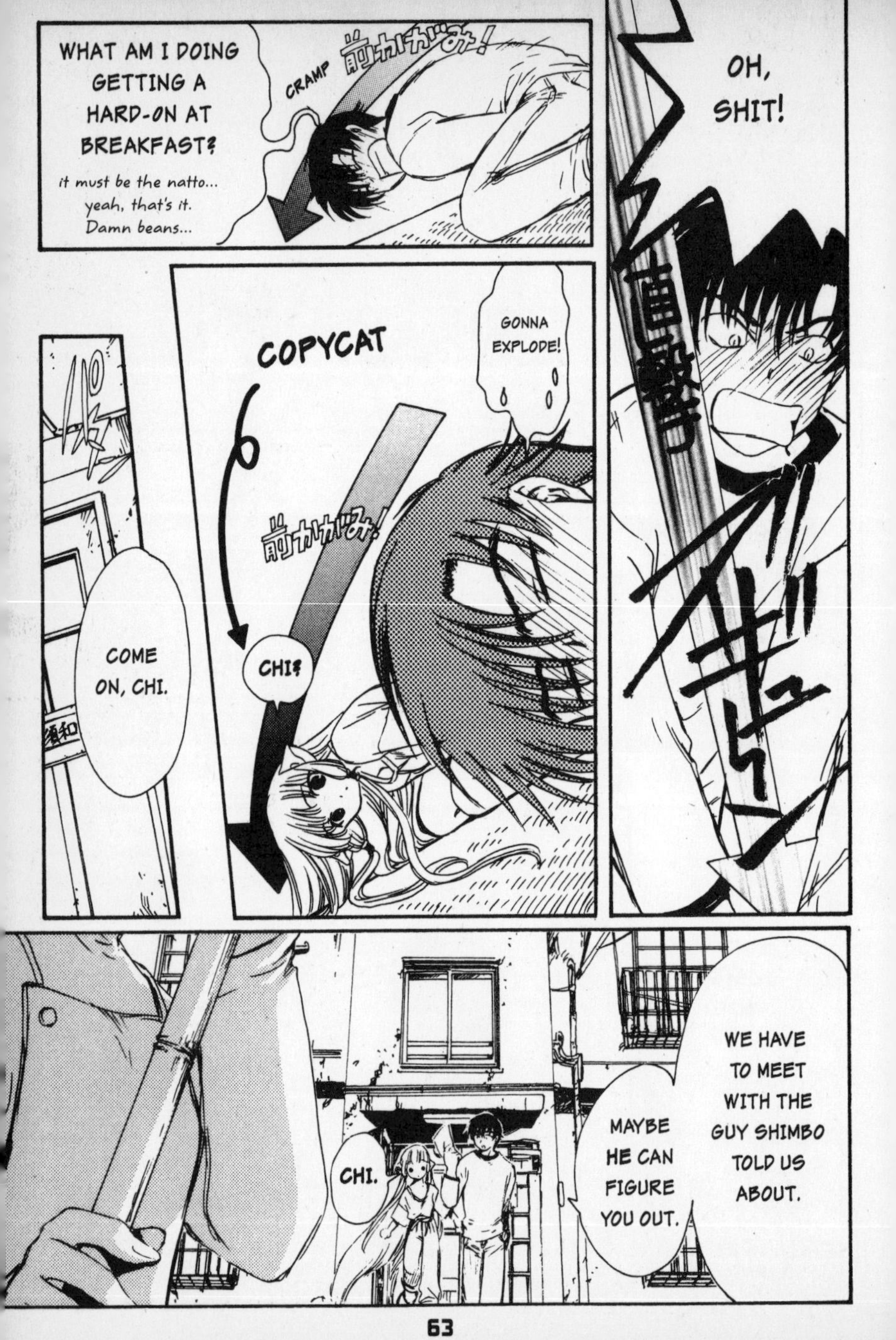
OH, SHIT!
WHAT AM I DOING GETTING A HARD-ON AT BREAKFAST?
it must be the natto... yeah, that's it. Damn beans...
CRAMP
前かがみ!
GONNA EXPLODE!
COPYCAT
前かがみ!
CHI?
COME ON, CHI.
WE HAVE TO MEET WITH THE GUY SHIMBO TOLD US ABOUT.
MAYBE HE CAN FIGURE YOU OUT.
CHI.

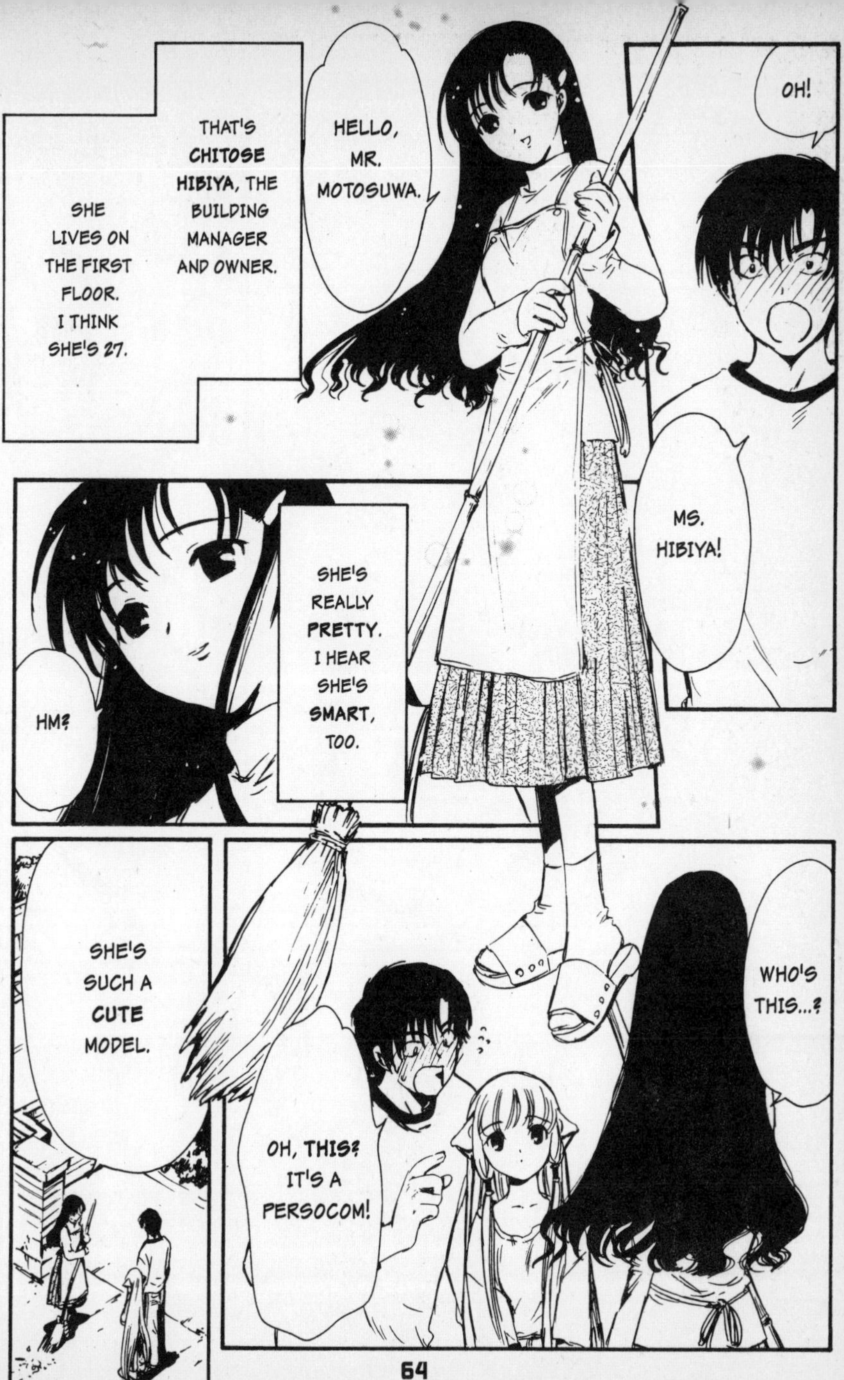
OH!
MS. HIBIYA!
HELLO, MR. MOTOSUWA.
THAT'S CHITOSE HIBIYA, THE BUILDING MANAGER AND OWNER.
SHE LIVES ON THE FIRST FLOOR. I THINK SHE'S 27.
SHE'S REALLY PRETTY. I HEAR SHE'S SMART, TOO.
HM?
WHO'S THIS...?
OH, THIS? IT'S A PERSOCOM!
SHE'S SUCH A CUTE MODEL.

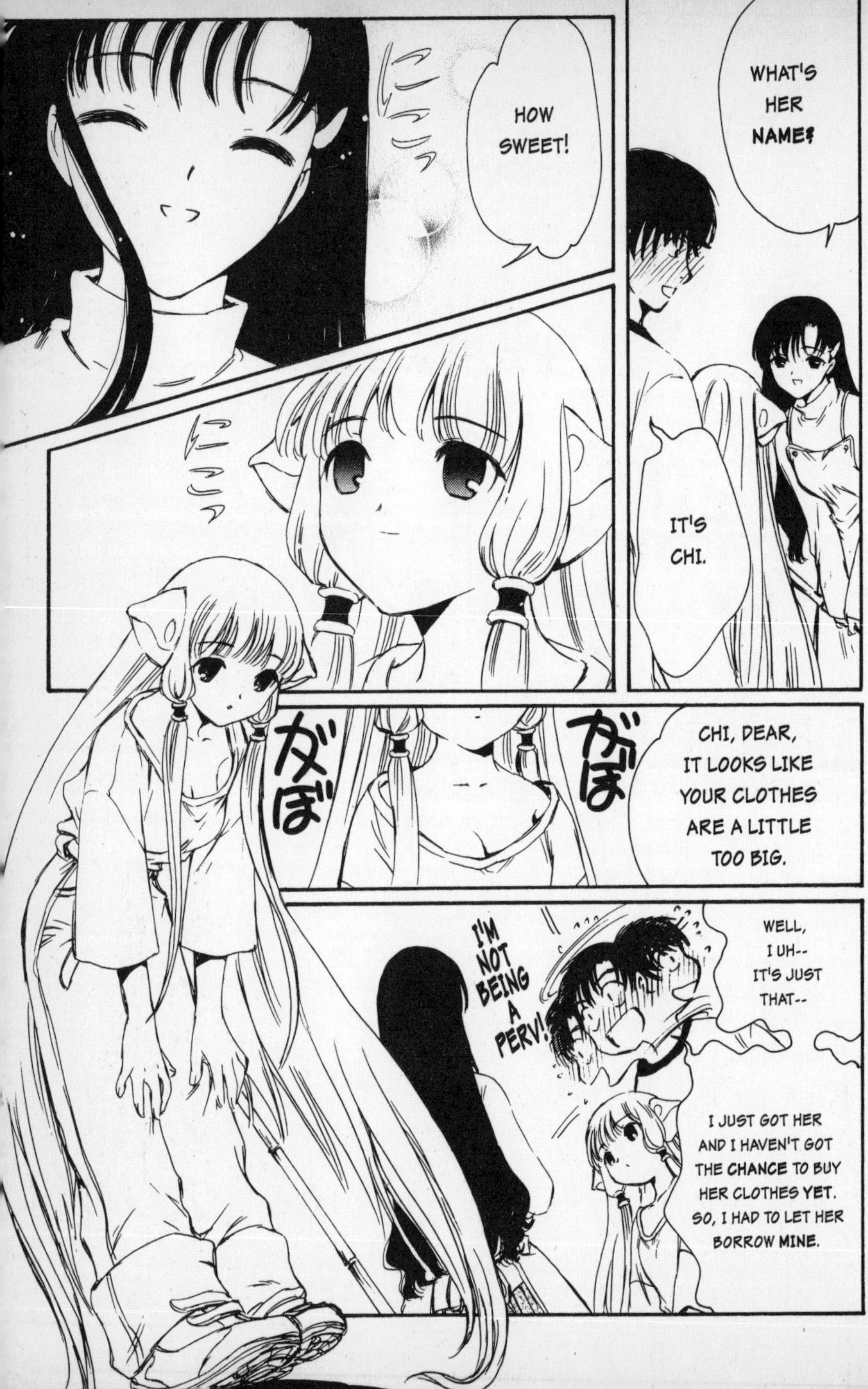
WHAT'S HER NAME?
IT'S CHI.
にこっ
HOW SWEET!
にこっ
がぼ
がぼ
CHI, DEAR, IT LOOKS LIKE YOUR CLOTHES ARE A LITTLE TOO BIG.
WELL, I UH-- IT'S JUST THAT--
I'M NOT BEING A PERV!
I JUST GOT HER AND I HAVEN'T GOT THE CHANCE TO BUY HER CLOTHES YET. SO, I HAD TO LET HER BORROW MINE.

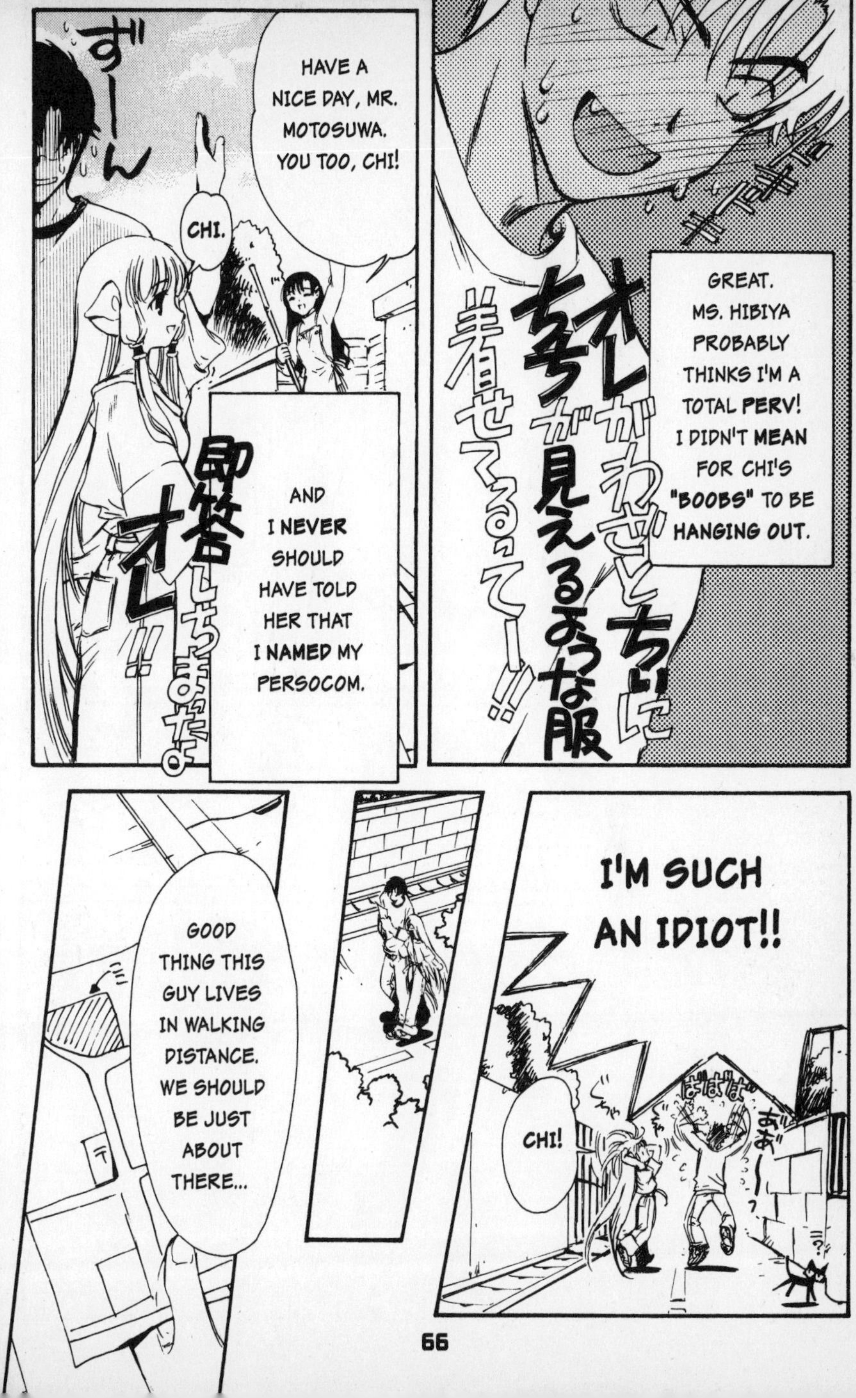

GREAT. MS. HIBIYA PROBABLY THINKS I'M A TOTAL PERV! I DIDN'T MEAN FOR CHI'S "BOOBS" TO BE HANGING OUT.
オレがわざとちぃに
ちちが見えるような服
着せてるって―!!
ずーん
HAVE A NICE DAY, MR. MOTOSUWA. YOU TOO, CHI!
CHI.
AND I NEVER SHOULD HAVE TOLD HER THAT I NAMED MY PERSOCOM.
即答しちまったよ
オレ!!
I'M SUCH AN IDIOT!!
CHI!
GOOD THING THIS GUY LIVES IN WALKING DISTANCE. WE SHOULD BE JUST ABOUT THERE...

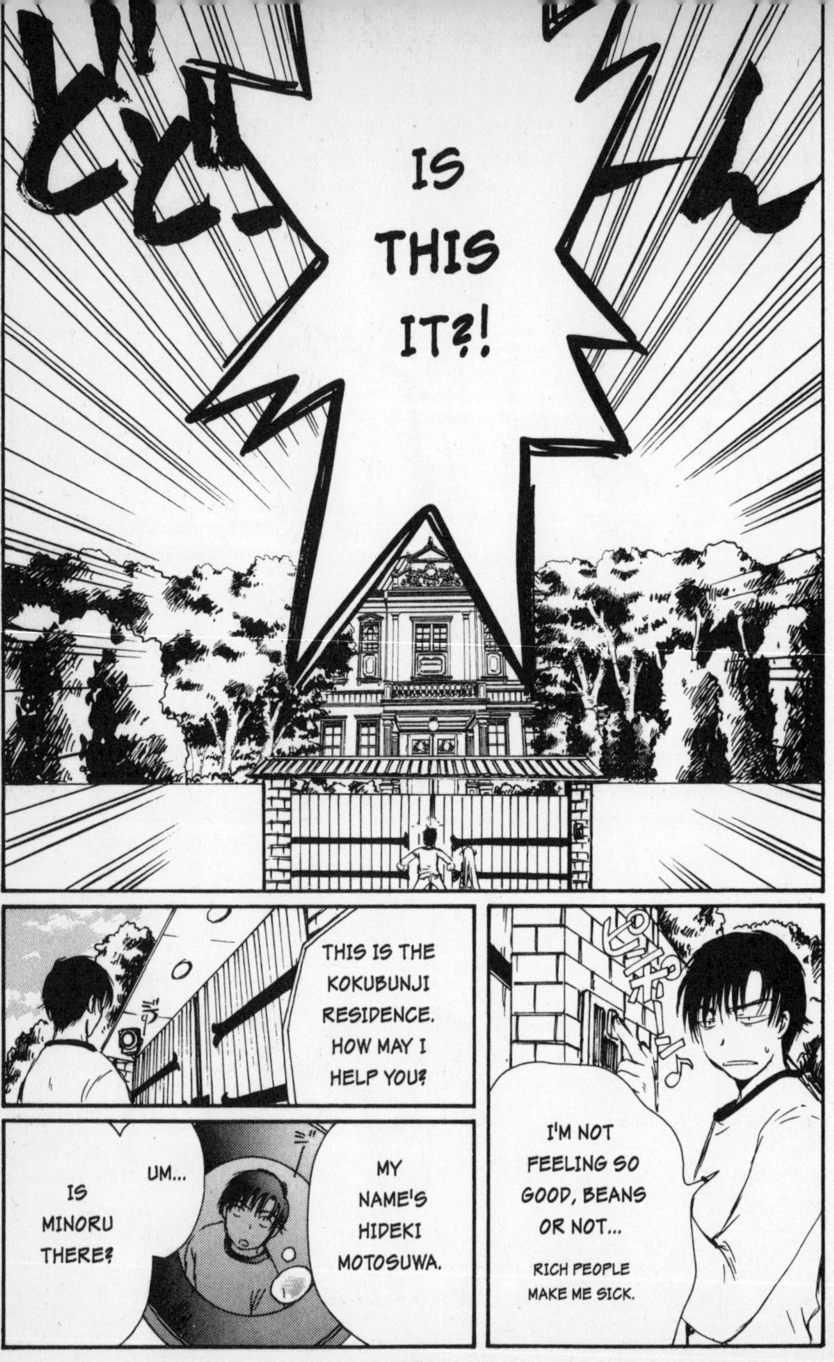
どどーん
IS THIS IT?!
ピンポーン♪
I'M NOT FEELING SO GOOD, BEANS OR NOT...
RICH PEOPLE MAKE ME SICK.
THIS IS THE KOKUBUNJI RESIDENCE. HOW MAY I HELP YOU?
MY NAME'S HIDEKI MOTOSUWA.
UM...
IS MINORU THERE?

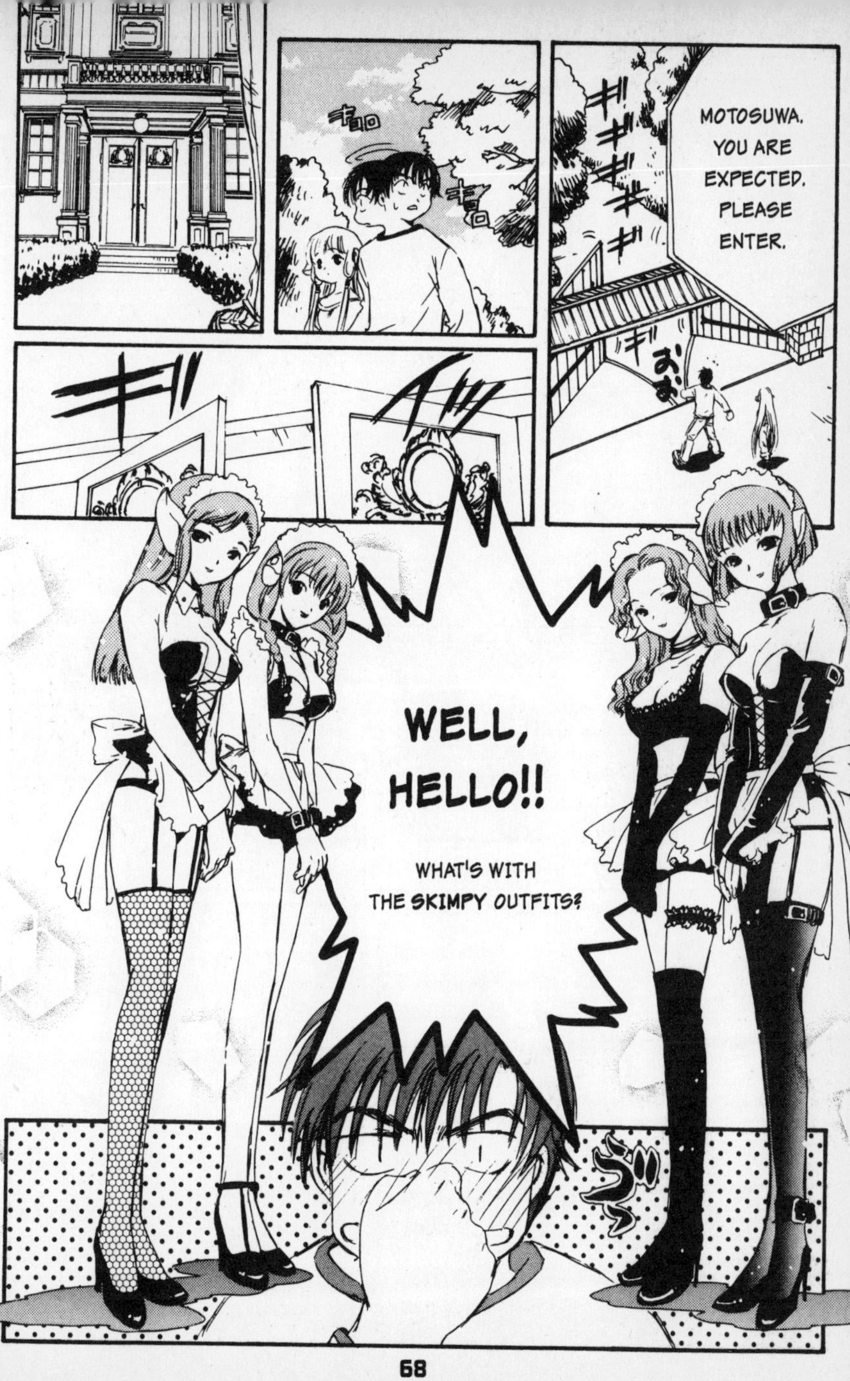
MOTOSUWA. YOU ARE EXPECTED. PLEASE ENTER.
WELL, HELLO!!
WHAT'S WITH THE SKIMPY OUTFITS?

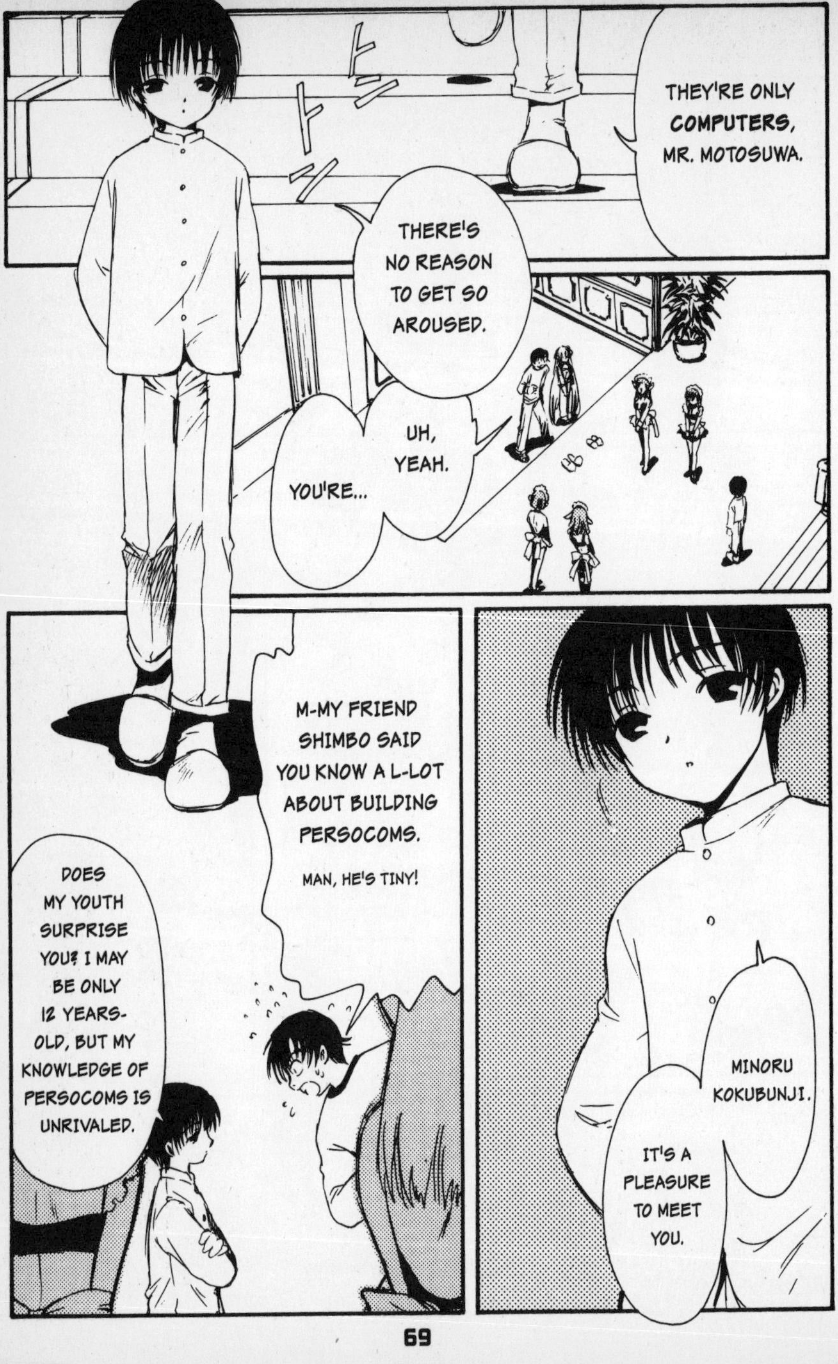

THEY'RE ONLY COMPUTERS, MR. MOTOSUWA.
THERE'S NO REASON TO GET SO AROUSED.
UH, YEAH.
YOU'RE...
MINORU KOKUBUNJI.
IT'S A PLEASURE TO MEET YOU.
M-MY FRIEND SHIMBO SAID YOU KNOW A L-LOT ABOUT BUILDING PERSOCOMS.
MAN, HE'S TINY!
DOES MY YOUTH SURPRISE YOU? I MAY BE ONLY 12 YEARS-OLD, BUT MY KNOWLEDGE OF PERSOCOMS IS UNRIVALED.

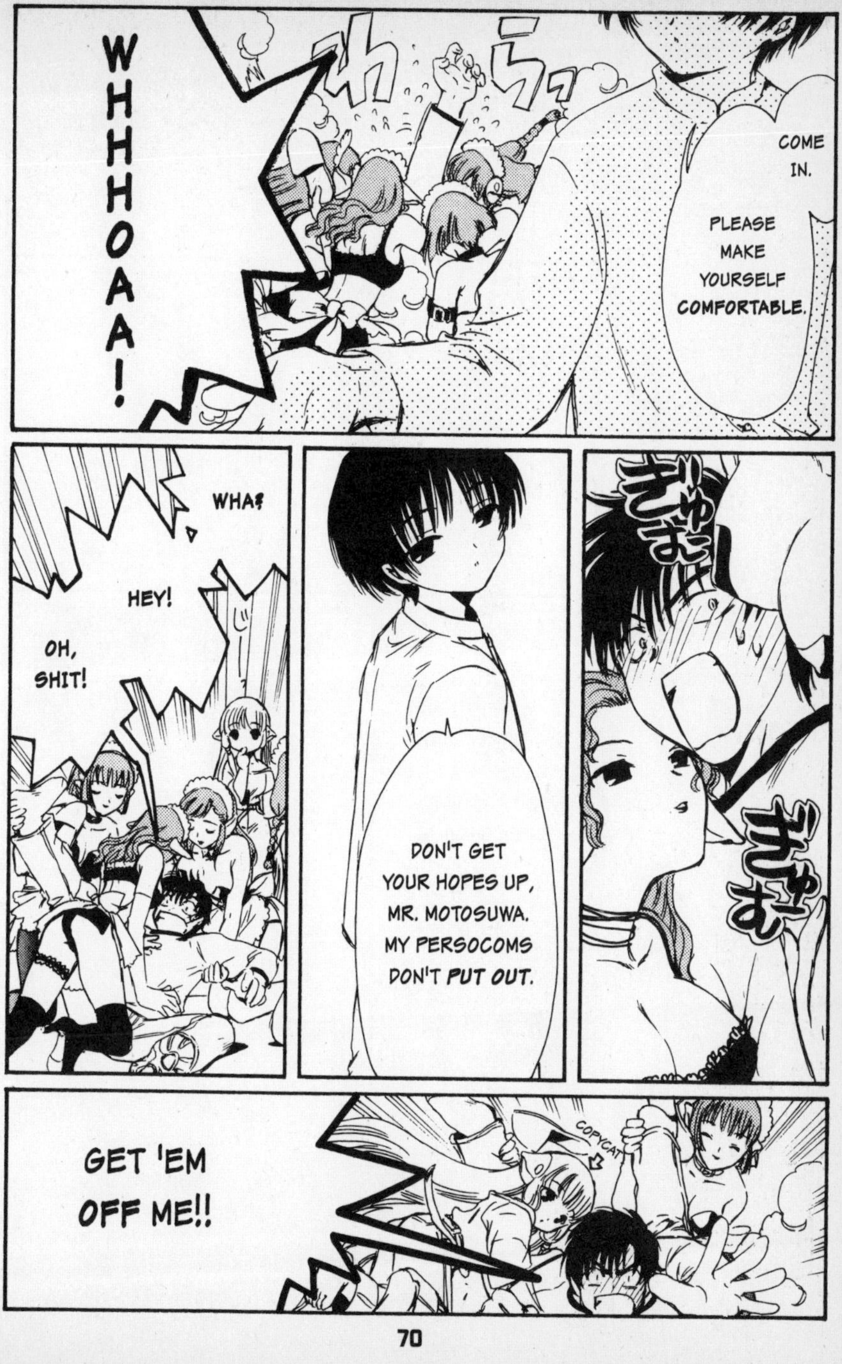
COME IN.
PLEASE MAKE YOURSELF COMFORTABLE.
WHHHOAA!
DON'T GET YOUR HOPES UP, MR. MOTOSUWA. MY PERSOCOMS DON'T PUT OUT.
WHA?
HEY!
OH, SHIT!
COPYCAT
GET 'EM OFF ME!!

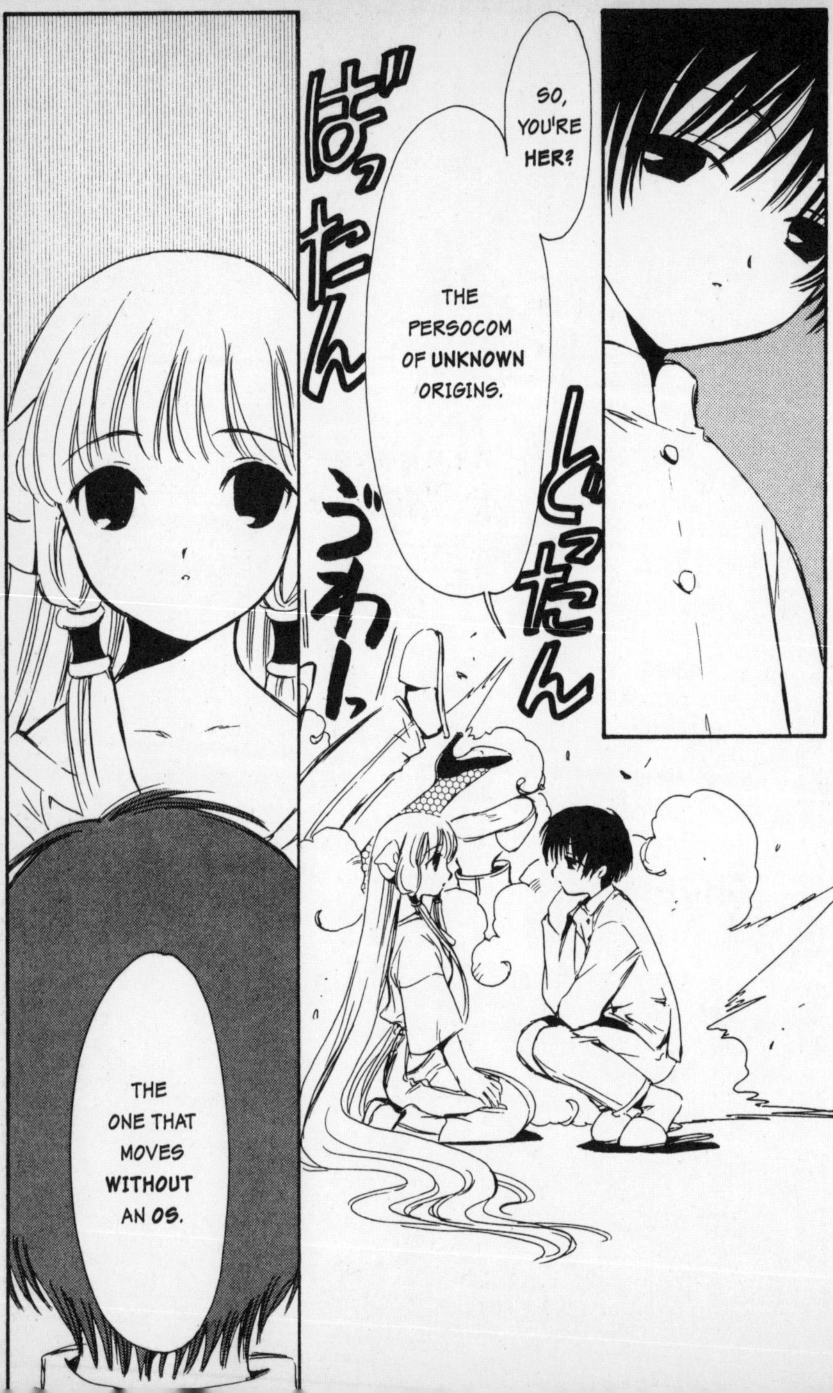
SO, YOU'RE HER?
THE PERSOCOM OF UNKNOWN ORIGINS.
どったん
ばったん
うわーっ
THE ONE THAT MOVES WITHOUT AN OS.

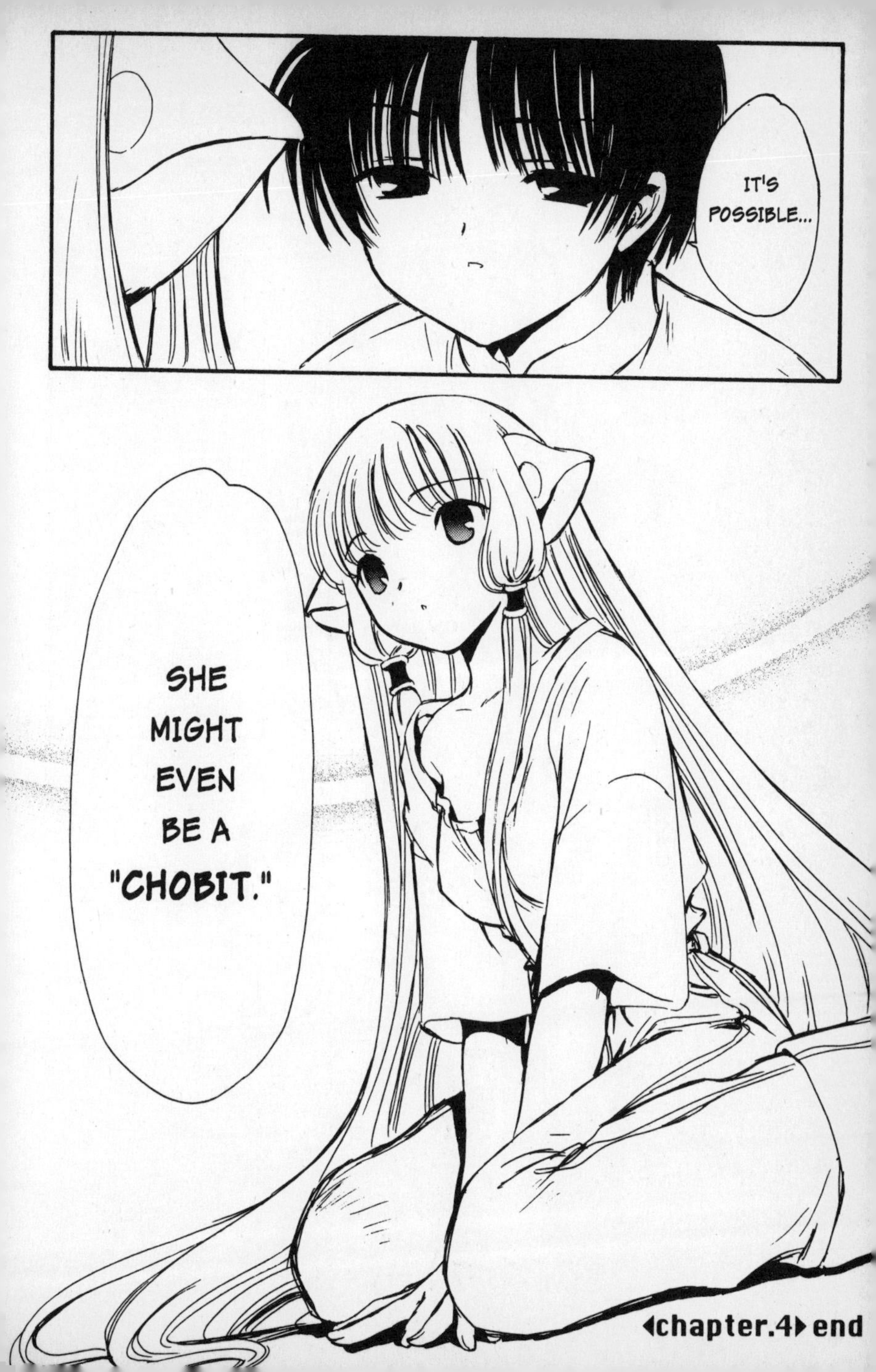
IT'S POSSIBLE...
SHE MIGHT EVEN BE A "CHOBIT."
◀chapter.4▶ end

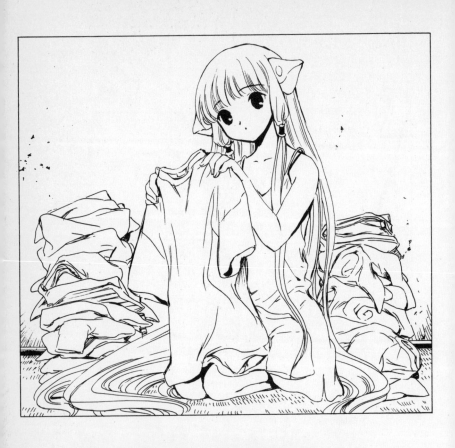

ちょびっツ
Chobits

◀chapter.5▶

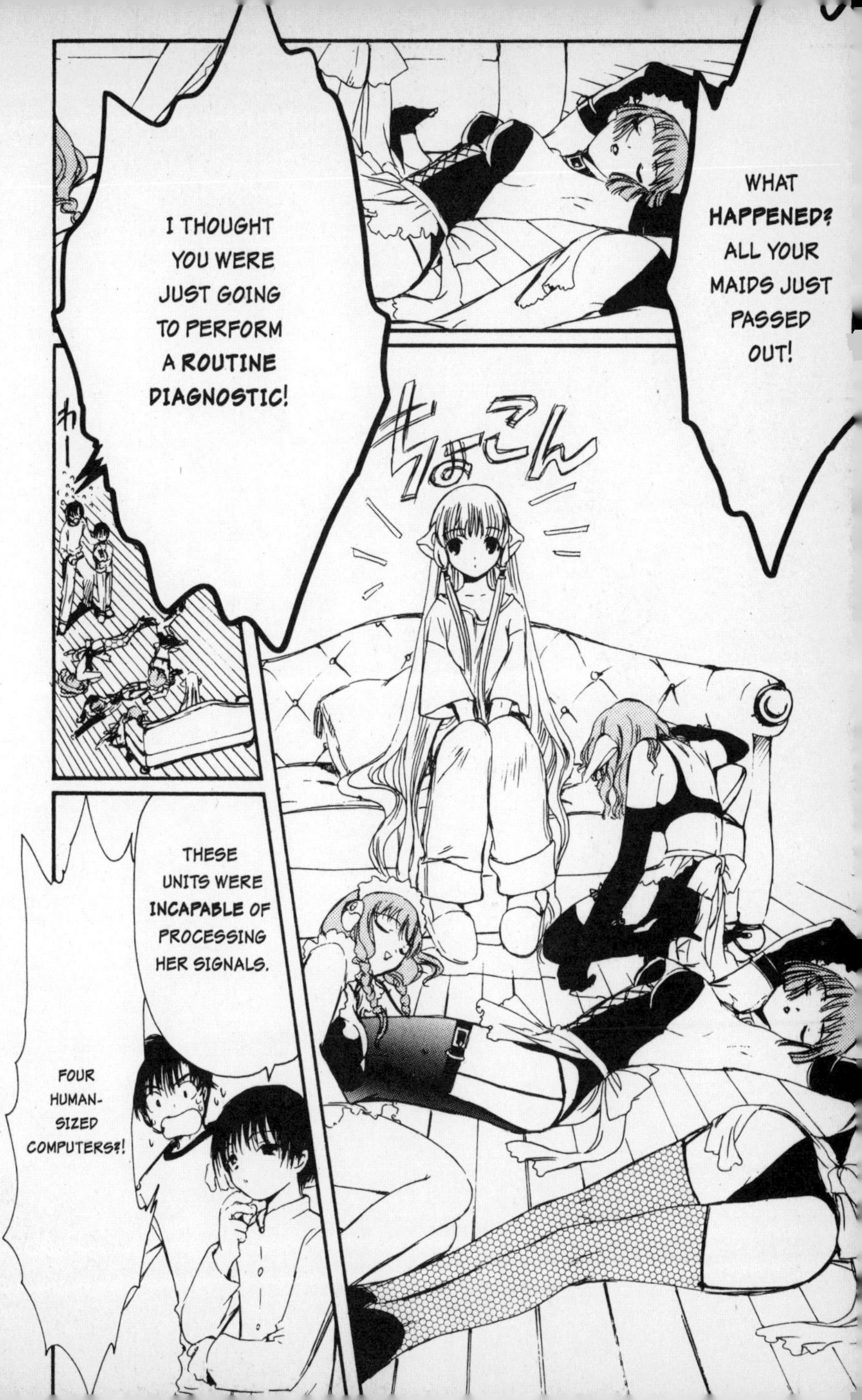
WHAT HAPPENED? ALL YOUR MAIDS JUST PASSED OUT!
I THOUGHT YOU WERE JUST GOING TO PERFORM A ROUTINE DIAGNOSTIC!
ちょこん
わー
THESE UNITS WERE INCAPABLE OF PROCESSING HER SIGNALS.
FOUR HUMAN-SIZED COMPUTERS?!

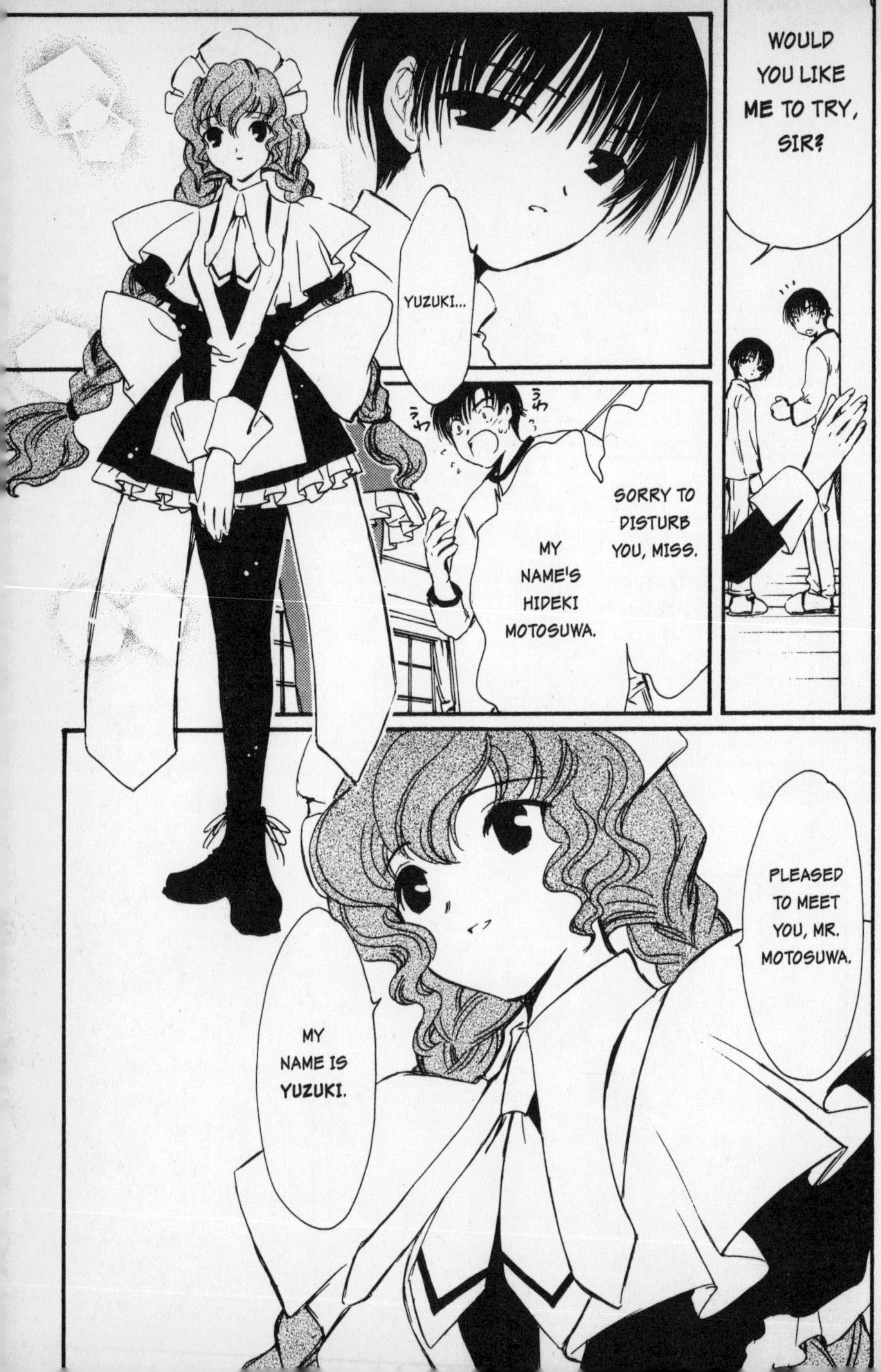
WOULD YOU LIKE ME TO TRY, SIR?
YUZUKI...
SORRY TO DISTURB YOU, MISS.
MY NAME'S HIDEKI MOTOSUWA.
PLEASED TO MEET YOU, MR. MOTOSUWA.
MY NAME IS YUZUKI.

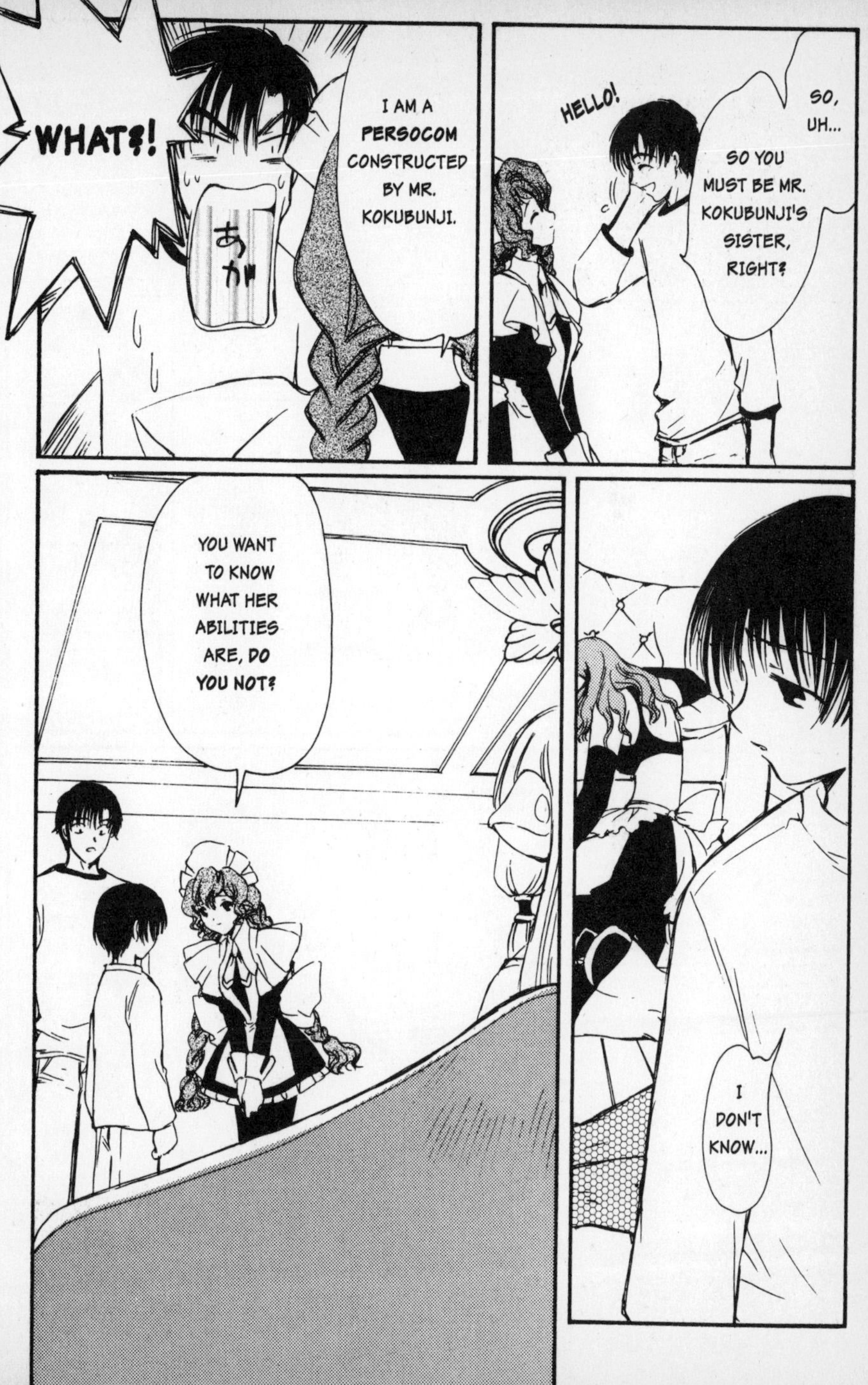
SO, UH...
HELLO!
SO YOU MUST BE MR. KOKUBUNJI'S SISTER, RIGHT?
I AM A PERSOCOM CONSTRUCTED BY MR. KOKUBUNJI.
WHAT?!
あか
I DON'T KNOW...
YOU WANT TO KNOW WHAT HER ABILITIES ARE, DO YOU NOT?

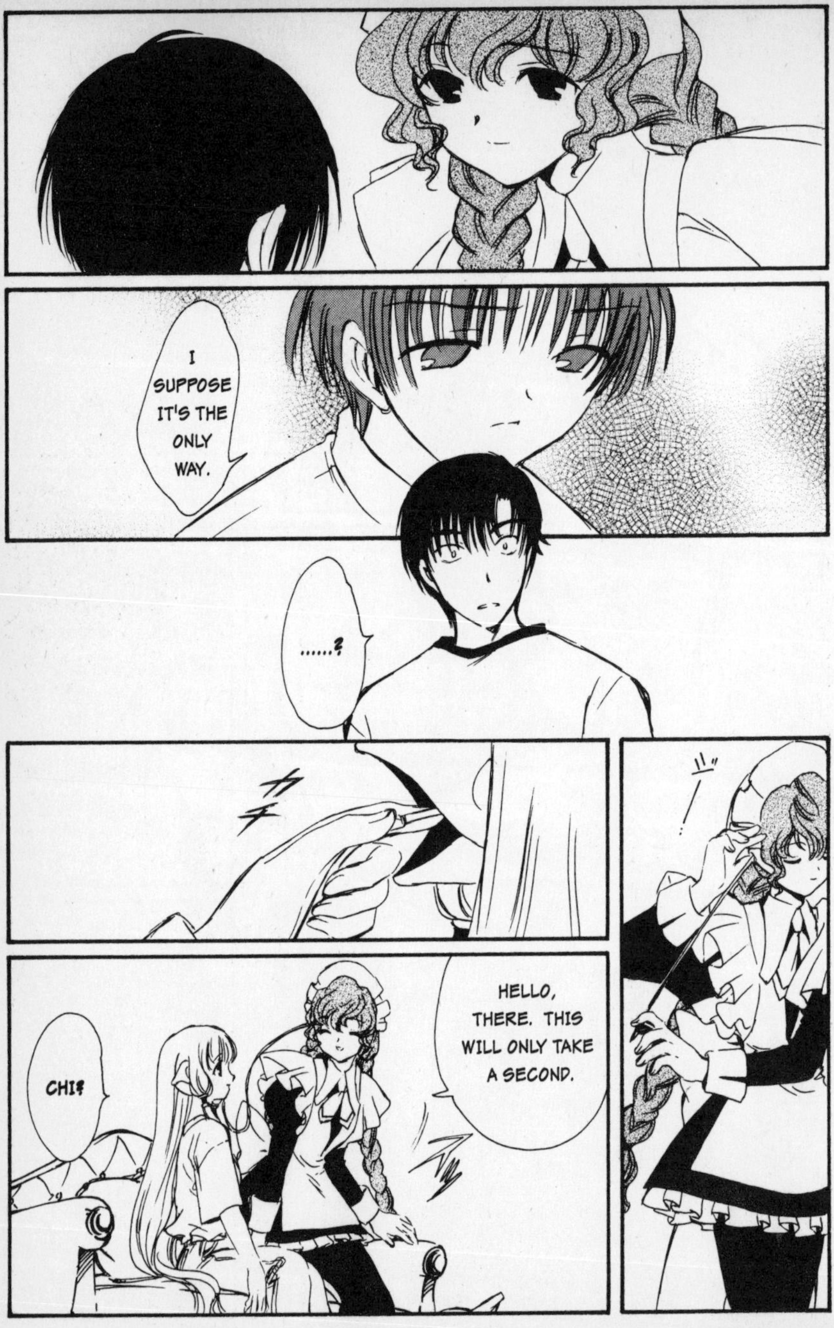
I SUPPOSE IT'S THE ONLY WAY.
......?
HELLO, THERE. THIS WILL ONLY TAKE A SECOND.
CHI?

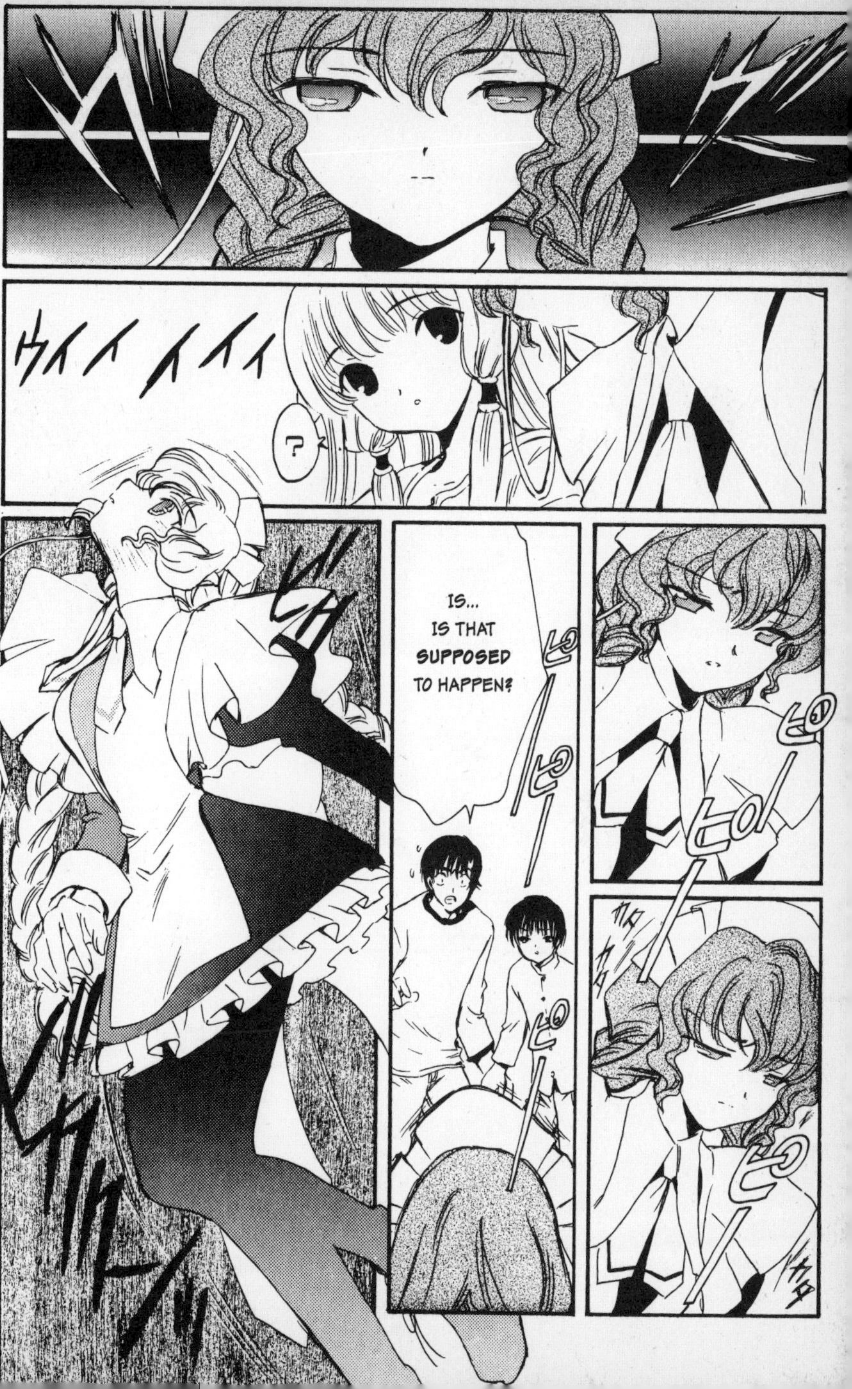
ウィイ イイイ
?
IS... IS THAT SUPPOSED TO HAPPEN?

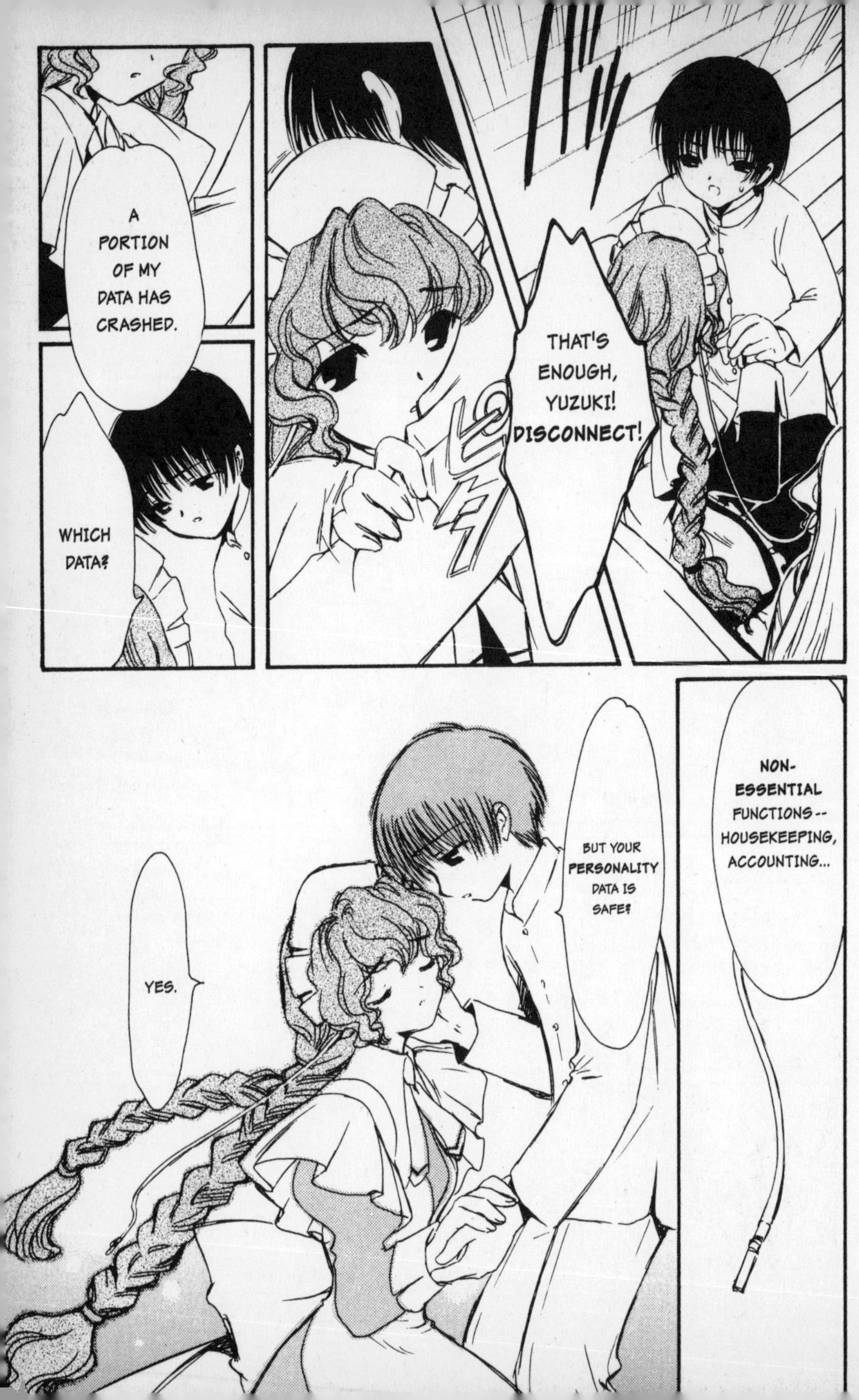
THAT'S ENOUGH, YUZUKI! DISCONNECT!
A PORTION OF MY DATA HAS CRASHED.
WHICH DATA?
NON-ESSENTIAL FUNCTIONS-- HOUSEKEEPING, ACCOUNTING...
BUT YOUR PERSONALITY DATA IS SAFE?
YES.

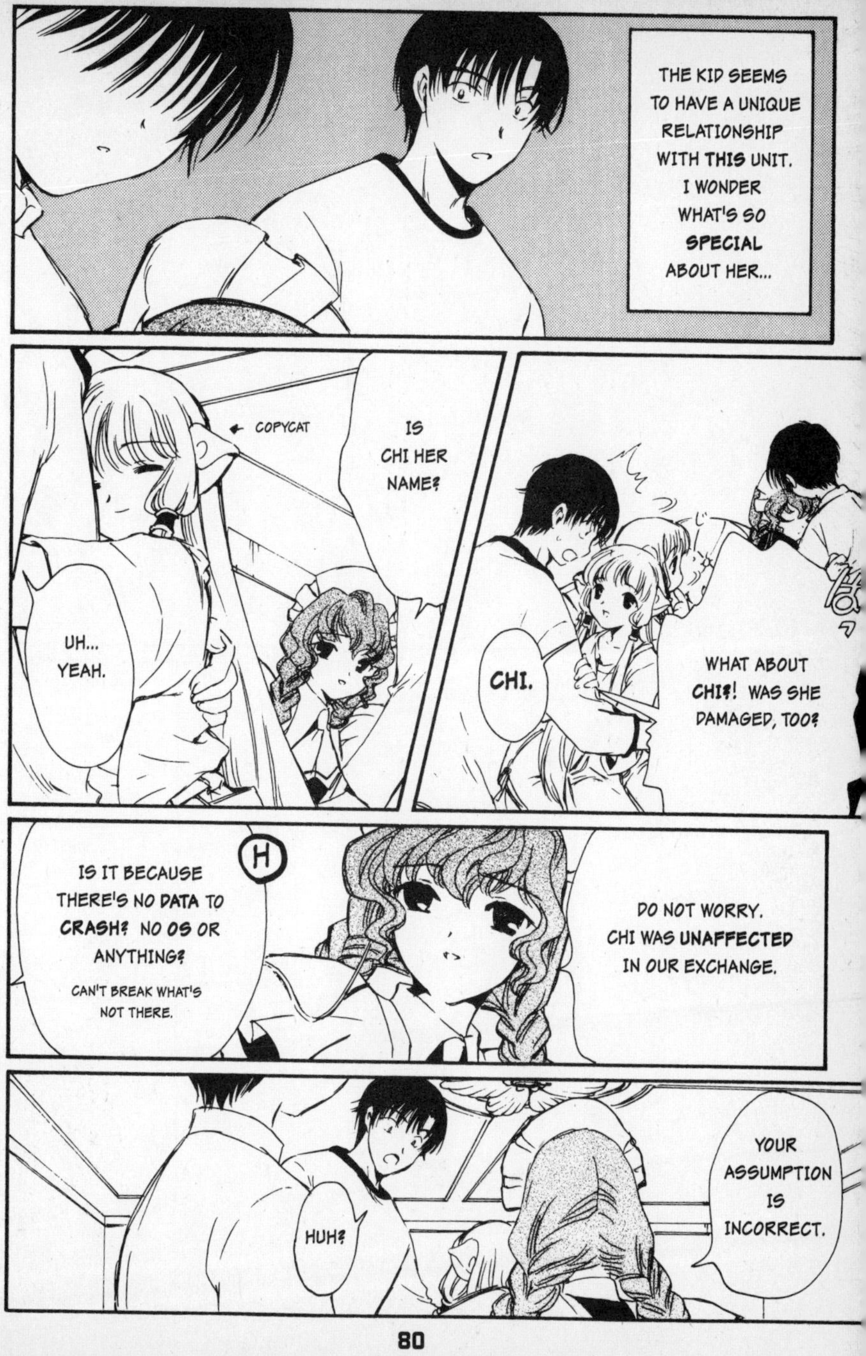
THE KID SEEMS TO HAVE A UNIQUE RELATIONSHIP WITH THIS UNIT. I WONDER WHAT'S SO SPECIAL ABOUT HER...
WHAT ABOUT CHI?! WAS SHE DAMAGED, TOO?
CHI.
IS CHI HER NAME?
COPYCAT
UH... YEAH.
DO NOT WORRY. CHI WAS UNAFFECTED IN OUR EXCHANGE.
IS IT BECAUSE THERE'S NO DATA TO CRASH? NO OS OR ANYTHING?
CAN'T BREAK WHAT'S NOT THERE.
YOUR ASSUMPTION IS INCORRECT.
HUH?

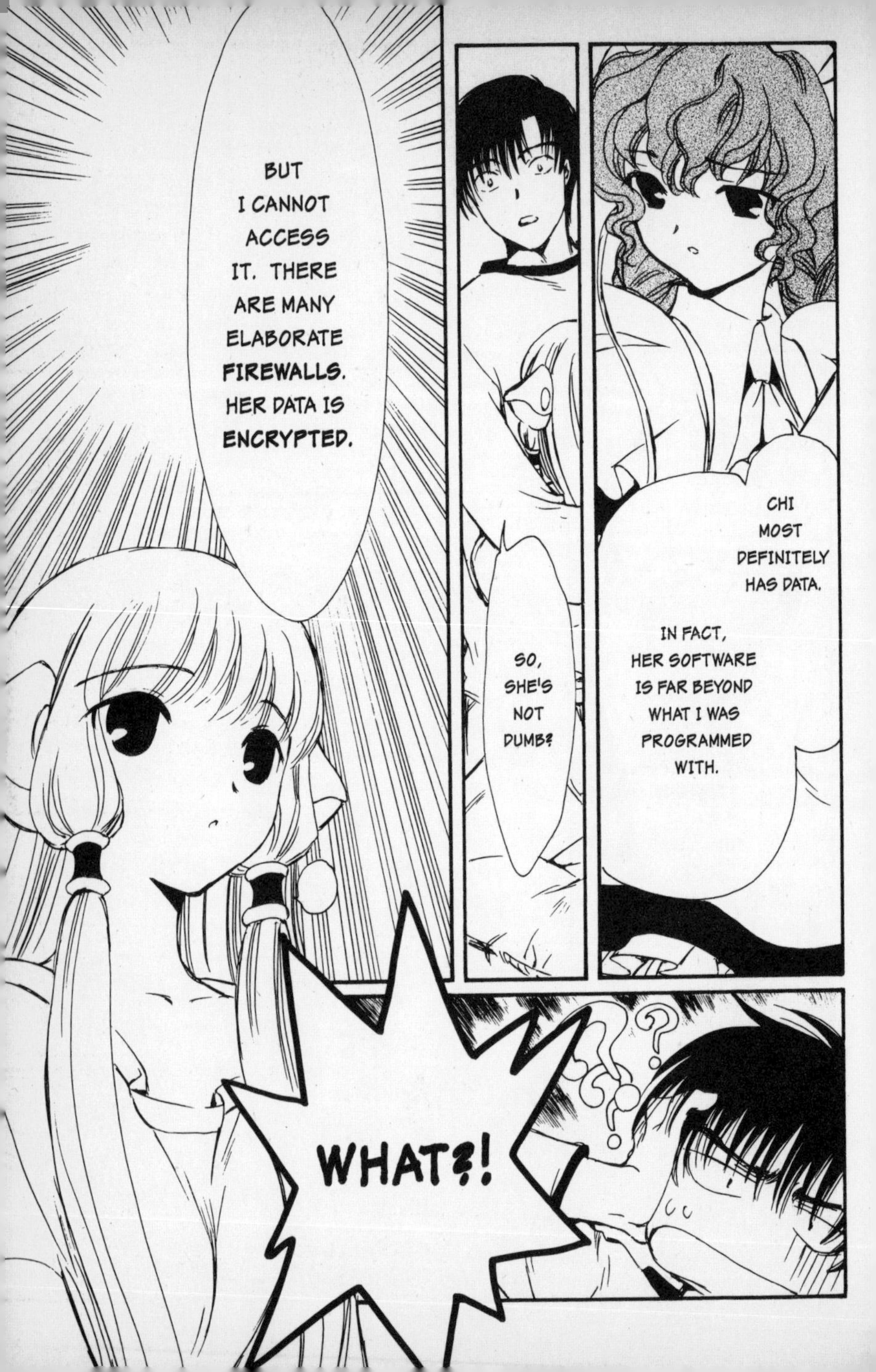
CHI MOST DEFINITELY HAS DATA.
IN FACT, HER SOFTWARE IS FAR BEYOND WHAT I WAS PROGRAMMED WITH.
SO, SHE'S NOT DUMB?
WHAT?!
BUT I CANNOT ACCESS IT. THERE ARE MANY ELABORATE FIREWALLS. HER DATA IS ENCRYPTED.

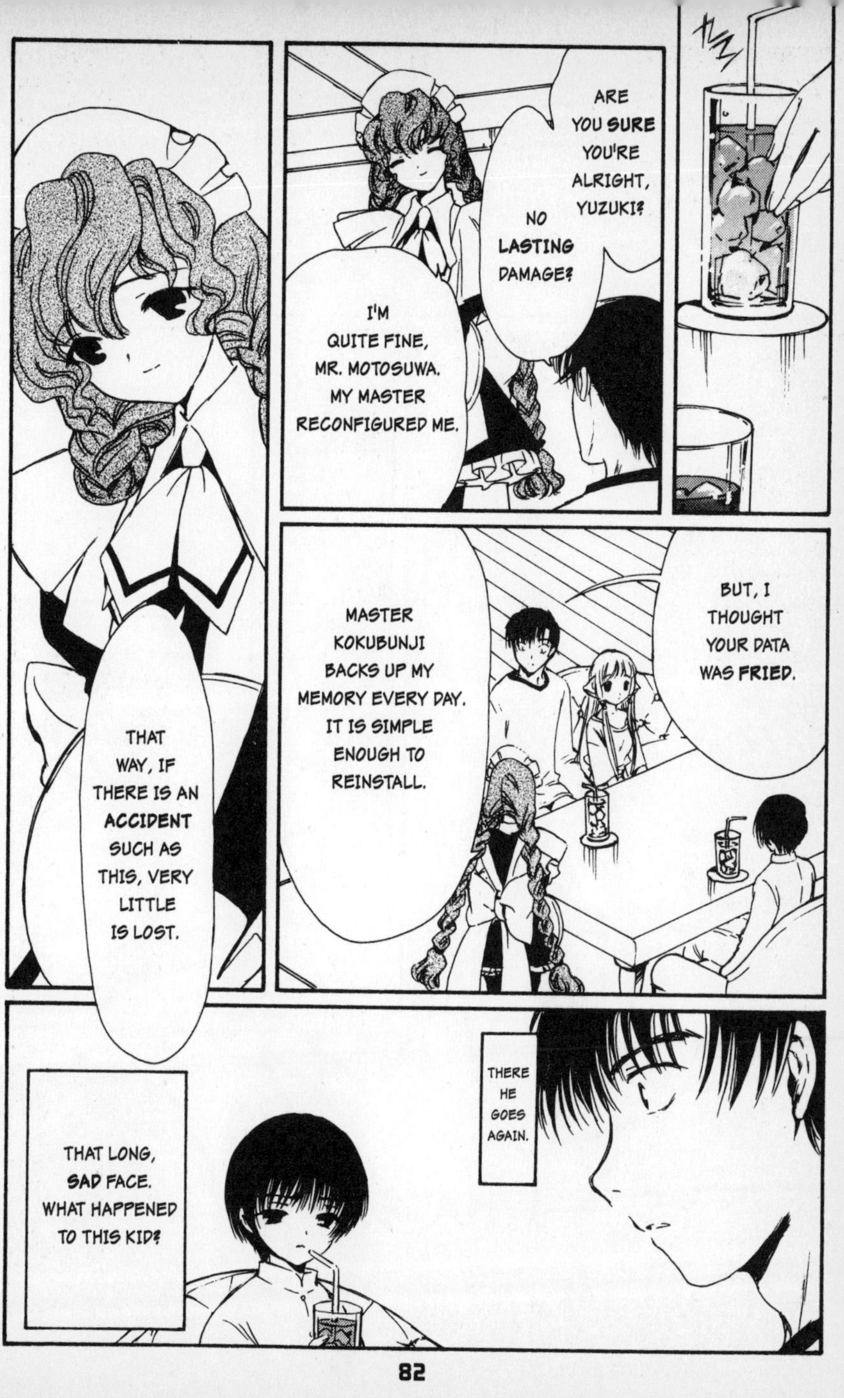
ARE YOU SURE YOU'RE ALRIGHT, YUZUKI?
NO LASTING DAMAGE?
I'M QUITE FINE, MR. MOTOSUWA. MY MASTER RECONFIGURED ME.
BUT, I THOUGHT YOUR DATA WAS FRIED.
MASTER KOKUBUNJI BACKS UP MY MEMORY EVERY DAY. IT IS SIMPLE ENOUGH TO REINSTALL.
THAT WAY, IF THERE IS AN ACCIDENT SUCH AS THIS, VERY LITTLE IS LOST.
THERE HE GOES AGAIN.
THAT LONG, SAD FACE. WHAT HAPPENED TO THIS KID?

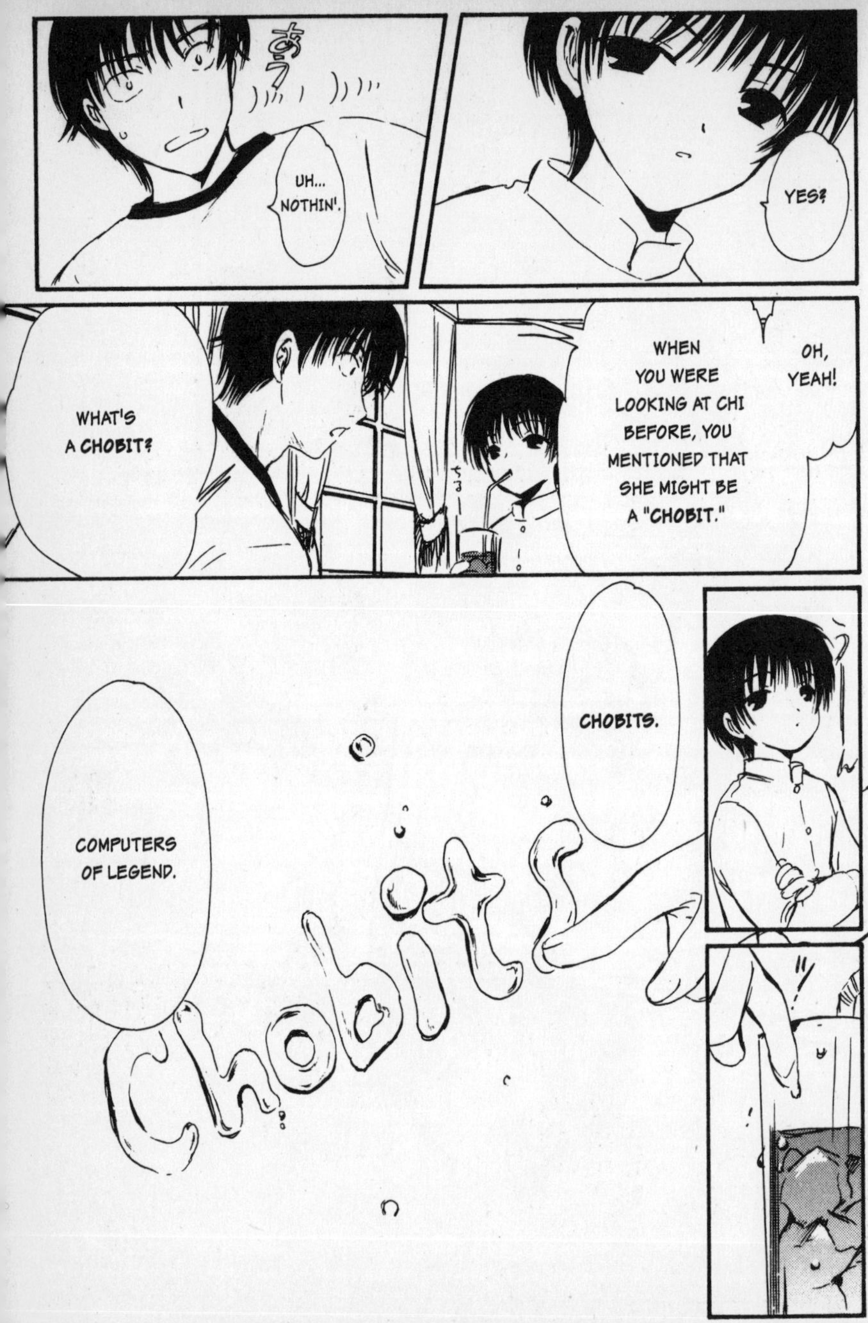
YES?
あう
UH... NOTHIN'.
OH, YEAH!
WHEN YOU WERE LOOKING AT CHI BEFORE, YOU MENTIONED THAT SHE MIGHT BE A "CHOBIT."
WHAT'S A CHOBIT?
CHOBITS.
Chobit
COMPUTERS OF LEGEND.

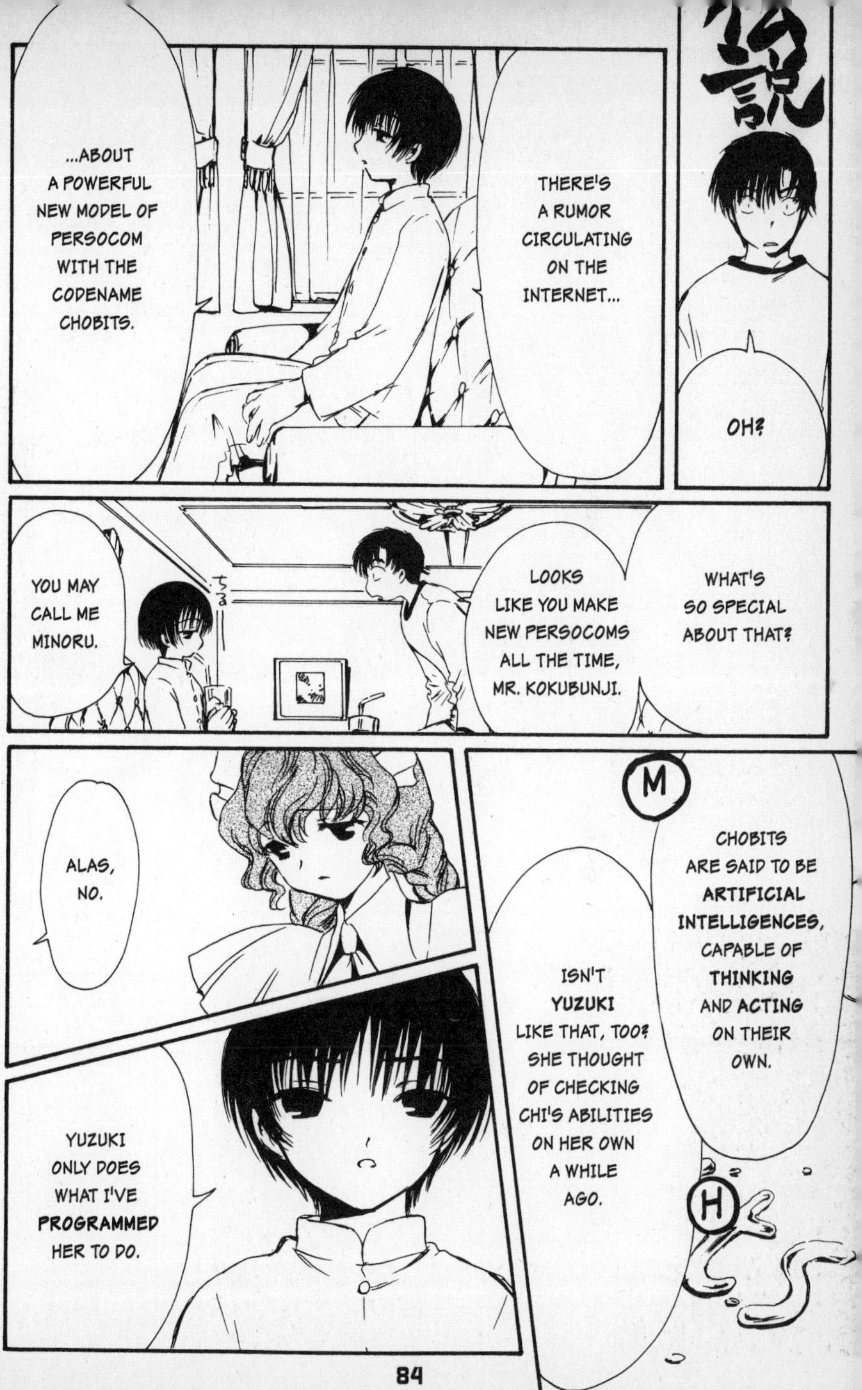
OH?
THERE'S A RUMOR CIRCULATING ON THE INTERNET...
...ABOUT A POWERFUL NEW MODEL OF PERSOCOM WITH THE CODENAME CHOBITS.
WHAT'S SO SPECIAL ABOUT THAT?
LOOKS LIKE YOU MAKE NEW PERSOCOMS ALL THE TIME, MR. KOKUBUNJI.
YOU MAY CALL ME MINORU.
M
CHOBITS ARE SAID TO BE ARTIFICIAL INTELLIGENCES, CAPABLE OF THINKING AND ACTING ON THEIR OWN.
ISN'T YUZUKI LIKE THAT, TOO? SHE THOUGHT OF CHECKING CHI'S ABILITIES ON HER OWN A WHILE AGO.
H
ALAS, NO.
YUZUKI ONLY DOES WHAT I'VE PROGRAMMED HER TO DO.

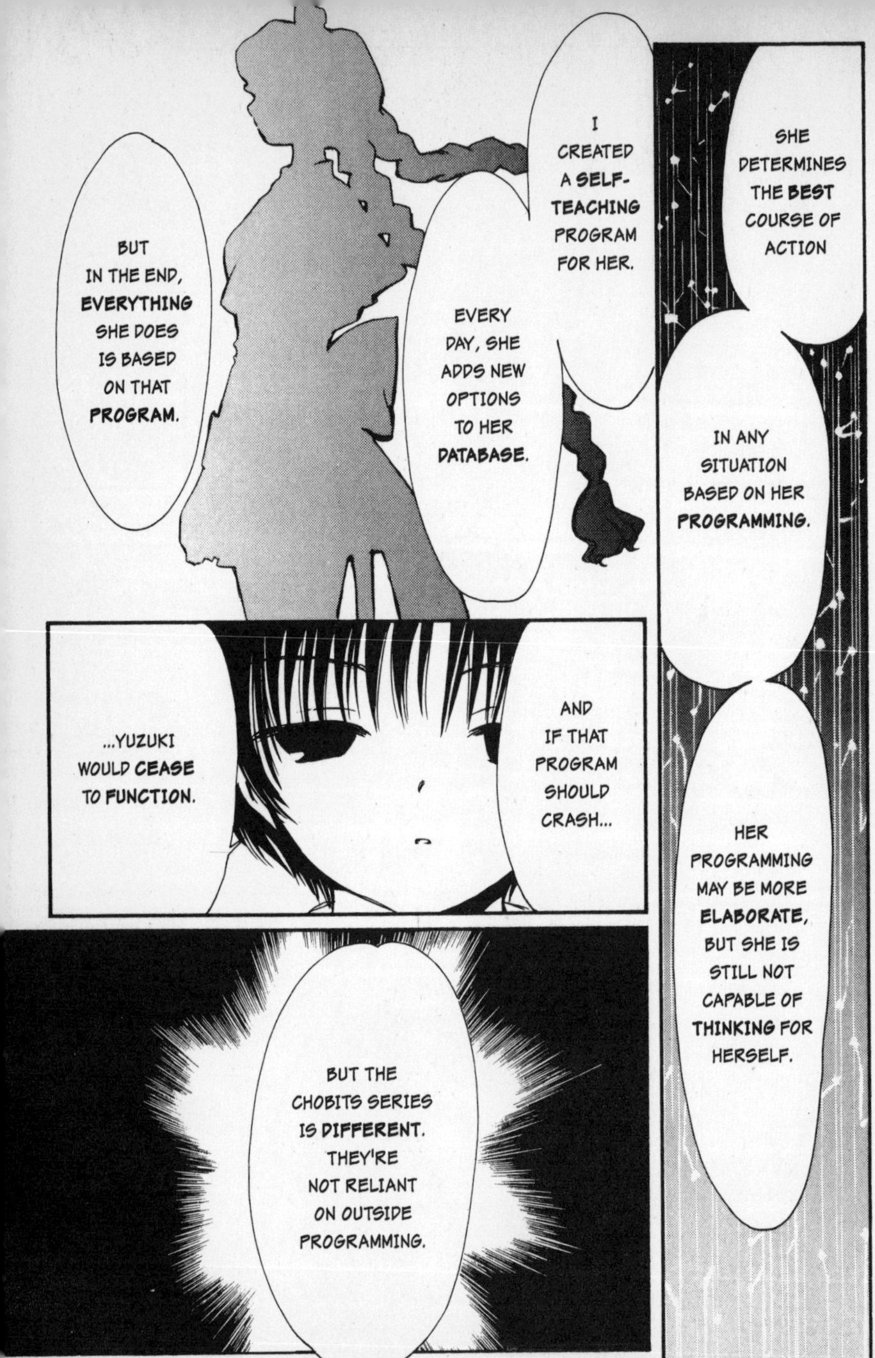
SHE DETERMINES THE BEST COURSE OF ACTION
IN ANY SITUATION BASED ON HER PROGRAMMING.
HER PROGRAMMING MAY BE MORE ELABORATE, BUT SHE IS STILL NOT CAPABLE OF THINKING FOR HERSELF.
I CREATED A SELF-TEACHING PROGRAM FOR HER.
EVERY DAY, SHE ADDS NEW OPTIONS TO HER DATABASE.
BUT IN THE END, EVERYTHING SHE DOES IS BASED ON THAT PROGRAM.
AND IF THAT PROGRAM SHOULD CRASH...
...YUZUKI WOULD CEASE TO FUNCTION.
BUT THE CHOBITS SERIES IS DIFFERENT. THEY'RE NOT RELIANT ON OUTSIDE PROGRAMMING.

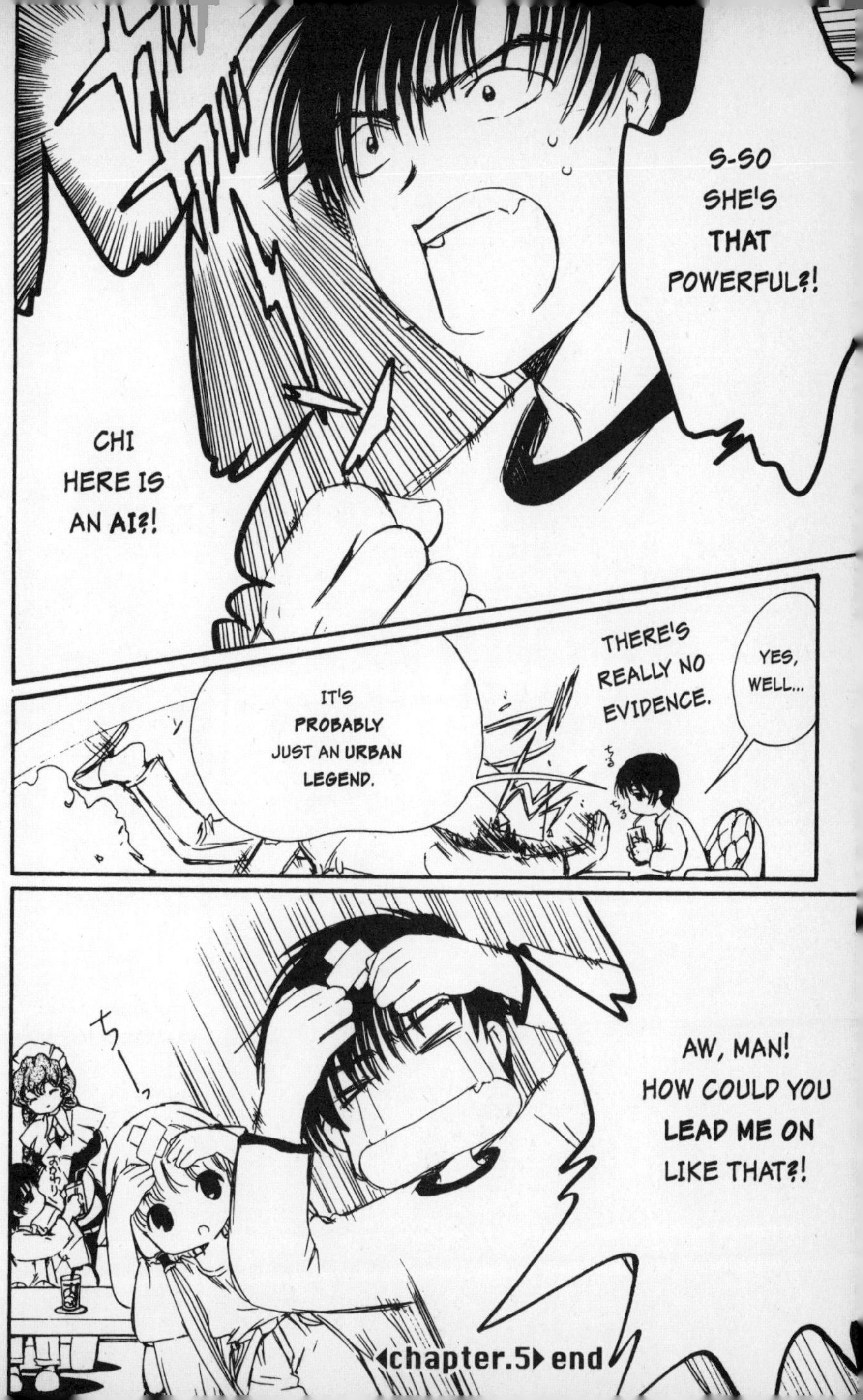
S-SO SHE'S THAT POWERFUL?!
CHI HERE IS AN AI?!
YES, WELL...
THERE'S REALLY NO EVIDENCE.
IT'S PROBABLY JUST AN URBAN LEGEND.
AW, MAN! HOW COULD YOU LEAD ME ON LIKE THAT?!
chapter.5 end

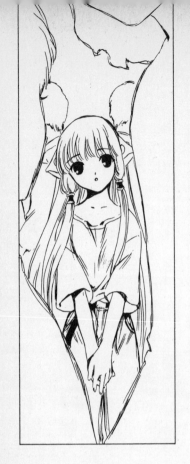
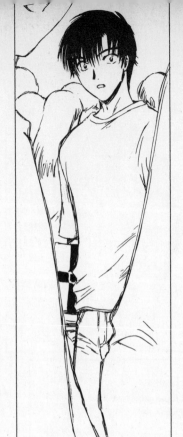

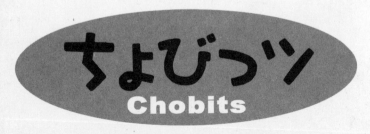

ちょびっツ
Chobits

◀chapter.6▶

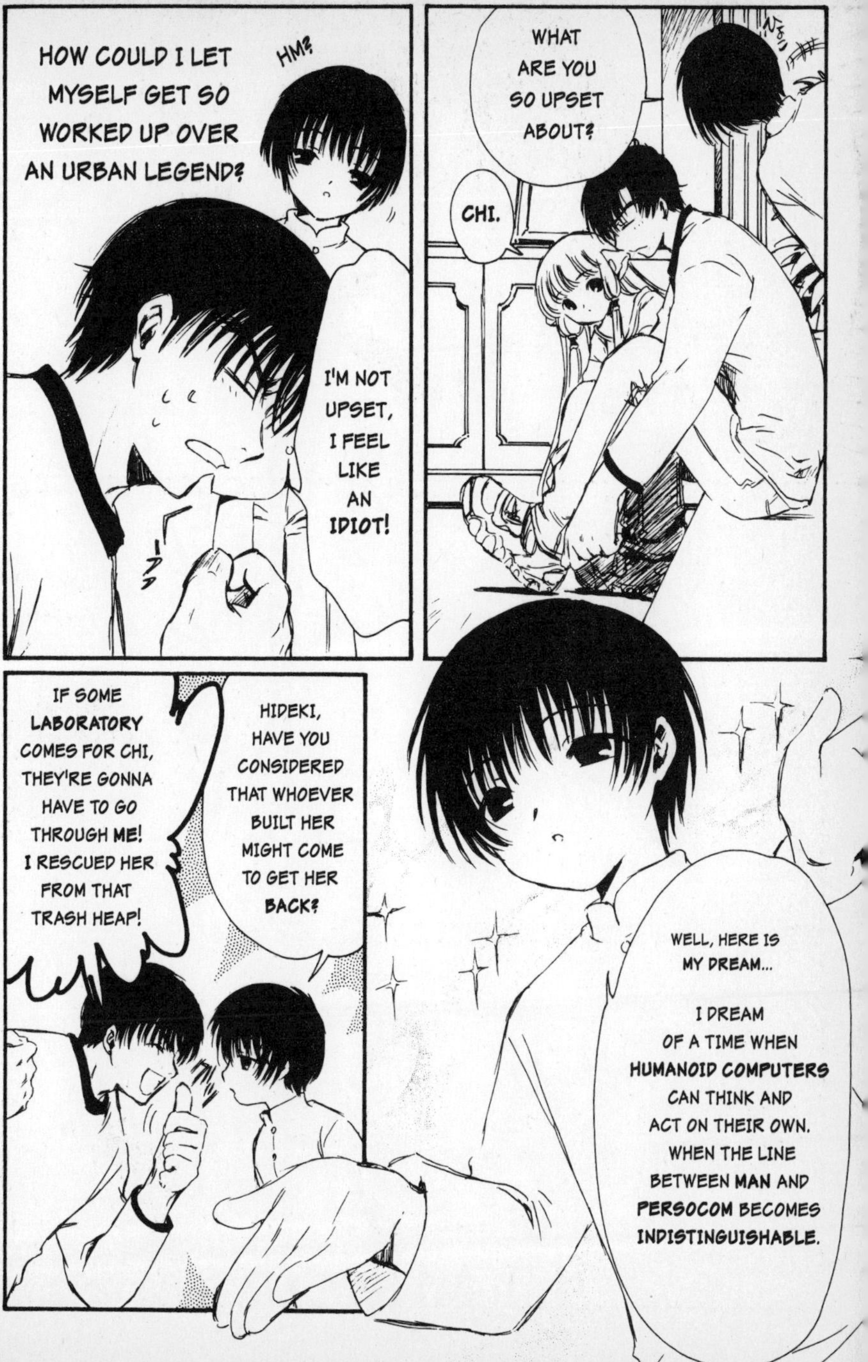
WHAT ARE YOU SO UPSET ABOUT?
CHI.
HOW COULD I LET MYSELF GET SO WORKED UP OVER AN URBAN LEGEND?
HM?
I'M NOT UPSET, I FEEL LIKE AN IDIOT!
WELL, HERE IS MY DREAM...
I DREAM OF A TIME WHEN HUMANOID COMPUTERS CAN THINK AND ACT ON THEIR OWN. WHEN THE LINE BETWEEN MAN AND PERSOCOM BECOMES INDISTINGUISHABLE.
HIDEKI, HAVE YOU CONSIDERED THAT WHOEVER BUILT HER MIGHT COME TO GET HER BACK?
IF SOME LABORATORY COMES FOR CHI, THEY'RE GONNA HAVE TO GO THROUGH ME! I RESCUED HER FROM THAT TRASH HEAP!

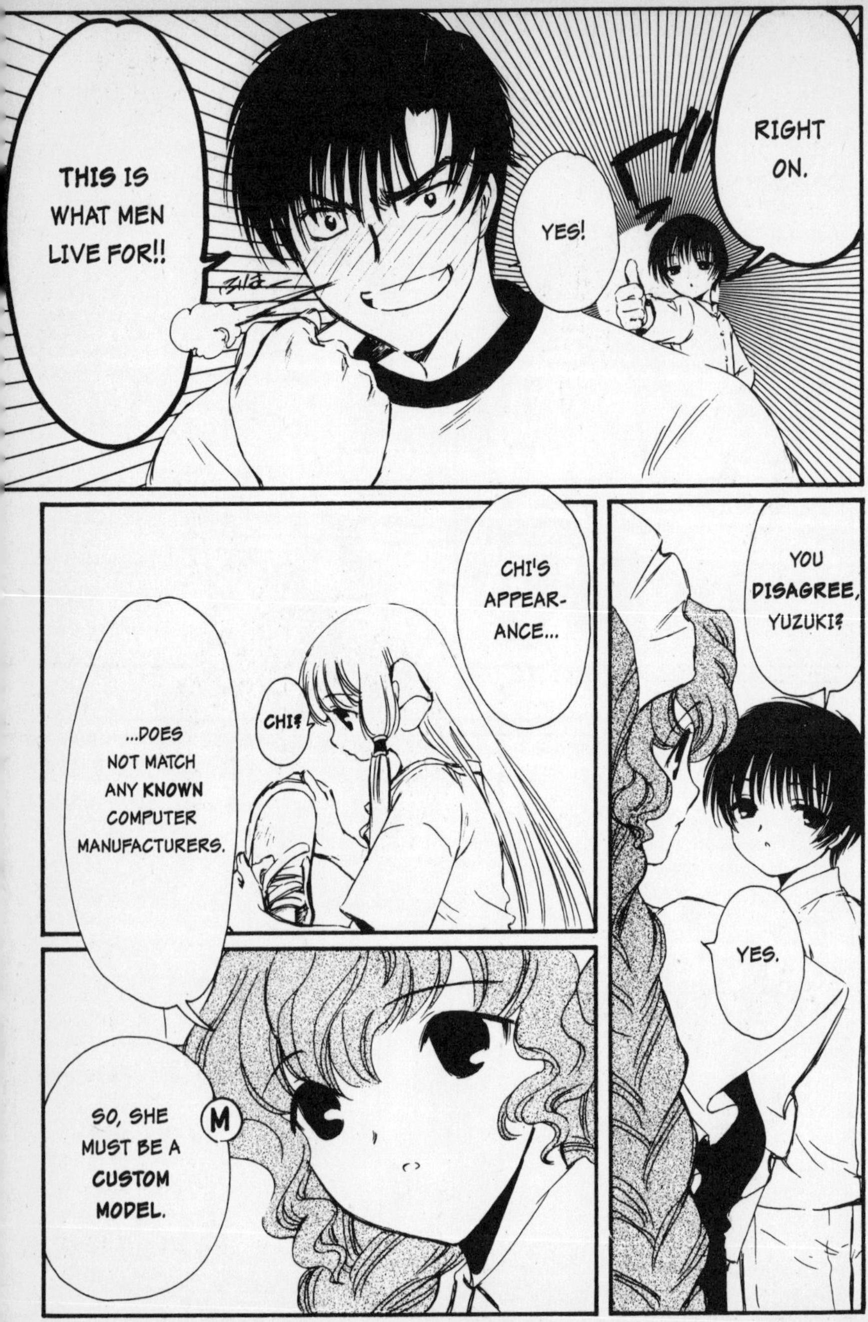
RIGHT ON.
YES!
THIS IS WHAT MEN LIVE FOR!!
YOU DISAGREE, YUZUKI?
YES.
CHI'S APPEAR-ANCE...
CHI?
...DOES NOT MATCH ANY KNOWN COMPUTER MANUFACTURERS.
M
SO, SHE MUST BE A CUSTOM MODEL.

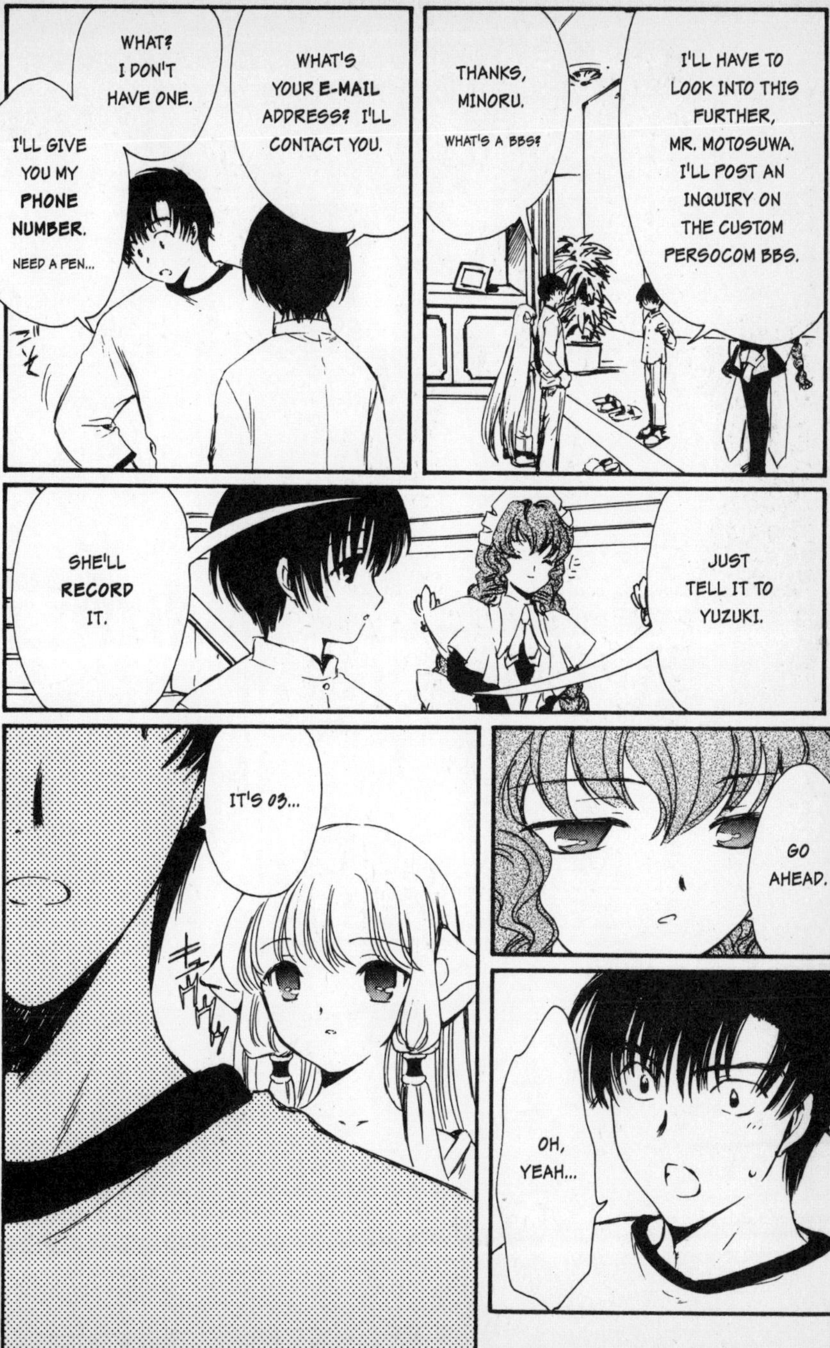
I'LL HAVE TO LOOK INTO THIS FURTHER, MR. MOTOSUWA. I'LL POST AN INQUIRY ON THE CUSTOM PERSOCOM BBS.
THANKS, MINORU.
WHAT'S A BBS?
WHAT'S YOUR E-MAIL ADDRESS? I'LL CONTACT YOU.
WHAT? I DON'T HAVE ONE.
I'LL GIVE YOU MY PHONE NUMBER.
NEED A PEN...
JUST TELL IT TO YUZUKI.
SHE'LL RECORD IT.
GO AHEAD.
OH, YEAH...
IT'S 03...

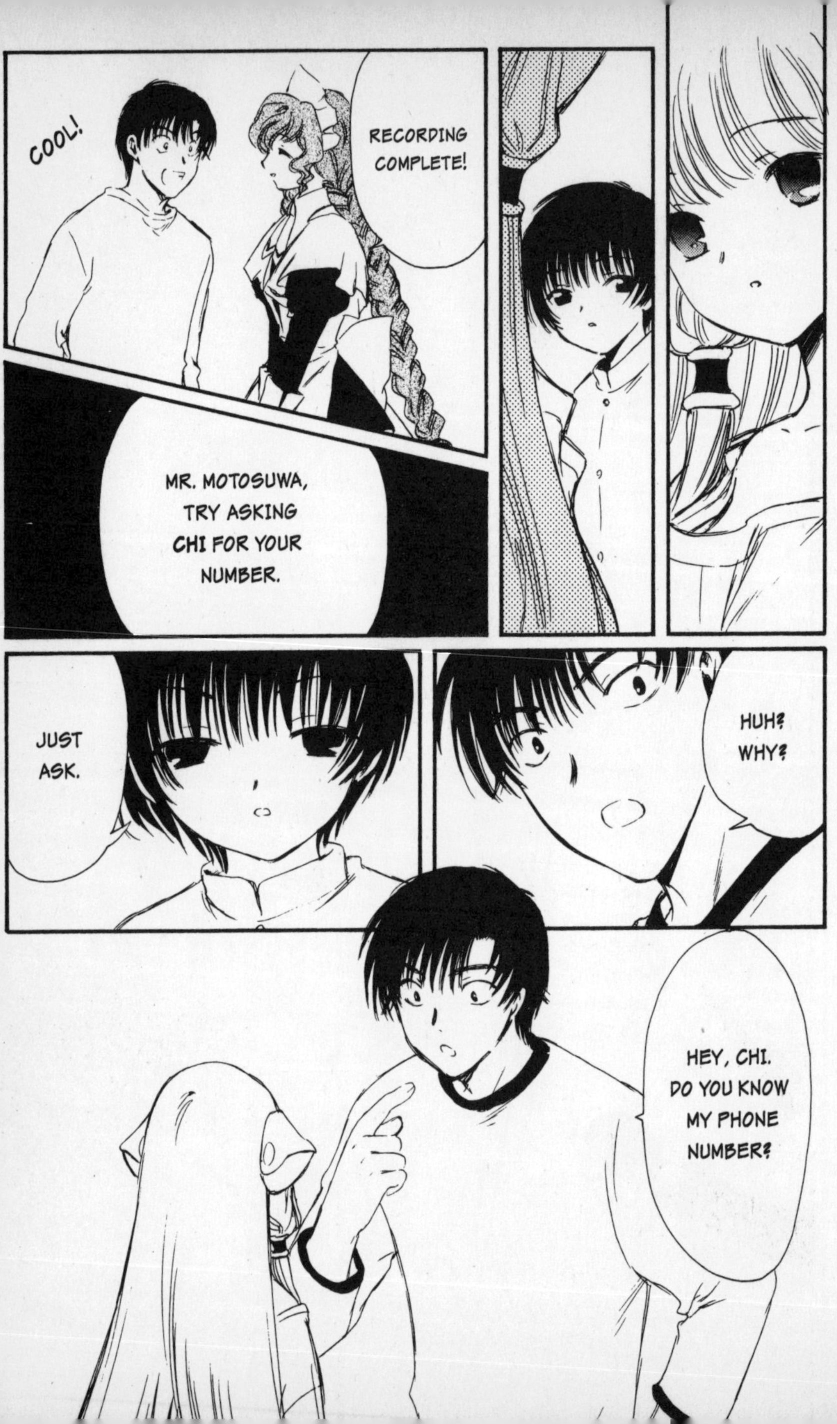
RECORDING COMPLETE!
COOL!
MR. MOTOSUWA, TRY ASKING CHI FOR YOUR NUMBER.
HUH? WHY?
JUST ASK.
HEY, CHI. DO YOU KNOW MY PHONE NUMBER?

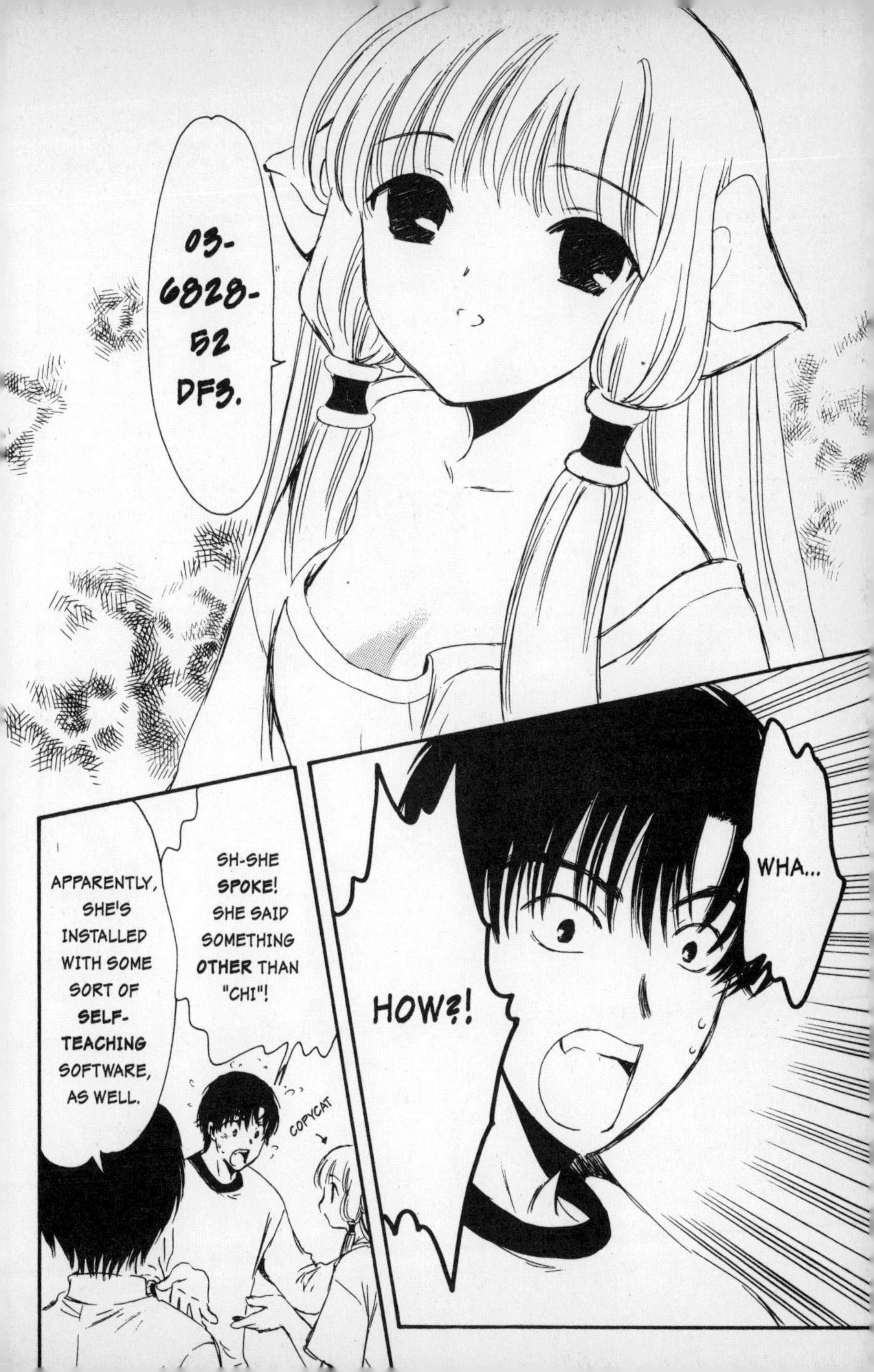
03-6828-52 DF3.
WHA...
HOW?!
SH-SHE SPOKE! SHE SAID SOMETHING OTHER THAN "CHI"!
APPARENTLY, SHE'S INSTALLED WITH SOME SORT OF SELF-TEACHING SOFTWARE, AS WELL.
COPYCAT

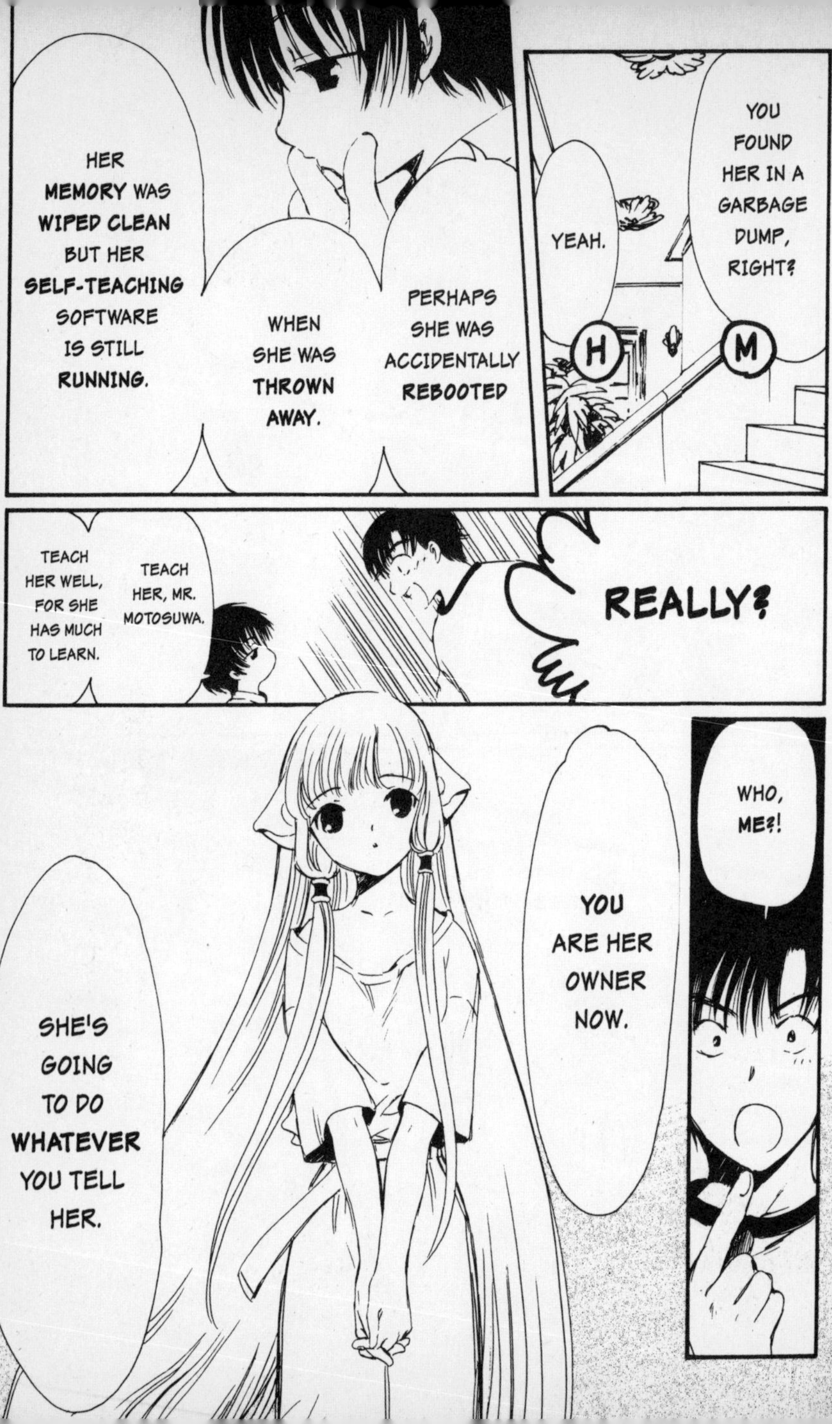
YOU FOUND HER IN A GARBAGE DUMP, RIGHT?
M
YEAH.
H
PERHAPS SHE WAS ACCIDENTALLY REBOOTED
WHEN SHE WAS THROWN AWAY.
HER MEMORY WAS WIPED CLEAN BUT HER SELF-TEACHING SOFTWARE IS STILL RUNNING.
REALLY?
TEACH HER, MR. MOTOSUWA.
TEACH HER WELL, FOR SHE HAS MUCH TO LEARN.
WHO, ME?!
YOU ARE HER OWNER NOW.
SHE'S GOING TO DO WHATEVER YOU TELL HER.

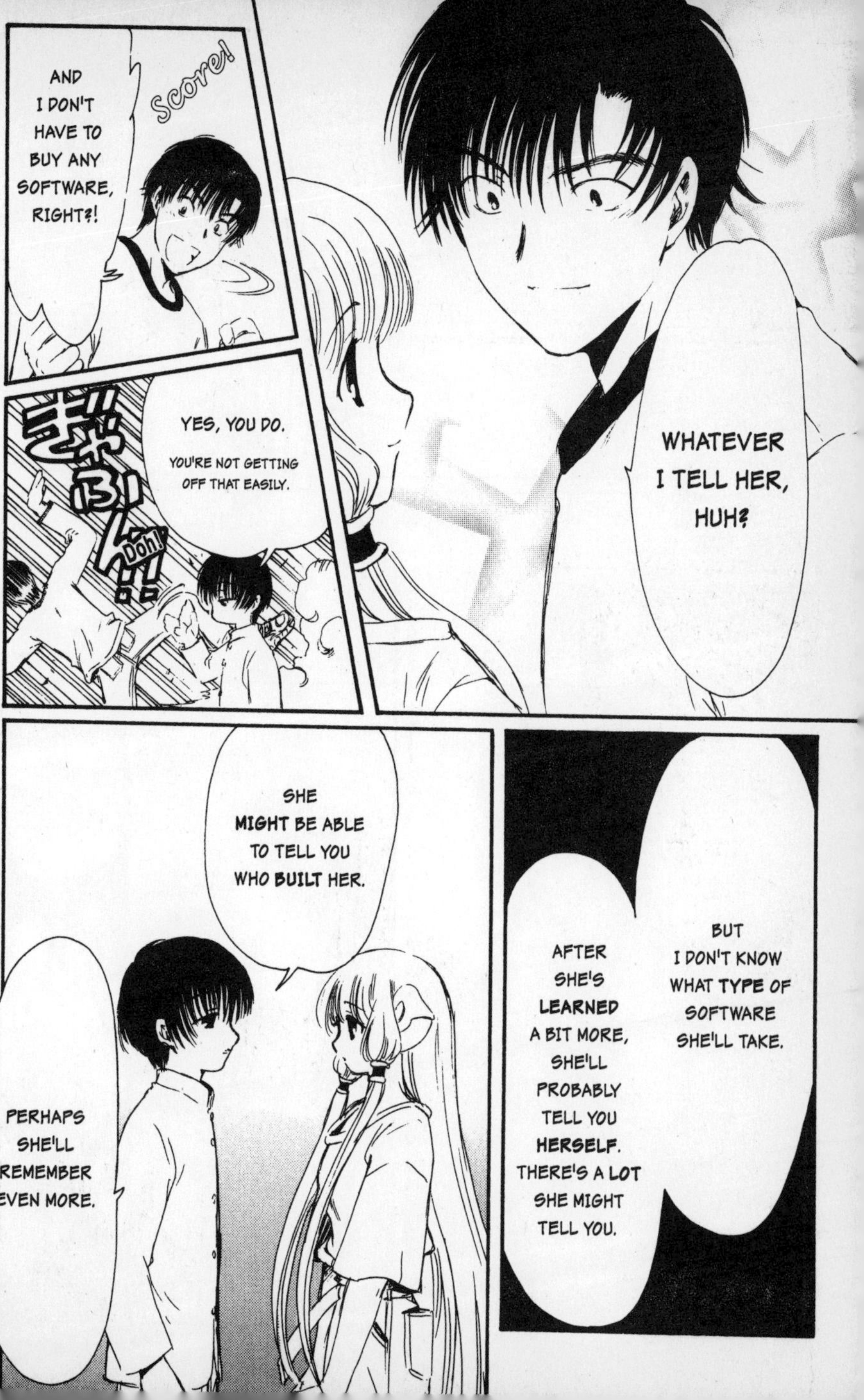
WHATEVER I TELL HER, HUH?
AND I DON'T HAVE TO BUY ANY SOFTWARE, RIGHT?!
Score!
YES, YOU DO.
YOU'RE NOT GETTING OFF THAT EASILY.
ぎゃふん!!
Doh!
BUT I DON'T KNOW WHAT TYPE OF SOFTWARE SHE'LL TAKE.
AFTER SHE'S LEARNED A BIT MORE, SHE'LL PROBABLY TELL YOU HERSELF. THERE'S A LOT SHE MIGHT TELL YOU.
SHE MIGHT BE ABLE TO TELL YOU WHO BUILT HER.
PERHAPS SHE'LL REMEMBER EVEN MORE.

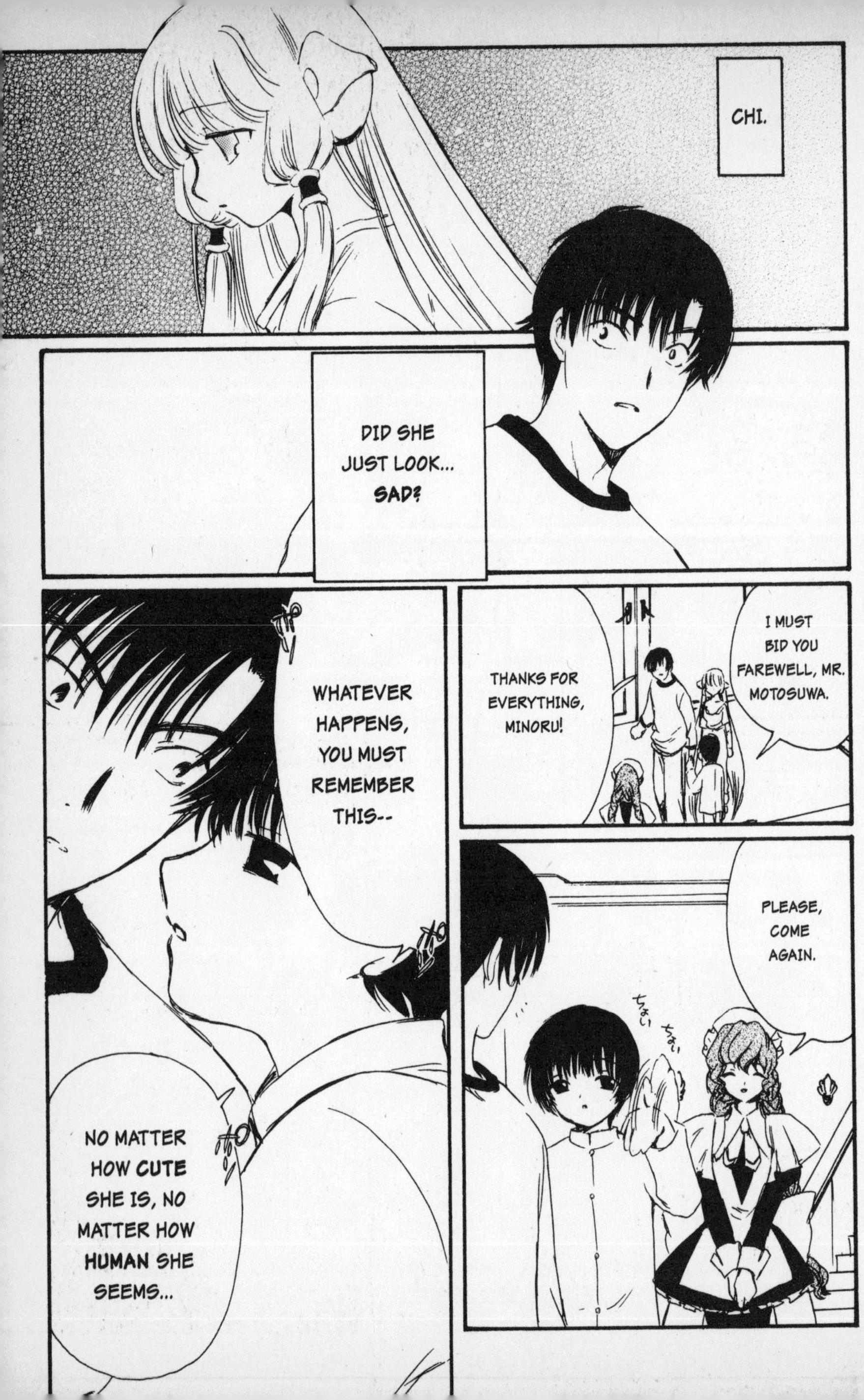
CHI.
DID SHE JUST LOOK... SAD?
I MUST BID YOU FAREWELL, MR. MOTOSUWA.
THANKS FOR EVERYTHING, MINORU!
PLEASE, COME AGAIN.
ちょい ちょい
WHATEVER HAPPENS, YOU MUST REMEMBER THIS--
NO MATTER HOW CUTE SHE IS, NO MATTER HOW HUMAN SHE SEEMS...

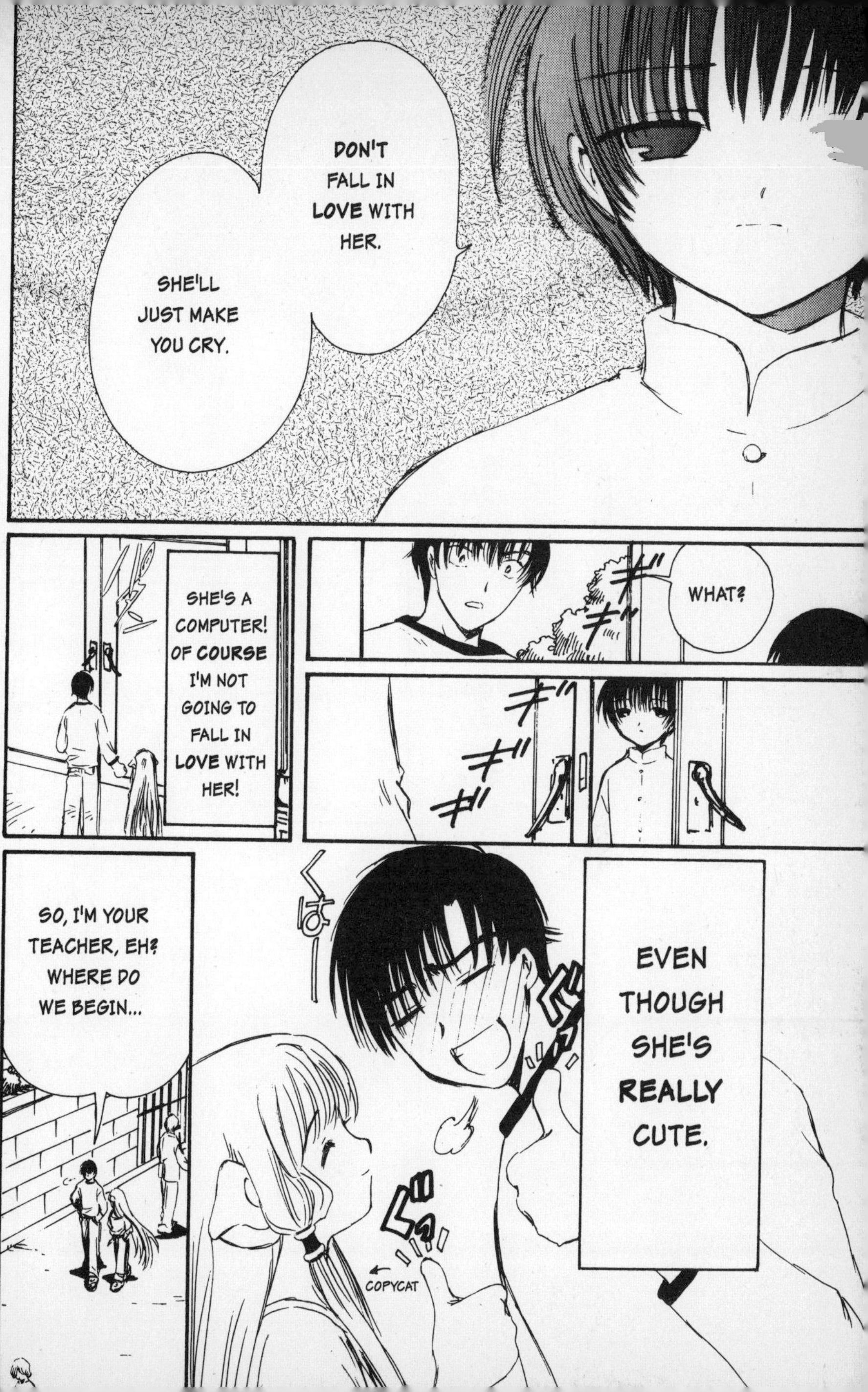
DON'T FALL IN LOVE WITH HER.
SHE'LL JUST MAKE YOU CRY.
WHAT?
SHE'S A COMPUTER! OF COURSE I'M NOT GOING TO FALL IN LOVE WITH HER!
EVEN THOUGH SHE'S REALLY CUTE.
COPYCAT
SO, I'M YOUR TEACHER, EH? WHERE DO WE BEGIN...

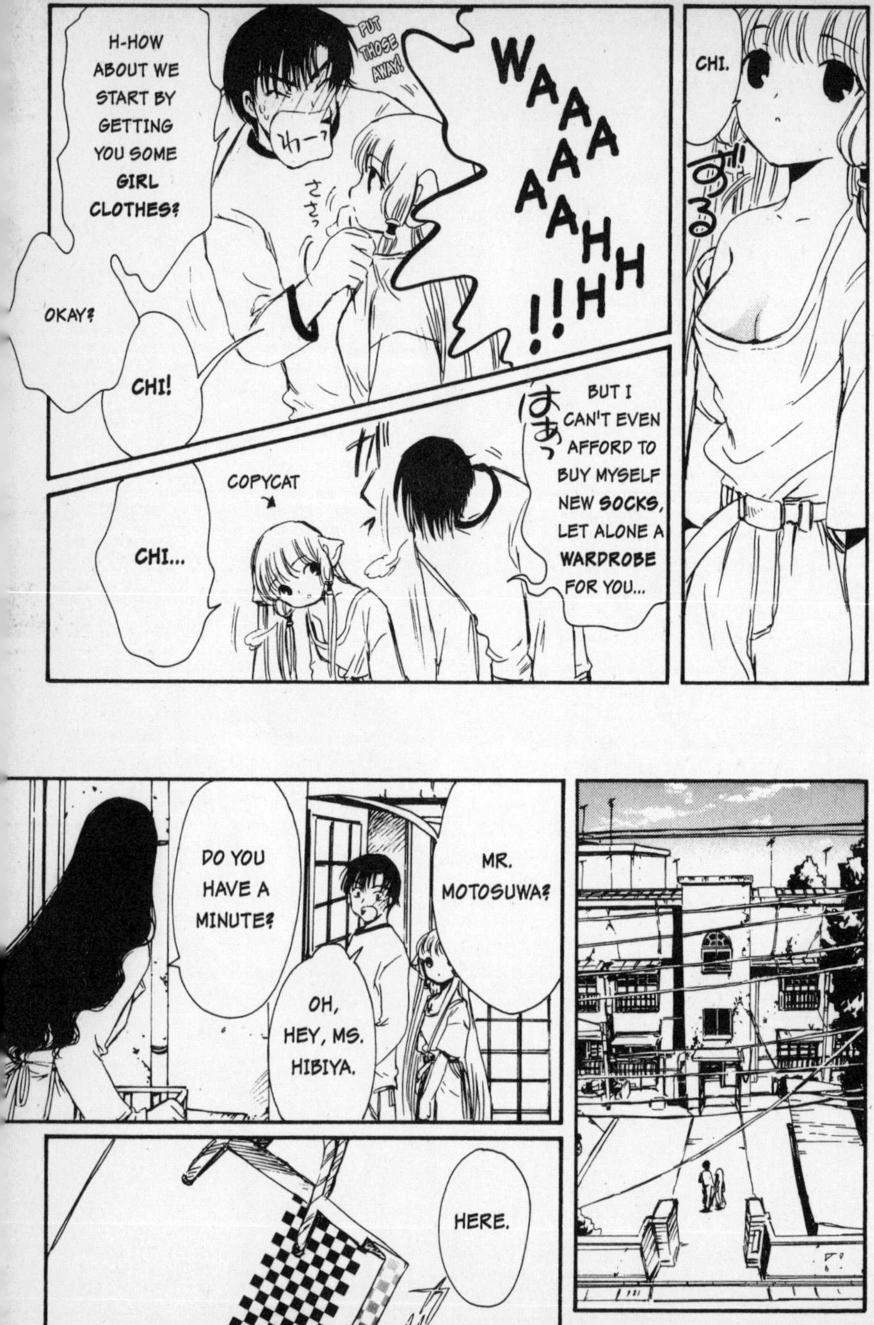
CHI.
ずる
WAAAAAAHHH!!!
PUT THOSE AWAY!
H-HOW ABOUT WE START BY GETTING YOU SOME GIRL CLOTHES?
ささっ
OKAY?
CHI!
BUT I CAN'T EVEN AFFORD TO BUY MYSELF NEW SOCKS, LET ALONE A WARDROBE FOR YOU...
はぁっ
COPYCAT
CHI...
MR. MOTOSUWA?
DO YOU HAVE A MINUTE?
OH, HEY, MS. HIBIYA.
HERE.

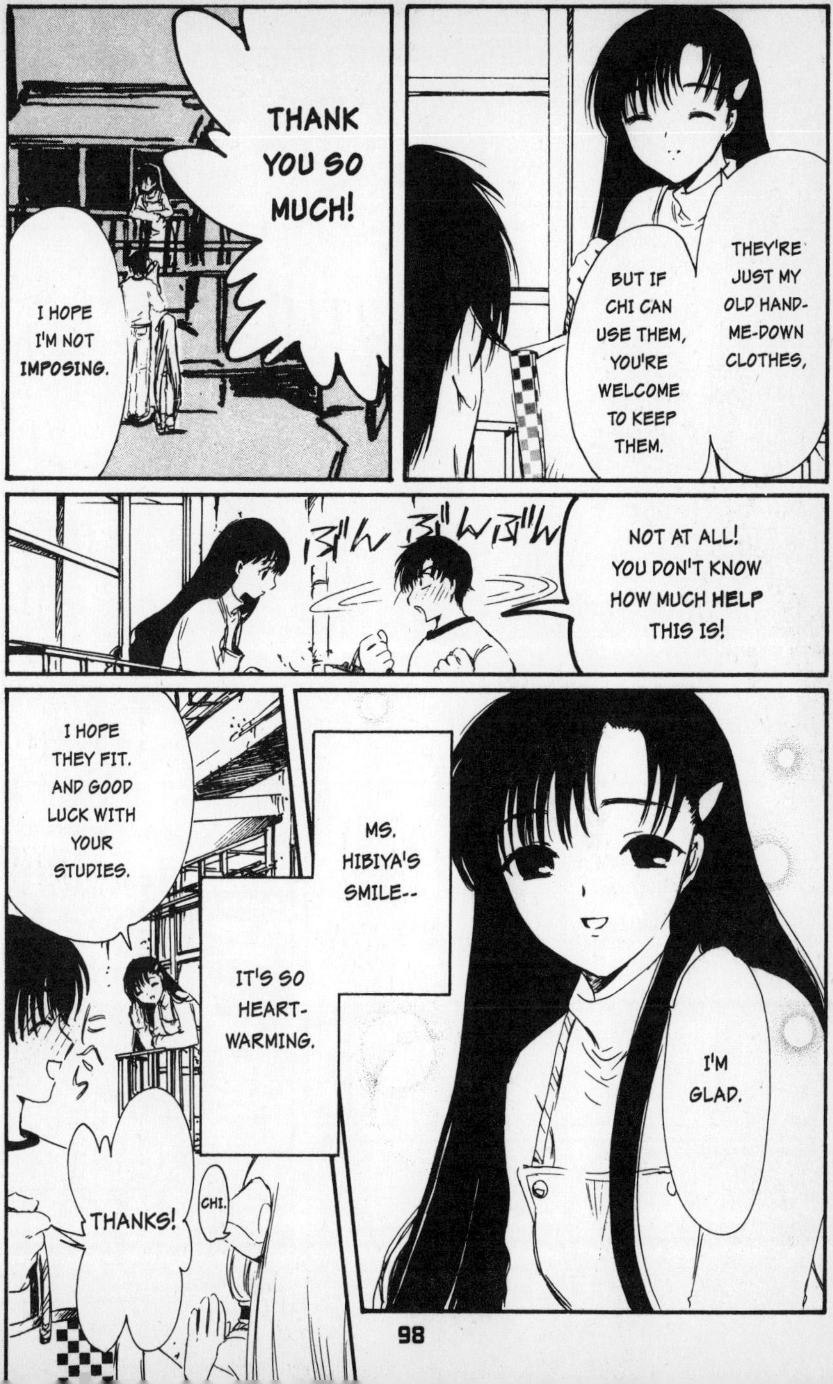
THEY'RE JUST MY OLD HAND-ME-DOWN CLOTHES,
BUT IF CHI CAN USE THEM, YOU'RE WELCOME TO KEEP THEM.
THANK YOU SO MUCH!
I HOPE I'M NOT IMPOSING.
ぶんぶんぶん
NOT AT ALL! YOU DON'T KNOW HOW MUCH HELP THIS IS!
I'M GLAD.
MS. HIBIYA'S SMILE--
IT'S SO HEART-WARMING.
I HOPE THEY FIT. AND GOOD LUCK WITH YOUR STUDIES.
へら
THANKS!
CHI.

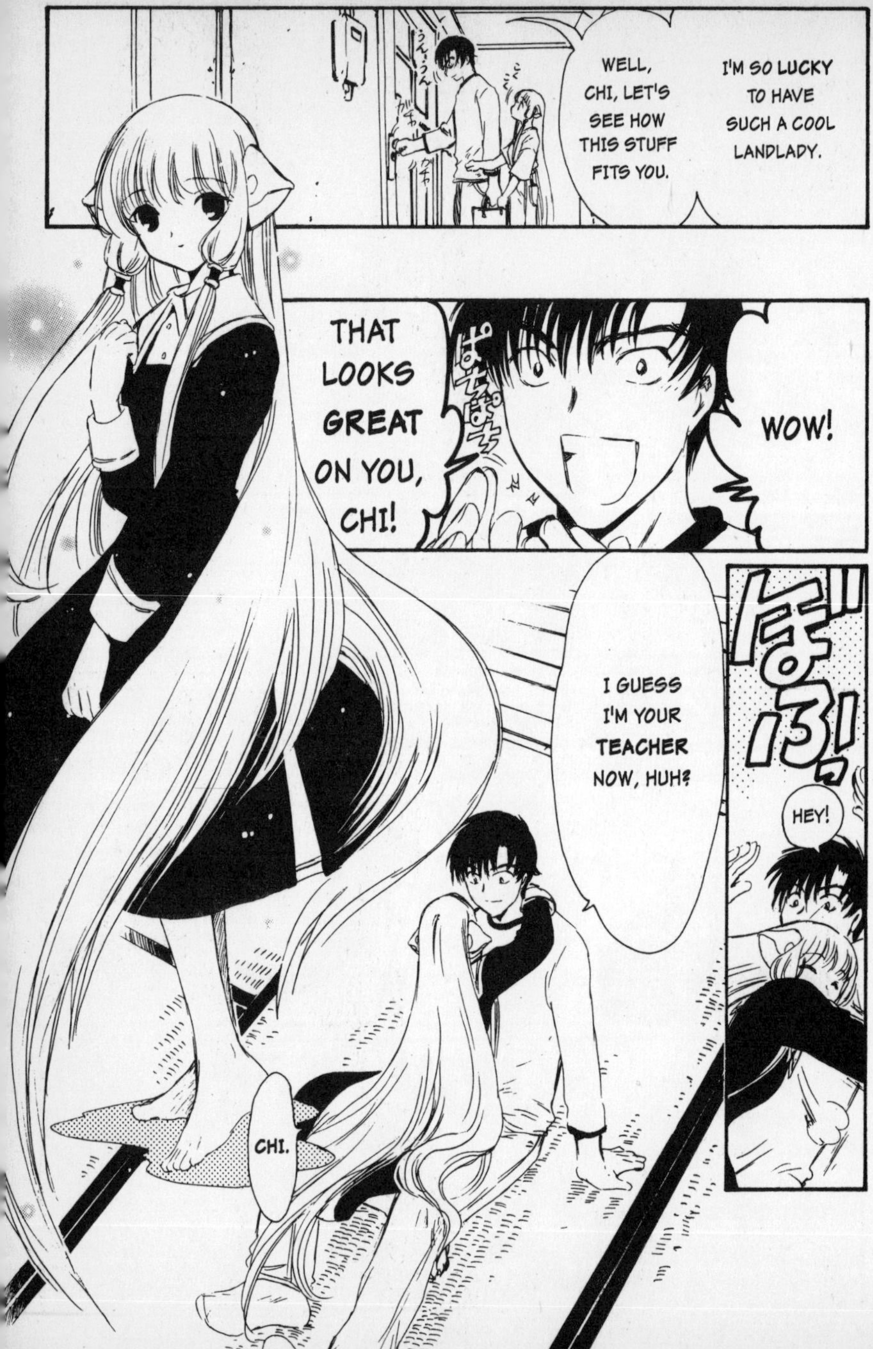
I'M SO LUCKY TO HAVE SUCH A COOL LANDLADY.
WELL, CHI, LET'S SEE HOW THIS STUFF FITS YOU.
WOW!
THAT LOOKS GREAT ON YOU, CHI!
ぼふっ!
HEY!
I GUESS I'M YOUR TEACHER NOW, HUH?
CHI.

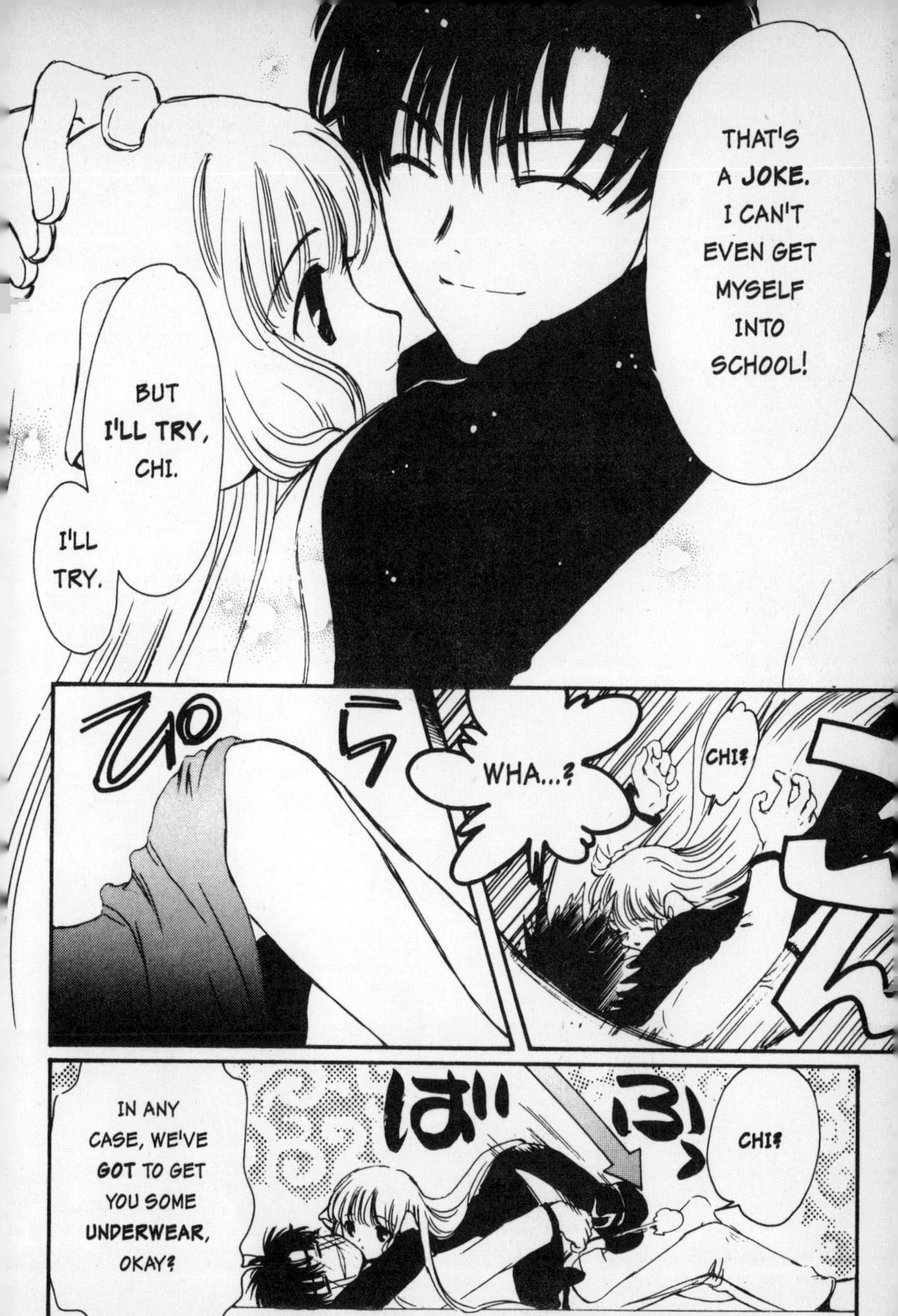
THAT'S A JOKE. I CAN'T EVEN GET MYSELF INTO SCHOOL!
BUT I'LL TRY, CHI.
I'LL TRY.
CHI?
WHA...?
ぴら
CHI?
ばふっ
IN ANY CASE, WE'VE GOT TO GET YOU SOME UNDERWEAR, OKAY?

◀chapter.6▶ end

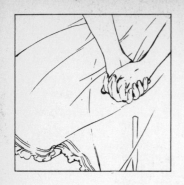
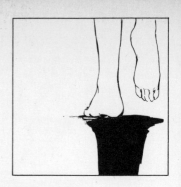
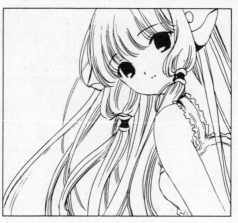

ちょびっツ
Chobits

◀chapter.7▶

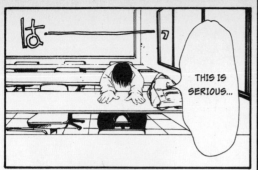

THIS IS SERIOUS...

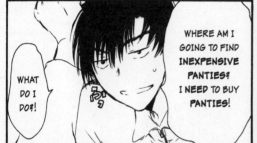

WHAT DO I DO?!

WHERE AM I GOING TO FIND INEXPENSIVE PANTIES? I NEED TO BUY PANTIES!

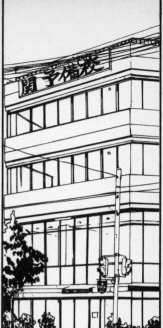

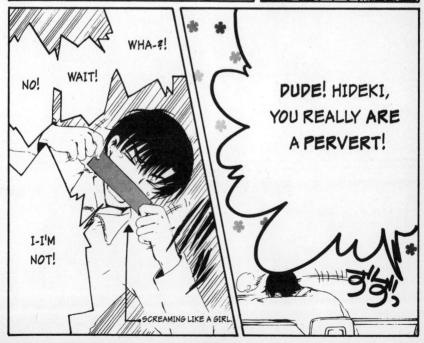

WHA-?!

NO!

WAIT!

DUDE! HIDEKI, YOU REALLY ARE A PERVERT!

I-I'M NOT!

SCREAMING LIKE A GIRL.

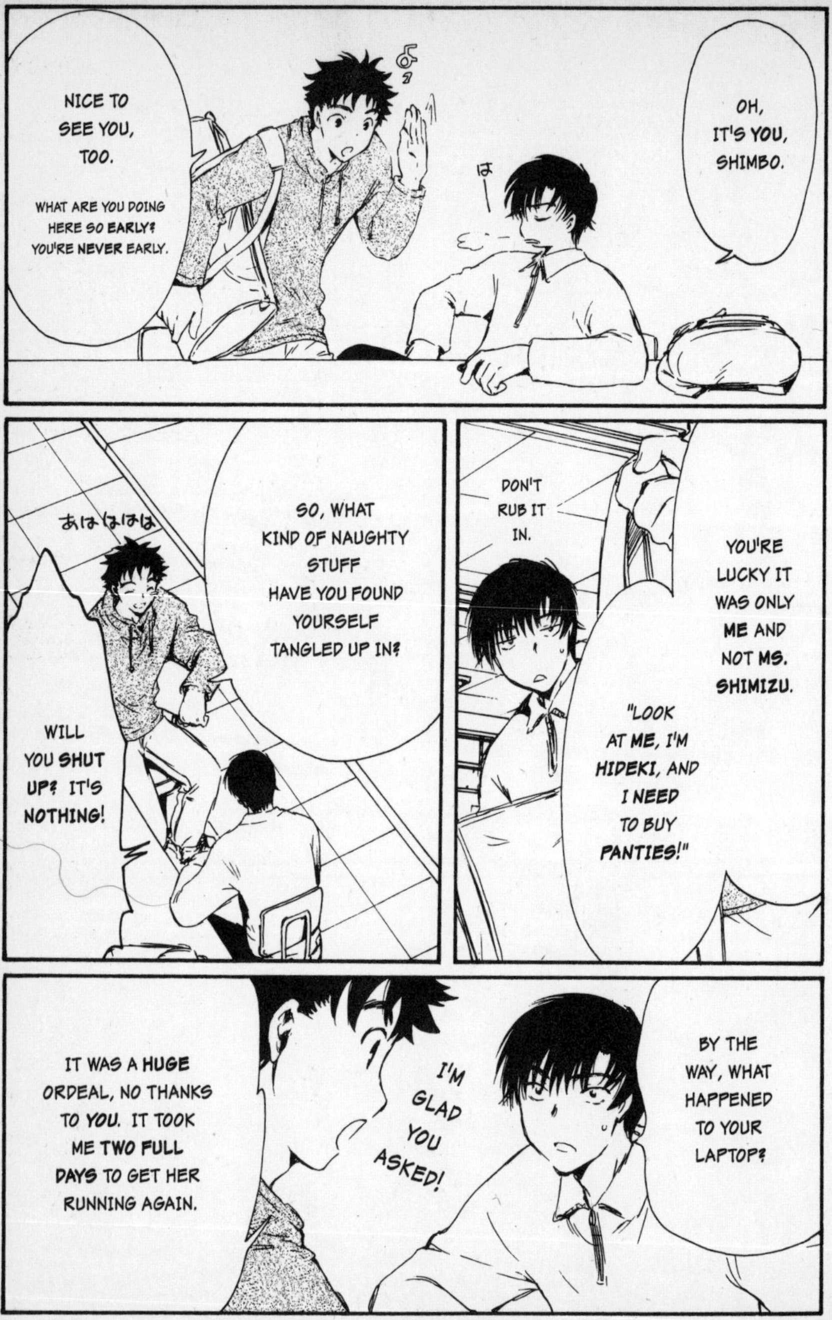
OH, IT'S YOU, SHIMBO.
は―
NICE TO SEE YOU, TOO.
WHAT ARE YOU DOING HERE SO EARLY? YOU'RE NEVER EARLY.
YOU'RE LUCKY IT WAS ONLY ME AND NOT MS. SHIMIZU.
DON'T RUB IT IN.
"LOOK AT ME, I'M HIDEKI, AND I NEED TO BUY PANTIES!"
SO, WHAT KIND OF NAUGHTY STUFF HAVE YOU FOUND YOURSELF TANGLED UP IN?
あはははは
WILL YOU SHUT UP? IT'S NOTHING!
BY THE WAY, WHAT HAPPENED TO YOUR LAPTOP?
I'M GLAD YOU ASKED!
IT WAS A HUGE ORDEAL, NO THANKS TO YOU. IT TOOK ME TWO FULL DAYS TO GET HER RUNNING AGAIN.

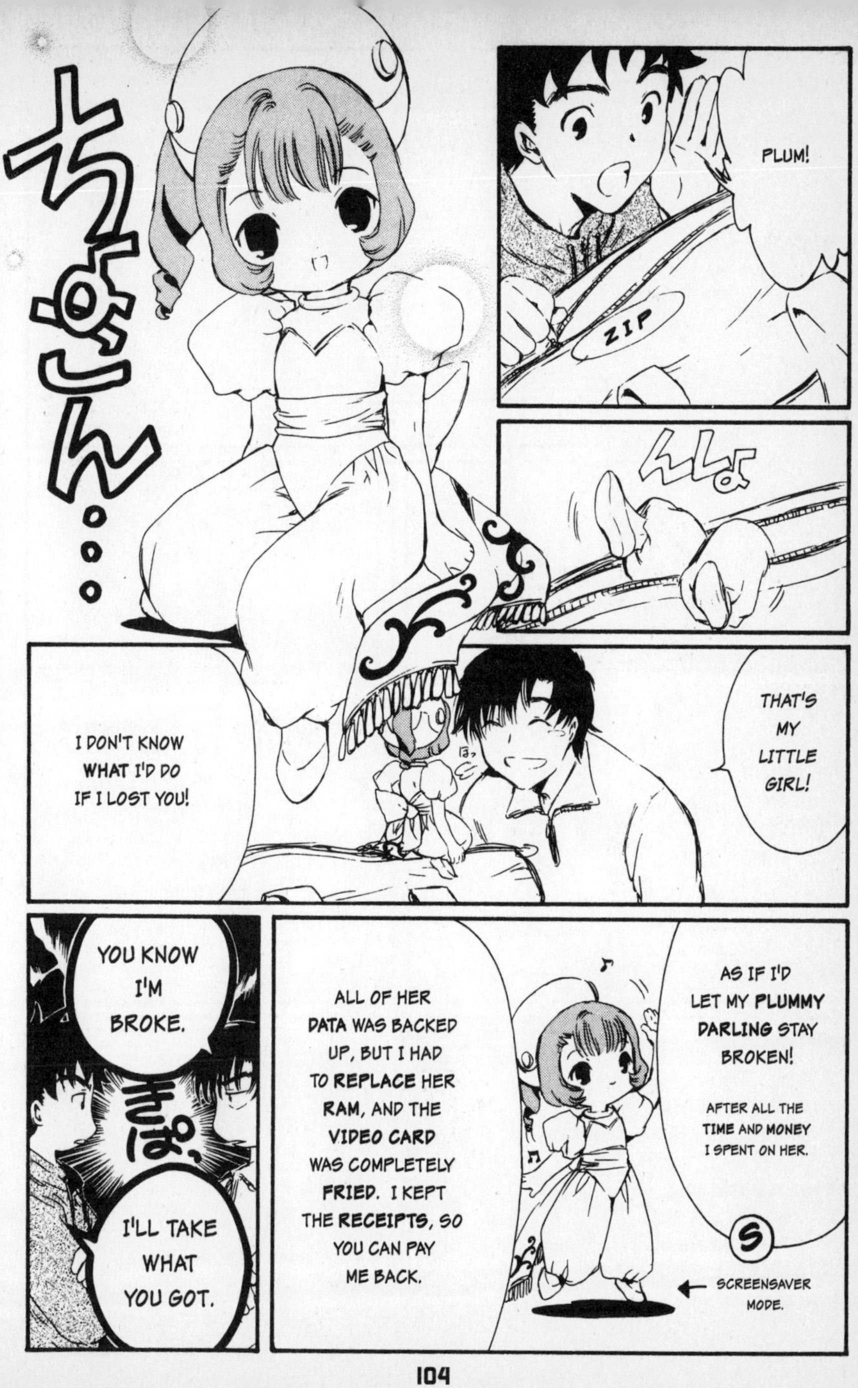
PLUM!
ZIP
んしょ
ちょこん…
THAT'S MY LITTLE GIRL!
I DON'T KNOW WHAT I'D DO IF I LOST YOU!
ほっ
AS IF I'D LET MY PLUMMY DARLING STAY BROKEN!
AFTER ALL THE TIME AND MONEY I SPENT ON HER.
S
← SCREENSAVER MODE.
ALL OF HER DATA WAS BACKED UP, BUT I HAD TO REPLACE HER RAM, AND THE VIDEO CARD WAS COMPLETELY FRIED. I KEPT THE RECEIPTS, SO YOU CAN PAY ME BACK.
YOU KNOW I'M BROKE.
きぱ
I'LL TAKE WHAT YOU GOT.

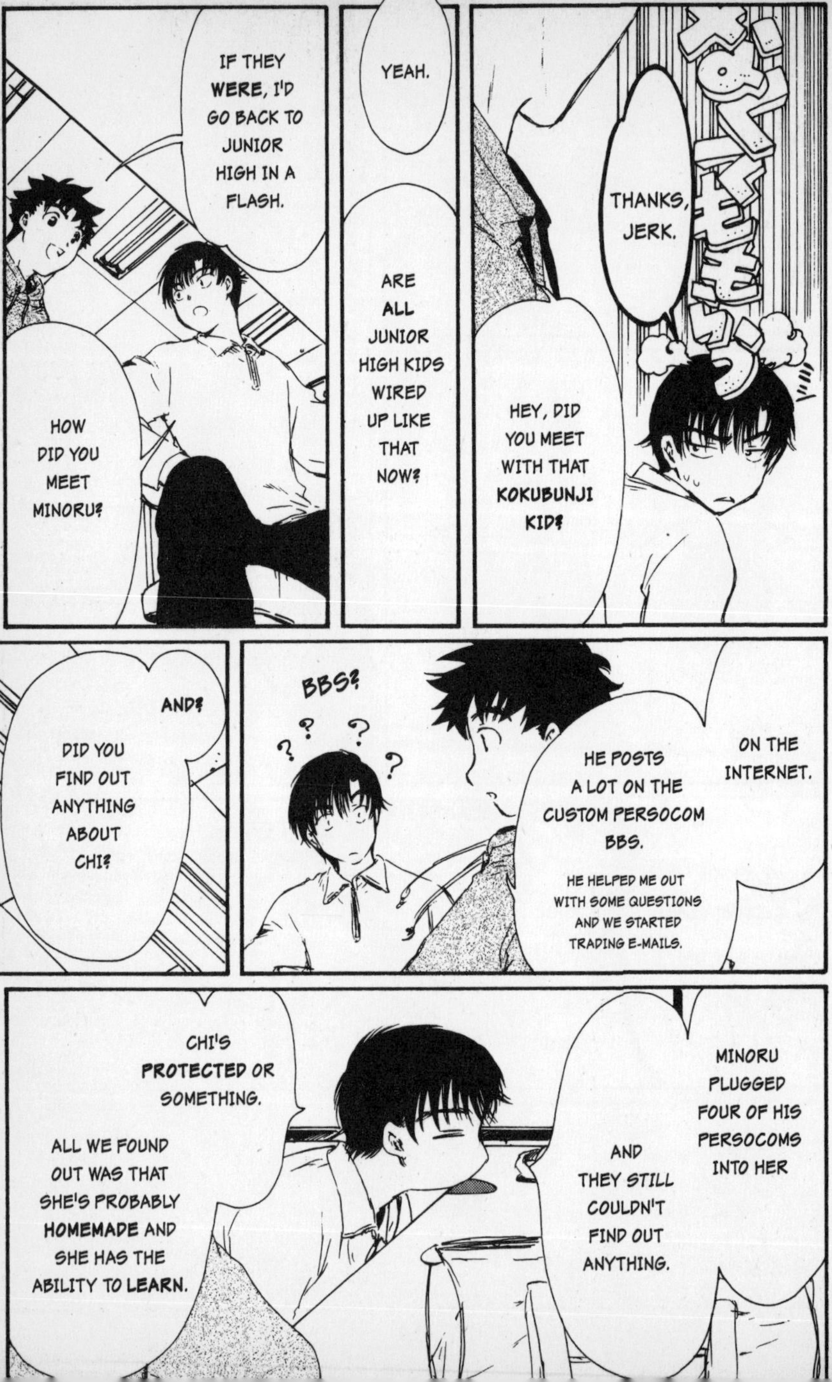
THANKS, JERK.
HEY, DID YOU MEET WITH THAT KOKUBUNJI KID?
YEAH.
ARE ALL JUNIOR HIGH KIDS WIRED UP LIKE THAT NOW?
IF THEY WERE, I'D GO BACK TO JUNIOR HIGH IN A FLASH.
HOW DID YOU MEET MINORU?
ON THE INTERNET.
HE POSTS A LOT ON THE CUSTOM PERSOCOM BBS.
HE HELPED ME OUT WITH SOME QUESTIONS AND WE STARTED TRADING E-MAILS.
BBS?
AND?
DID YOU FIND OUT ANYTHING ABOUT CHI?
MINORU PLUGGED FOUR OF HIS PERSOCOMS INTO HER
AND THEY STILL COULDN'T FIND OUT ANYTHING.
CHI'S PROTECTED OR SOMETHING.
ALL WE FOUND OUT WAS THAT SHE'S PROBABLY HOMEMADE AND SHE HAS THE ABILITY TO LEARN.

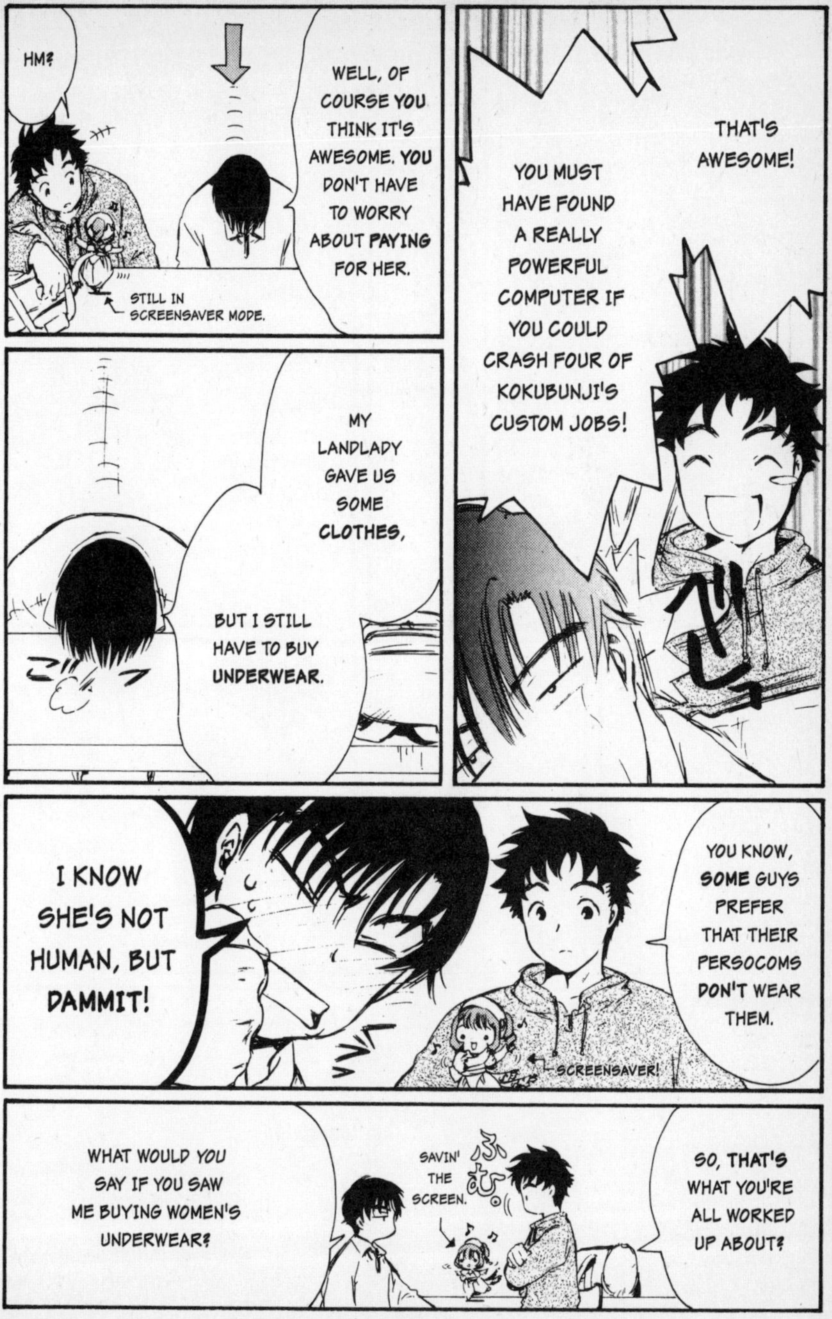
THAT'S AWESOME!
YOU MUST HAVE FOUND A REALLY POWERFUL COMPUTER IF YOU COULD CRASH FOUR OF KOKUBUNJI'S CUSTOM JOBS!
WELL, OF COURSE YOU THINK IT'S AWESOME. YOU DON'T HAVE TO WORRY ABOUT PAYING FOR HER.
HM?
STILL IN SCREENSAVER MODE.
MY LANDLADY GAVE US SOME CLOTHES,
BUT I STILL HAVE TO BUY UNDERWEAR.
YOU KNOW, SOME GUYS PREFER THAT THEIR PERSOCOMS DON'T WEAR THEM.
SCREENSAVER!
I KNOW SHE'S NOT HUMAN, BUT DAMMIT!
SO, THAT'S WHAT YOU'RE ALL WORKED UP ABOUT?
SAVIN' THE SCREEN.
WHAT WOULD YOU SAY IF YOU SAW ME BUYING WOMEN'S UNDERWEAR?

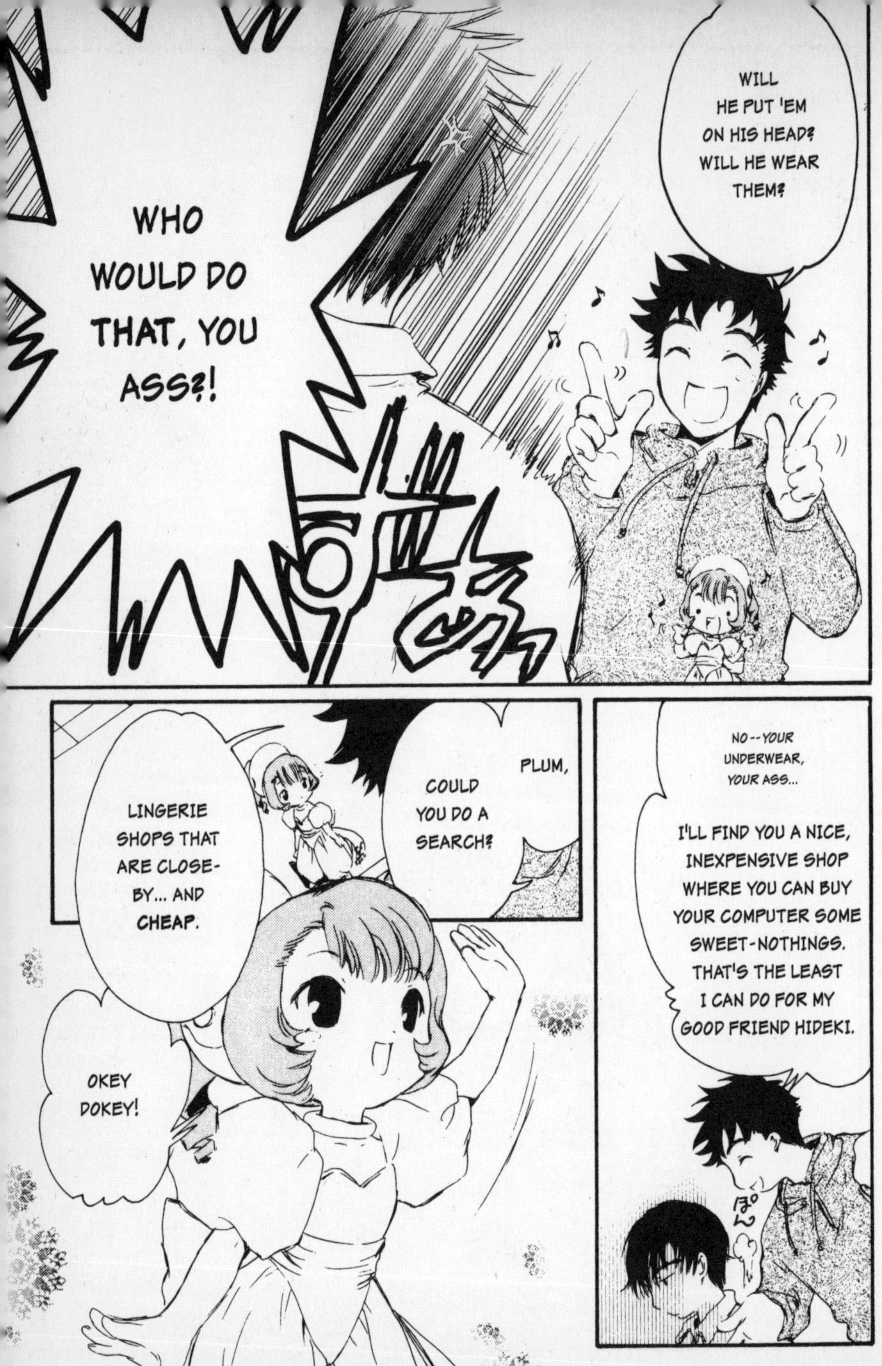
WILL HE PUT 'EM ON HIS HEAD? WILL HE WEAR THEM?
WHO WOULD DO THAT, YOU ASS?!
NO--YOUR UNDERWEAR, YOUR ASS...
I'LL FIND YOU A NICE, INEXPENSIVE SHOP WHERE YOU CAN BUY YOUR COMPUTER SOME SWEET-NOTHINGS. THAT'S THE LEAST I CAN DO FOR MY GOOD FRIEND HIDEKI.
ぽん
PLUM, COULD YOU DO A SEARCH?
LINGERIE SHOPS THAT ARE CLOSE-BY... AND CHEAP.
OKEY DOKEY!

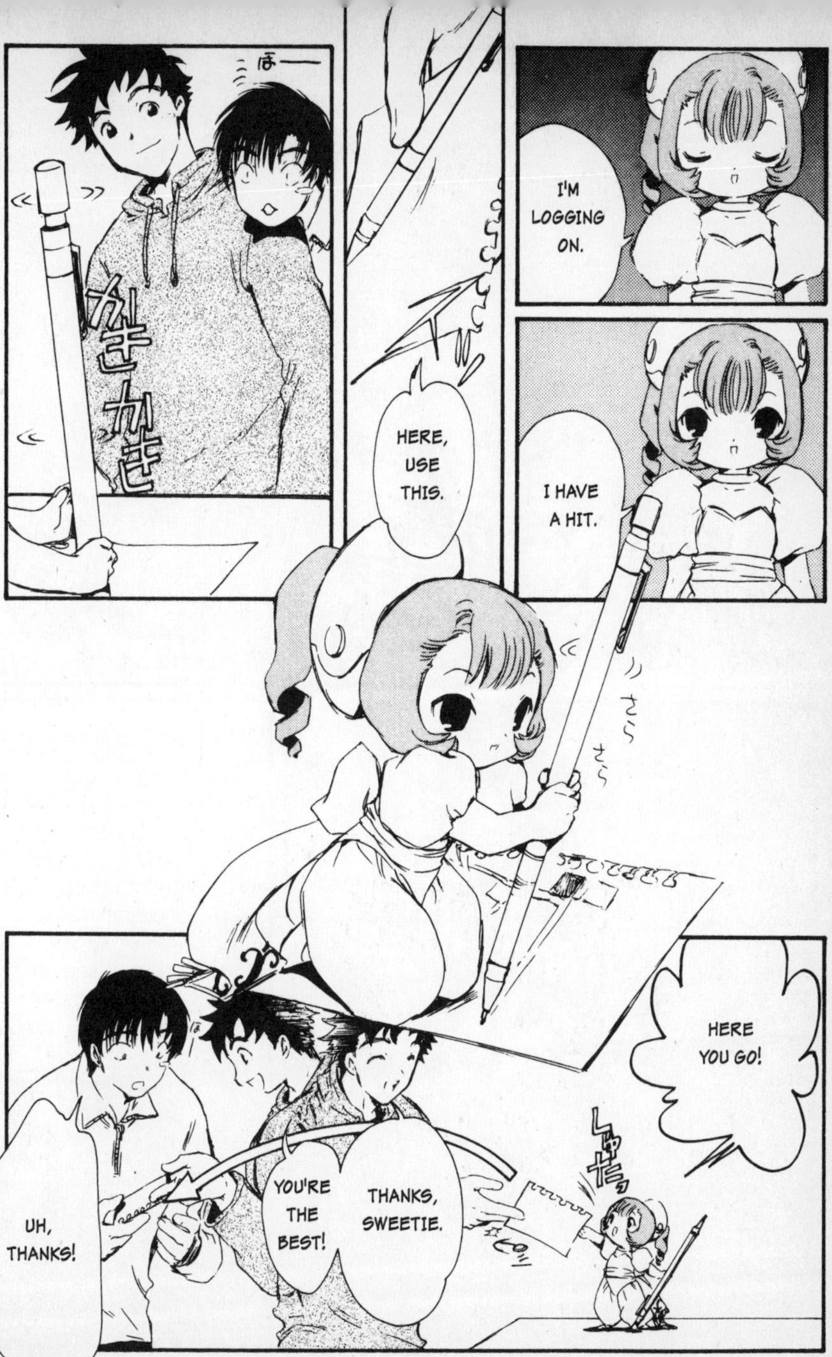
I'M LOGGING ON.
I HAVE A HIT.
HERE, USE THIS.
ほー
かきかき
さら
さら
HERE YOU GO!
THANKS, SWEETIE.
YOU'RE THE BEST!
UH, THANKS!

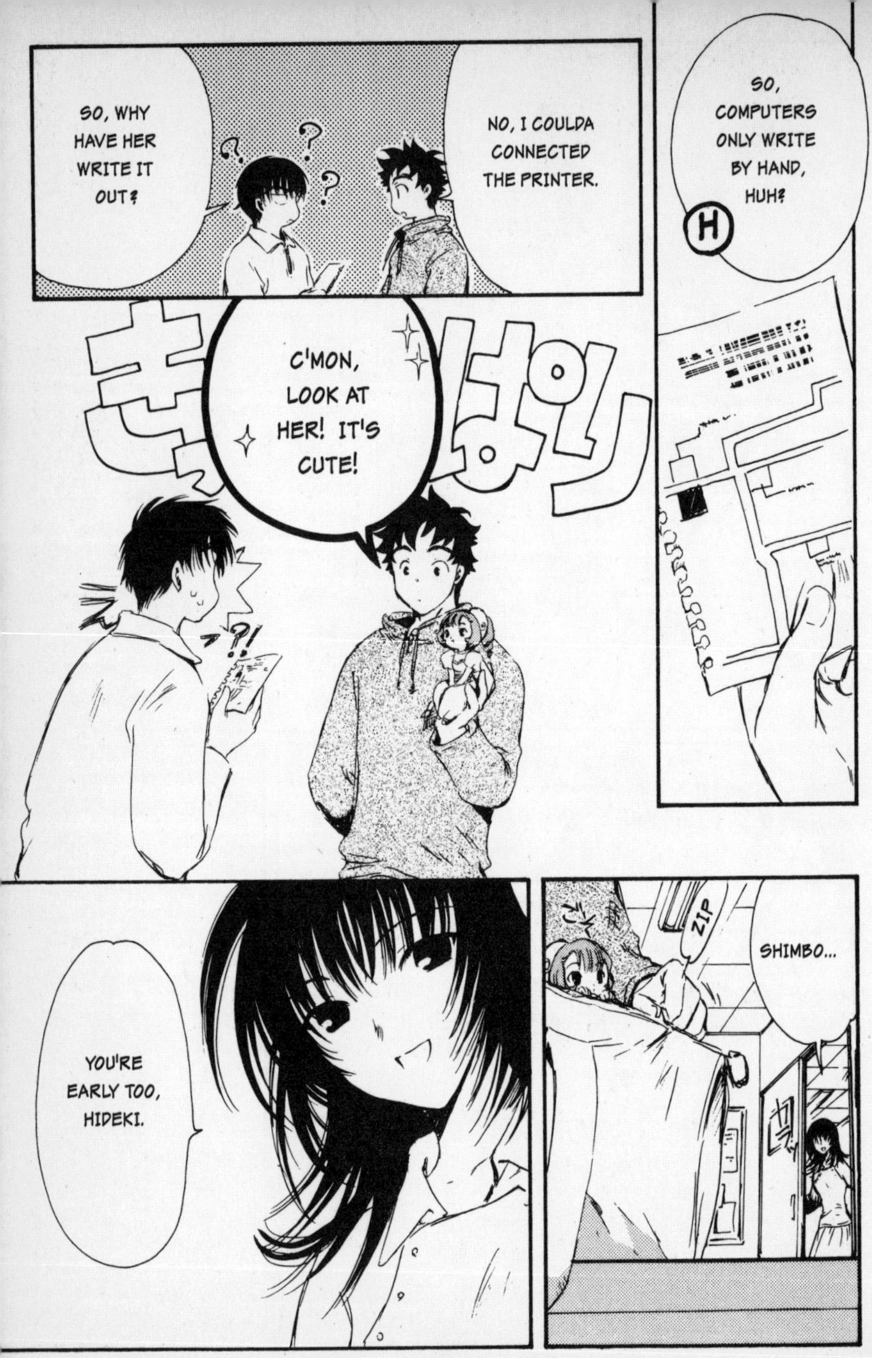
SO, COMPUTERS ONLY WRITE BY HAND, HUH?
H
NO, I COULDA CONNECTED THE PRINTER.
SO, WHY HAVE HER WRITE IT OUT?
C'MON, LOOK AT HER! IT'S CUTE!
ZIP
SHIMBO...
YOU'RE EARLY TOO, HIDEKI.

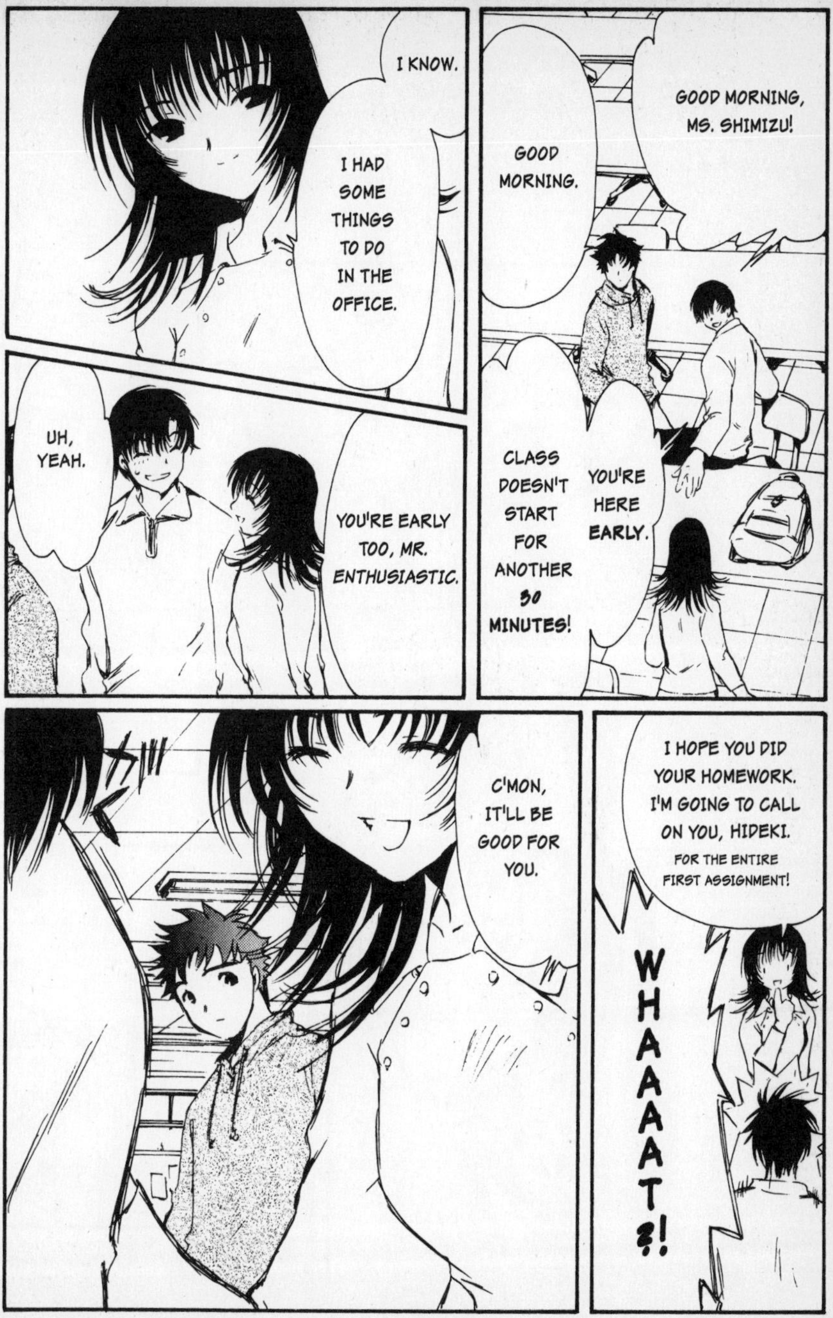
GOOD MORNING, MS. SHIMIZU!
GOOD MORNING.
YOU'RE HERE EARLY.
CLASS DOESN'T START FOR ANOTHER 30 MINUTES!
I KNOW.
I HAD SOME THINGS TO DO IN THE OFFICE.
YOU'RE EARLY TOO, MR. ENTHUSIASTIC.
UH, YEAH.
I HOPE YOU DID YOUR HOMEWORK. I'M GOING TO CALL ON YOU, HIDEKI. FOR THE ENTIRE FIRST ASSIGNMENT!
WHAAAAT?!
C'MON, IT'LL BE GOOD FOR YOU.

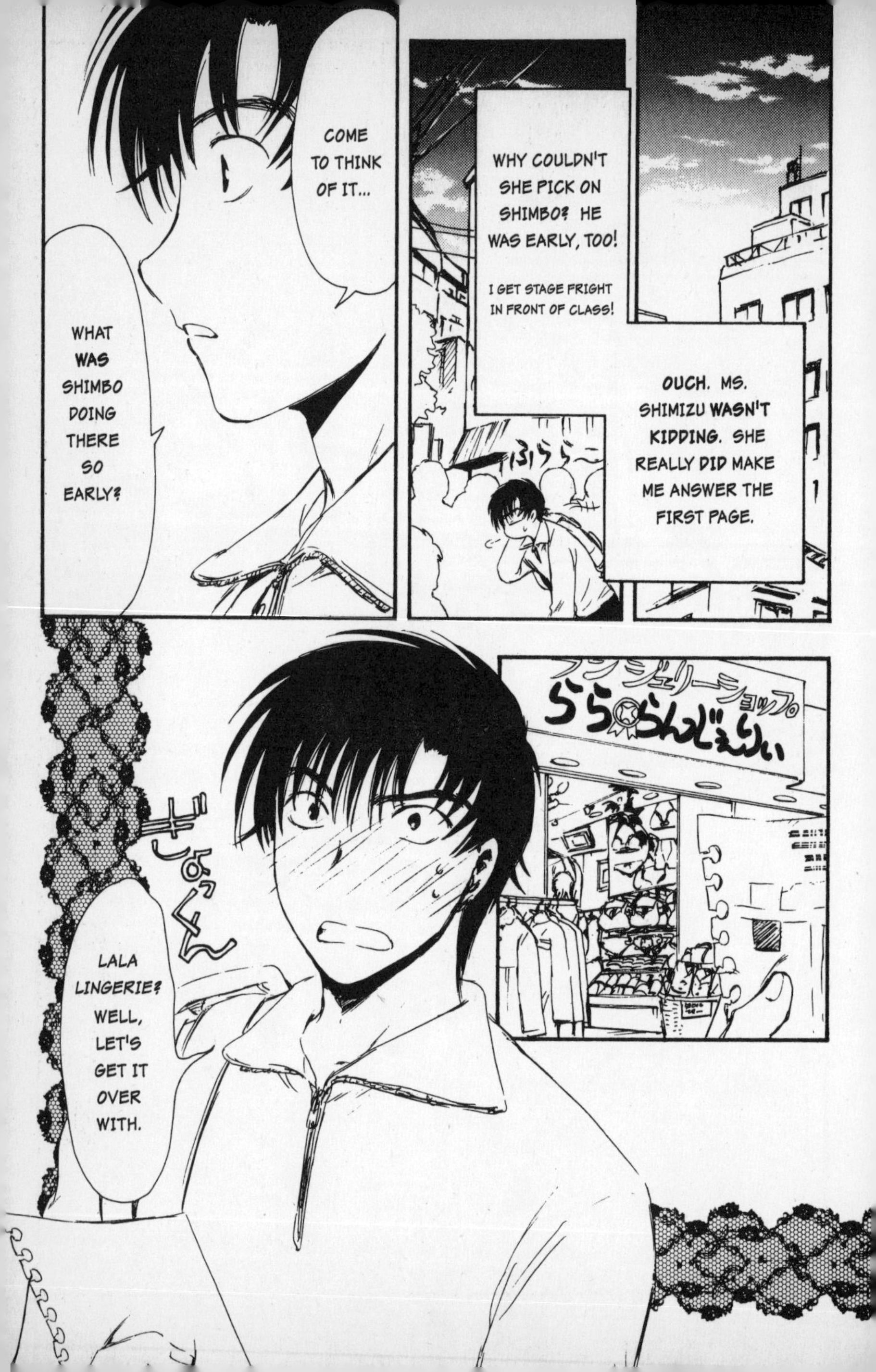
OUCH. MS. SHIMIZU WASN'T KIDDING. SHE REALLY DID MAKE ME ANSWER THE FIRST PAGE.
WHY COULDN'T SHE PICK ON SHIMBO? HE WAS EARLY, TOO!
I GET STAGE FRIGHT IN FRONT OF CLASS!
ふらら～
COME TO THINK OF IT...
WHAT WAS SHIMBO DOING THERE SO EARLY?
ランジェリーショップ
らららんじぇりぃ
LALA LINGERIE? WELL, LET'S GET IT OVER WITH.

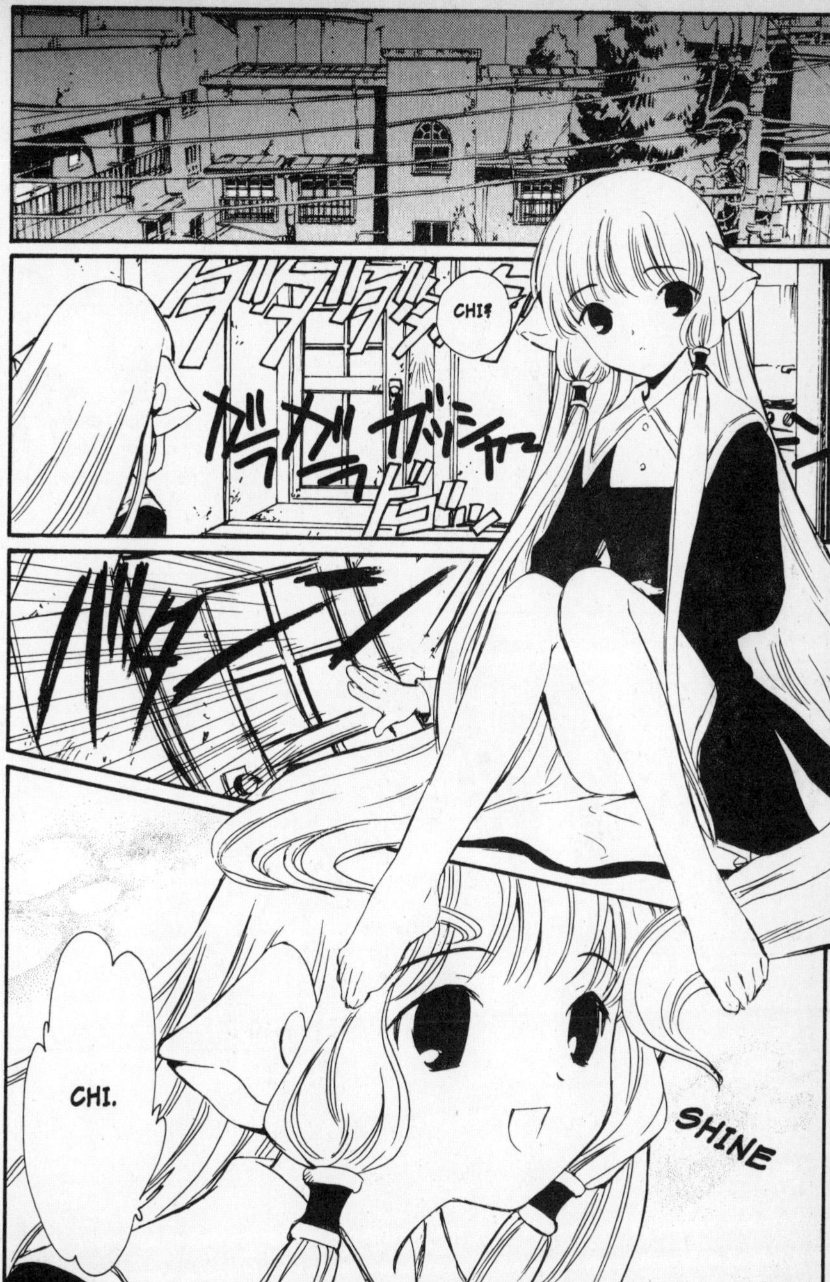
CHI?
SHINE
CHI.

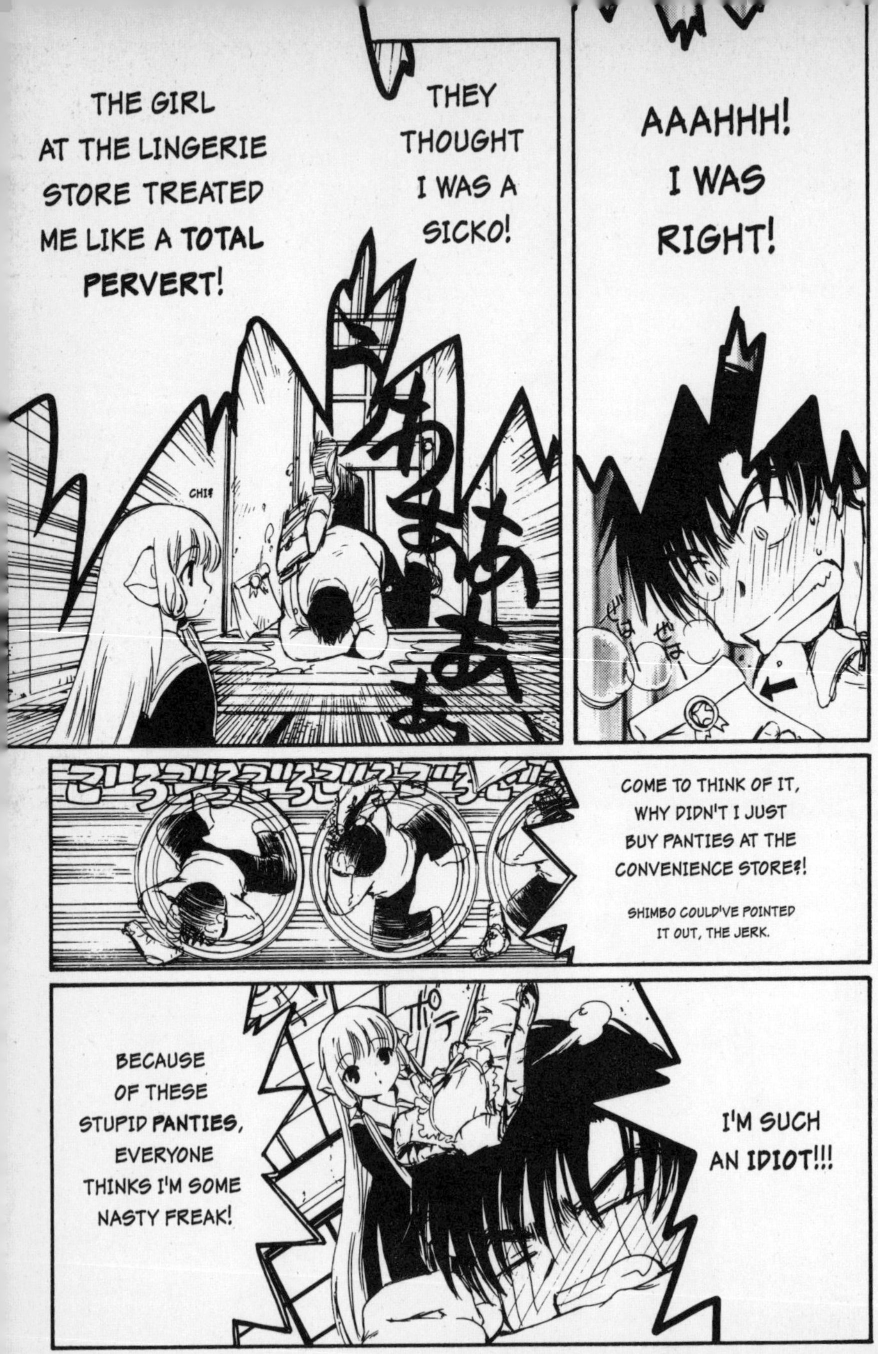
AAAHHH! I WAS RIGHT!
THEY THOUGHT I WAS A SICKO!
THE GIRL AT THE LINGERIE STORE TREATED ME LIKE A TOTAL PERVERT!
CHI?
COME TO THINK OF IT, WHY DIDN'T I JUST BUY PANTIES AT THE CONVENIENCE STORE?!
SHIMBO COULD'VE POINTED IT OUT, THE JERK.
I'M SUCH AN IDIOT!!!
BECAUSE OF THESE STUPID PANTIES, EVERYONE THINKS I'M SOME NASTY FREAK!

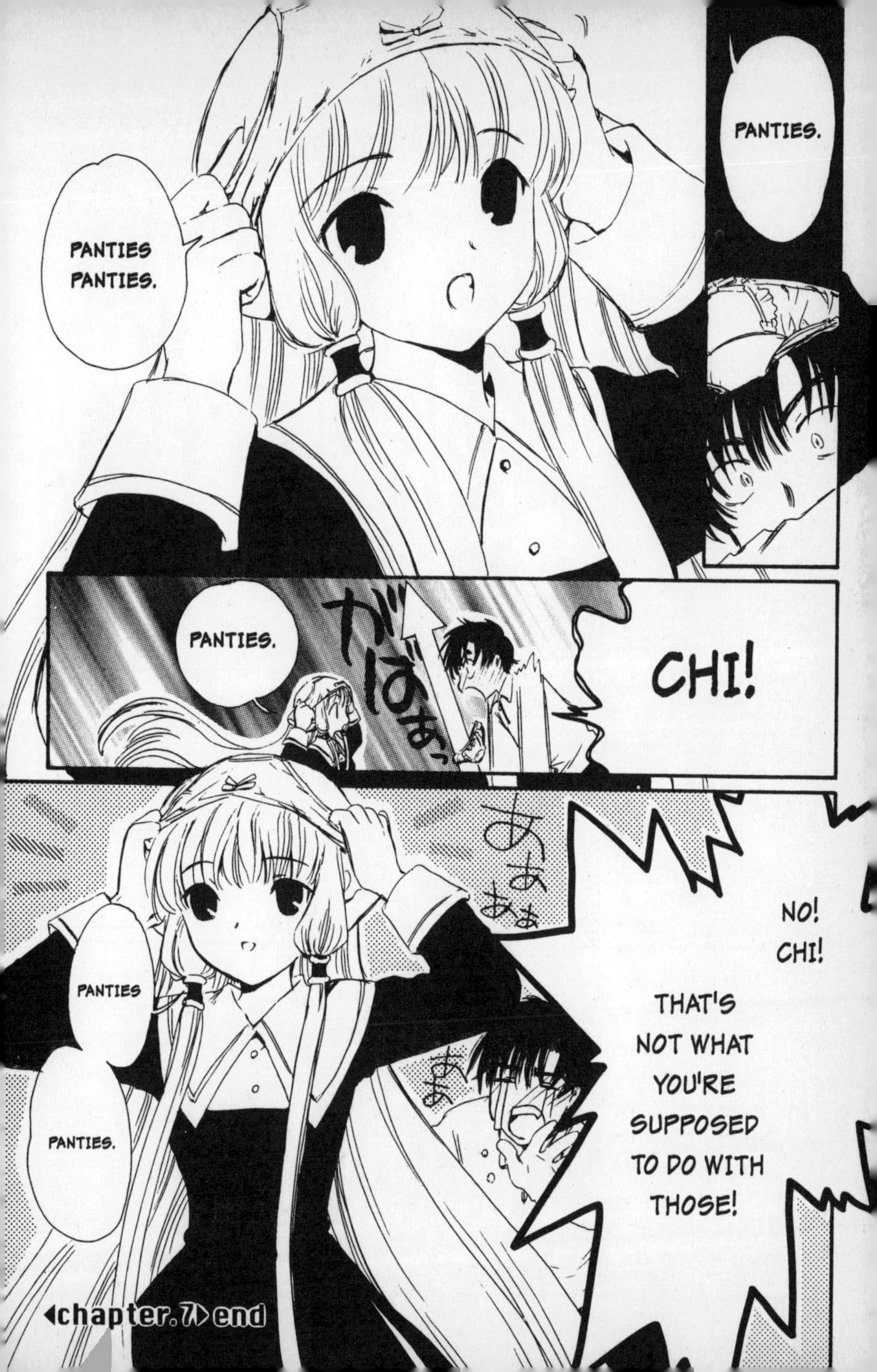
PANTIES.
PANTIES PANTIES.
CHI!
PANTIES.
NO! CHI!
THAT'S NOT WHAT YOU'RE SUPPOSED TO DO WITH THOSE!
PANTIES
PANTIES.
◀chapter. 7▶ end

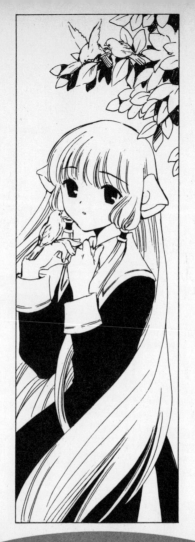

ちょびっツ
Chobits
◀chapter.8▶

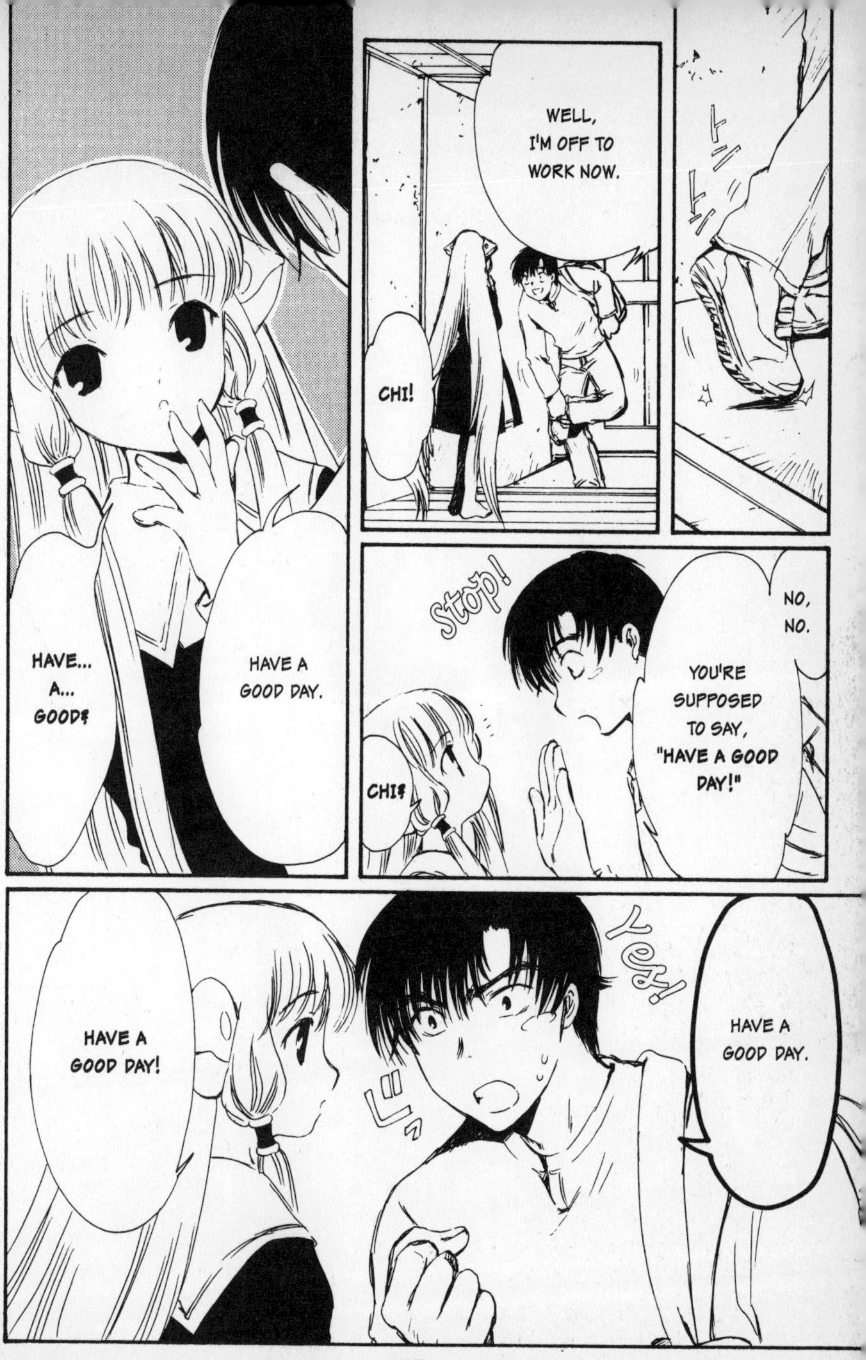
WELL, I'M OFF TO WORK NOW.
CHI!
NO, NO.
YOU'RE SUPPOSED TO SAY, "HAVE A GOOD DAY!"
Stop!
CHI?
HAVE A GOOD DAY.
HAVE... A... GOOD?
HAVE A GOOD DAY.
Yea!
HAVE A GOOD DAY!

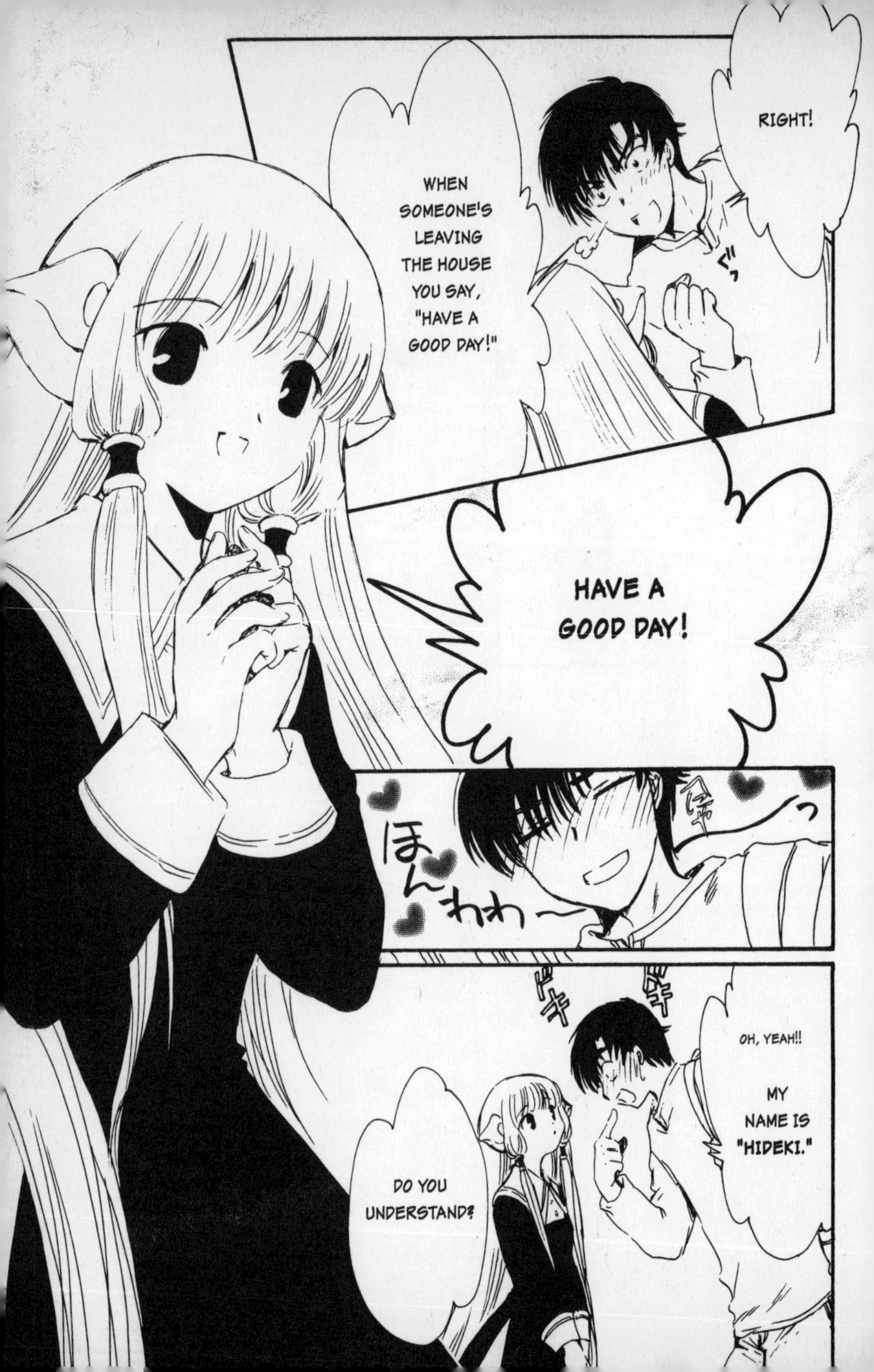
RIGHT!
WHEN SOMEONE'S LEAVING THE HOUSE YOU SAY, "HAVE A GOOD DAY!"
ぐっ
HAVE A GOOD DAY!
ほんわわ~
ドキ ドキ
OH, YEAH!!
MY NAME IS "HIDEKI."
DO YOU UNDERSTAND?

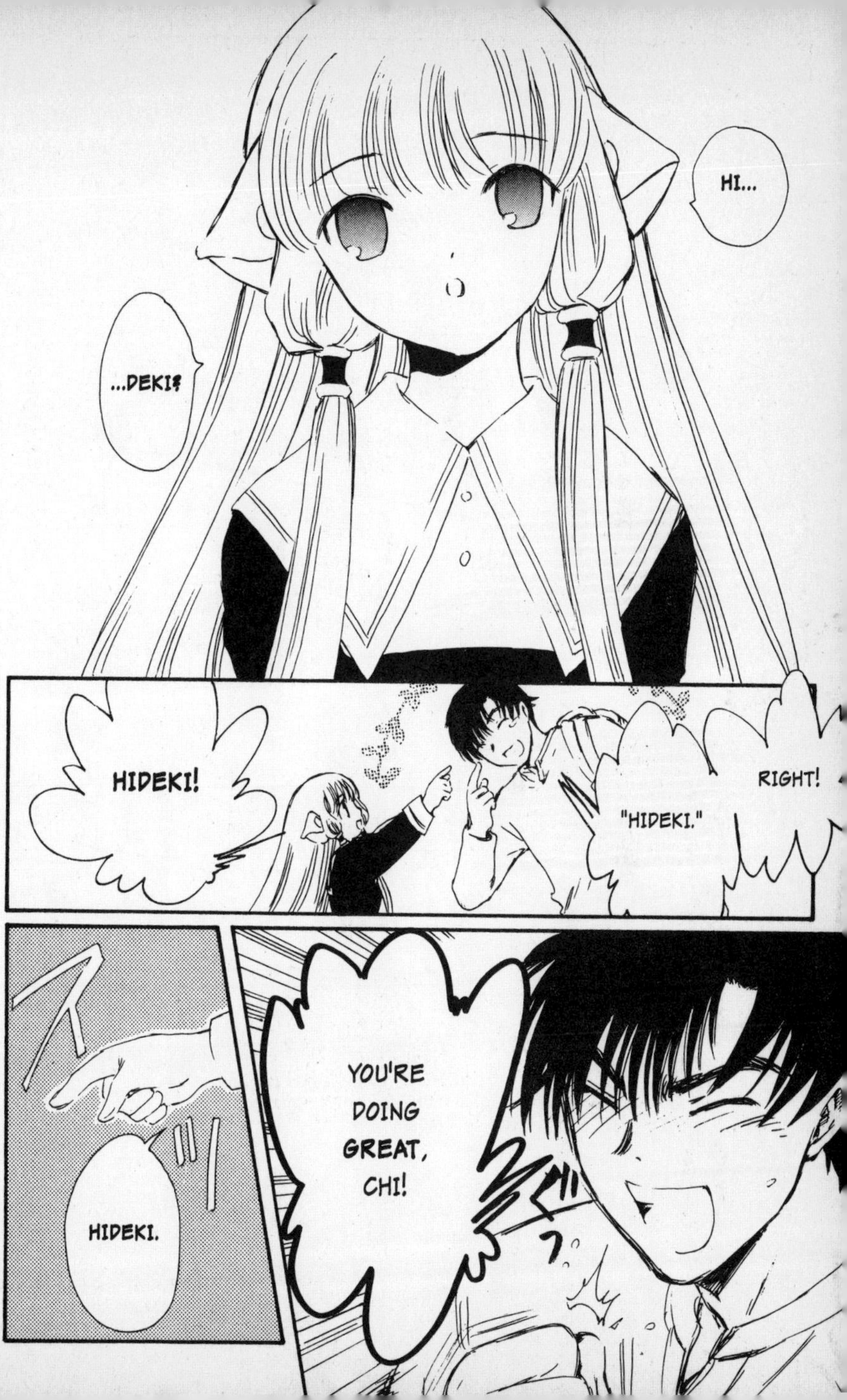
HI...
...DEKI?
RIGHT!
"HIDEKI."
HIDEKI!
YOU'RE DOING GREAT, CHI!
HIDEKI.

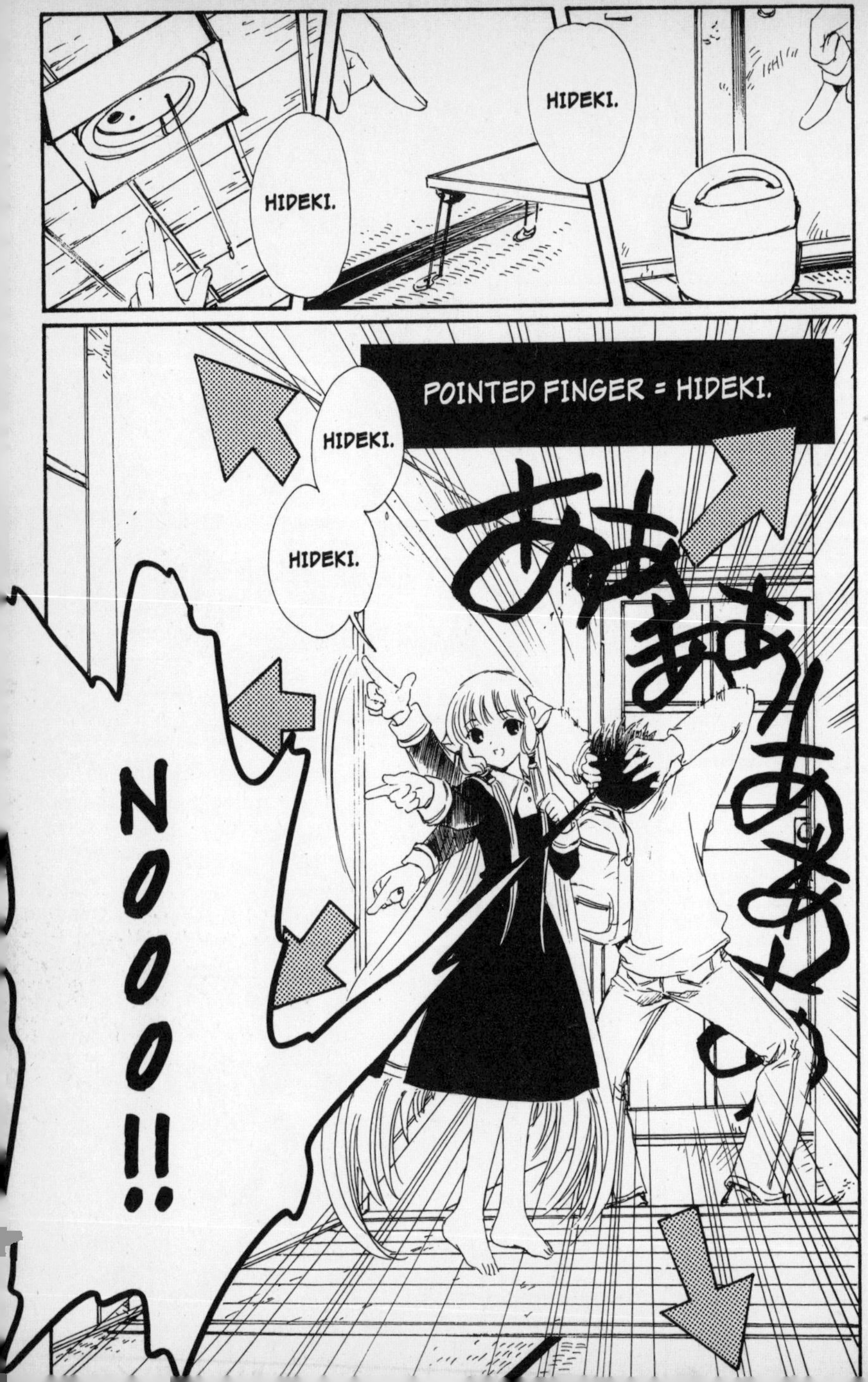
HIDEKI.
HIDEKI.
POINTED FINGER = HIDEKI.
HIDEKI.
HIDEKI.
NOOO!!

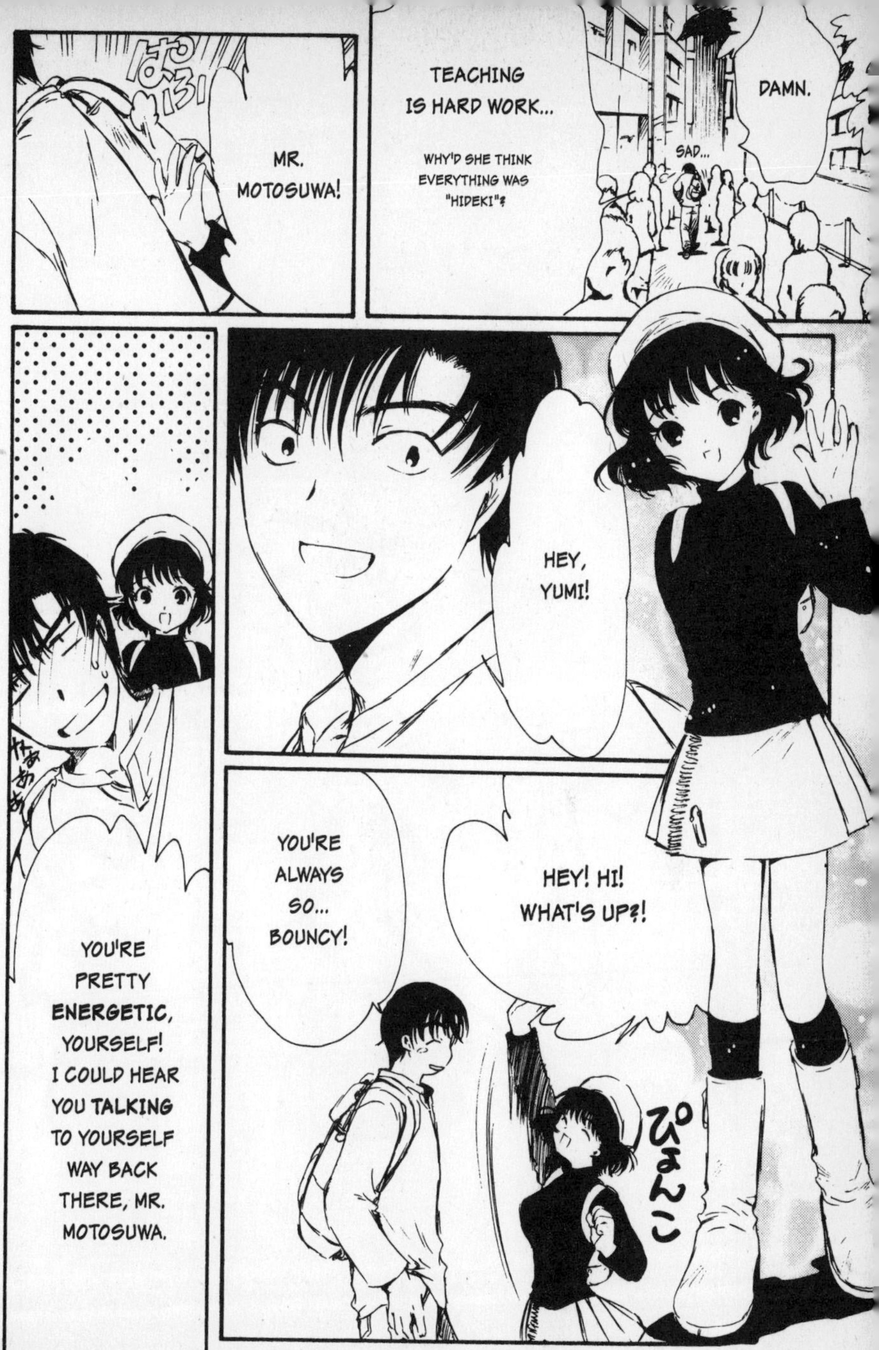
DAMN.
TEACHING IS HARD WORK...
WHY'D SHE THINK EVERYTHING WAS "HIDEKI"?
SAD...
MR. MOTOSUWA!
HEY, YUMI!
HEY! HI! WHAT'S UP?!
ぴょんこ
YOU'RE ALWAYS SO... BOUNCY!
YOU'RE PRETTY ENERGETIC, YOURSELF! I COULD HEAR YOU TALKING TO YOURSELF WAY BACK THERE, MR. MOTOSUWA.

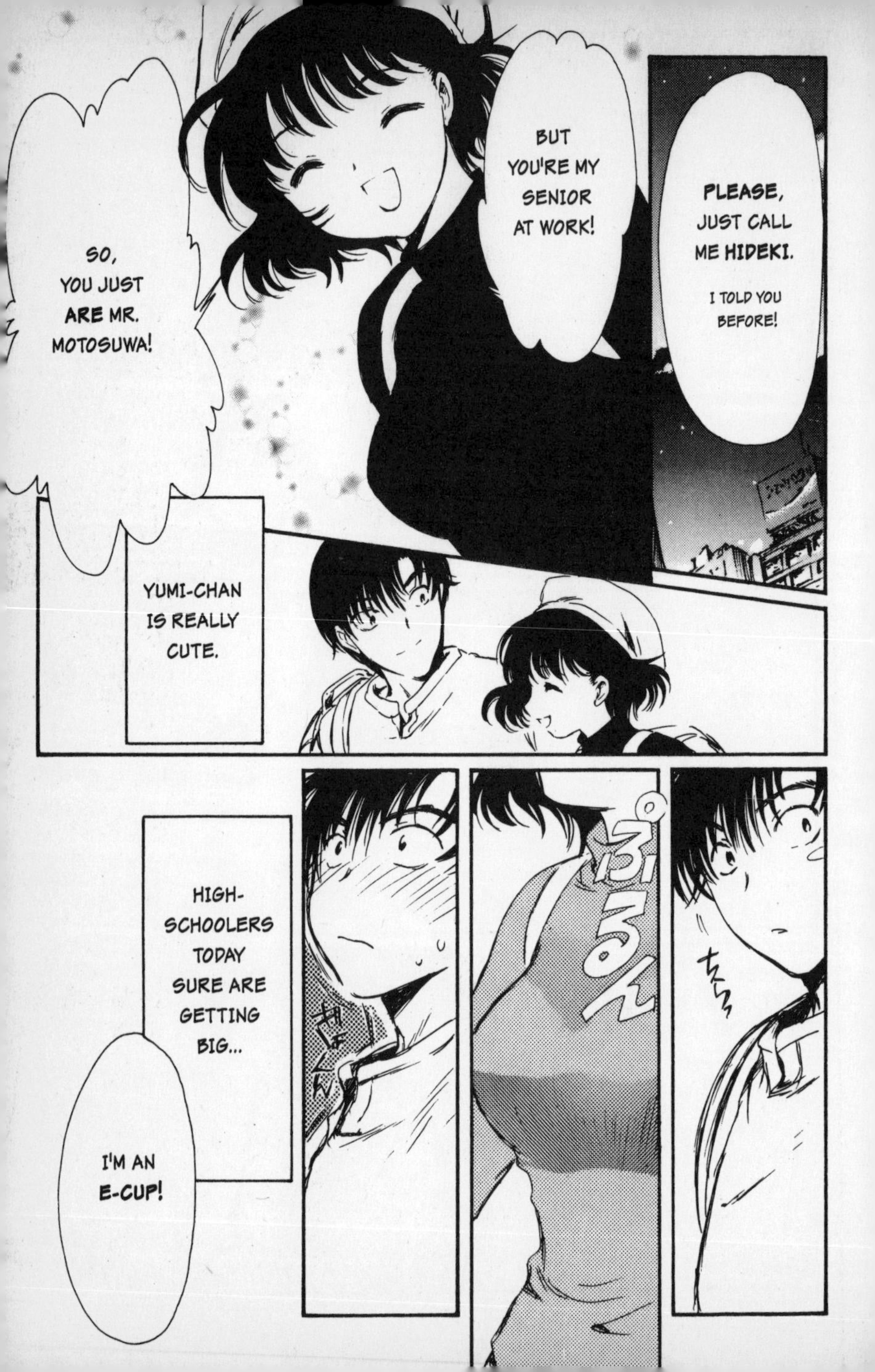
PLEASE, JUST CALL ME HIDEKI.
I TOLD YOU BEFORE!
BUT YOU'RE MY SENIOR AT WORK!
SO, YOU JUST ARE MR. MOTOSUWA!
YUMI-CHAN IS REALLY CUTE.
ぷるん
HIGH-SCHOOLERS TODAY SURE ARE GETTING BIG...
I'M AN E-CUP!

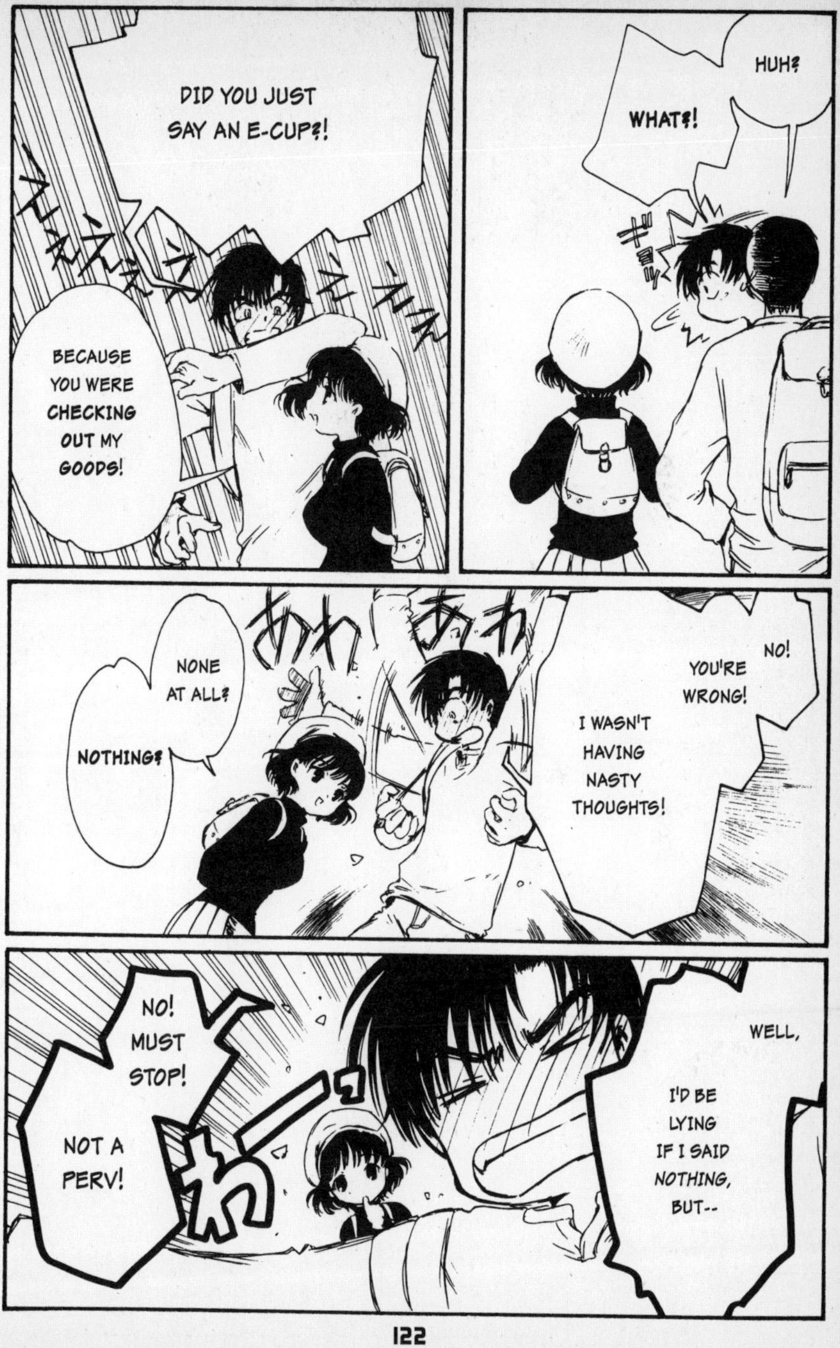
HUH?
WHAT?!
DID YOU JUST SAY AN E-CUP?!
BECAUSE YOU WERE CHECKING OUT MY GOODS!
NO!
YOU'RE WRONG!
I WASN'T HAVING NASTY THOUGHTS!
あわ
あわ
NONE AT ALL?
NOTHING?
WELL,
I'D BE LYING IF I SAID NOTHING, BUT--
NO! MUST STOP!
NOT A PERV!

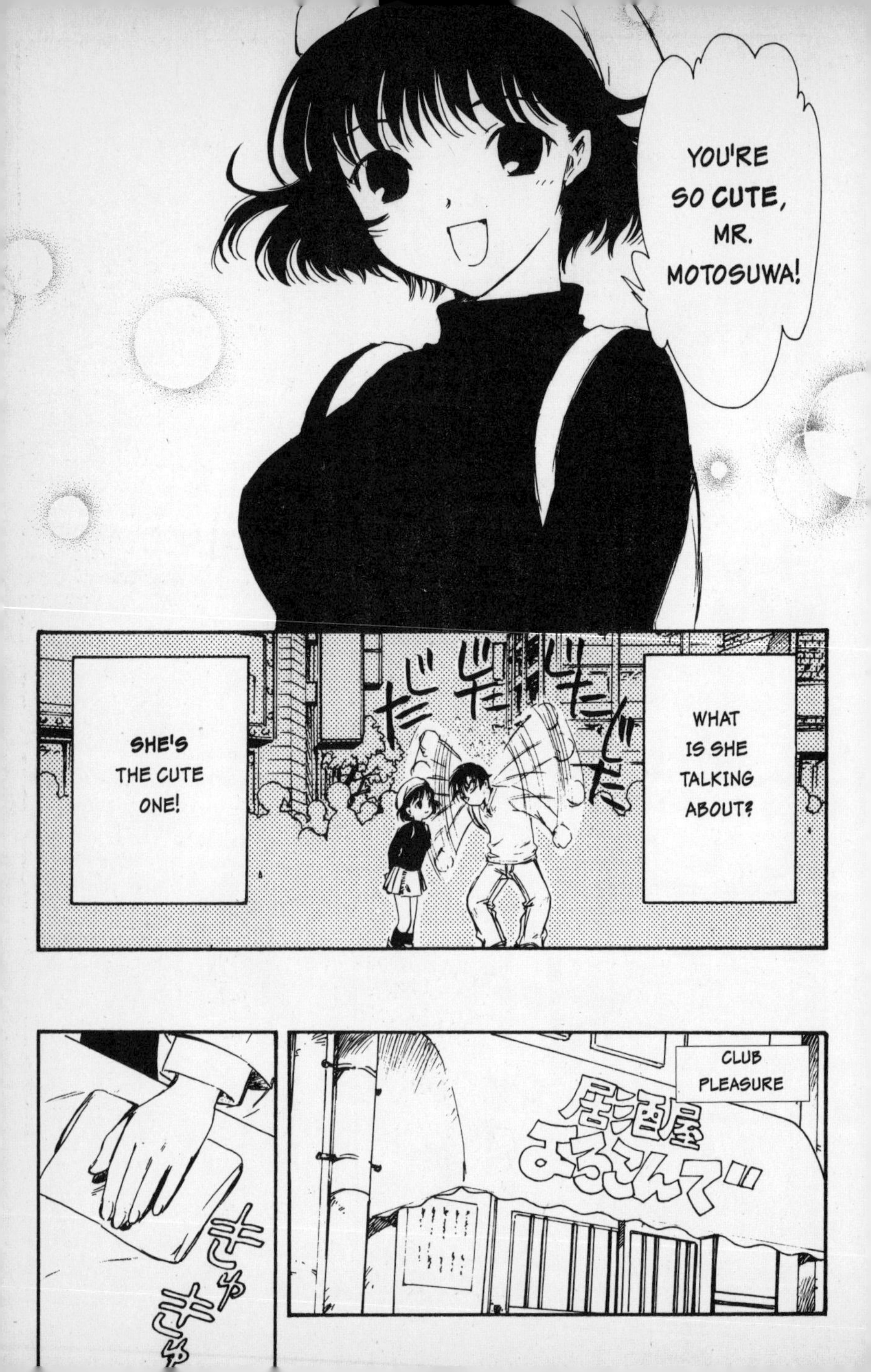
YOU'RE SO CUTE, MR. MOTOSUWA!
WHAT IS SHE TALKING ABOUT?
SHE'S THE CUTE ONE!
CLUB PLEASURE
居酒屋

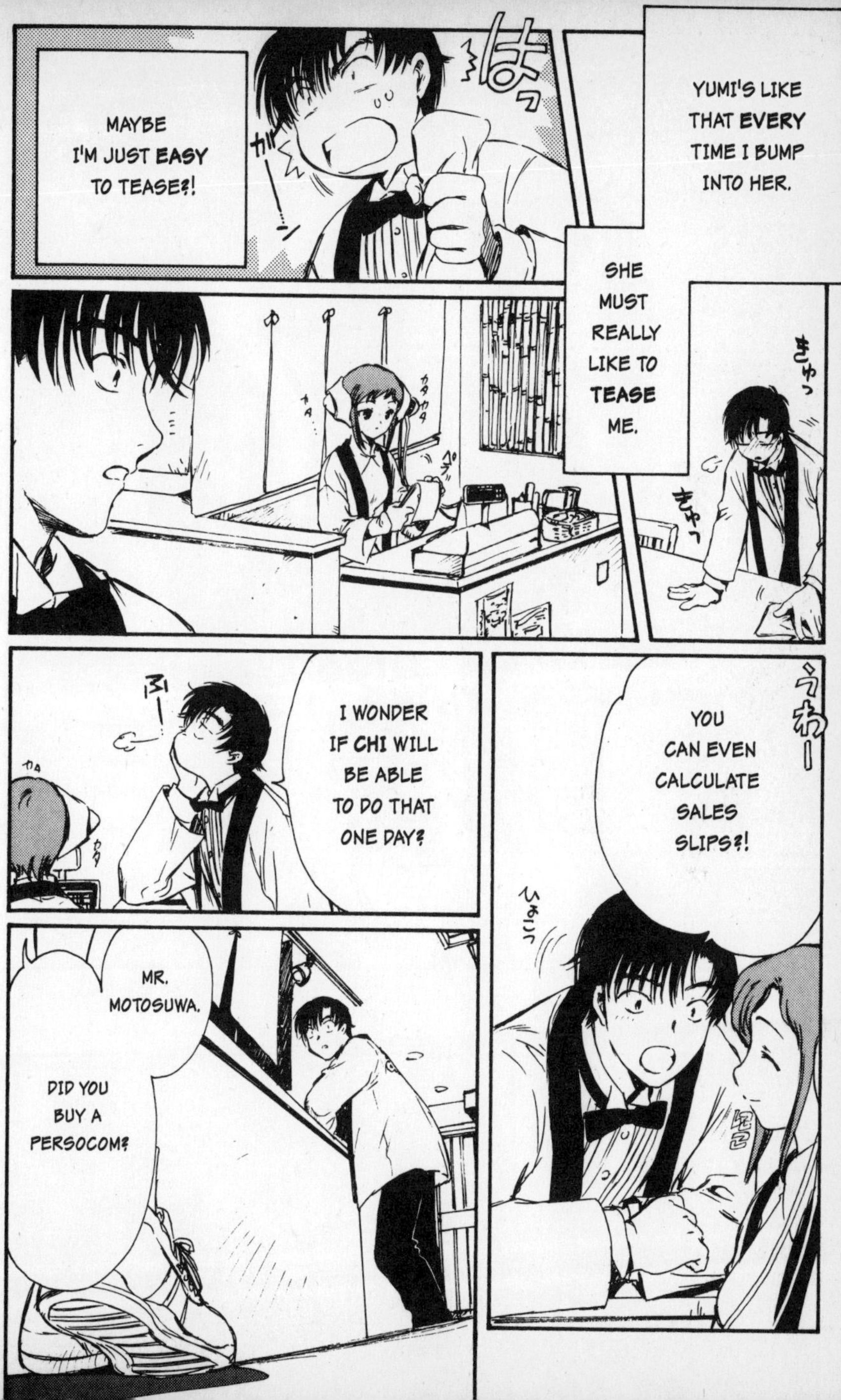
YUMI'S LIKE THAT EVERY TIME I BUMP INTO HER.
SHE MUST REALLY LIKE TO TEASE ME.
はっ
MAYBE I'M JUST EASY TO TEASE?!
きゅっ
きゅっ
うわー
YOU CAN EVEN CALCULATE SALES SLIPS?!
ひょこっ
ふー
I WONDER IF CHI WILL BE ABLE TO DO THAT ONE DAY?
MR. MOTOSUWA.
DID YOU BUY A PERSOCOM?

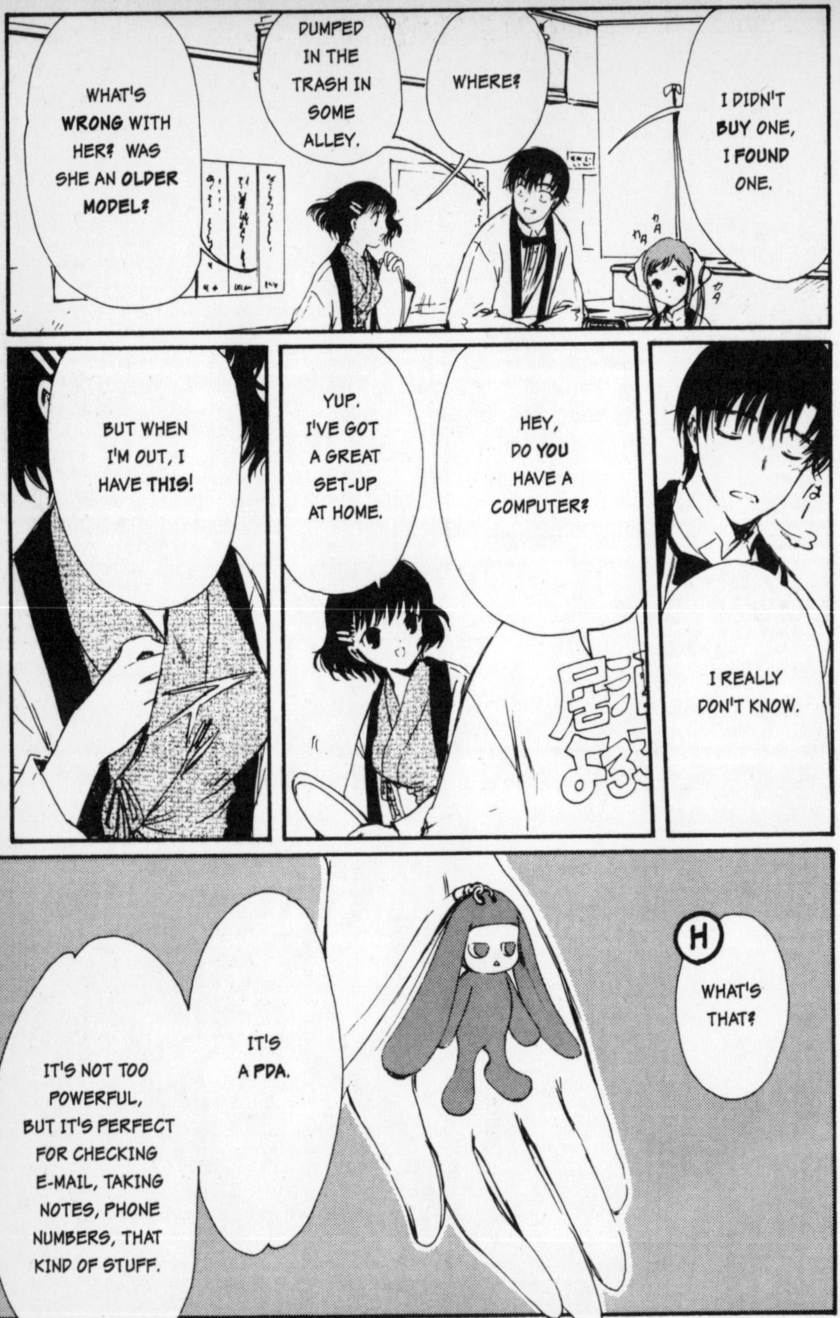
I DIDN'T BUY ONE, I FOUND ONE.
WHERE?
DUMPED IN THE TRASH IN SOME ALLEY.
WHAT'S WRONG WITH HER? WAS SHE AN OLDER MODEL?
I REALLY DON'T KNOW.
HEY, DO YOU HAVE A COMPUTER?
YUP. I'VE GOT A GREAT SET-UP AT HOME.
BUT WHEN I'M OUT, I HAVE THIS!
H
WHAT'S THAT?
IT'S A PDA.
IT'S NOT TOO POWERFUL, BUT IT'S PERFECT FOR CHECKING E-MAIL, TAKING NOTES, PHONE NUMBERS, THAT KIND OF STUFF.

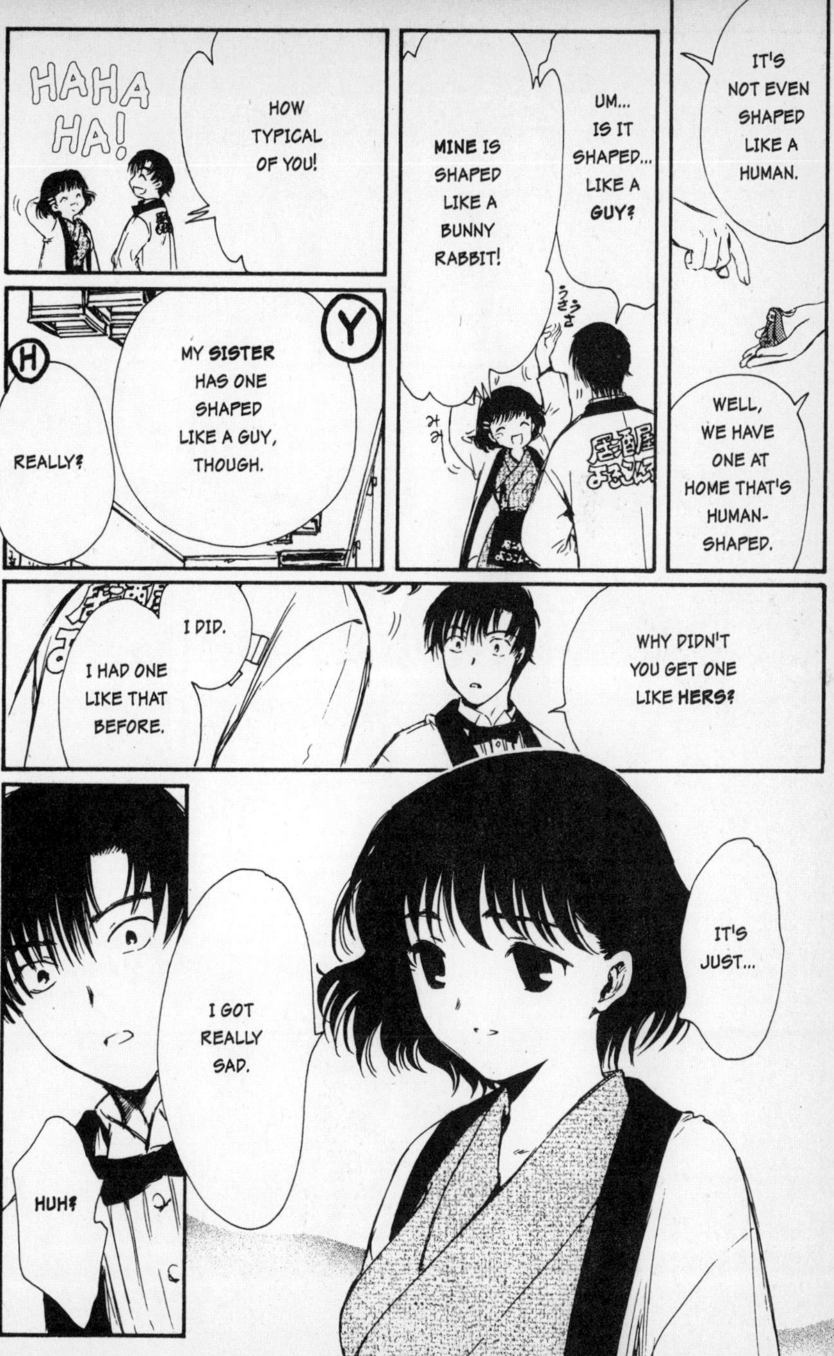
IT'S NOT EVEN SHAPED LIKE A HUMAN.
WELL, WE HAVE ONE AT HOME THAT'S HUMAN-SHAPED.
UM... IS IT SHAPED... LIKE A GUY?
MINE IS SHAPED LIKE A BUNNY RABBIT!
うさうさ
みみ
HAHA HA!
HOW TYPICAL OF YOU!
Y
MY SISTER HAS ONE SHAPED LIKE A GUY, THOUGH.
H
REALLY?
WHY DIDN'T YOU GET ONE LIKE HERS?
I DID.
I HAD ONE LIKE THAT BEFORE.
IT'S JUST...
I GOT REALLY SAD.
HUH?

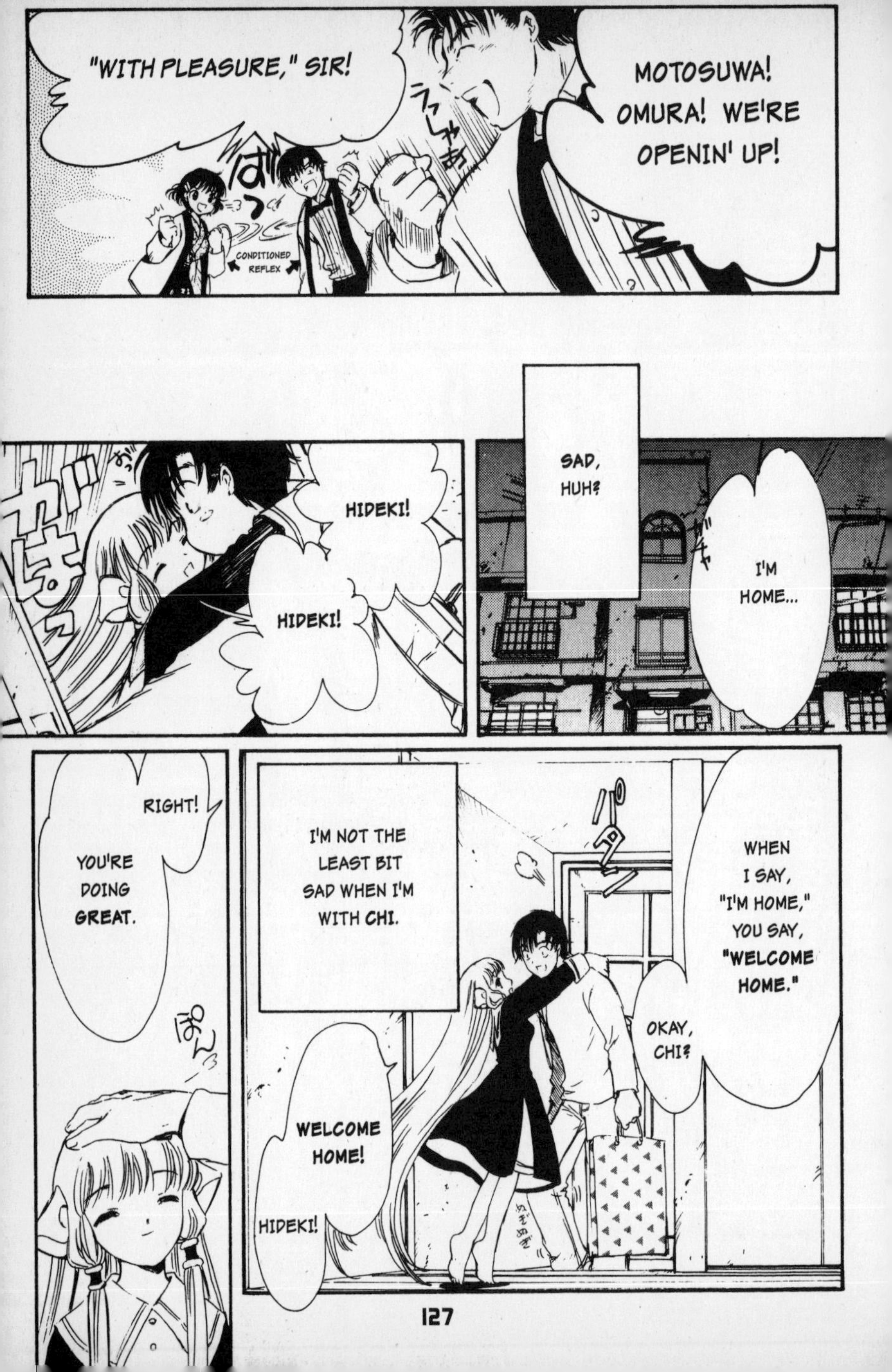
MOTOSUWA! OMURA! WE'RE OPENIN' UP!
"WITH PLEASURE," SIR!
CONDITIONED REFLEX
SAD, HUH?
I'M HOME...
HIDEKI!
HIDEKI!
WHEN I SAY, "I'M HOME," YOU SAY, "WELCOME HOME."
OKAY, CHI?
I'M NOT THE LEAST BIT SAD WHEN I'M WITH CHI.
WELCOME HOME!
HIDEKI!
RIGHT!
YOU'RE DOING GREAT.

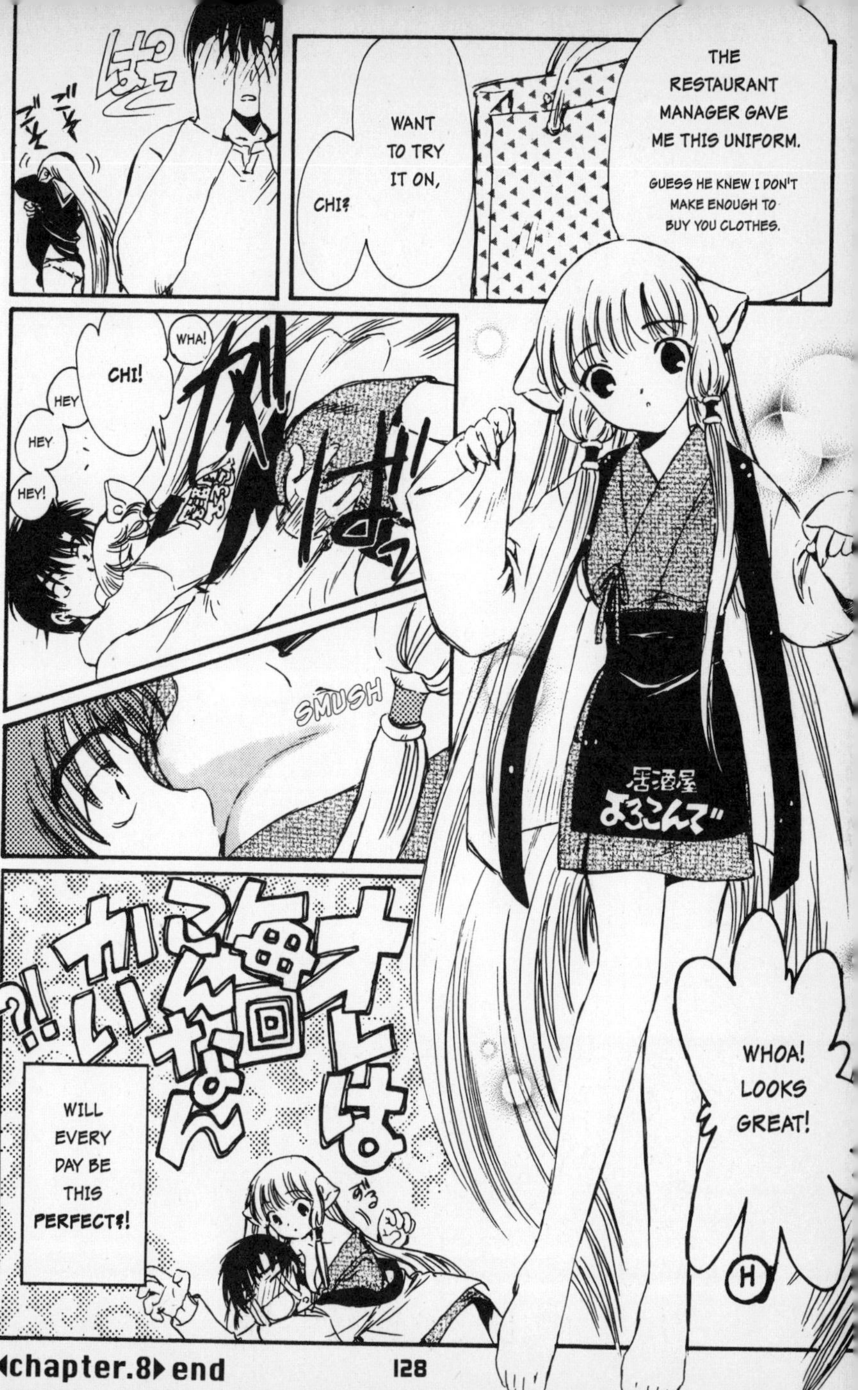

THE RESTAURANT MANAGER GAVE ME THIS UNIFORM.
GUESS HE KNEW I DON'T MAKE ENOUGH TO BUY YOU CLOTHES.
WANT TO TRY IT ON, CHI?
WHOA! LOOKS GREAT!
H
居酒屋
よろこんで
WHA!
CHI!
HEY
HEY
HEY!
SMUSH
WILL EVERY DAY BE THIS PERFECT?!

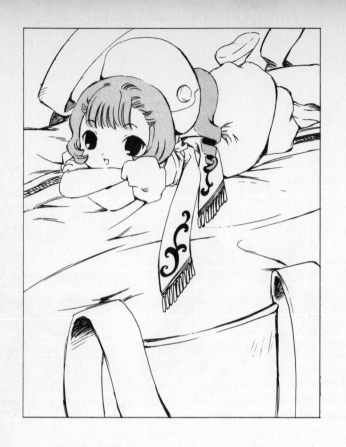

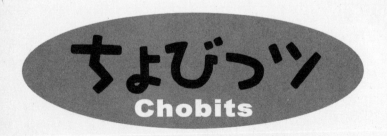

ちょびっツ
Chobits

◀chapter.9▶

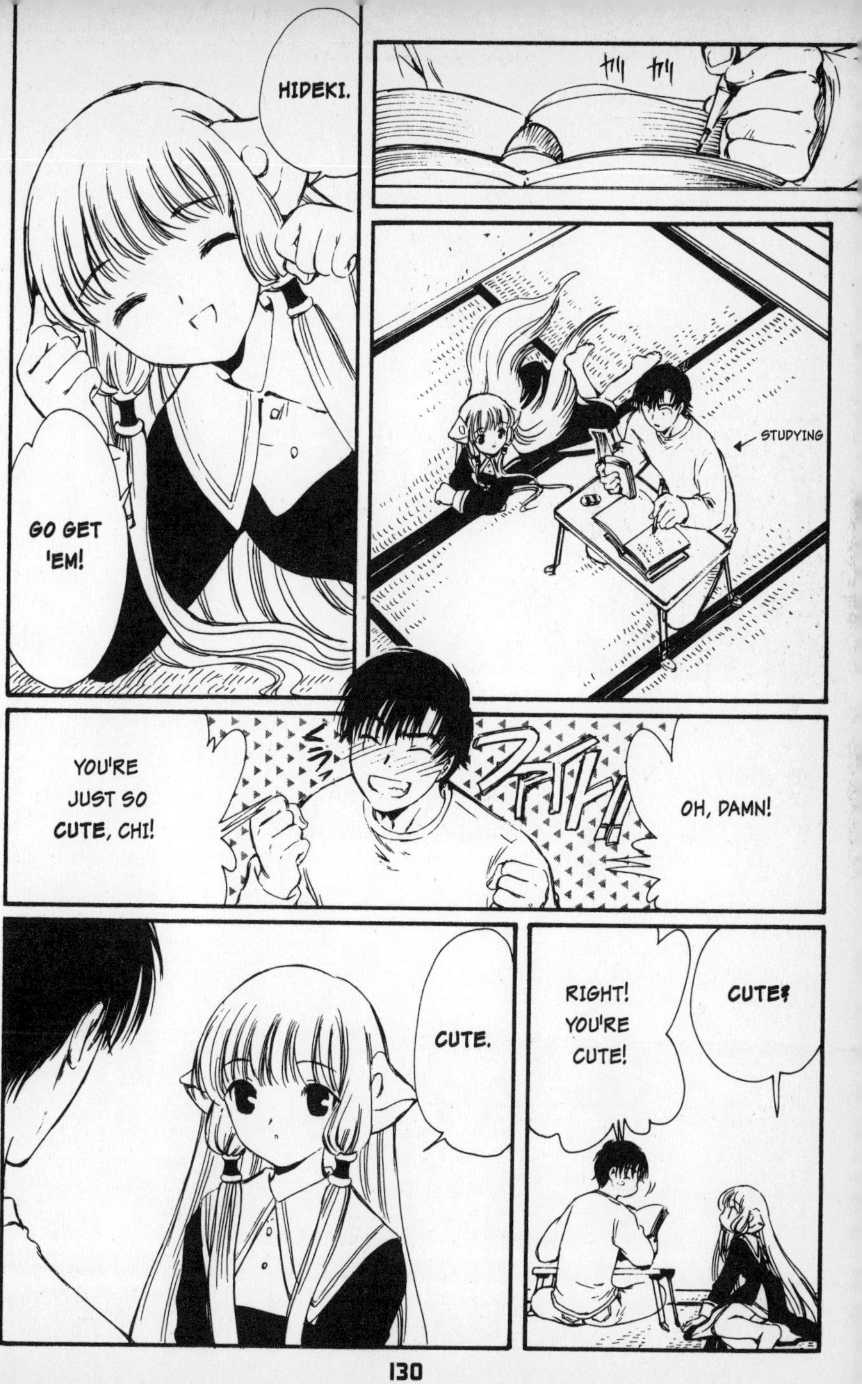
STUDYING
HIDEKI.
GO GET 'EM!
OH, DAMN!
YOU'RE JUST SO CUTE, CHI!
CUTE?
RIGHT! YOU'RE CUTE!
CUTE.

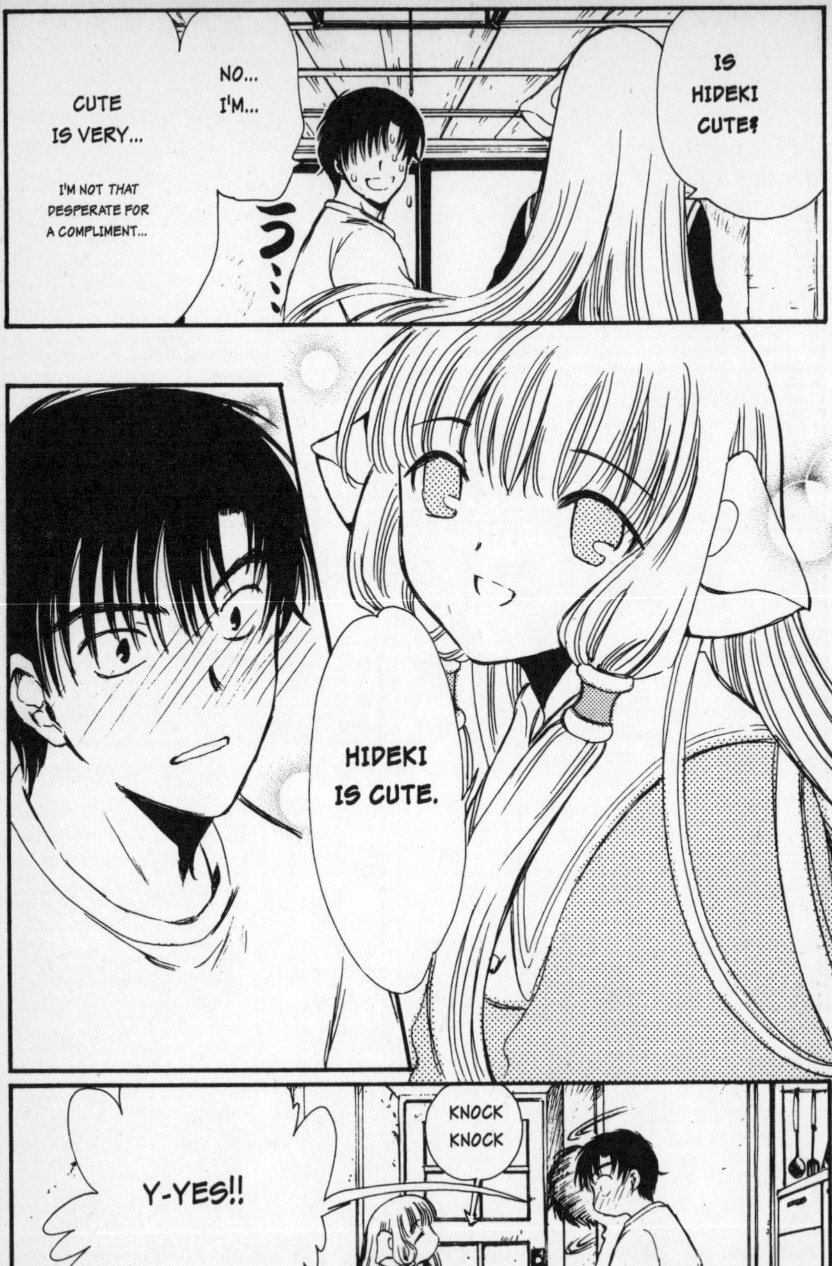
IS HIDEKI CUTE?
NO... I'M...
う…
CUTE IS VERY...
I'M NOT THAT DESPERATE FOR A COMPLIMENT...
HIDEKI IS CUTE.
KNOCK KNOCK
Y-YES!!

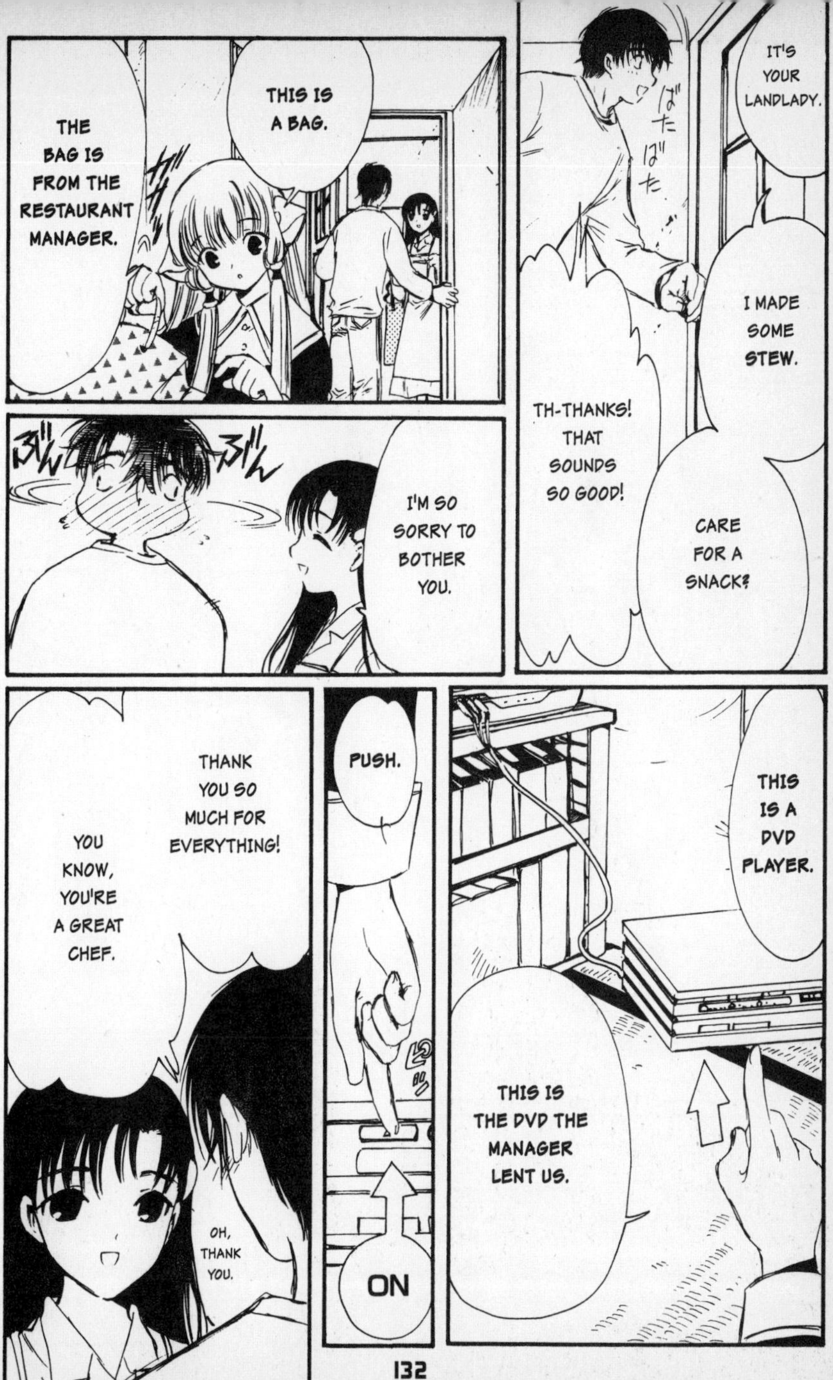
IT'S YOUR LANDLADY.
ばた ばた
I MADE SOME STEW.
CARE FOR A SNACK?
TH-THANKS! THAT SOUNDS SO GOOD!
THIS IS A BAG.
THE BAG IS FROM THE RESTAURANT MANAGER.
ぶん ぶん
I'M SO SORRY TO BOTHER YOU.
THIS IS A DVD PLAYER.
THIS IS THE DVD THE MANAGER LENT US.
PUSH.
ON
THANK YOU SO MUCH FOR EVERYTHING!
YOU KNOW, YOU'RE A GREAT CHEF.
OH, THANK YOU.

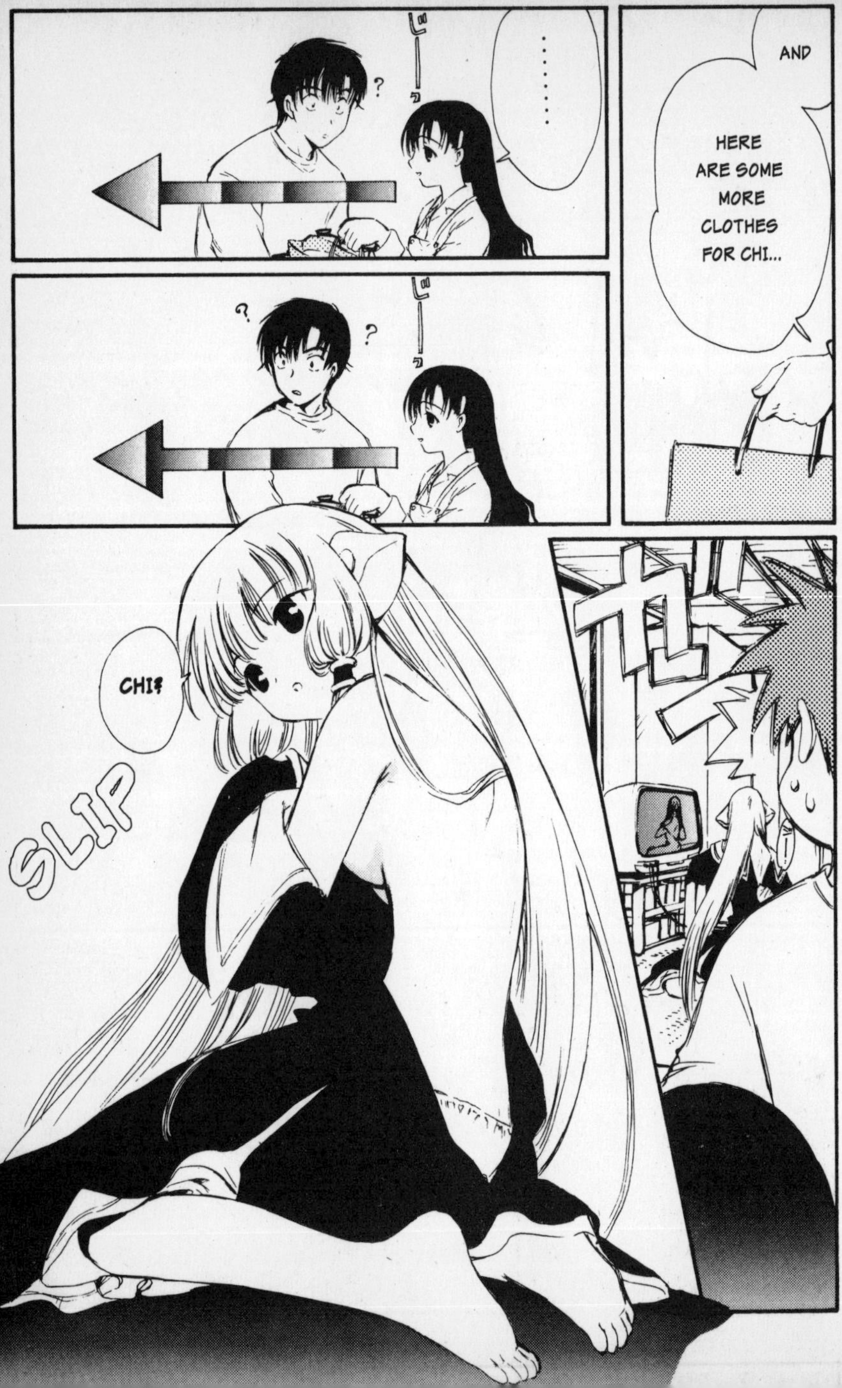
AND
HERE ARE SOME MORE CLOTHES FOR CHI...
......
ジーッ
ジーッ
CHI?
SLIP

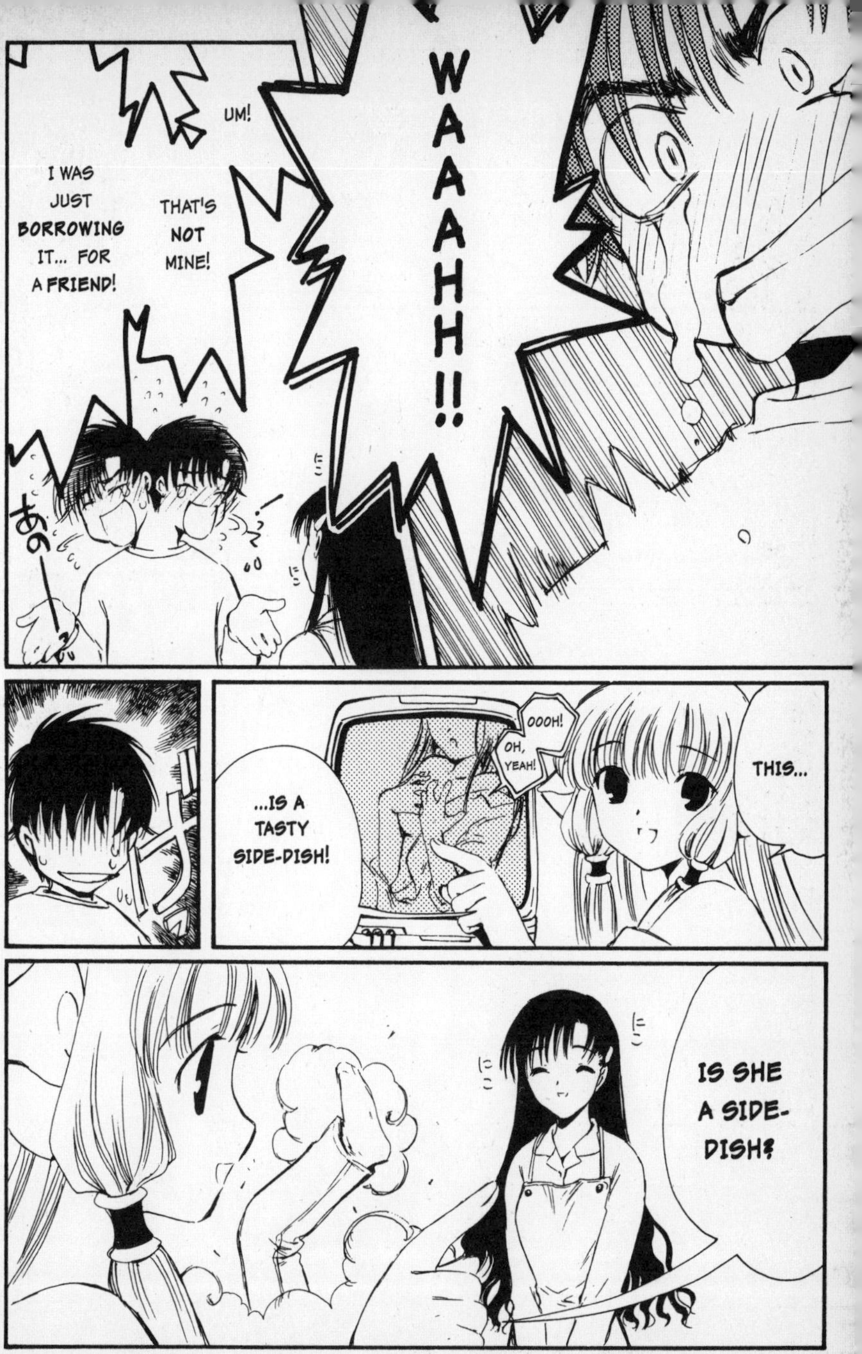
WAAAAHH!!
UM!
THAT'S NOT MINE!
I WAS JUST BORROWING IT... FOR A FRIEND!
あの—
にこ
にこ
THIS...
OOOH!
OH, YEAH!
...IS A TASTY SIDE-DISH!
IS SHE A SIDE-DISH?
にこ
にこ

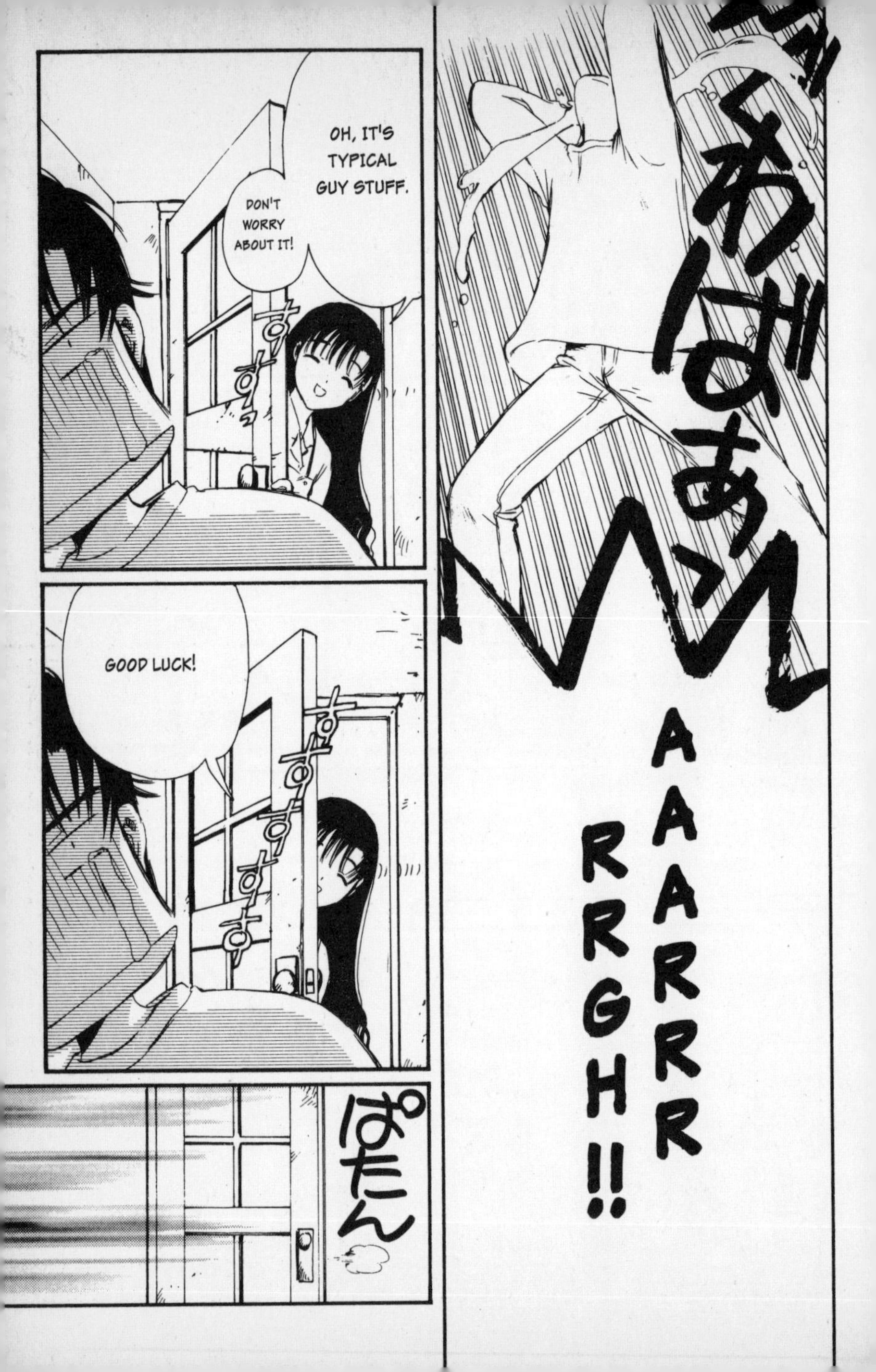
AAARRRRRGH!!
OH, IT'S TYPICAL GUY STUFF.
DON'T WORRY ABOUT IT!
GOOD LUCK!
ぱたん

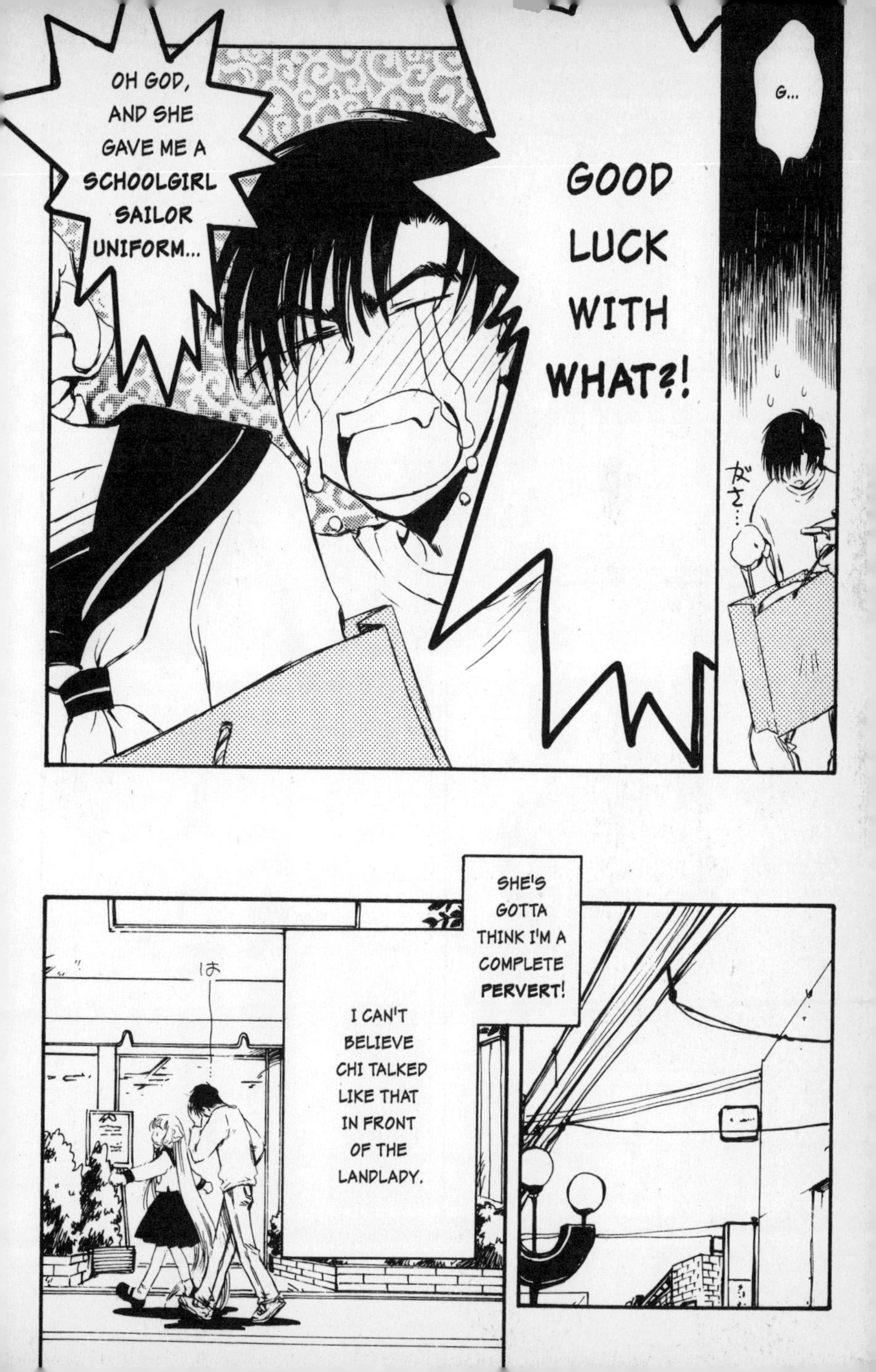
G...
がさ…
GOOD LUCK WITH WHAT?!
OH GOD, AND SHE GAVE ME A SCHOOLGIRL SAILOR UNIFORM...
は
I CAN'T BELIEVE CHI TALKED LIKE THAT IN FRONT OF THE LANDLADY.
SHE'S GOTTA THINK I'M A COMPLETE PERVERT!

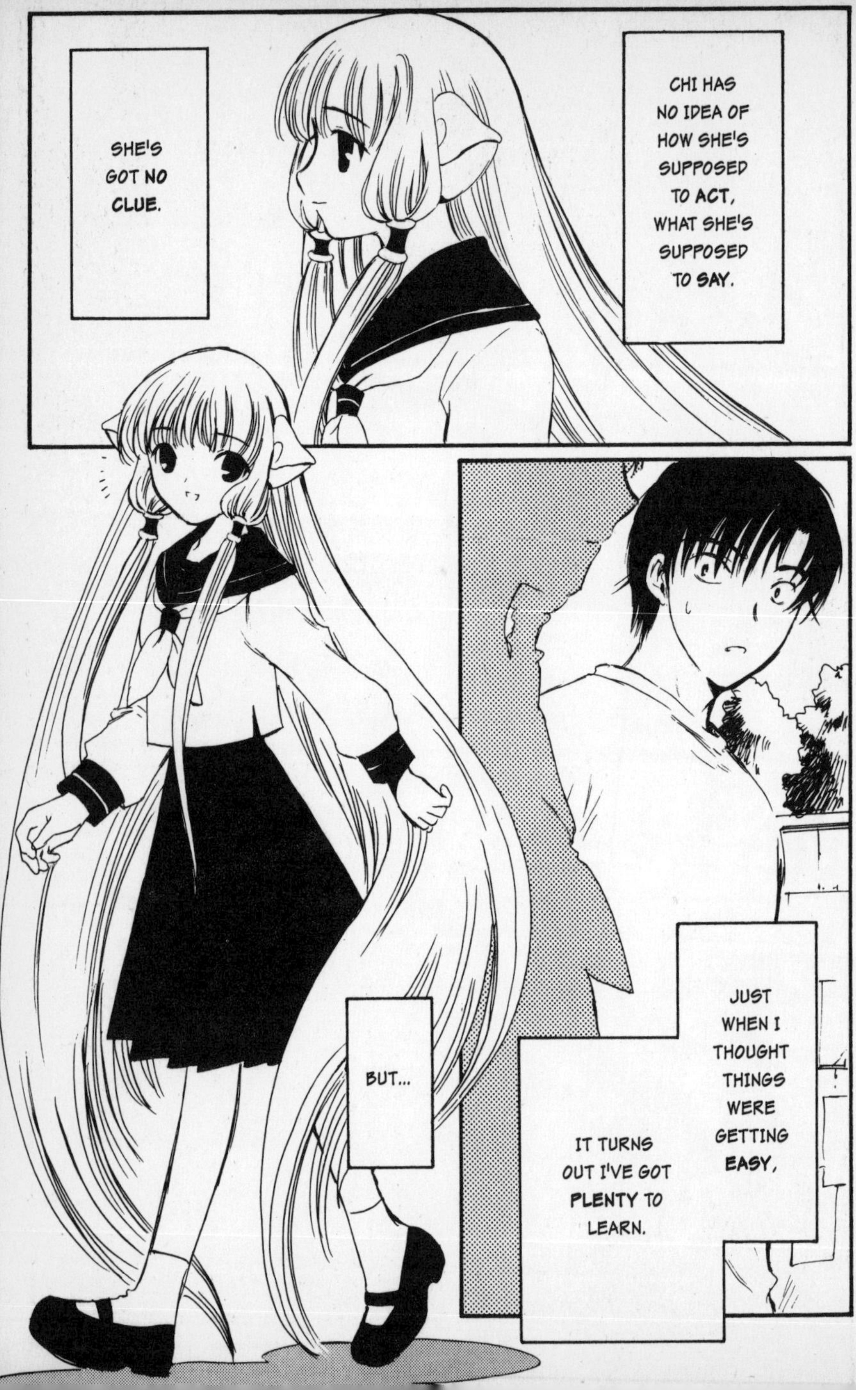
CHI HAS NO IDEA OF HOW SHE'S SUPPOSED TO ACT, WHAT SHE'S SUPPOSED TO SAY.
SHE'S GOT NO CLUE.
BUT...
JUST WHEN I THOUGHT THINGS WERE GETTING EASY,
IT TURNS OUT I'VE GOT PLENTY TO LEARN.

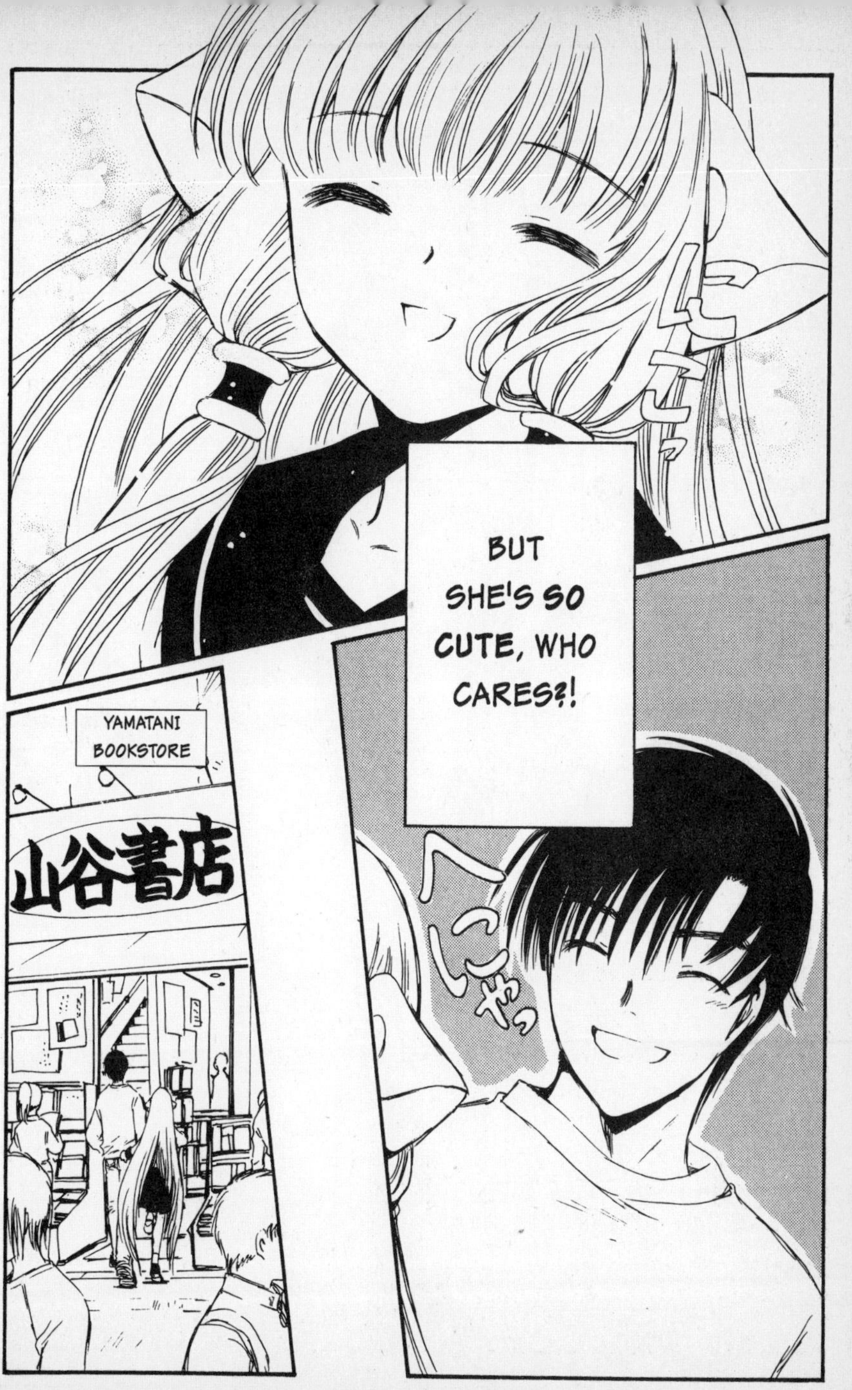
BUT SHE'S SO CUTE, WHO CARES?!
YAMATANI BOOKSTORE
山谷書店

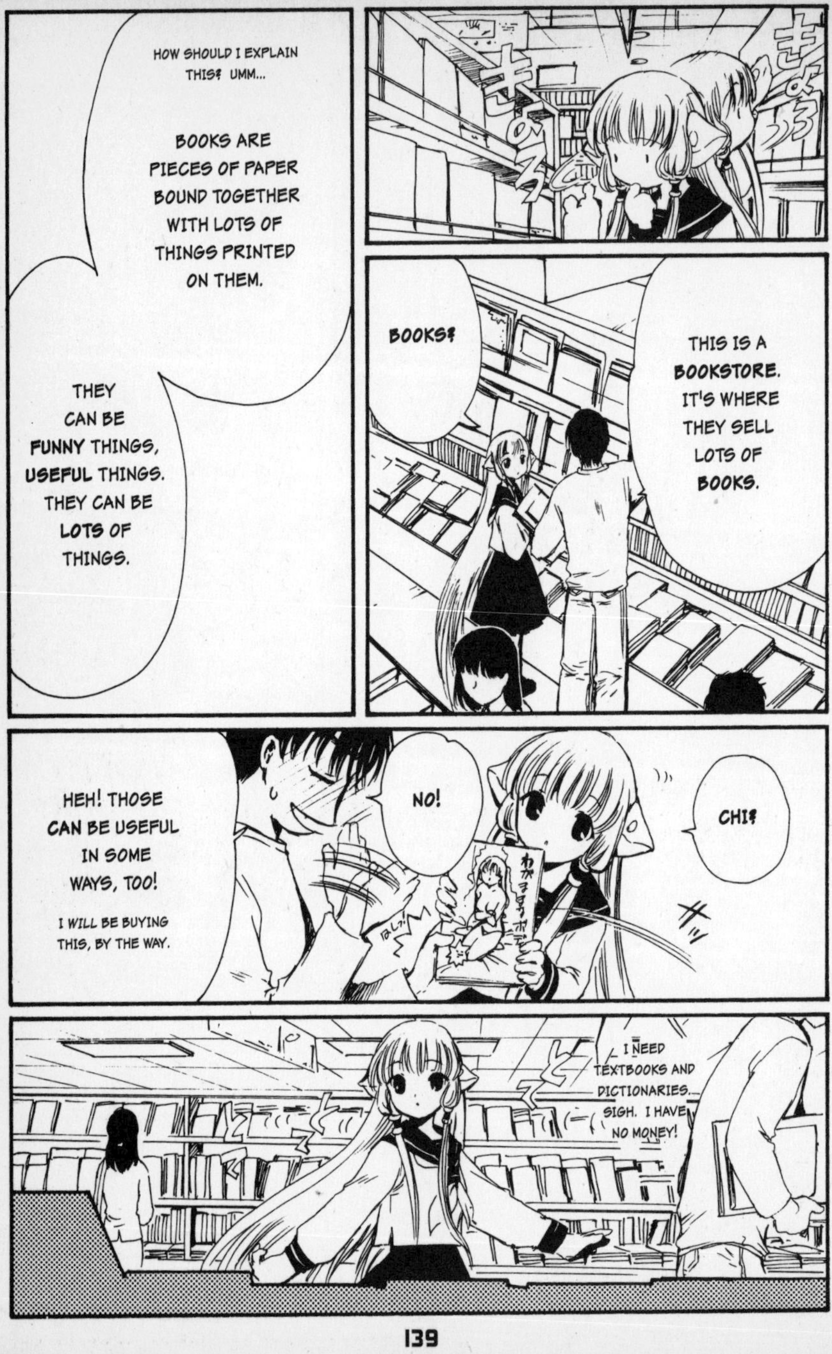
きょろ
きょろ
THIS IS A BOOKSTORE. IT'S WHERE THEY SELL LOTS OF BOOKS.
BOOKS?
HOW SHOULD I EXPLAIN THIS? UMM...
BOOKS ARE PIECES OF PAPER BOUND TOGETHER WITH LOTS OF THINGS PRINTED ON THEM.
THEY CAN BE FUNNY THINGS, USEFUL THINGS. THEY CAN BE LOTS OF THINGS.
CHI?
NO!
HEH! THOSE CAN BE USEFUL IN SOME WAYS, TOO!
I WILL BE BUYING THIS, BY THE WAY.
I NEED TEXTBOOKS AND DICTIONARIES... SIGH. I HAVE NO MONEY!

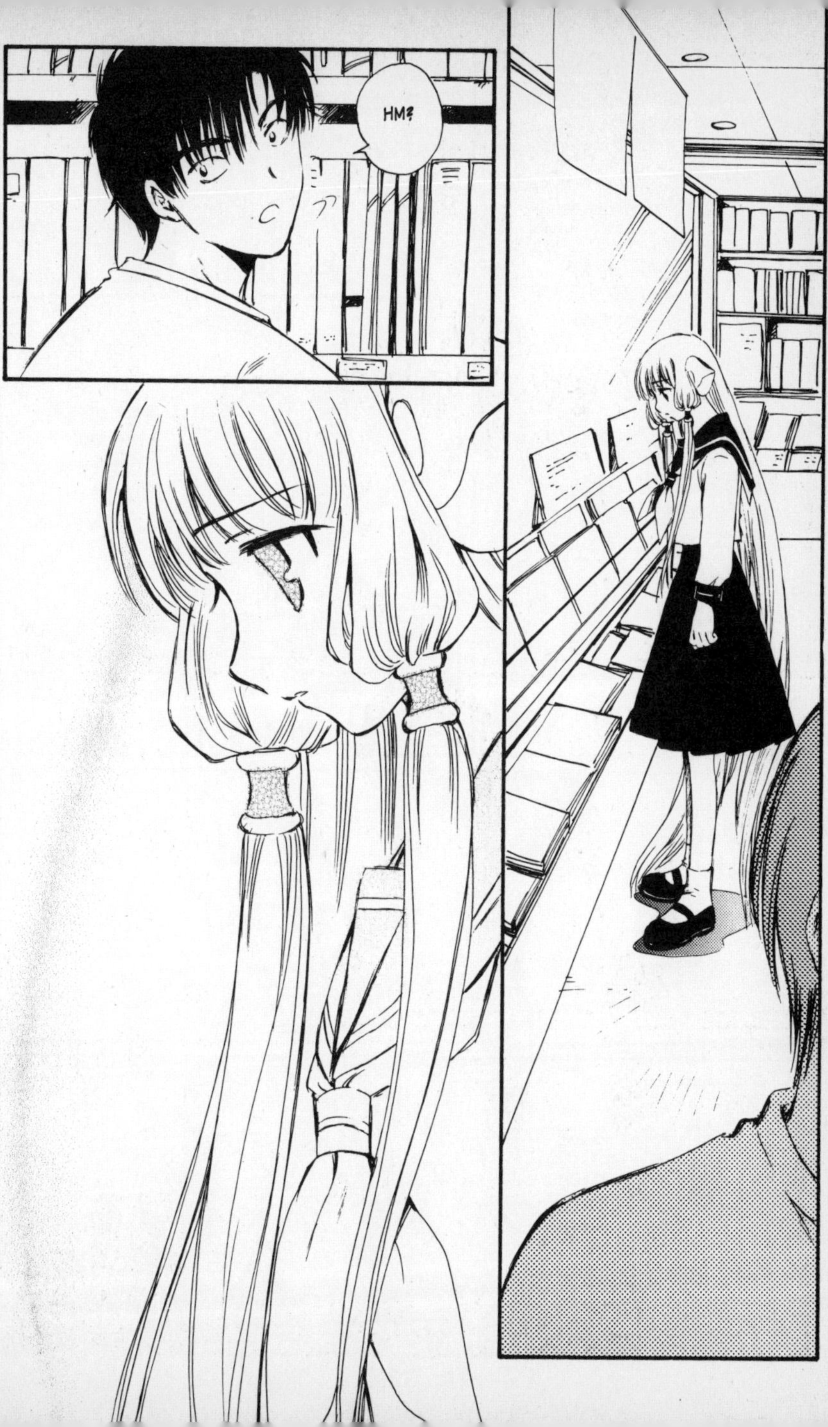
HM?

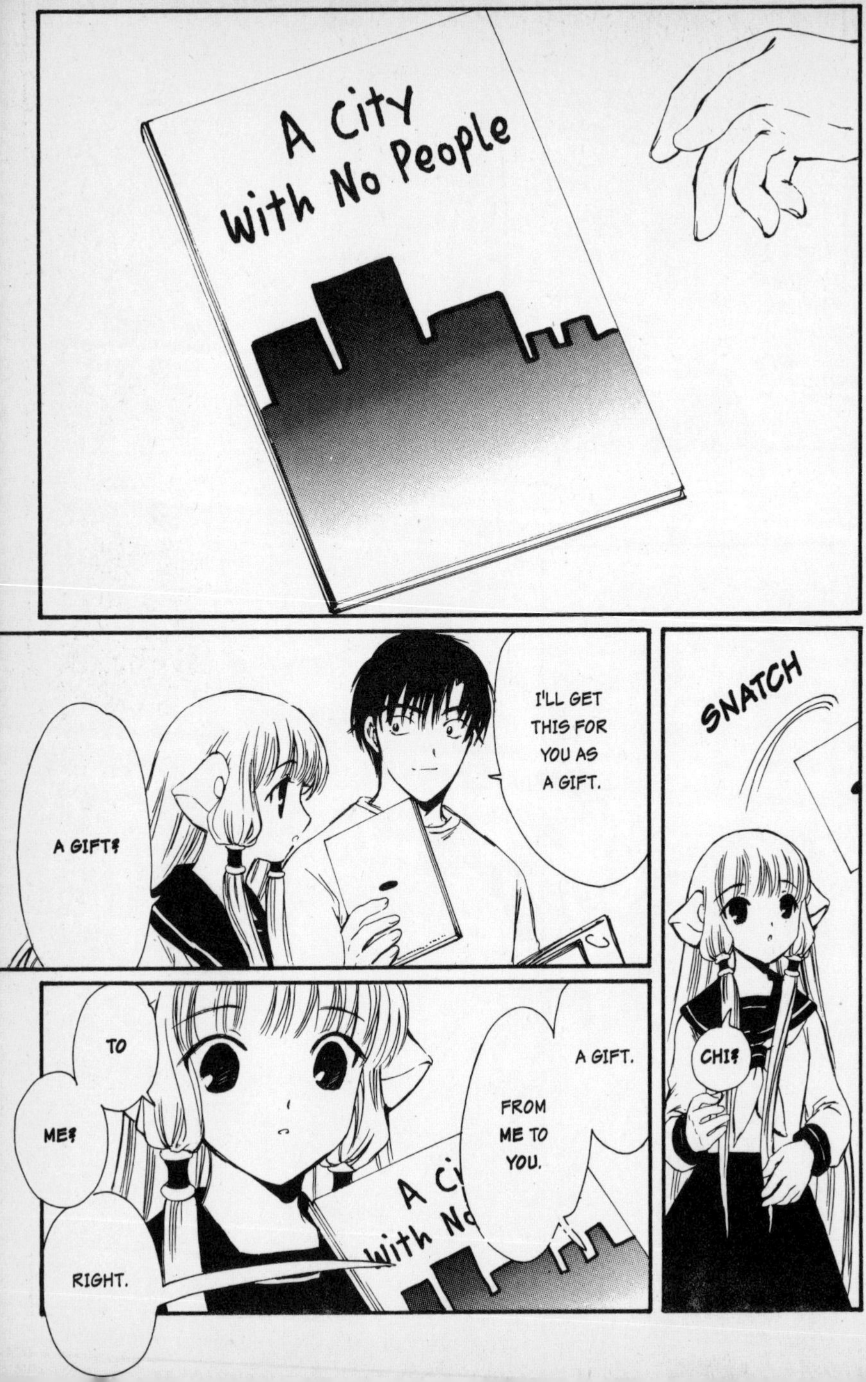
A City With No People
SNATCH
CHI?
I'LL GET THIS FOR YOU AS A GIFT.
A GIFT?
A GIFT.
FROM ME TO YOU.
TO ME?
RIGHT.

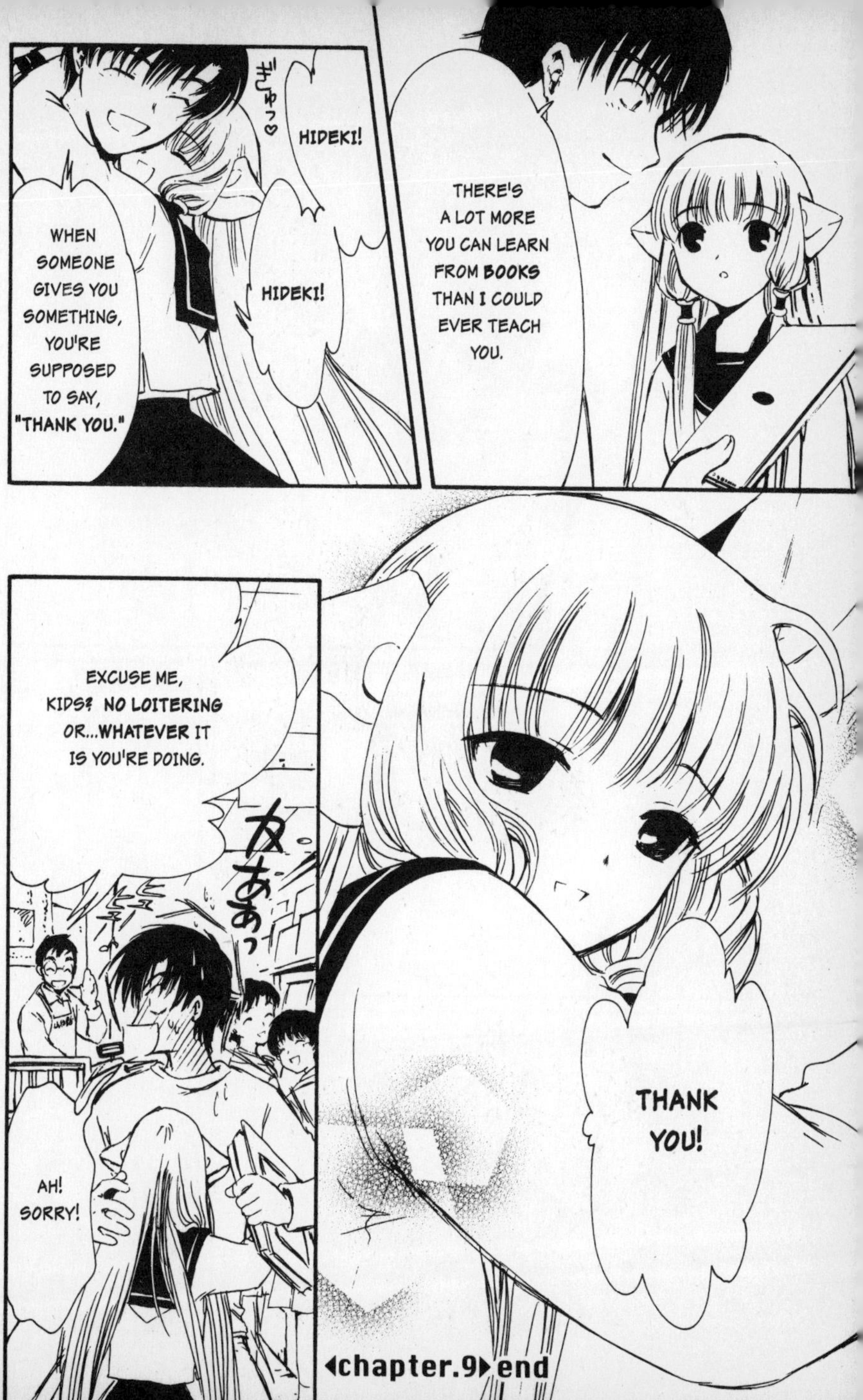
THERE'S A LOT MORE YOU CAN LEARN FROM BOOKS THAN I COULD EVER TEACH YOU.
ぎゅっ♡
HIDEKI!
HIDEKI!
WHEN SOMEONE GIVES YOU SOMETHING, YOU'RE SUPPOSED TO SAY, "THANK YOU."
THANK YOU!
EXCUSE ME, KIDS? NO LOITERING OR...WHATEVER IT IS YOU'RE DOING.
かあっ
AH! SORRY!

◀chapter.9▶ end

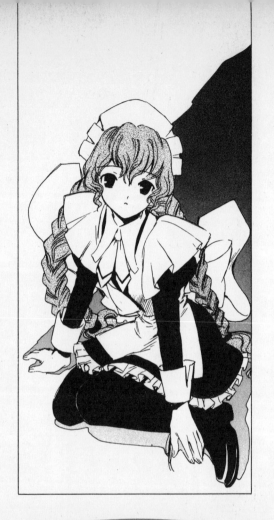

ちょびっツ
Chobits
◀chapter.10▶

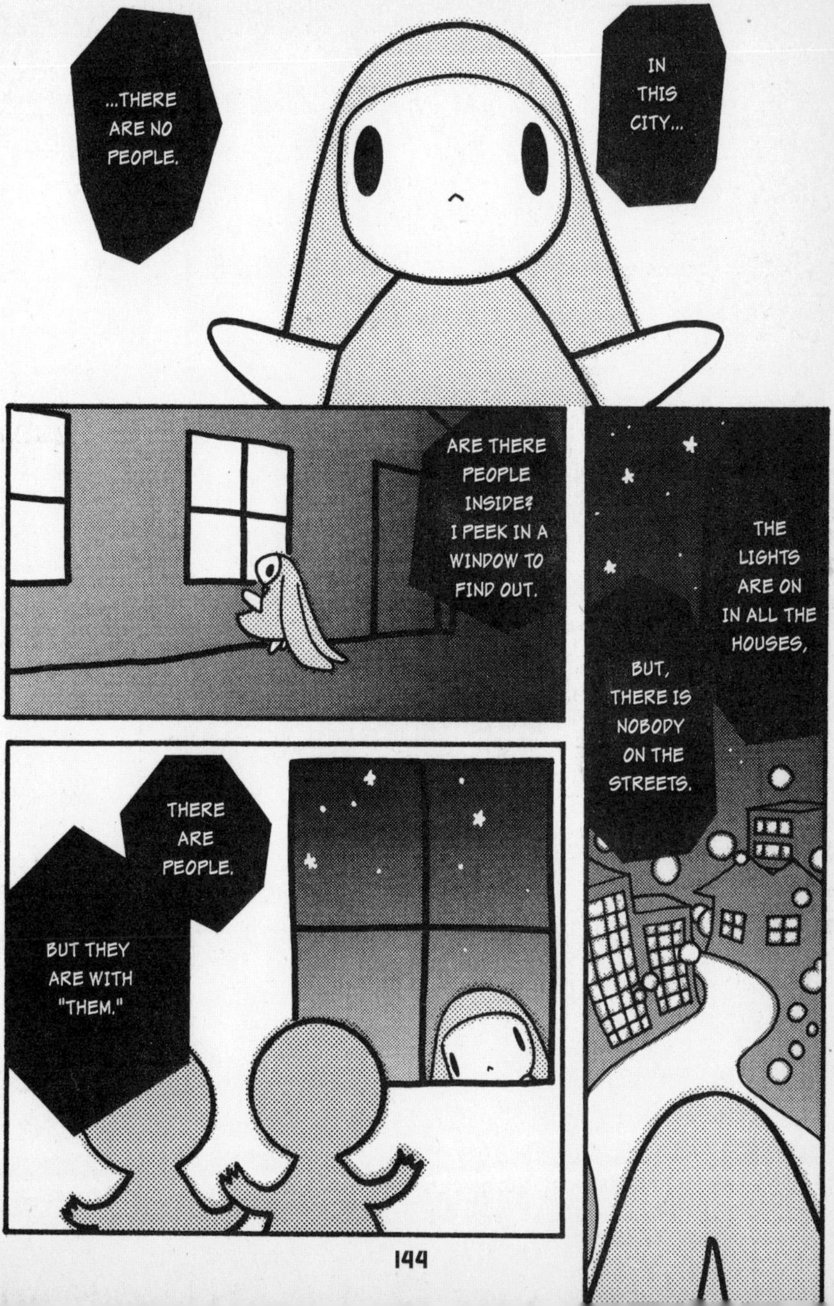
IN THIS CITY...
...THERE ARE NO PEOPLE.
THE LIGHTS ARE ON IN ALL THE HOUSES,
BUT, THERE IS NOBODY ON THE STREETS.
ARE THERE PEOPLE INSIDE? I PEEK IN A WINDOW TO FIND OUT.
THERE ARE PEOPLE.
BUT THEY ARE WITH "THEM."

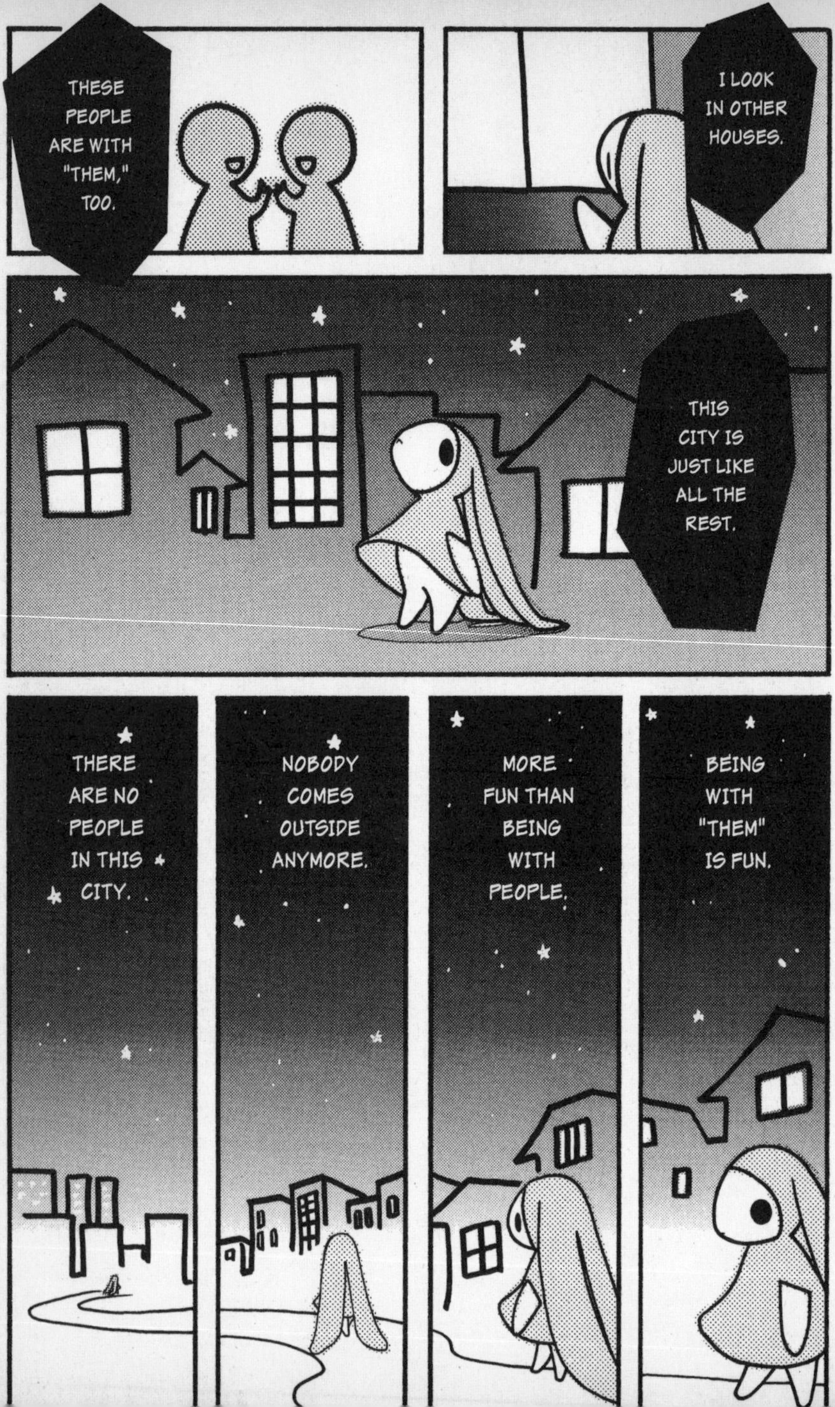
I LOOK IN OTHER HOUSES.
THESE PEOPLE ARE WITH "THEM," TOO.
THIS CITY IS JUST LIKE ALL THE REST.
BEING WITH "THEM" IS FUN.
MORE FUN THAN BEING WITH PEOPLE.
NOBODY COMES OUTSIDE ANYMORE.
THERE ARE NO PEOPLE IN THIS CITY.

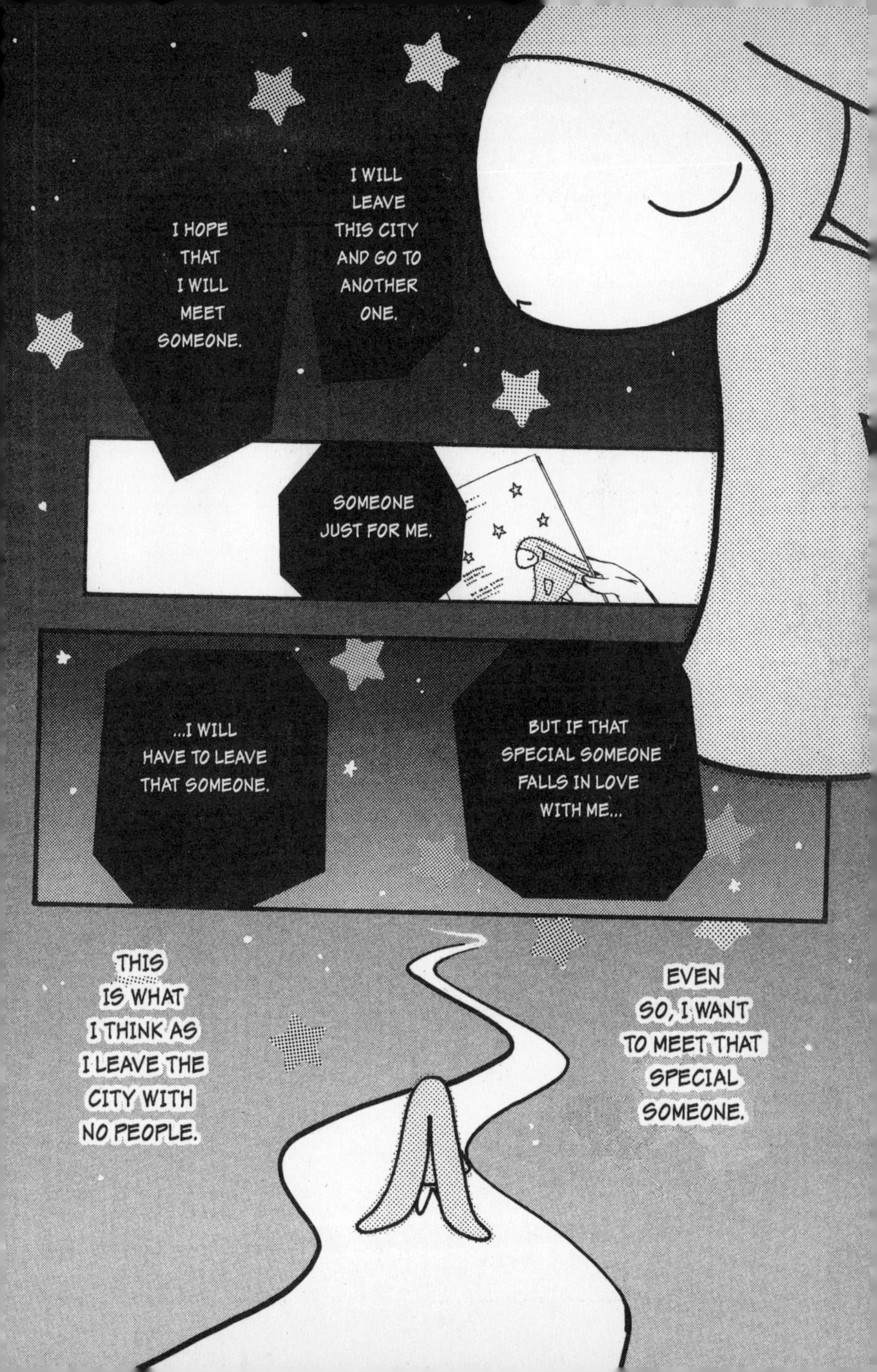
I WILL LEAVE THIS CITY AND GO TO ANOTHER ONE.
I HOPE THAT I WILL MEET SOMEONE.
SOMEONE JUST FOR ME.
BUT IF THAT SPECIAL SOMEONE FALLS IN LOVE WITH ME...
...I WILL HAVE TO LEAVE THAT SOMEONE.
EVEN SO, I WANT TO MEET THAT SPECIAL SOMEONE.
THIS IS WHAT I THINK AS I LEAVE THE CITY WITH NO PEOPLE.

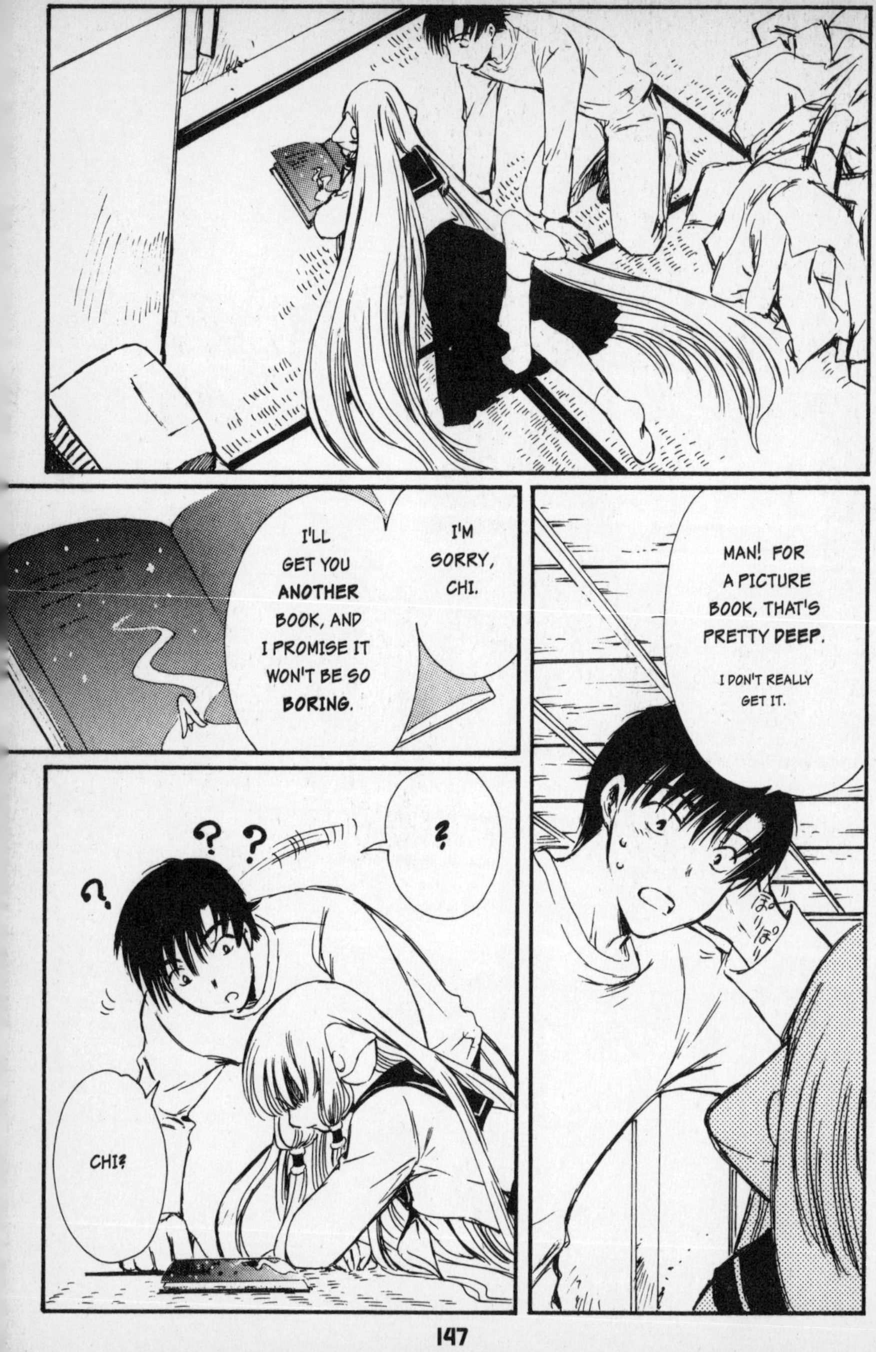
MAN! FOR A PICTURE BOOK, THAT'S PRETTY DEEP.
I DON'T REALLY GET IT.
I'M SORRY, CHI.
I'LL GET YOU ANOTHER BOOK, AND I PROMISE IT WON'T BE SO BORING.
?
? ? ?
CHI?

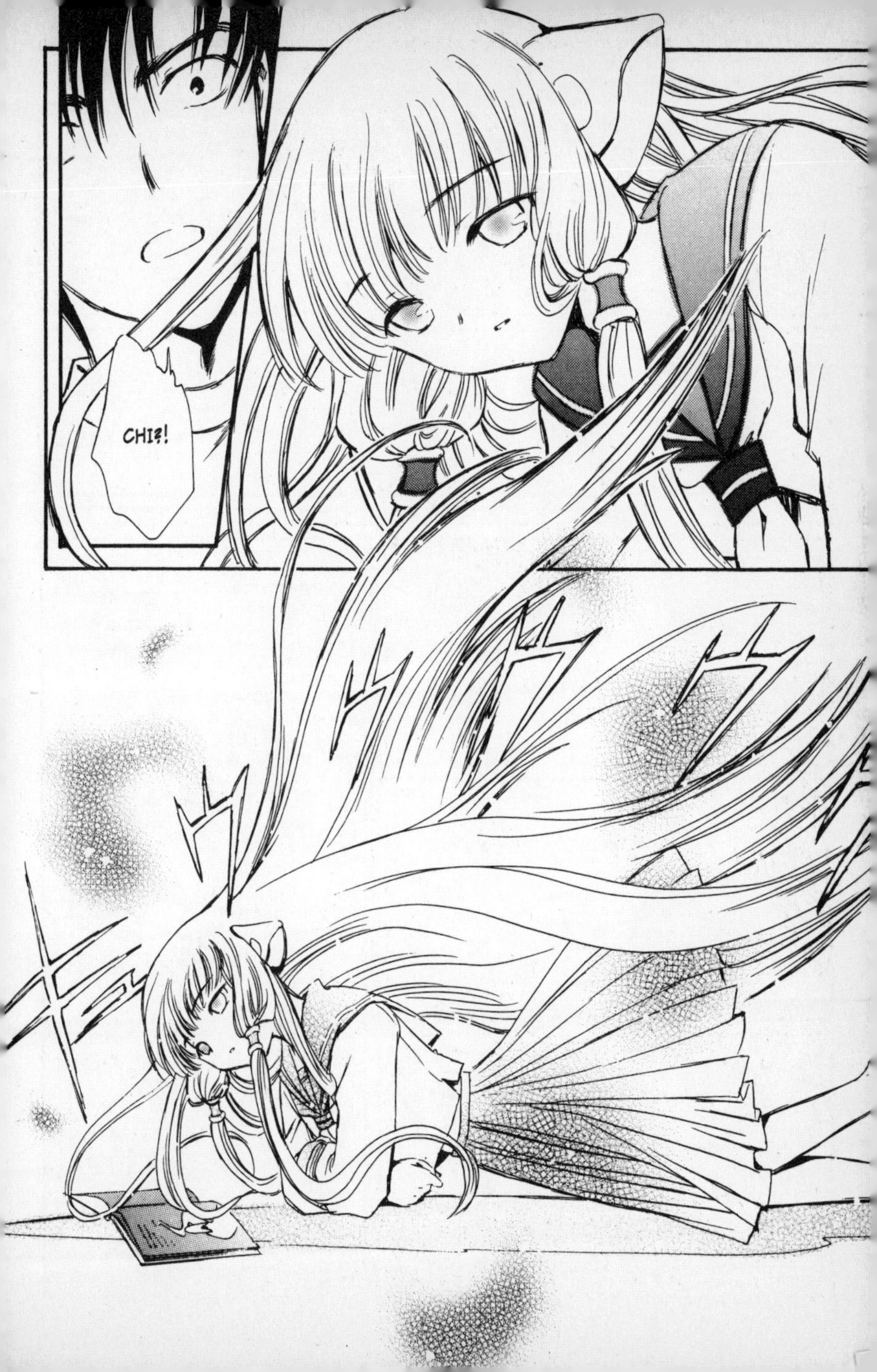
CHI?!

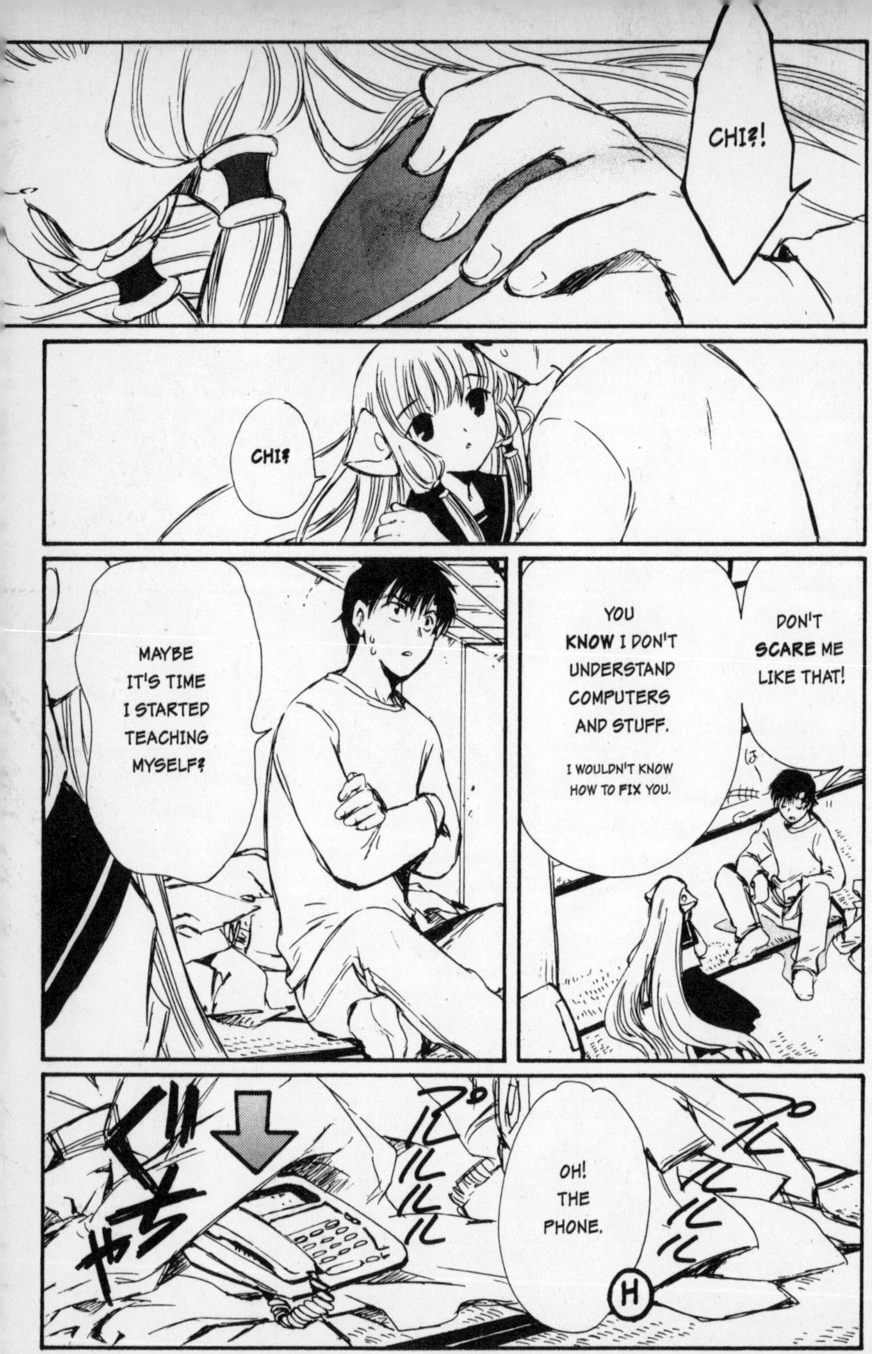
CHI?!
CHI?
DON'T SCARE ME LIKE THAT!
YOU KNOW I DON'T UNDERSTAND COMPUTERS AND STUFF.
I WOULDN'T KNOW HOW TO FIX YOU.
MAYBE IT'S TIME I STARTED TEACHING MYSELF?
OH! THE PHONE.

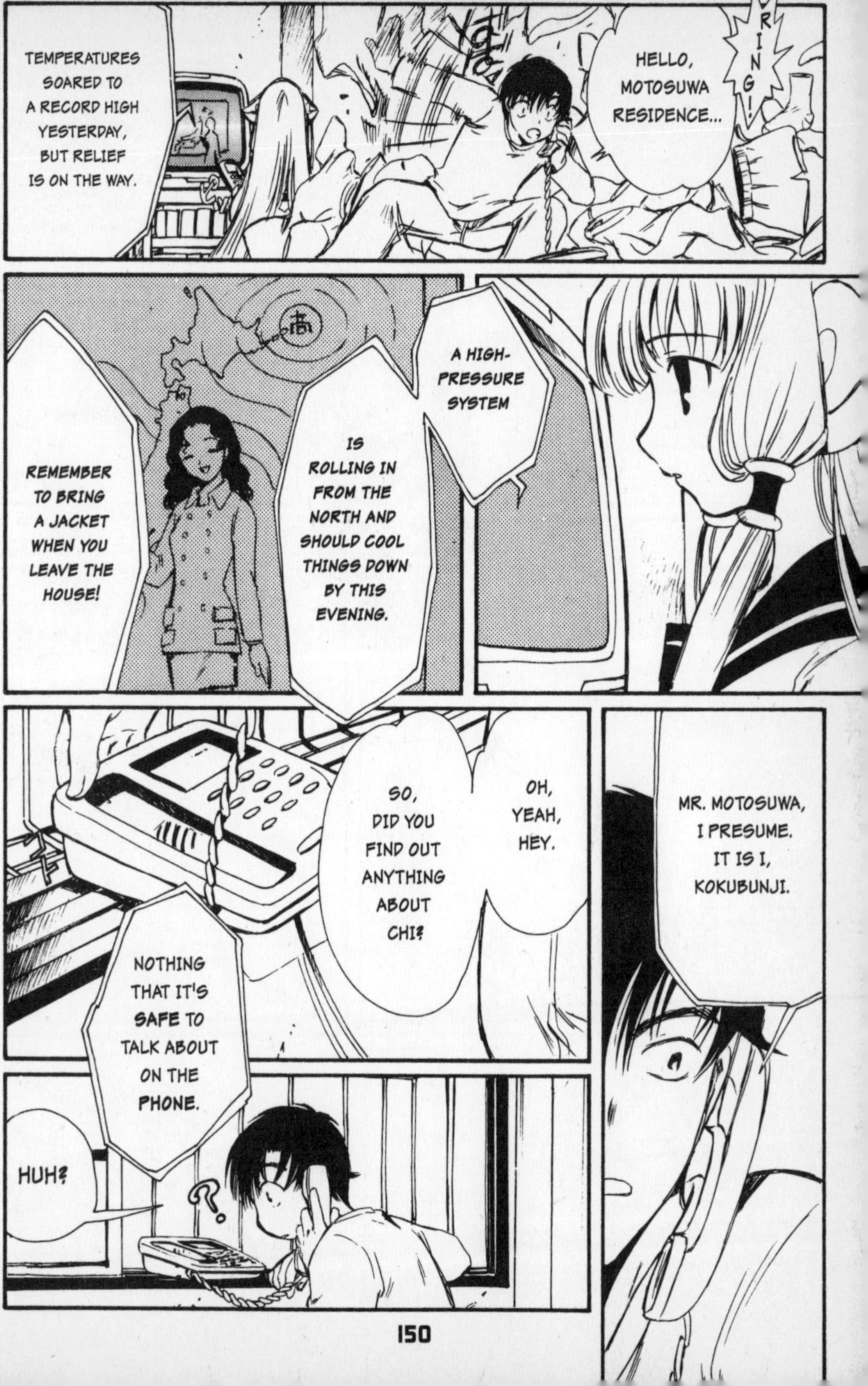
RING!
HELLO, MOTOSUWA RESIDENCE...
TEMPERATURES SOARED TO A RECORD HIGH YESTERDAY, BUT RELIEF IS ON THE WAY.
A HIGH-PRESSURE SYSTEM
IS ROLLING IN FROM THE NORTH AND SHOULD COOL THINGS DOWN BY THIS EVENING.
REMEMBER TO BRING A JACKET WHEN YOU LEAVE THE HOUSE!
MR. MOTOSUWA, I PRESUME. IT IS I, KOKUBUNJI.
OH, YEAH, HEY.
SO, DID YOU FIND OUT ANYTHING ABOUT CHI?
NOTHING THAT IT'S SAFE TO TALK ABOUT ON THE PHONE.
HUH?

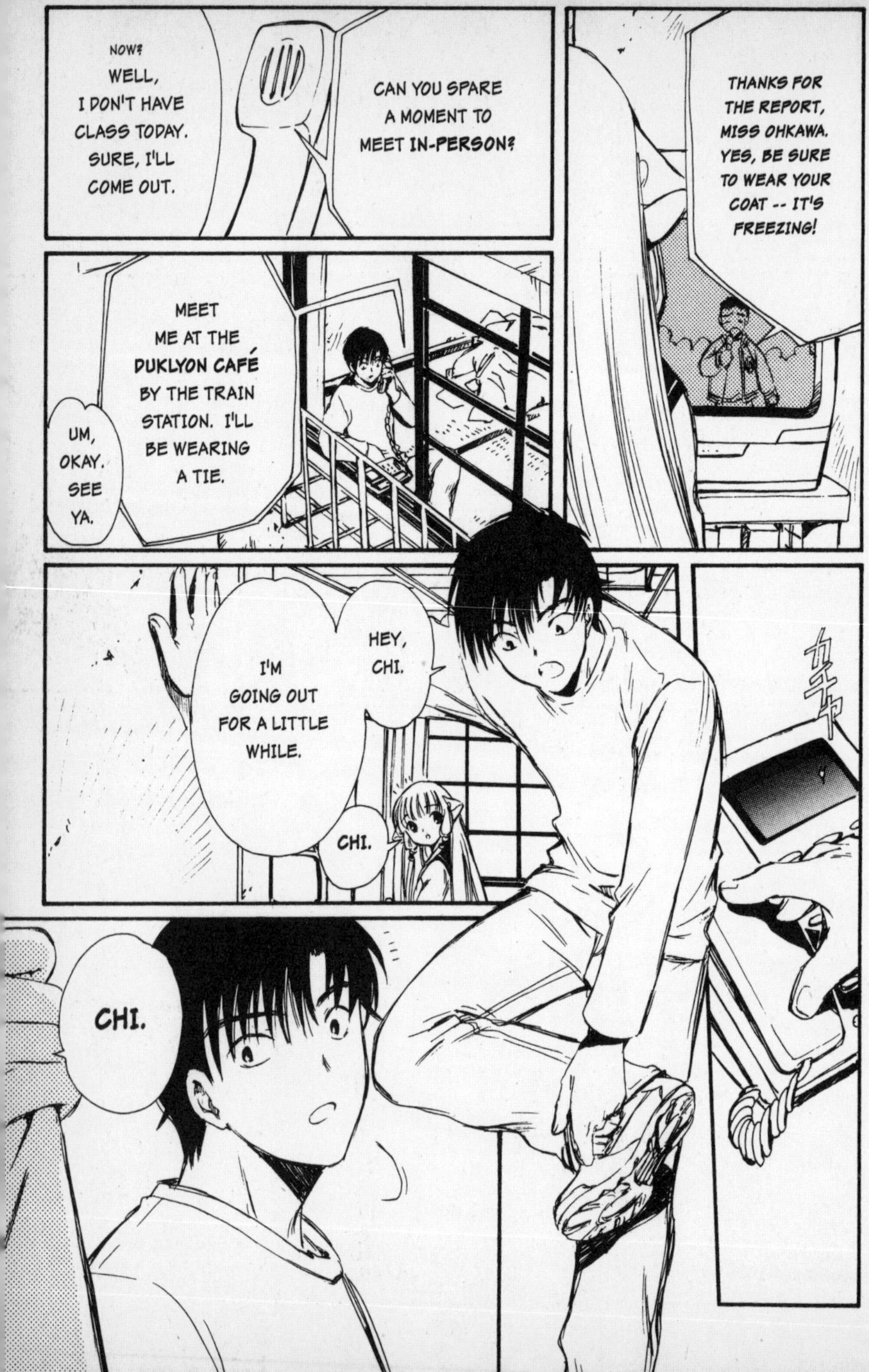
THANKS FOR THE REPORT, MISS OHKAWA. YES, BE SURE TO WEAR YOUR COAT -- IT'S FREEZING!
CAN YOU SPARE A MOMENT TO MEET IN-PERSON?
NOW? WELL, I DON'T HAVE CLASS TODAY. SURE, I'LL COME OUT.
MEET ME AT THE DUKLYON CAFÉ BY THE TRAIN STATION. I'LL BE WEARING A TIE.
UM, OKAY. SEE YA.
カチャ
HEY, CHI.
I'M GOING OUT FOR A LITTLE WHILE.
CHI.
CHI.

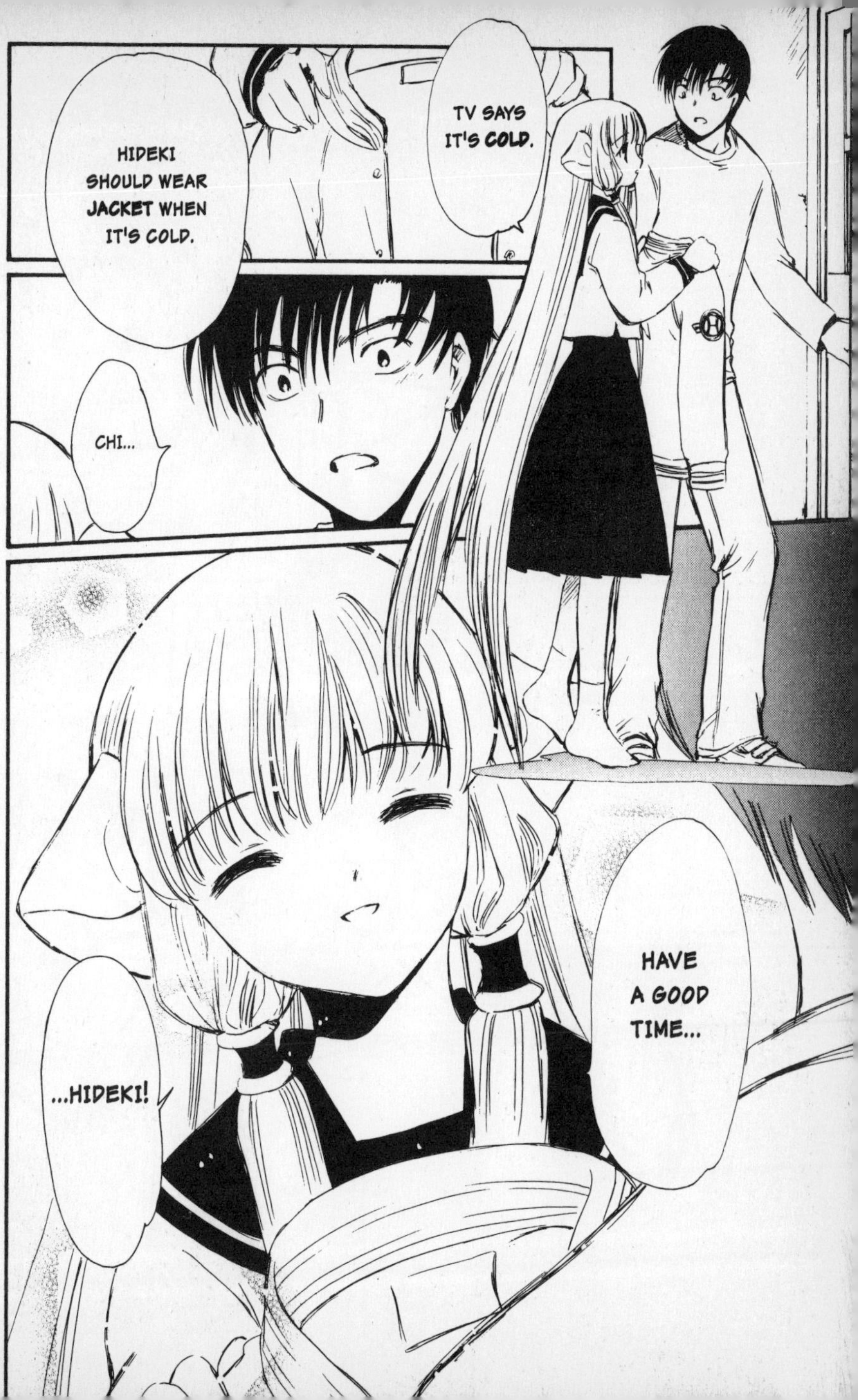
TV SAYS IT'S COLD.
HIDEKI SHOULD WEAR JACKET WHEN IT'S COLD.
CHI...
HAVE A GOOD TIME...
...HIDEKI!

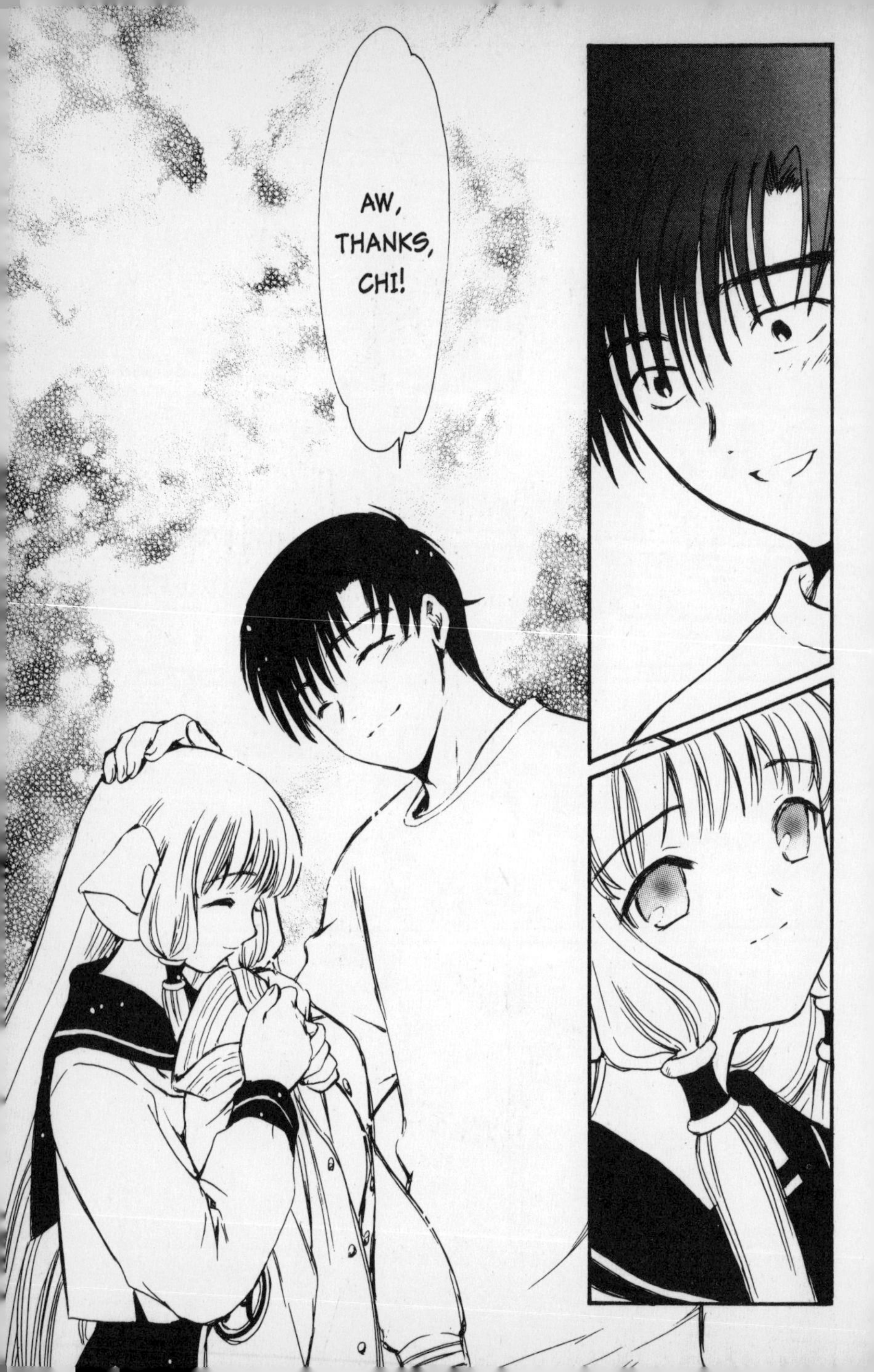
AW, THANKS, CHI!

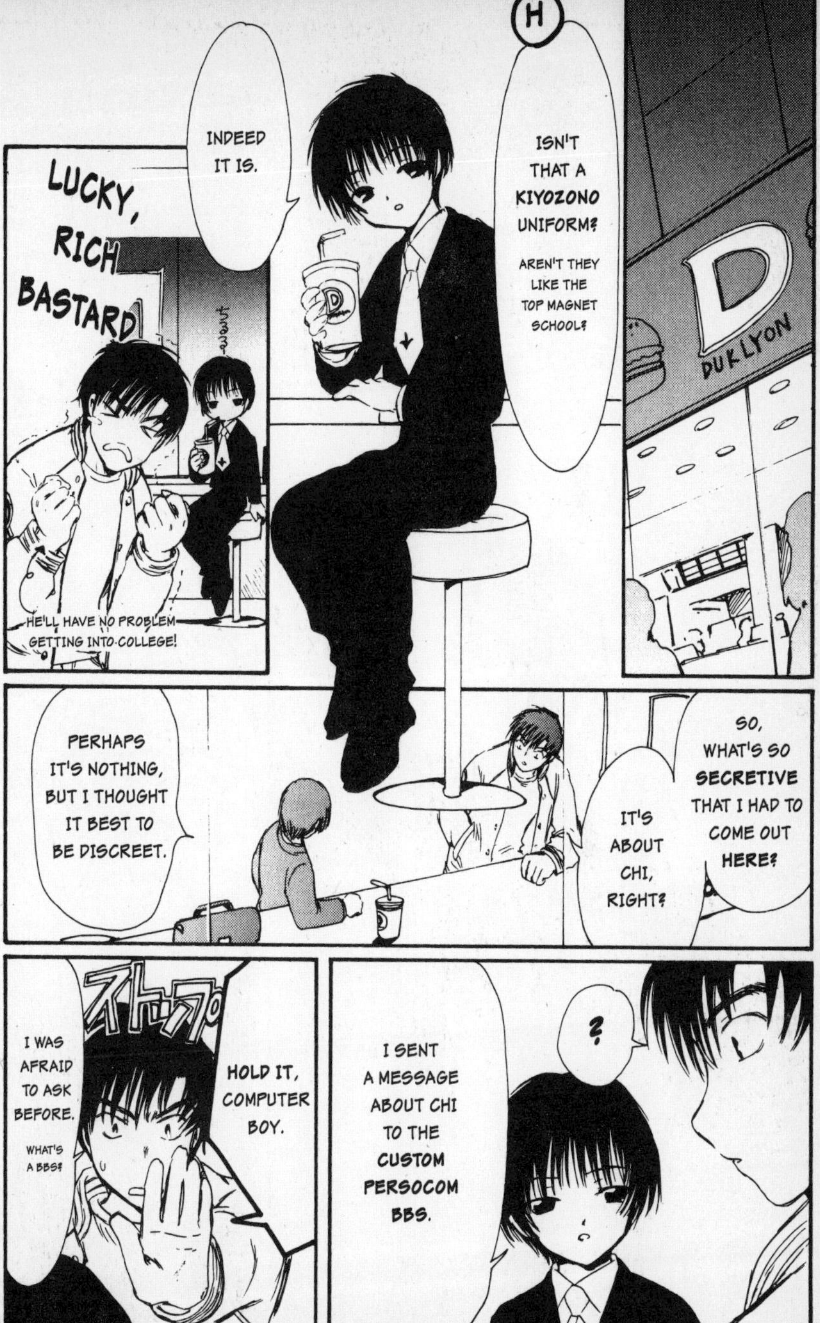
H
DUKLYON
ISN'T THAT A KIYOZONO UNIFORM?
AREN'T THEY LIKE THE TOP MAGNET SCHOOL?
INDEED IT IS.
LUCKY, RICH BASTARD
HE'LL HAVE NO PROBLEM GETTING INTO COLLEGE!
SO, WHAT'S SO SECRETIVE THAT I HAD TO COME OUT HERE?
IT'S ABOUT CHI, RIGHT?
PERHAPS IT'S NOTHING, BUT I THOUGHT IT BEST TO BE DISCREET.
?
I SENT A MESSAGE ABOUT CHI TO THE CUSTOM PERSOCOM BBS.
ストップ
HOLD IT, COMPUTER BOY.
I WAS AFRAID TO ASK BEFORE.
WHAT'S A BBS?

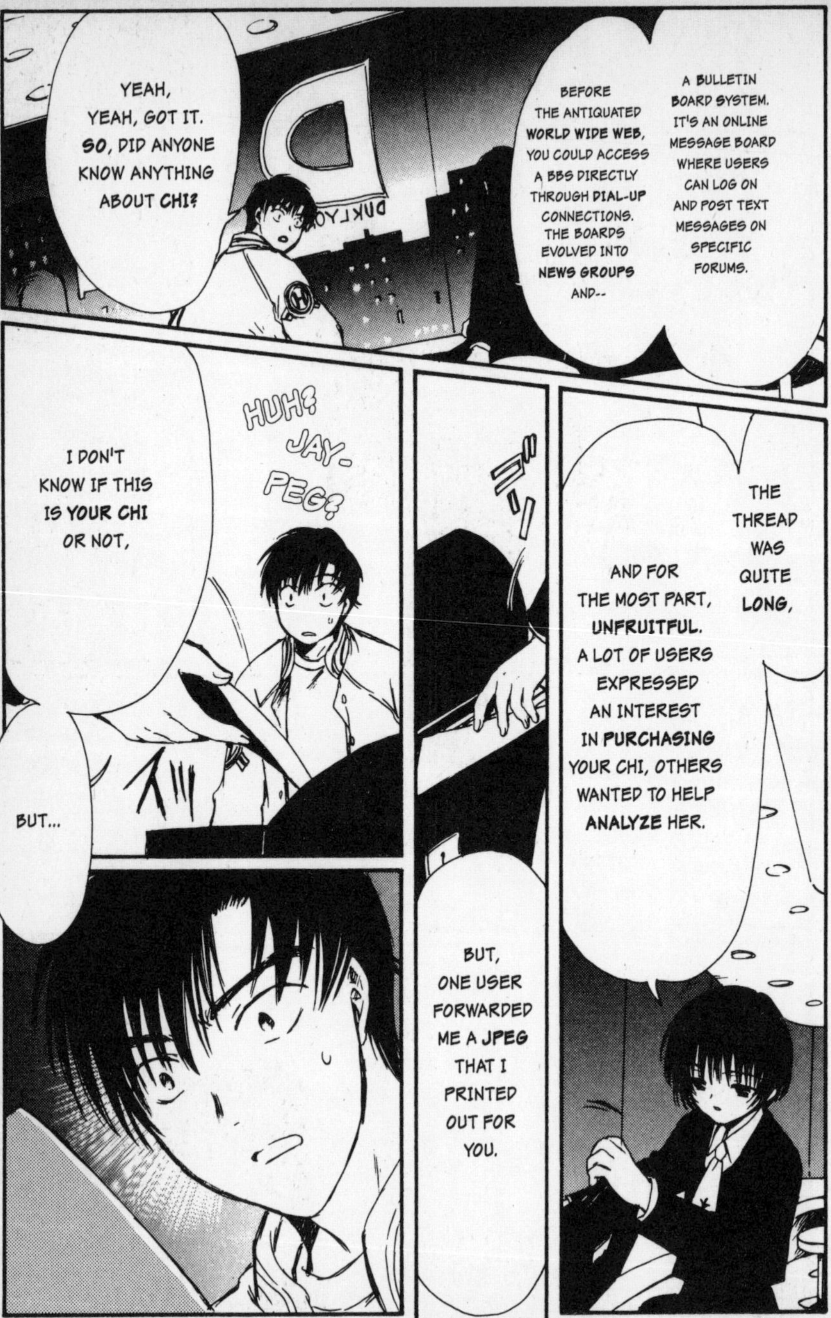
A BULLETIN BOARD SYSTEM. IT'S AN ONLINE MESSAGE BOARD WHERE USERS CAN LOG ON AND POST TEXT MESSAGES ON SPECIFIC FORUMS.
BEFORE THE ANTIQUATED WORLD WIDE WEB, YOU COULD ACCESS A BBS DIRECTLY THROUGH DIAL-UP CONNECTIONS. THE BOARDS EVOLVED INTO NEWS GROUPS AND--
YEAH, YEAH, GOT IT. SO, DID ANYONE KNOW ANYTHING ABOUT CHI?
THE THREAD WAS QUITE LONG,
AND FOR THE MOST PART, UNFRUITFUL. A LOT OF USERS EXPRESSED AN INTEREST IN PURCHASING YOUR CHI, OTHERS WANTED TO HELP ANALYZE HER.
BUT, ONE USER FORWARDED ME A JPEG THAT I PRINTED OUT FOR YOU.
HUH? JAY-PEG?
I DON'T KNOW IF THIS IS YOUR CHI OR NOT,
BUT...

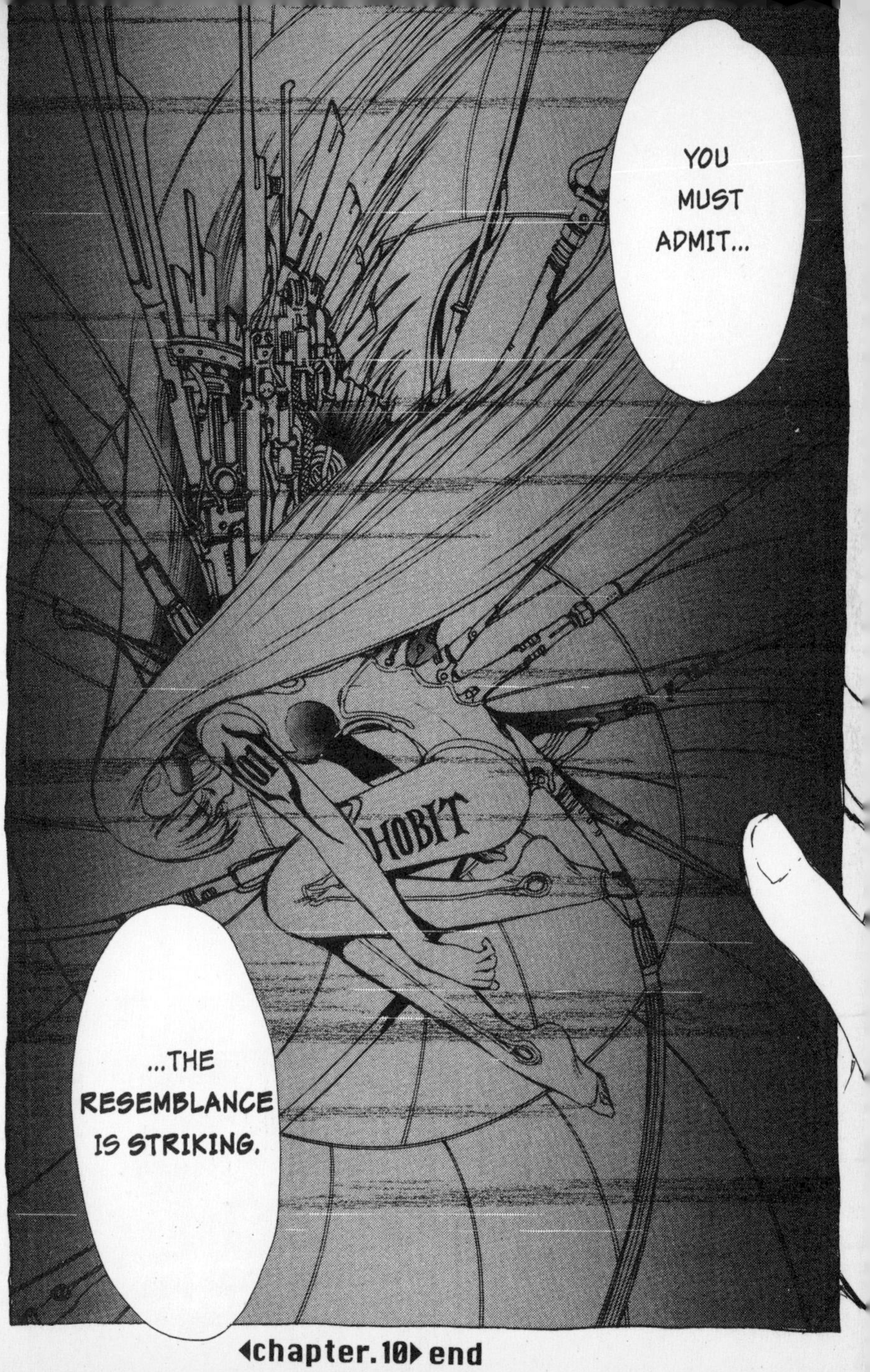
YOU MUST ADMIT...
HOBIT
...THE RESEMBLANCE IS STRIKING.

◀chapter. 10▶ end

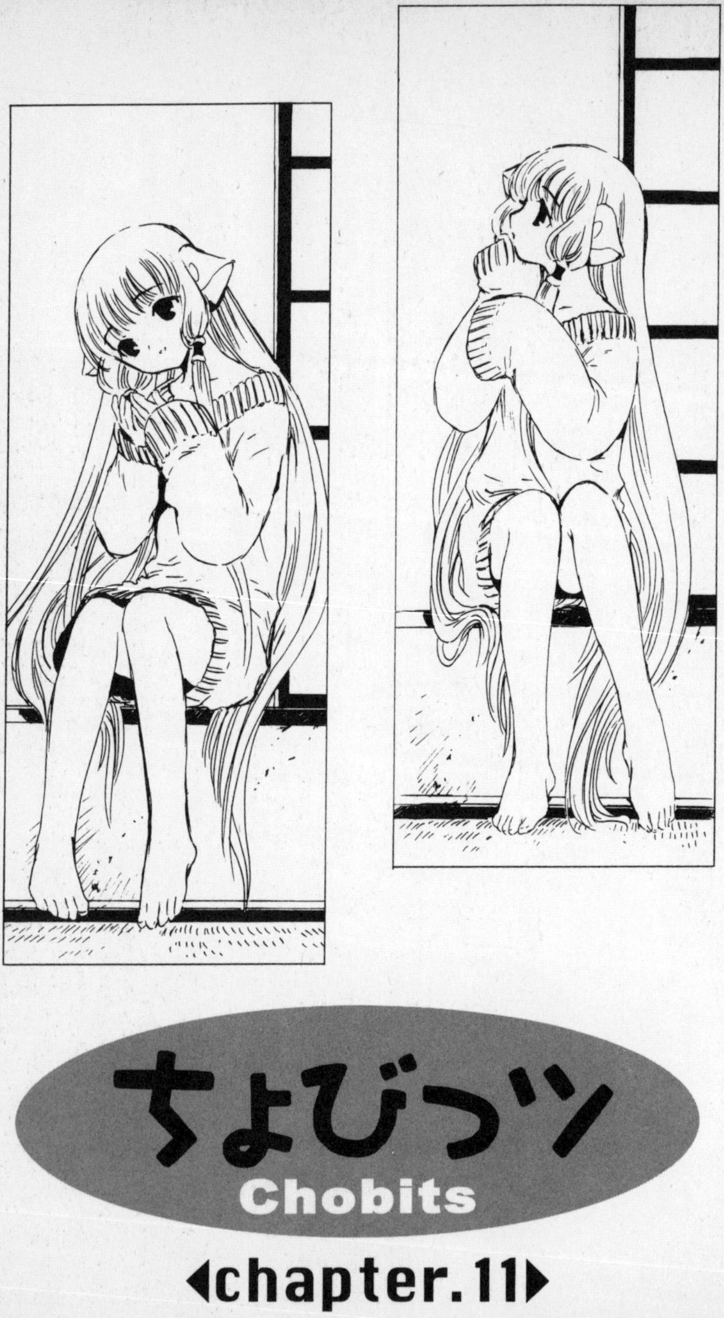

ちょびっツ

Chobits

chapter.11

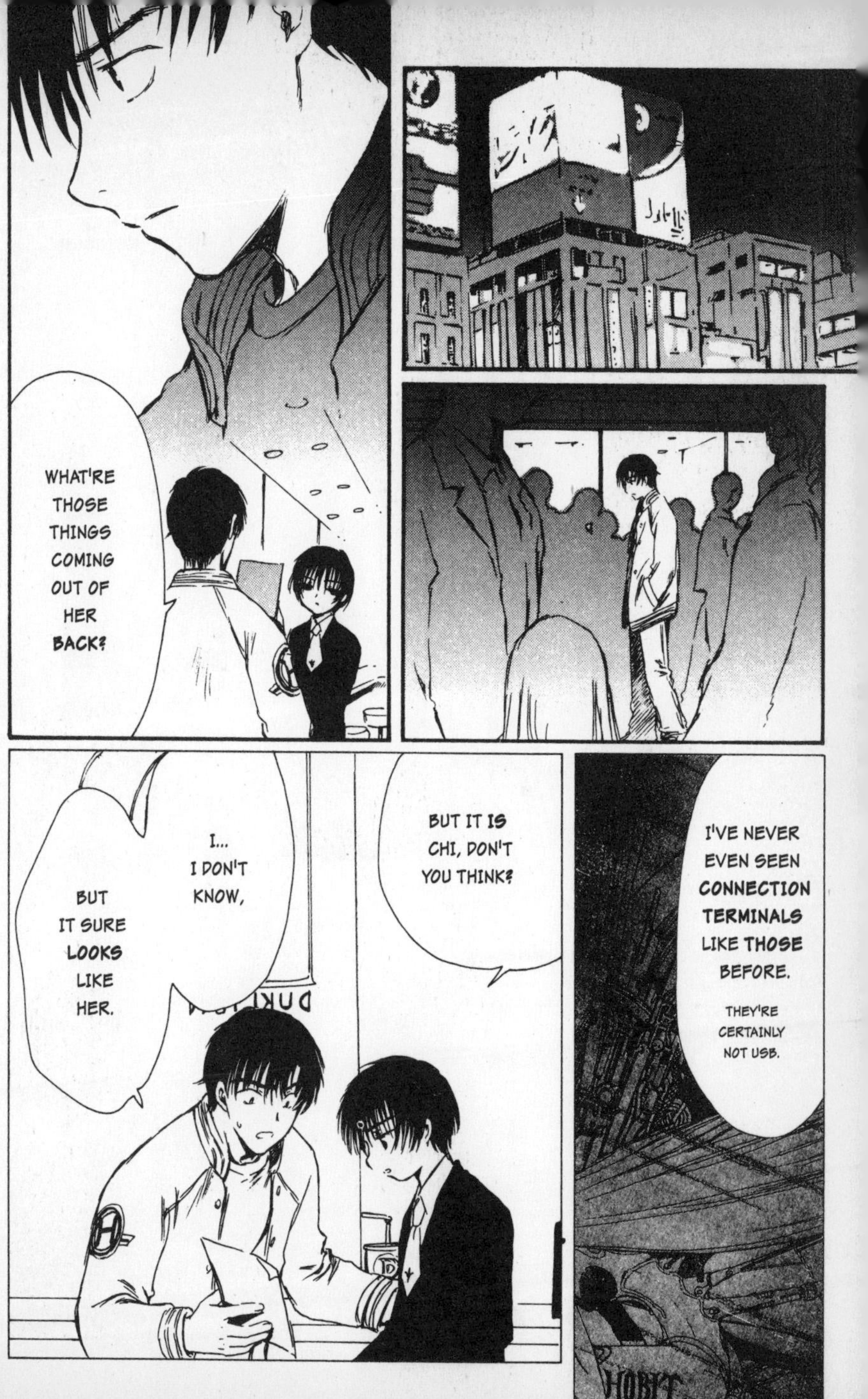
WHAT'RE THOSE THINGS COMING OUT OF HER BACK?
I'VE NEVER EVEN SEEN CONNECTION TERMINALS LIKE THOSE BEFORE.
THEY'RE CERTAINLY NOT USB.
HOBIT
BUT IT IS CHI, DON'T YOU THINK?
I... I DON'T KNOW,
BUT IT SURE LOOKS LIKE HER.

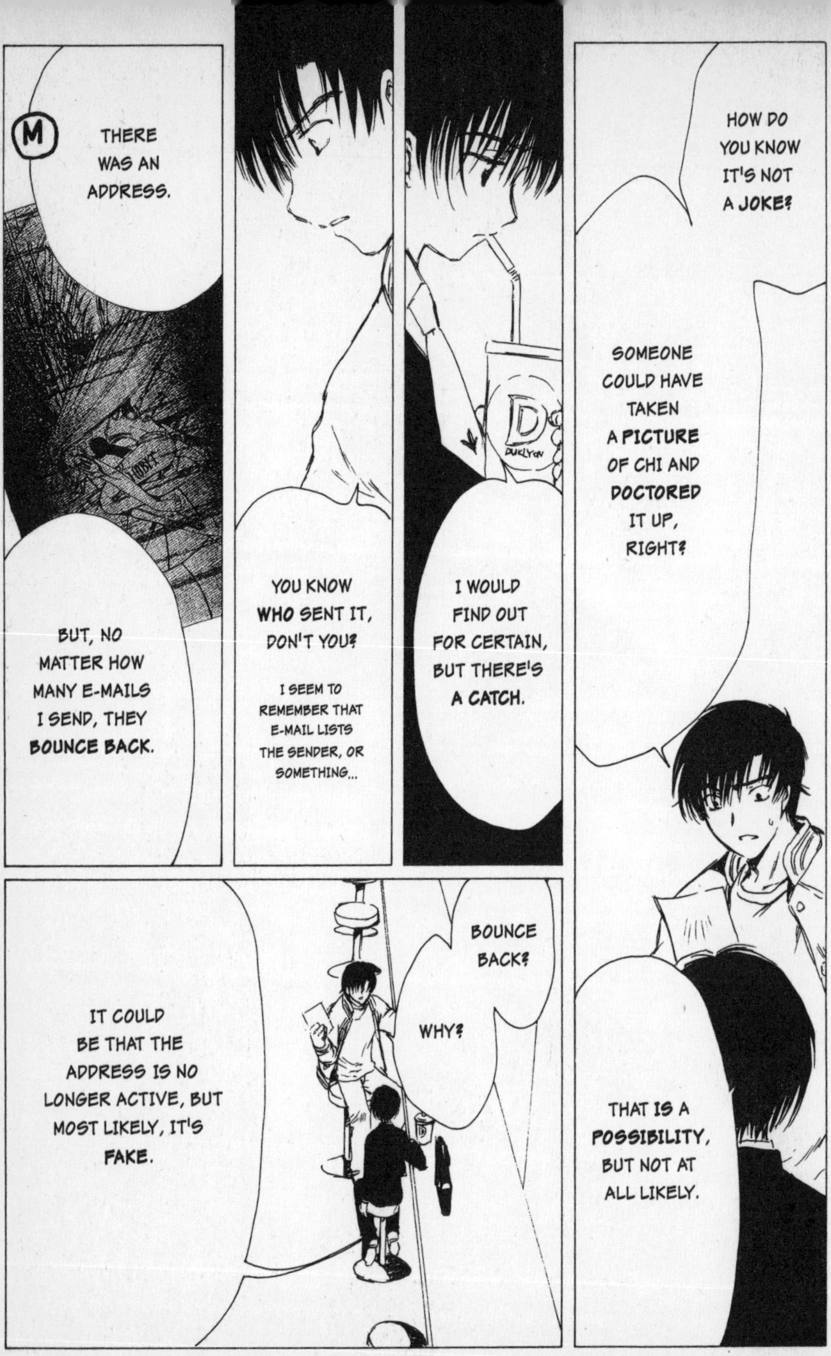
HOW DO YOU KNOW IT'S NOT A JOKE?
SOMEONE COULD HAVE TAKEN A PICTURE OF CHI AND DOCTORED IT UP, RIGHT?
THAT IS A POSSIBILITY, BUT NOT AT ALL LIKELY.
I WOULD FIND OUT FOR CERTAIN, BUT THERE'S A CATCH.
YOU KNOW WHO SENT IT, DON'T YOU?
I SEEM TO REMEMBER THAT E-MAIL LISTS THE SENDER, OR SOMETHING...
M
THERE WAS AN ADDRESS.
BUT, NO MATTER HOW MANY E-MAILS I SEND, THEY BOUNCE BACK.
BOUNCE BACK?
WHY?
IT COULD BE THAT THE ADDRESS IS NO LONGER ACTIVE, BUT MOST LIKELY, IT'S FAKE.

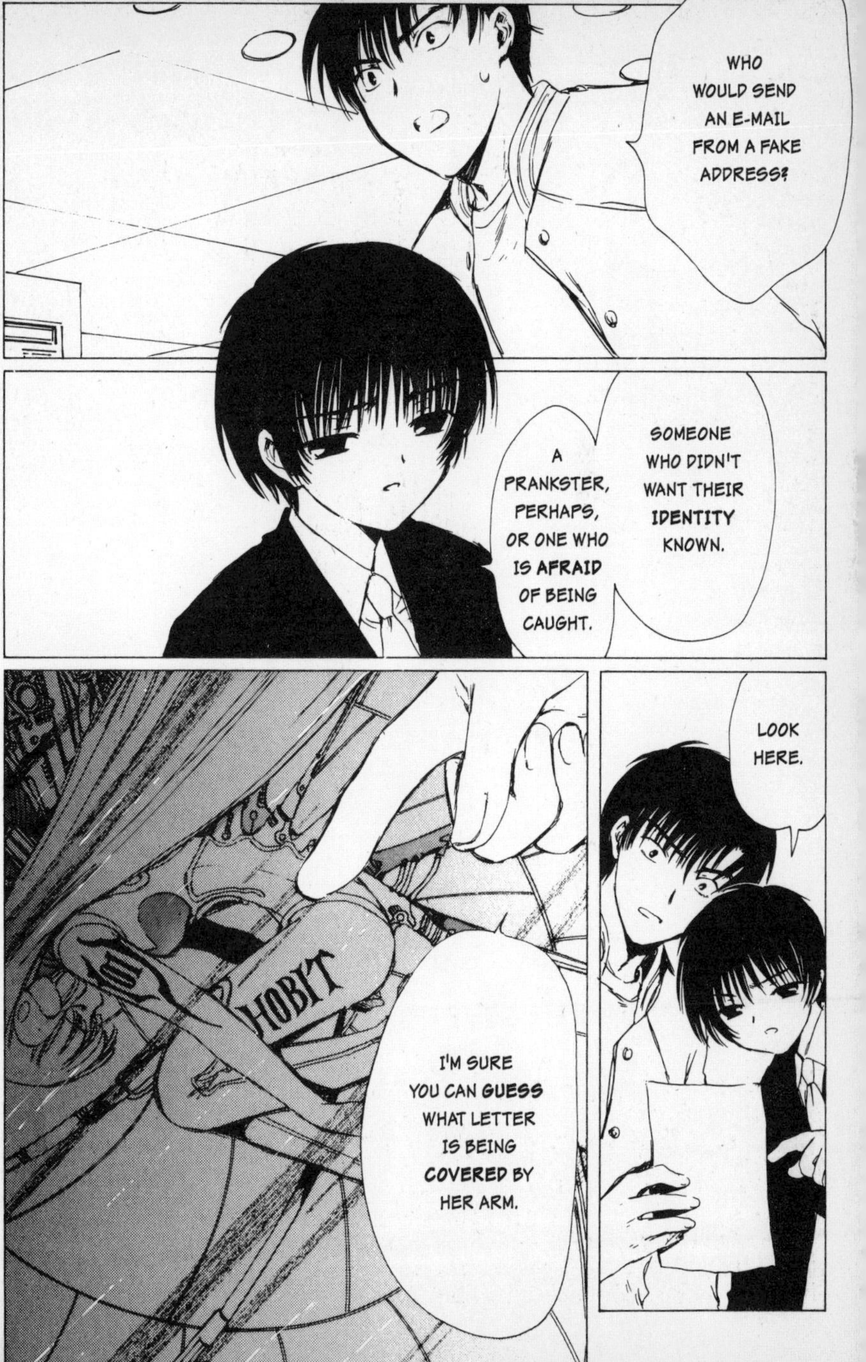
WHO WOULD SEND AN E-MAIL FROM A FAKE ADDRESS?
SOMEONE WHO DIDN'T WANT THEIR **IDENTITY** KNOWN.
A PRANKSTER, PERHAPS, OR ONE WHO IS **AFRAID** OF BEING CAUGHT.
LOOK HERE.
HOBIT
I'M SURE YOU CAN **GUESS** WHAT LETTER IS BEING **COVERED** BY HER ARM.

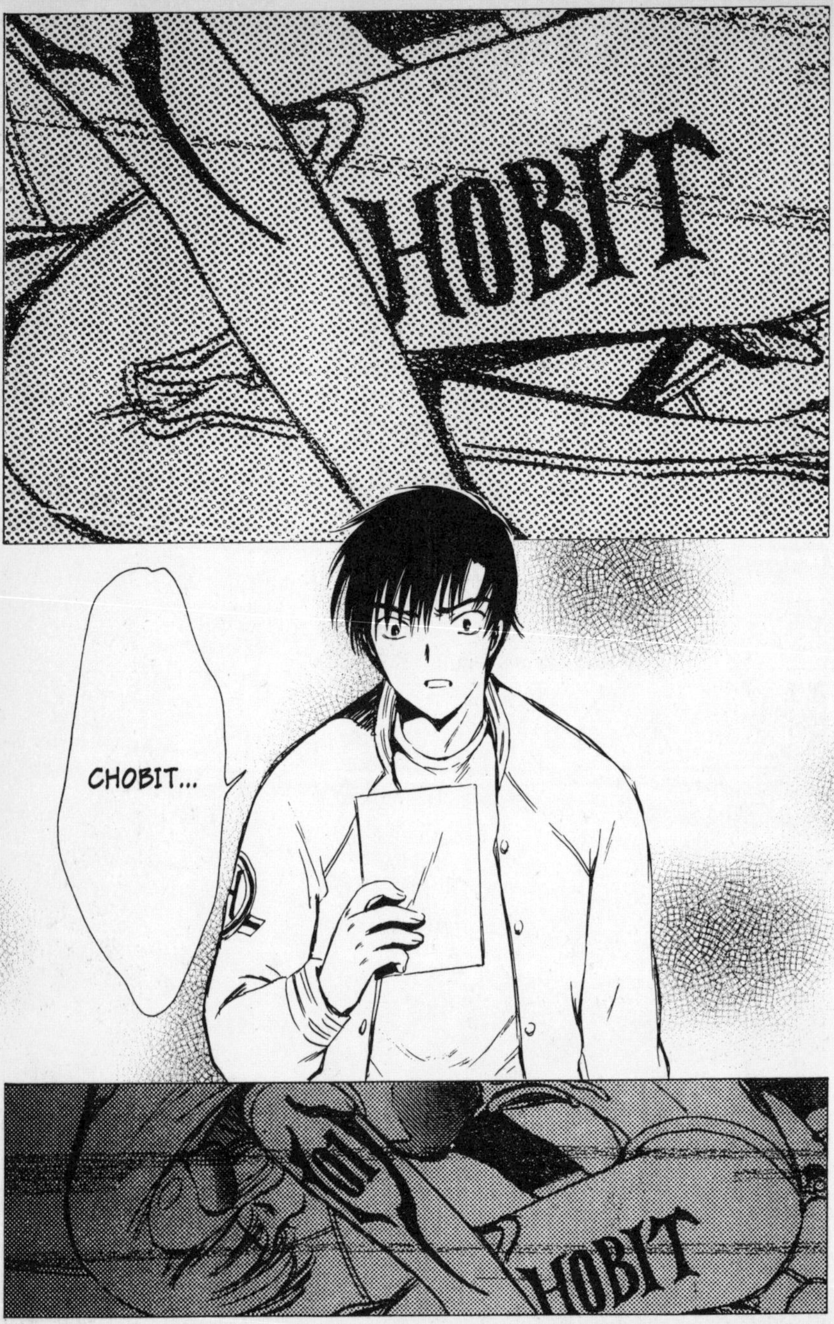
HOBIT
CHOBIT...
HOBIT

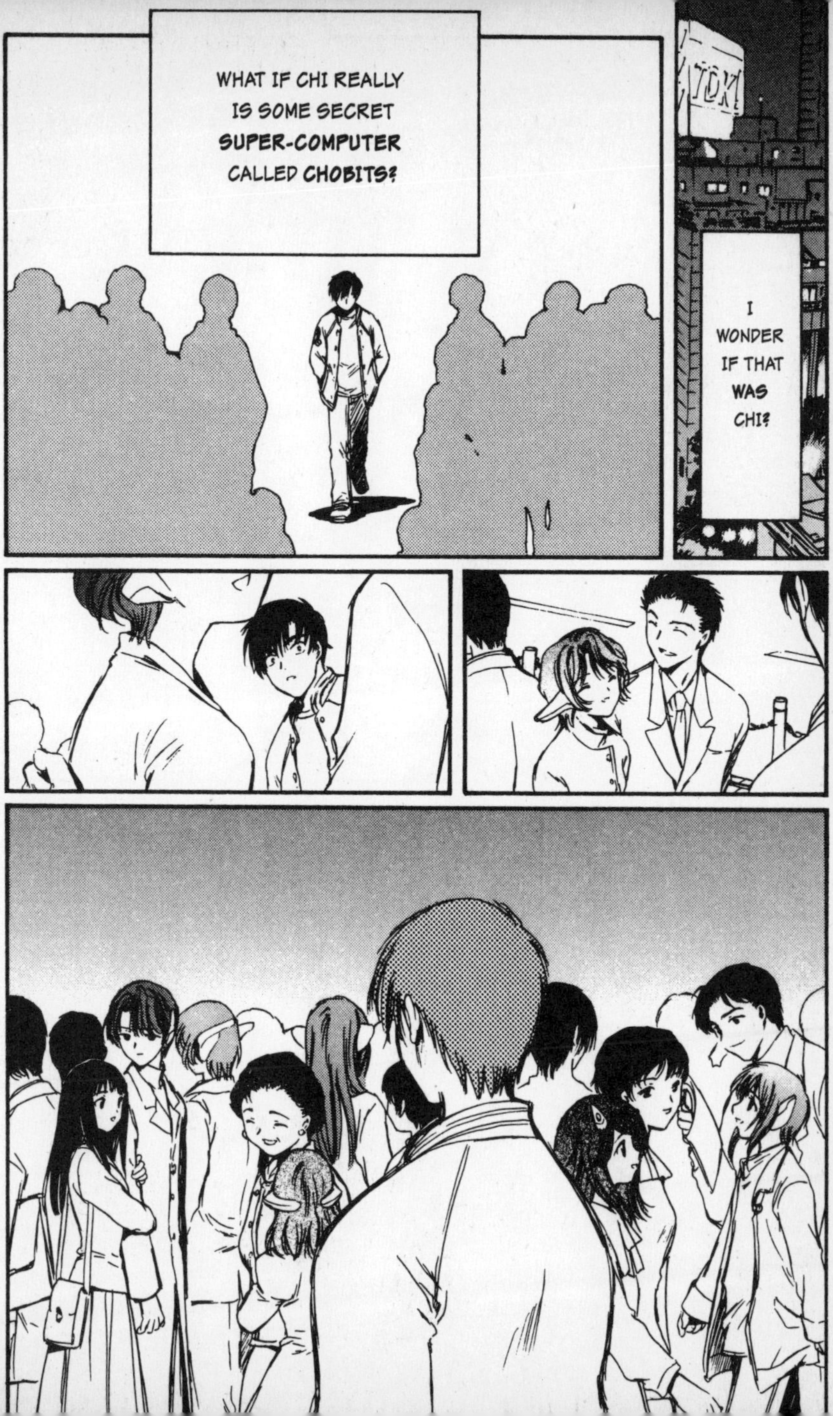
I WONDER IF THAT WAS CHI?
WHAT IF CHI REALLY IS SOME SECRET SUPER-COMPUTER CALLED CHOBITS?

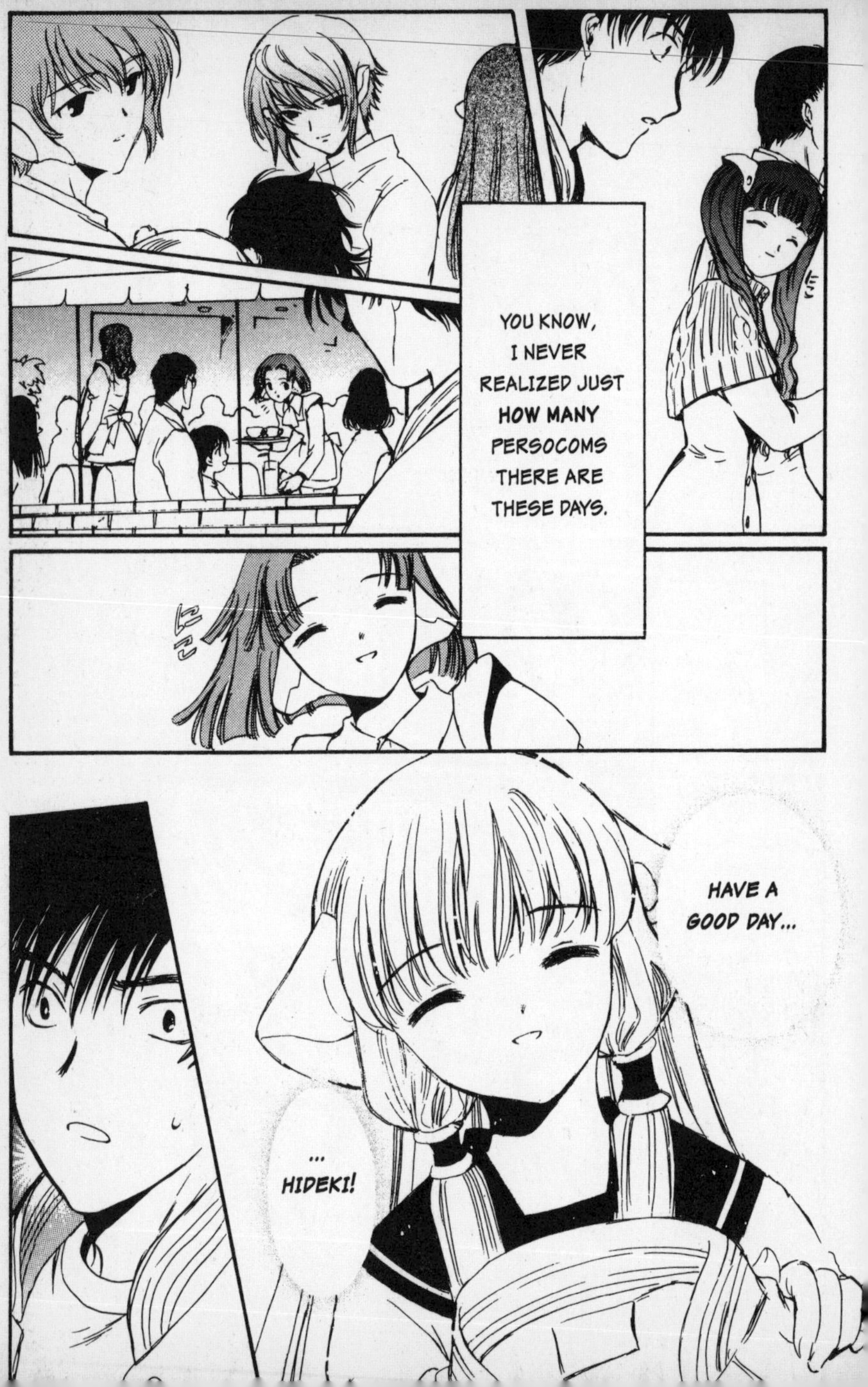
YOU KNOW, I NEVER REALIZED JUST HOW MANY PERSOCOMS THERE ARE THESE DAYS.
HAVE A GOOD DAY...
... HIDEKI!

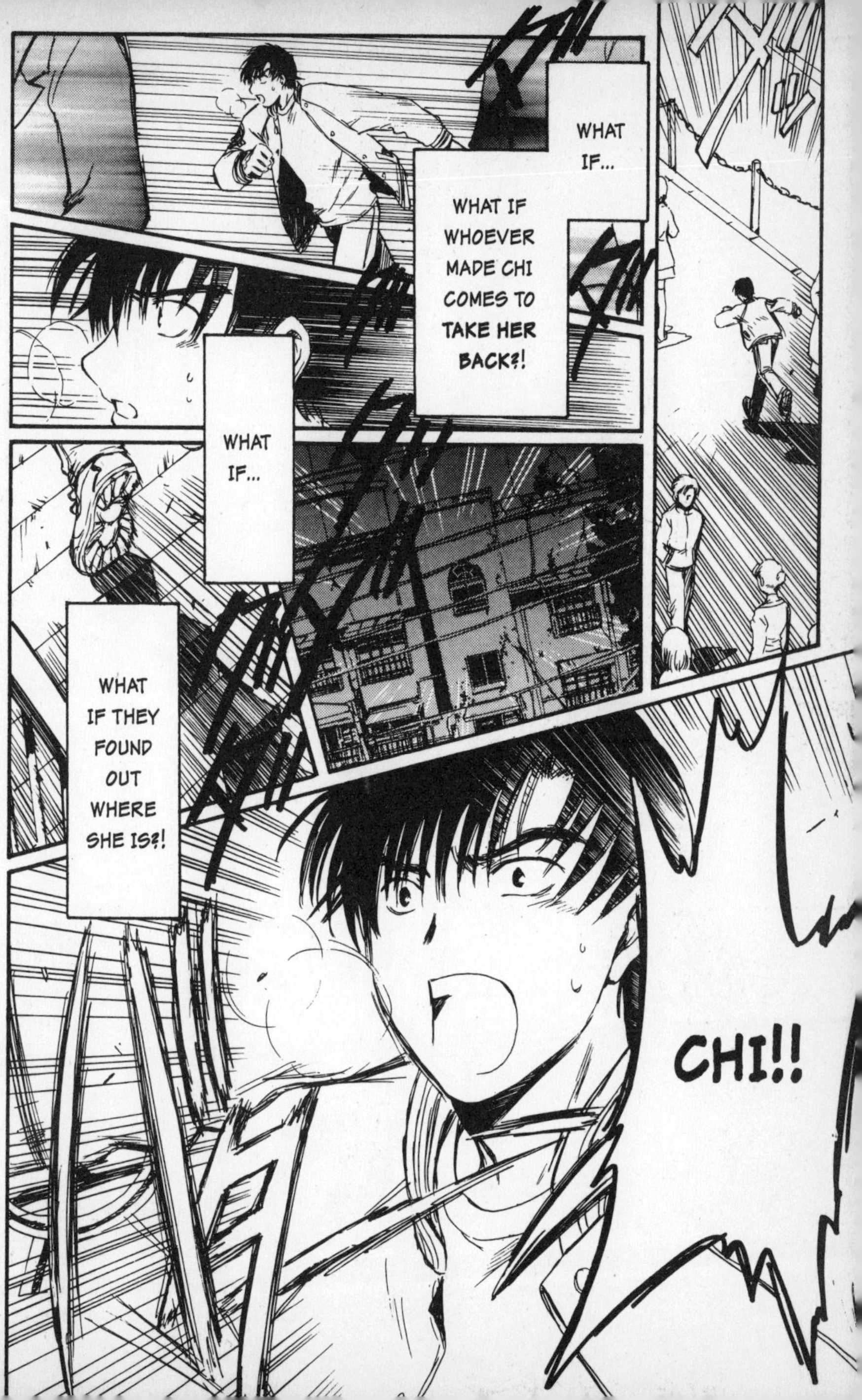
WHAT IF...
WHAT IF WHOEVER MADE CHI COMES TO TAKE HER BACK?!
WHAT IF...
WHAT IF THEY FOUND OUT WHERE SHE IS?!
CHI!!

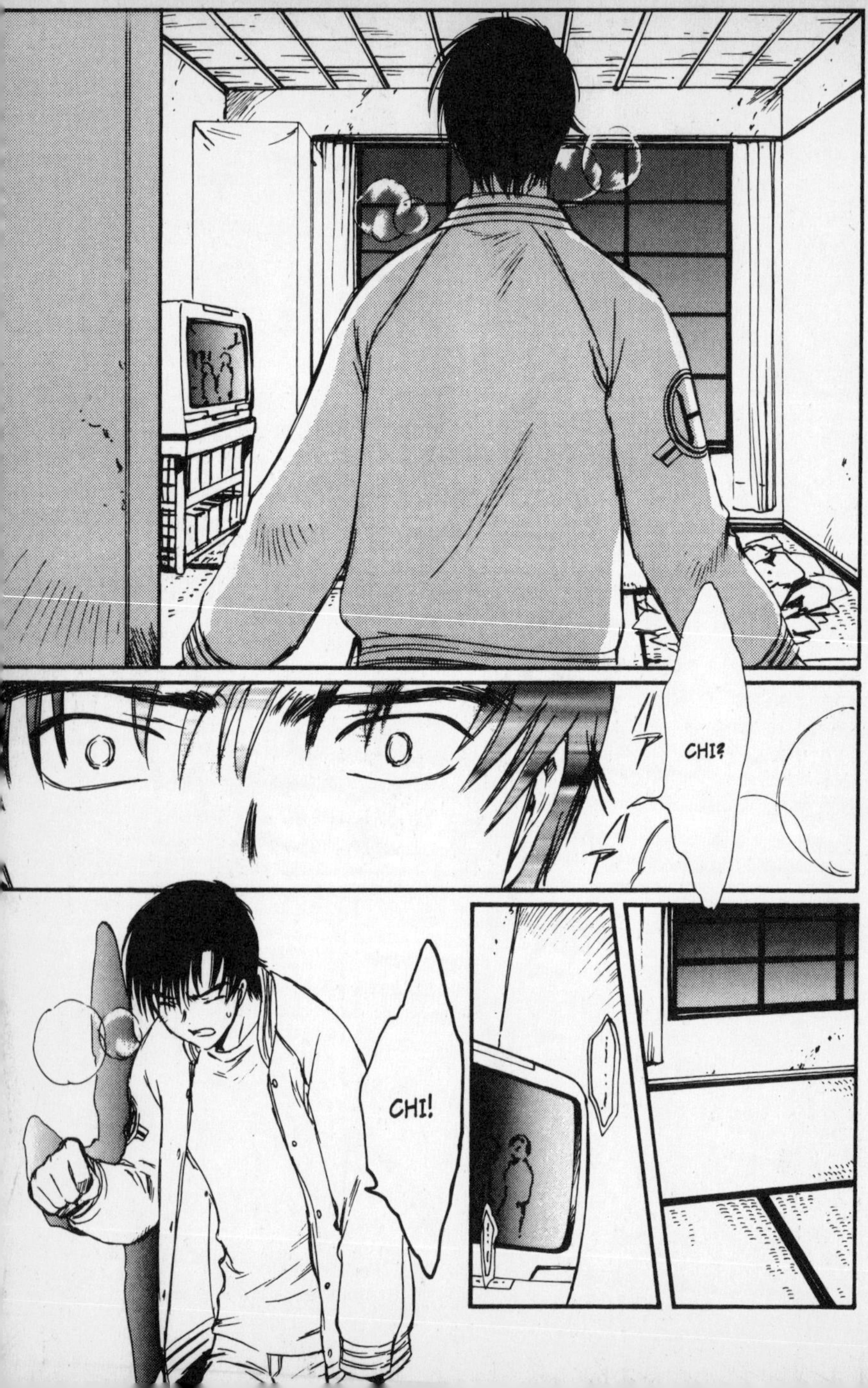
CHI?
CHI!

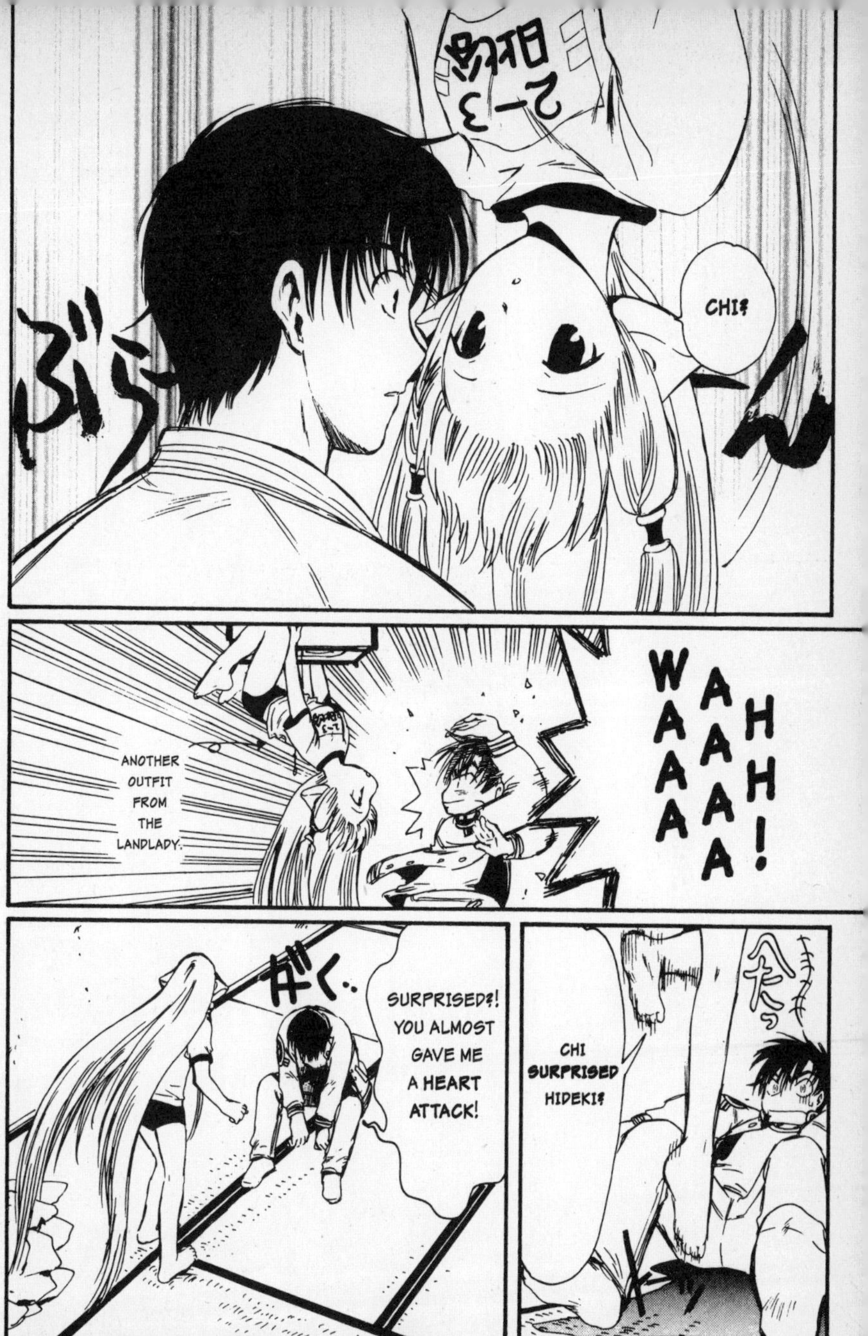

ぶら
ん
CHI?
WAAAAAAAAHH!
ANOTHER OUTFIT FROM THE LANDLADY.
CHI SURPRISED HIDEKI?
がく..
SURPRISED?! YOU ALMOST GAVE ME A HEART ATTACK!

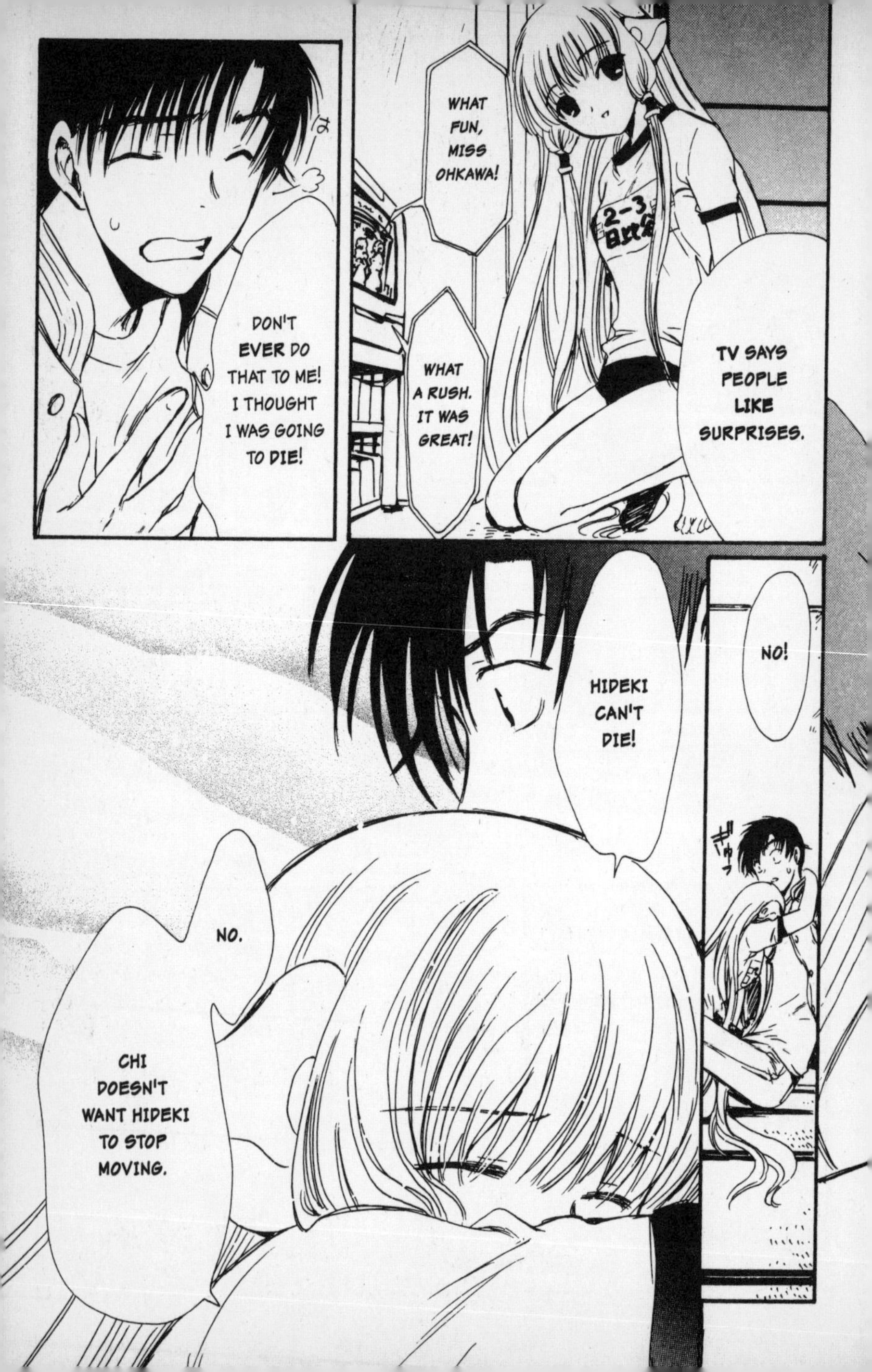
WHAT FUN, MISS OHKAWA!
WHAT A RUSH. IT WAS GREAT!
TV SAYS PEOPLE LIKE SURPRISES.
はーっ
DON'T EVER DO THAT TO ME! I THOUGHT I WAS GOING TO DIE!
ぎゅっ
NO!
HIDEKI CAN'T DIE!
NO.
CHI DOESN'T WANT HIDEKI TO STOP MOVING.

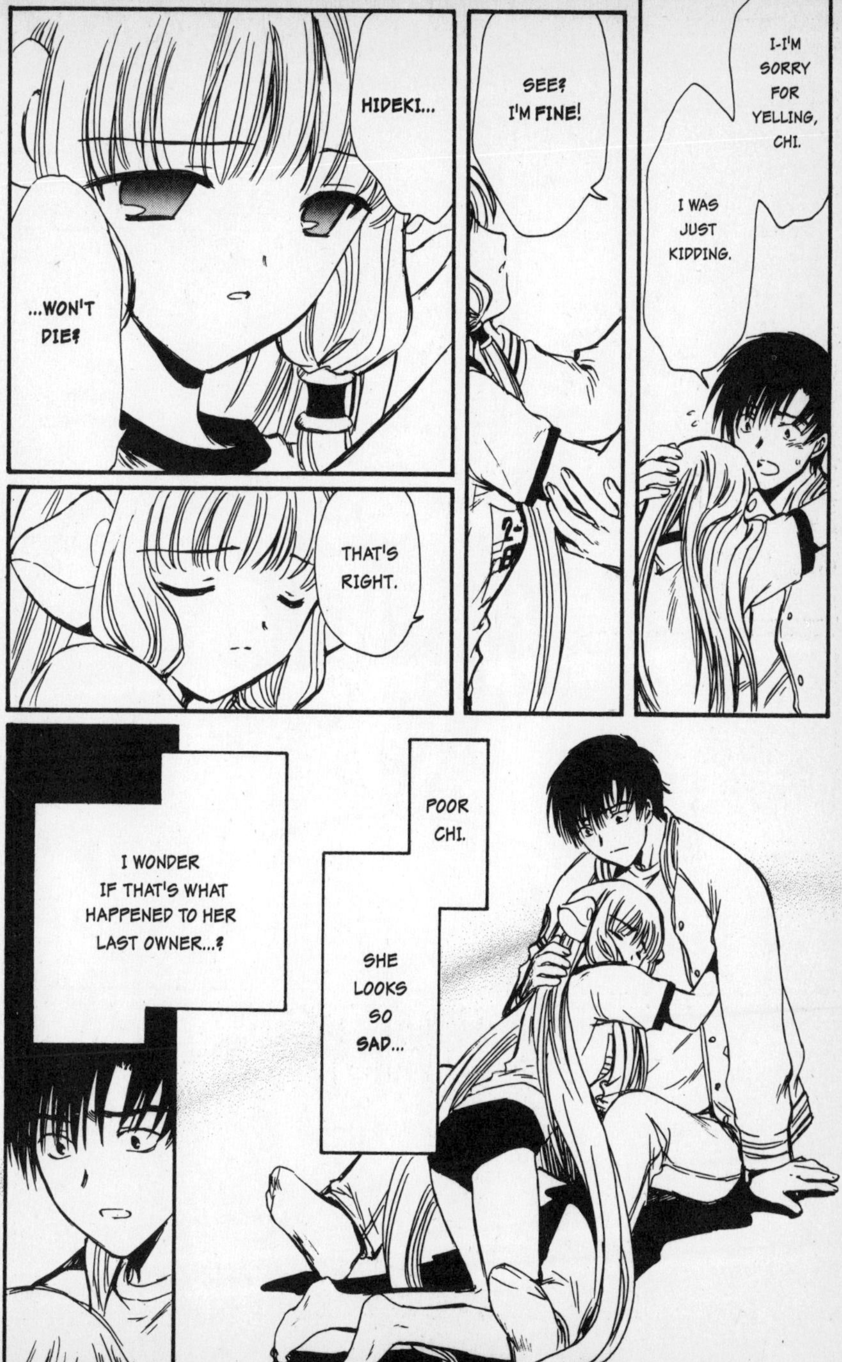
I-I'M SORRY FOR YELLING, CHI.
I WAS JUST KIDDING.
SEE? I'M FINE!
HIDEKI...
...WON'T DIE?
THAT'S RIGHT.
POOR CHI.
SHE LOOKS SO SAD...
I WONDER IF THAT'S WHAT HAPPENED TO HER LAST OWNER...?

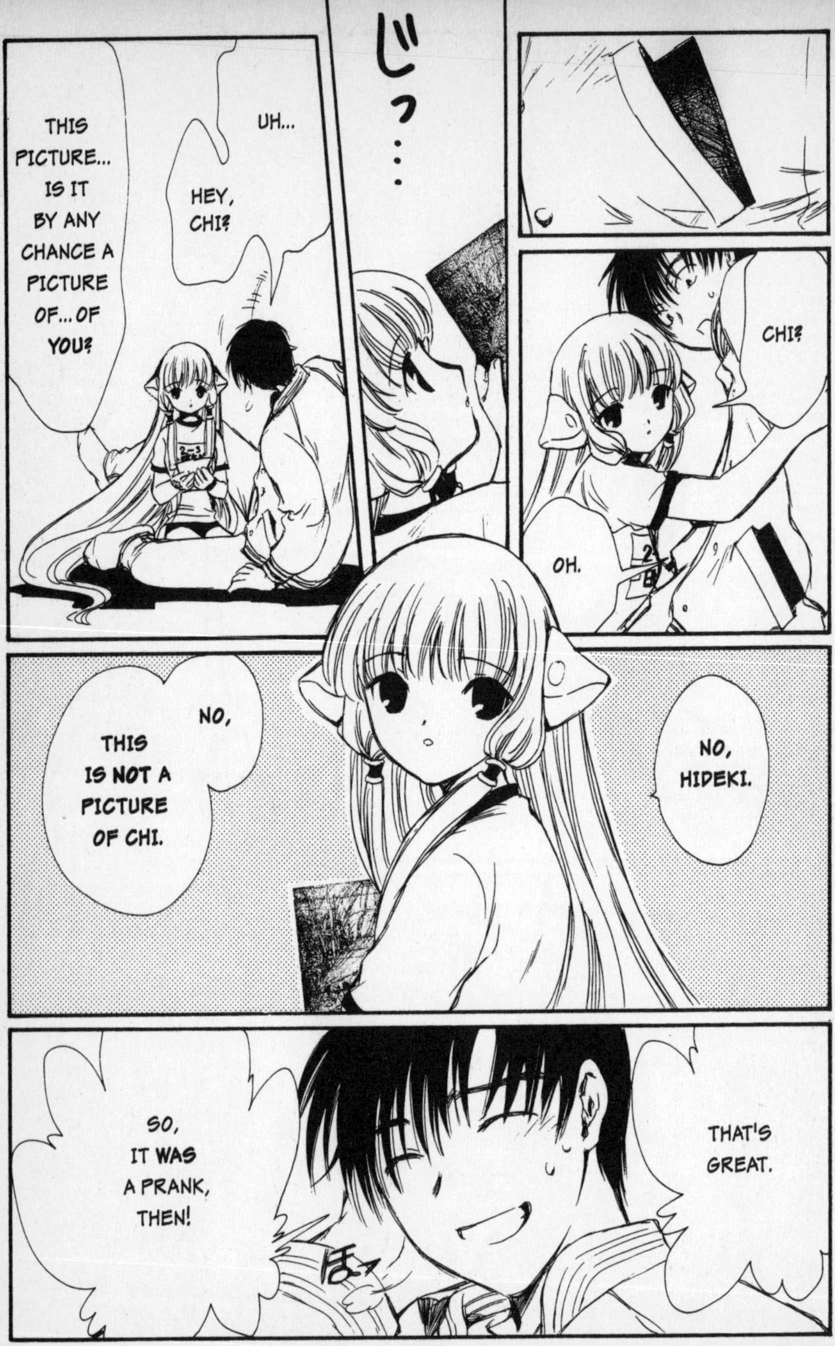
CHI?
OH.
じっ…
UH...
HEY, CHI?
THIS PICTURE... IS IT BY ANY CHANCE A PICTURE OF... OF YOU?
NO, HIDEKI.
NO, THIS IS NOT A PICTURE OF CHI.
THAT'S GREAT.
SO, IT WAS A PRANK, THEN!
ほっ

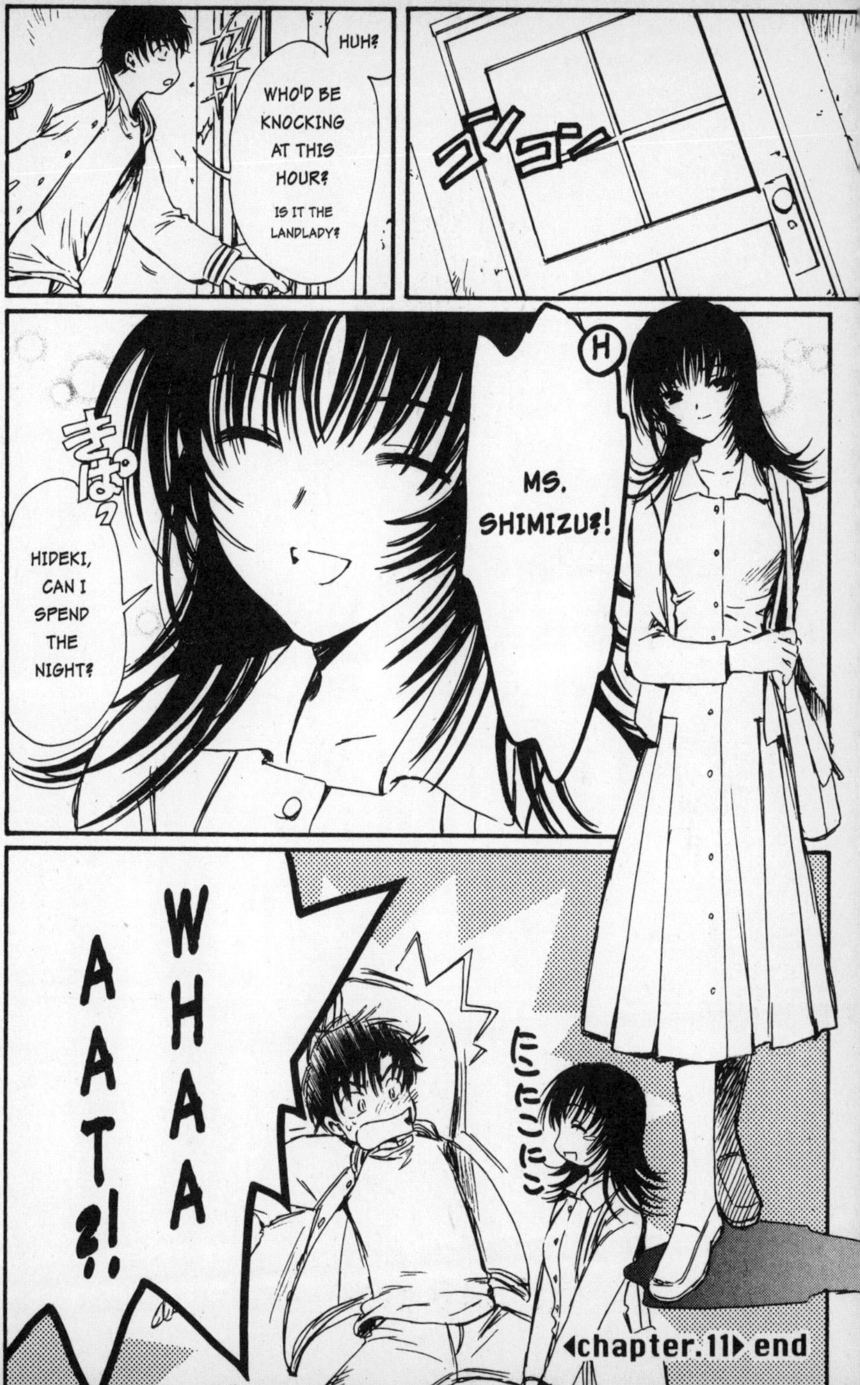
コンコン
HUH?
WHO'D BE KNOCKING AT THIS HOUR?
IS IT THE LANDLADY?
H
MS. SHIMIZU?!
きぱっ
HIDEKI, CAN I SPEND THE NIGHT?
WHAAAAT?!
ニコニコ
◂chapter.11▸ end

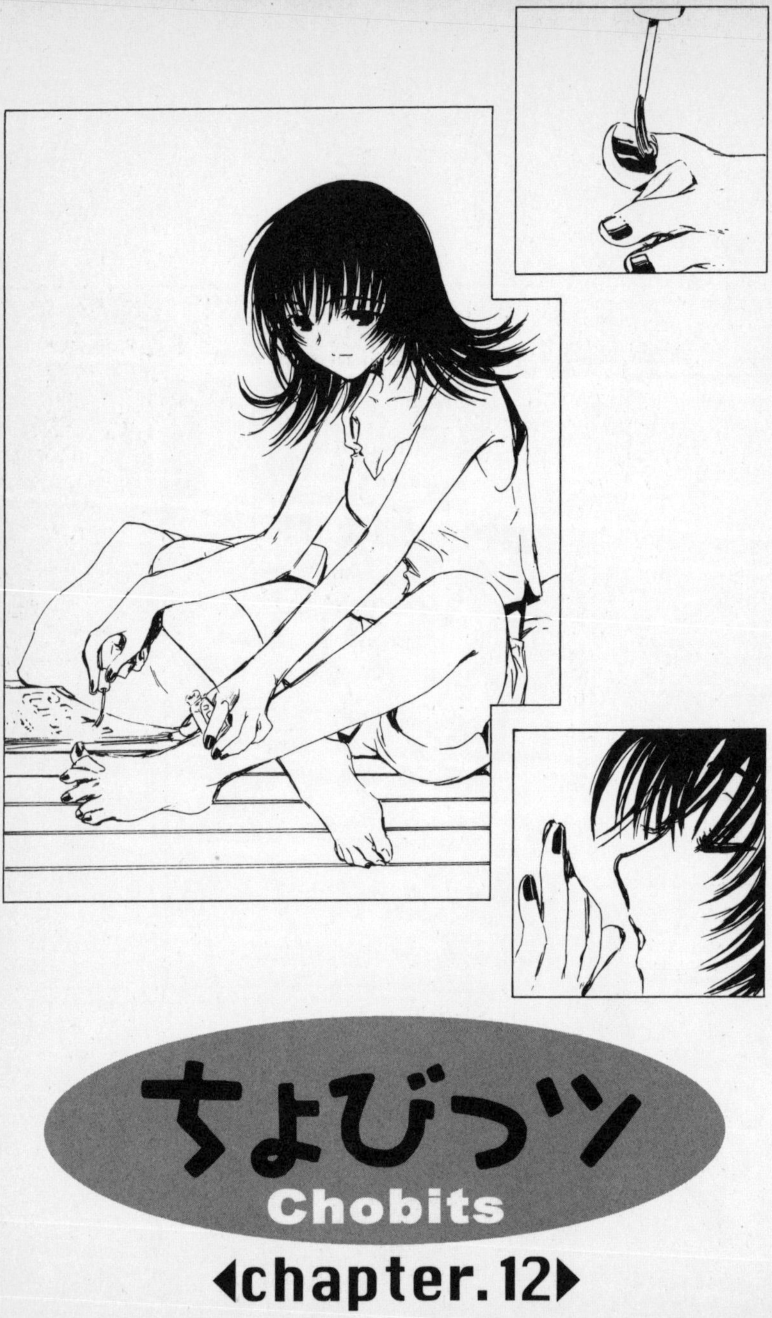

ちょびっツ
Chobits
◀chapter. 12▶

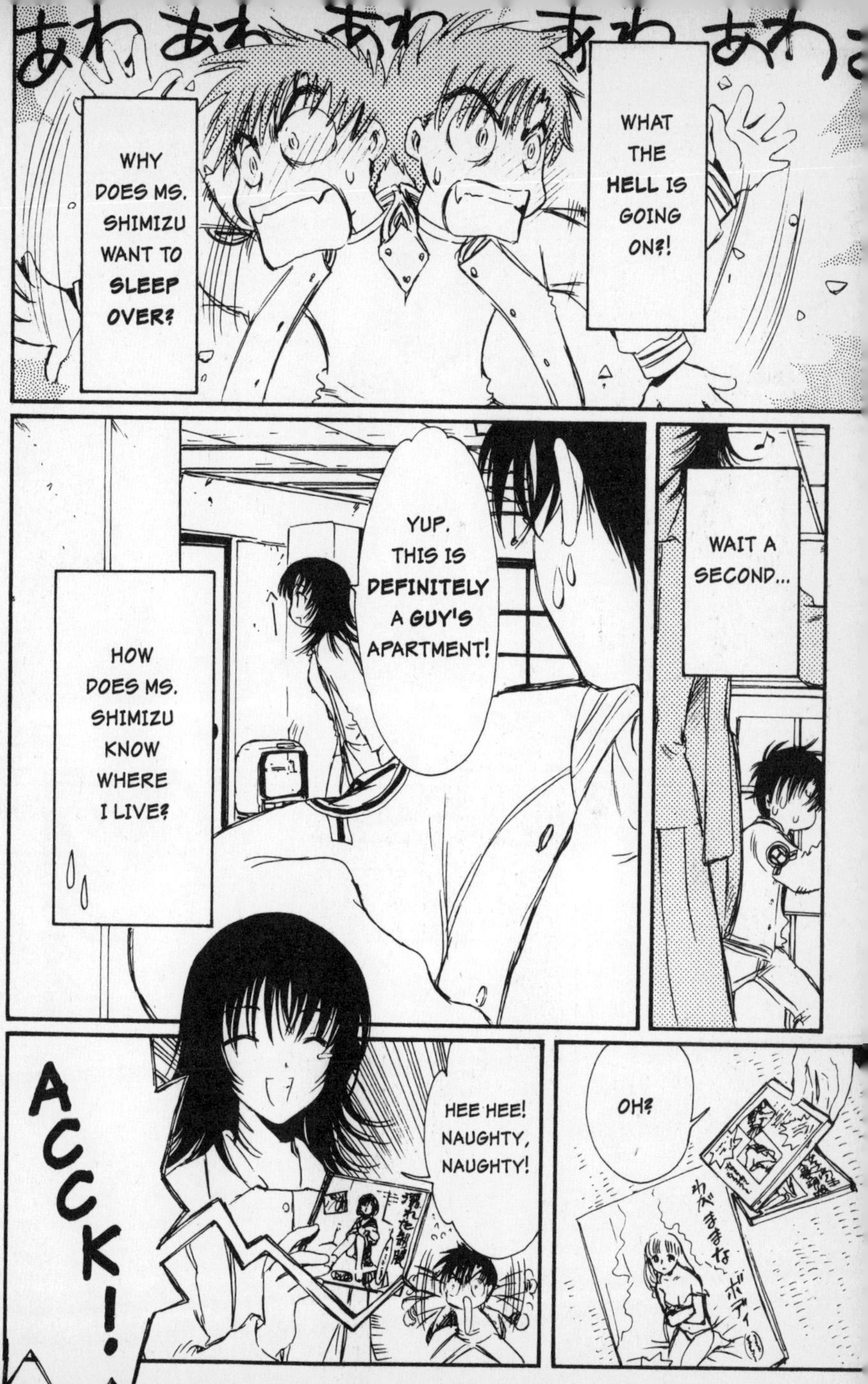
あわあわ あわ あわ あわ
WHAT THE HELL IS GOING ON?!
WHY DOES MS. SHIMIZU WANT TO SLEEP OVER?
WAIT A SECOND...
YUP. THIS IS DEFINITELY A GUY'S APARTMENT!
HOW DOES MS. SHIMIZU KNOW WHERE I LIVE?
OH?
HEE HEE! NAUGHTY, NAUGHTY!
ACCK!

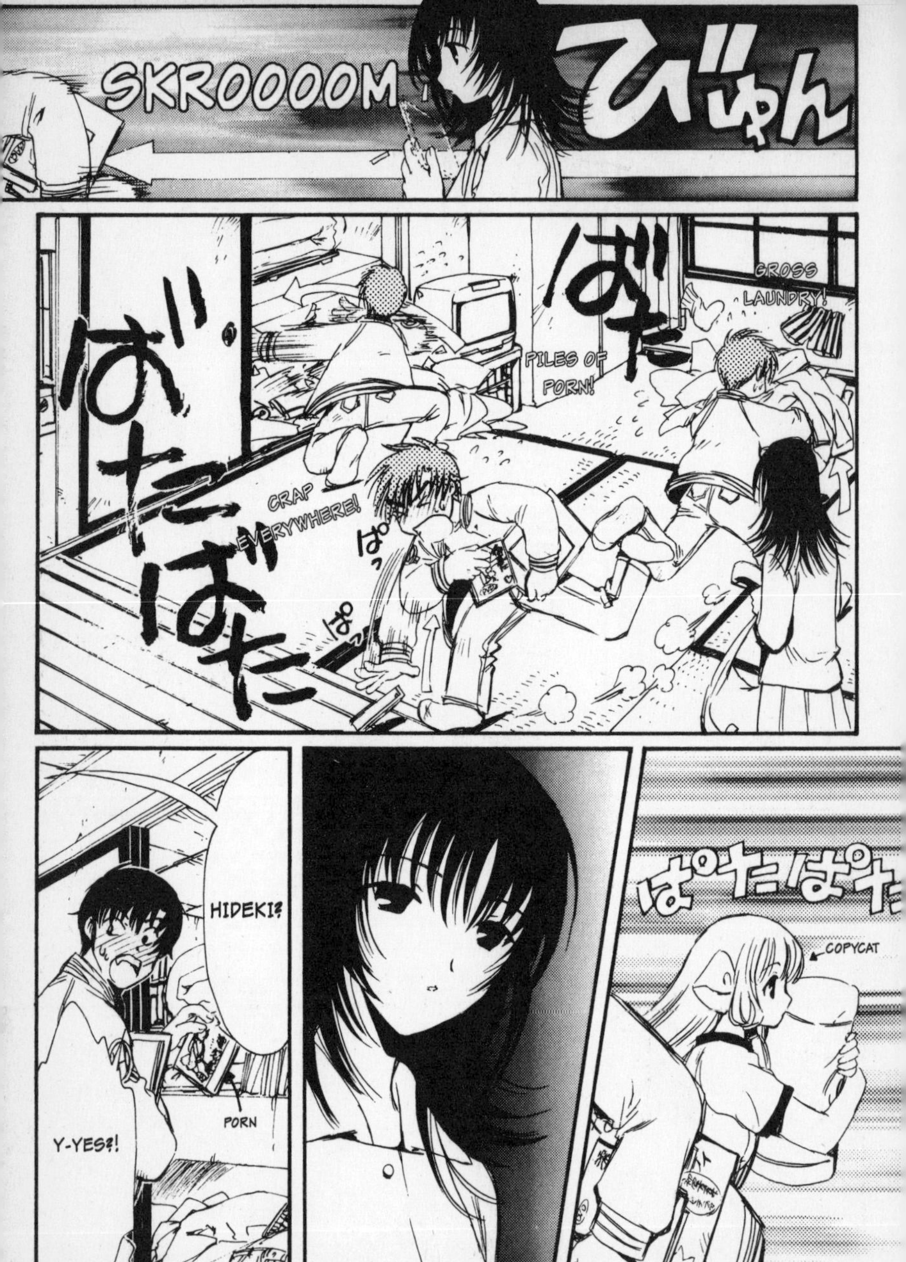
びゅん
SKROOOOM
ぱた
GROSS LAUNDRY!
PILES OF PORN!
ぱたぱた
CRAP EVERYWHERE!
ぱっ
ぱっ
ぱたぱた
COPYCAT
HIDEKI?
Y-YES?!
PORN

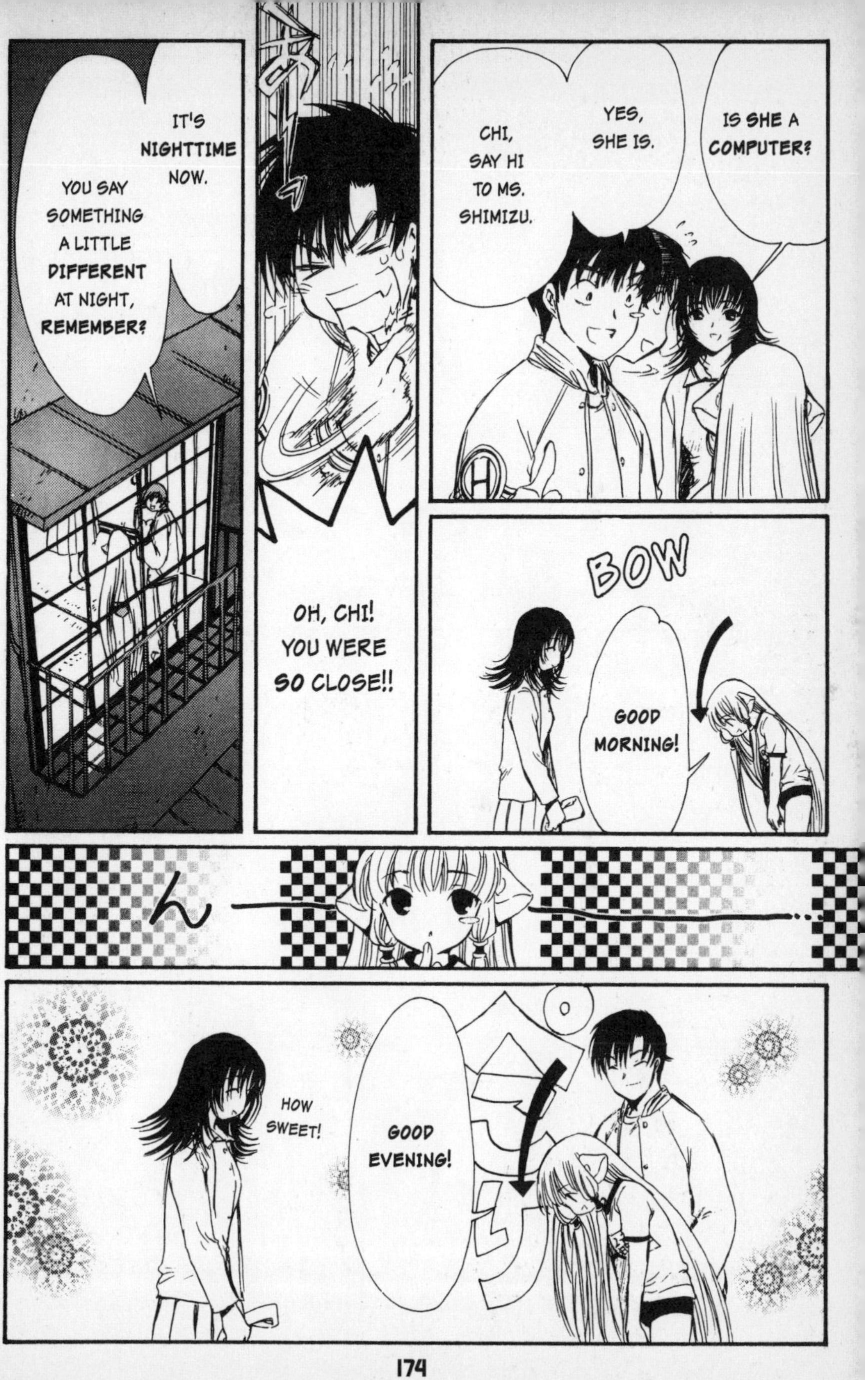
IS SHE A COMPUTER?
YES, SHE IS.
CHI, SAY HI TO MS. SHIMIZU.
BOW
GOOD MORNING!
OH, CHI! YOU WERE SO CLOSE!!
IT'S NIGHTTIME NOW.
YOU SAY SOMETHING A LITTLE DIFFERENT AT NIGHT, REMEMBER?
ん———————...
GOOD EVENING!
HOW SWEET!

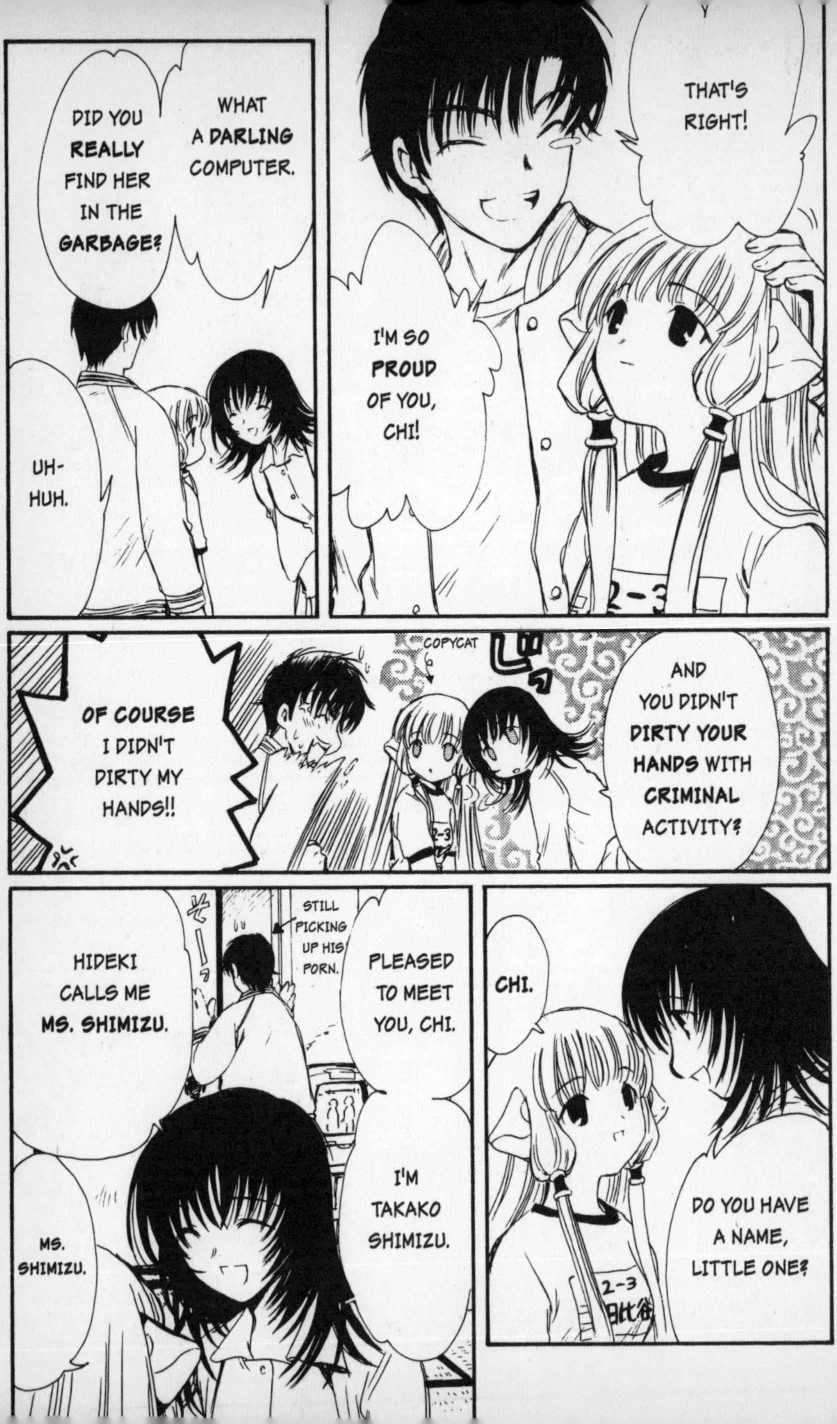

THAT'S RIGHT!
I'M SO PROUD OF YOU, CHI!
WHAT A DARLING COMPUTER.
DID YOU REALLY FIND HER IN THE GARBAGE?
UH-HUH.
AND YOU DIDN'T DIRTY YOUR HANDS WITH CRIMINAL ACTIVITY?
COPYCAT
OF COURSE I DIDN'T DIRTY MY HANDS!!
DO YOU HAVE A NAME, LITTLE ONE?
CHI.
PLEASED TO MEET YOU, CHI.
I'M TAKAKO SHIMIZU.
STILL PICKING UP HIS PORN.
HIDEKI CALLS ME MS. SHIMIZU.
MS. SHIMIZU.

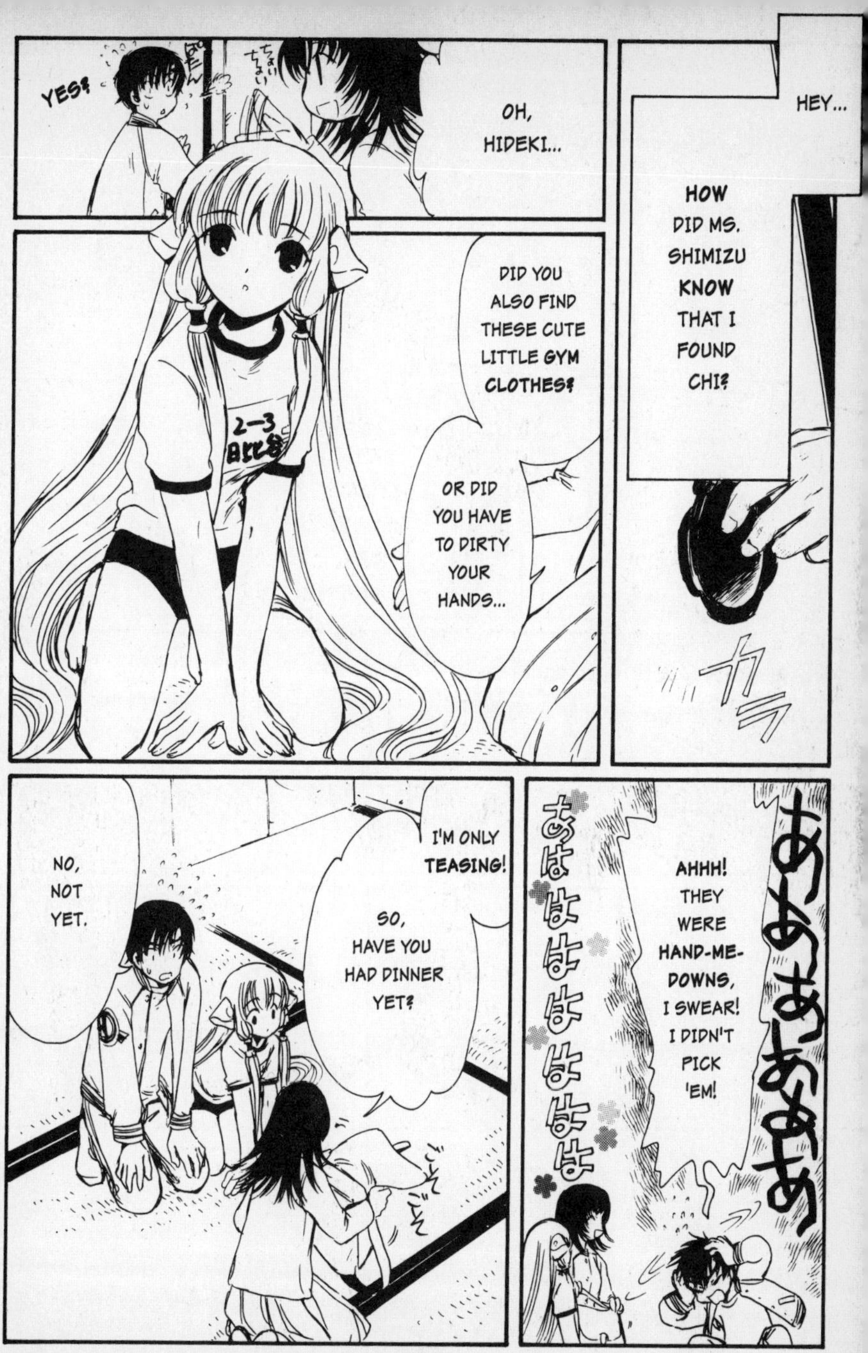
HEY...
HOW DID MS. SHIMIZU KNOW THAT I FOUND CHI?
カラ
OH, HIDEKI...
YES?
DID YOU ALSO FIND THESE CUTE LITTLE GYM CLOTHES?
OR DID YOU HAVE TO DIRTY YOUR HANDS...
AHHH! THEY WERE HAND-ME-DOWNS, I SWEAR! I DIDN'T PICK 'EM!
I'M ONLY TEASING!
SO, HAVE YOU HAD DINNER YET?
NO, NOT YET.

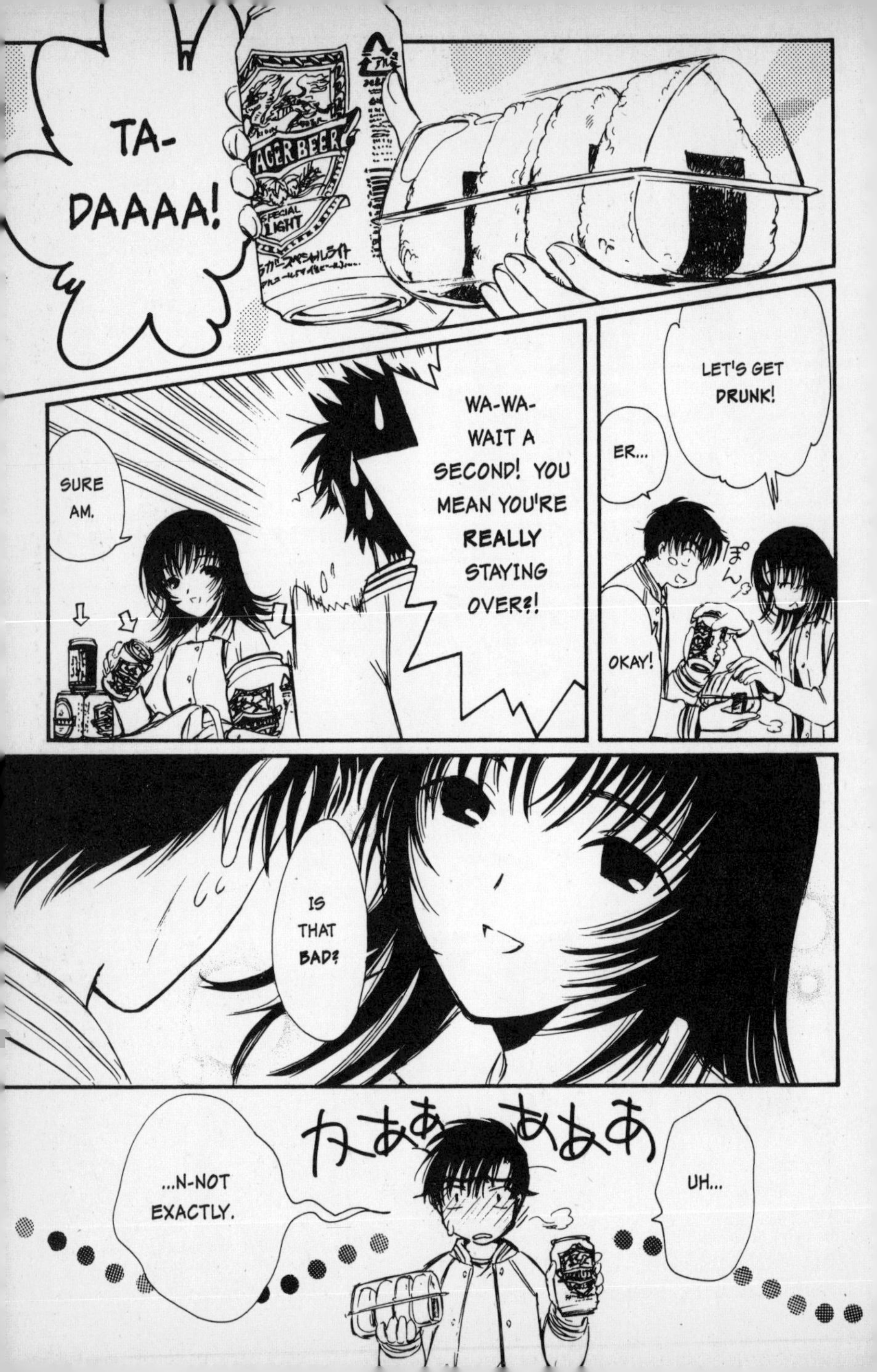
TA-DAAAA!
LET'S GET DRUNK!
ER...
ぽん
OKAY!
WA-WA-WAIT A SECOND! YOU MEAN YOU'RE REALLY STAYING OVER?!
SURE AM.
IS THAT BAD?
かあああああ
UH...
...N-NOT EXACTLY.

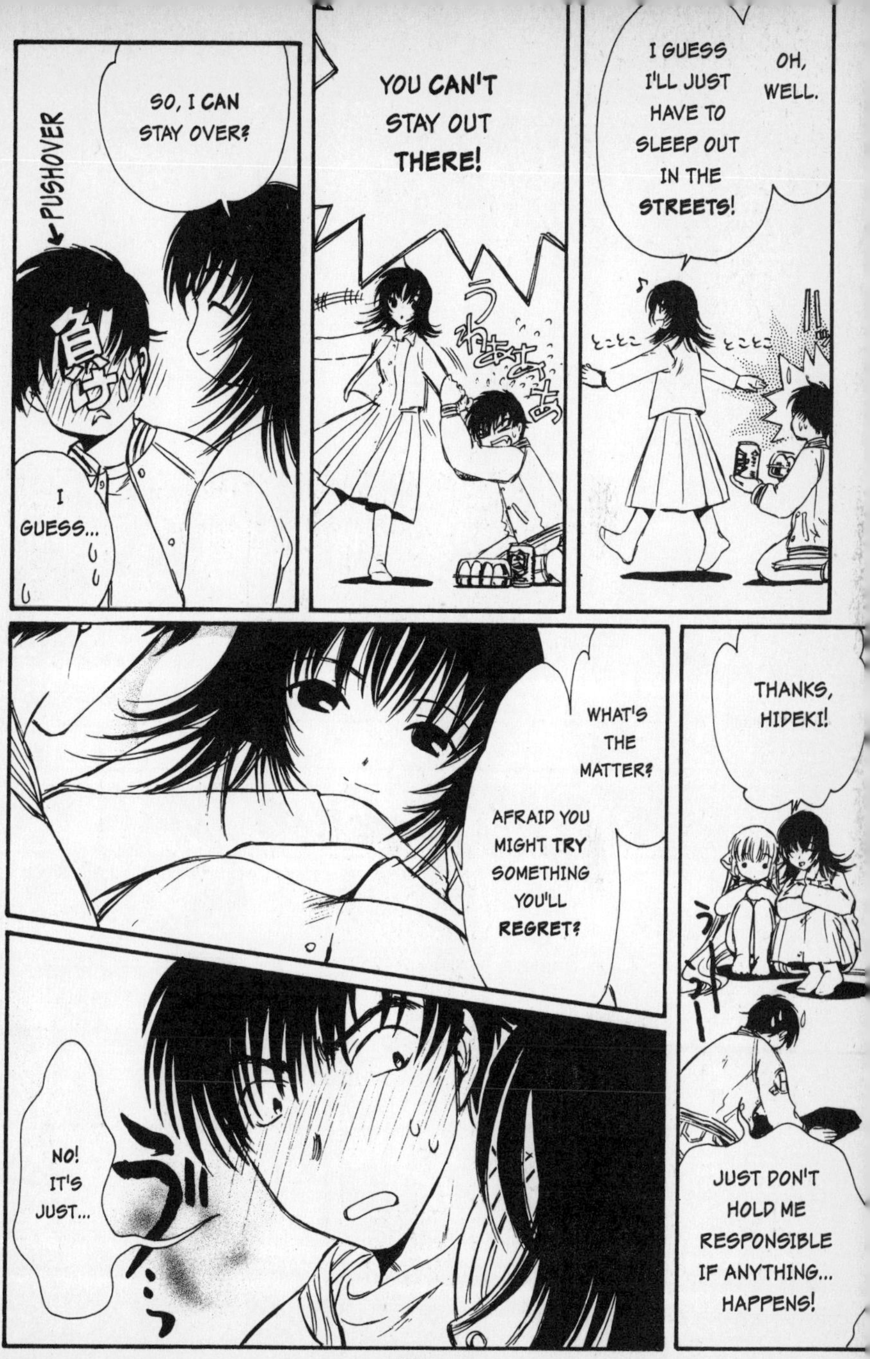
OH, WELL.
I GUESS I'LL JUST HAVE TO SLEEP OUT IN THE STREETS!
とことこ
とことこ
YOU CAN'T STAY OUT THERE!
SO, I CAN STAY OVER?
PUSHOVER
I GUESS...
THANKS, HIDEKI!
JUST DON'T HOLD ME RESPONSIBLE IF ANYTHING... HAPPENS!
WHAT'S THE MATTER?
AFRAID YOU MIGHT TRY SOMETHING YOU'LL REGRET?
NO! IT'S JUST...

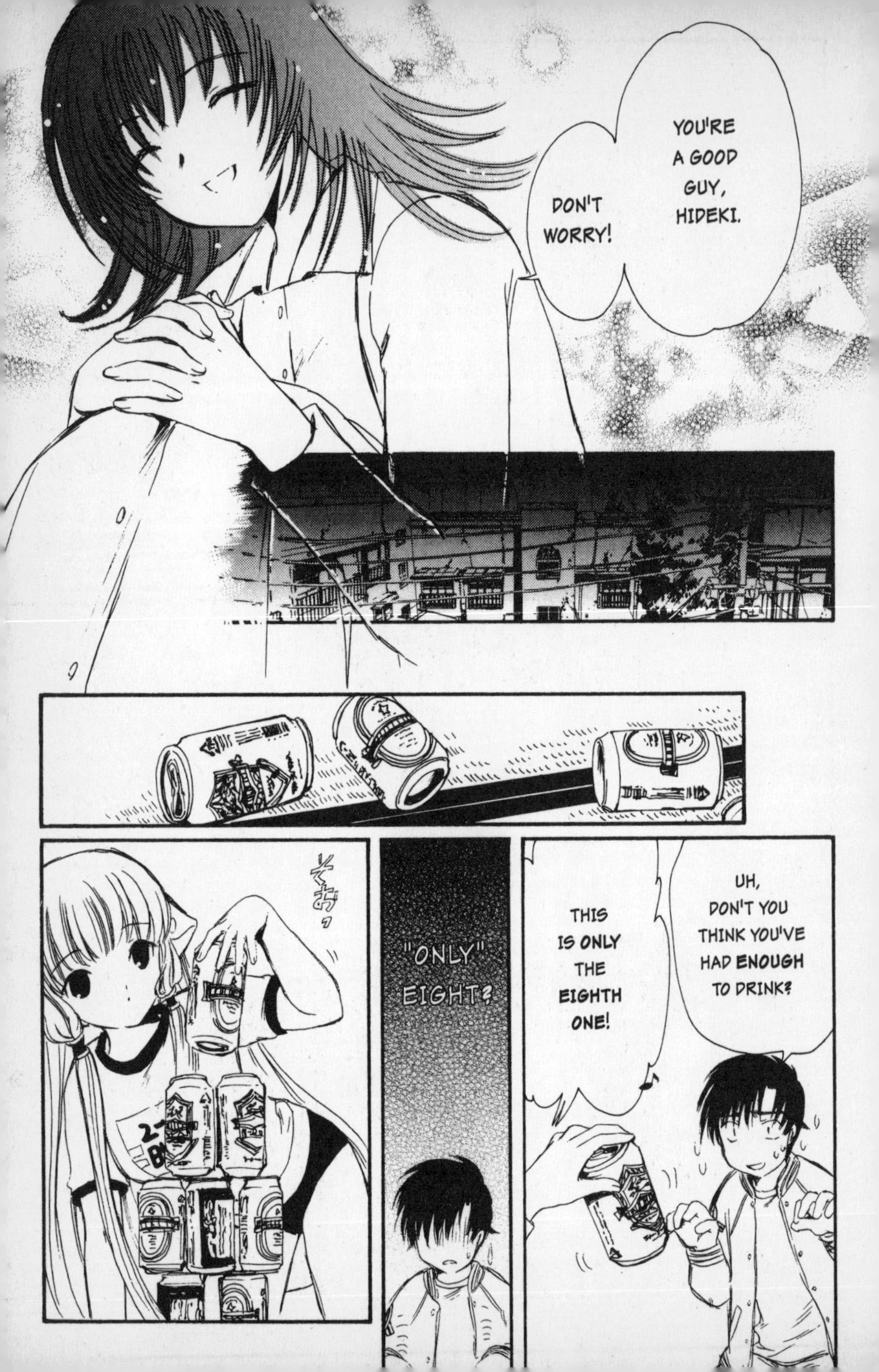
YOU'RE A GOOD GUY, HIDEKI.
DON'T WORRY!
UH, DON'T YOU THINK YOU'VE HAD ENOUGH TO DRINK?
THIS IS ONLY THE EIGHTH ONE!
"ONLY" EIGHT?
そおっ

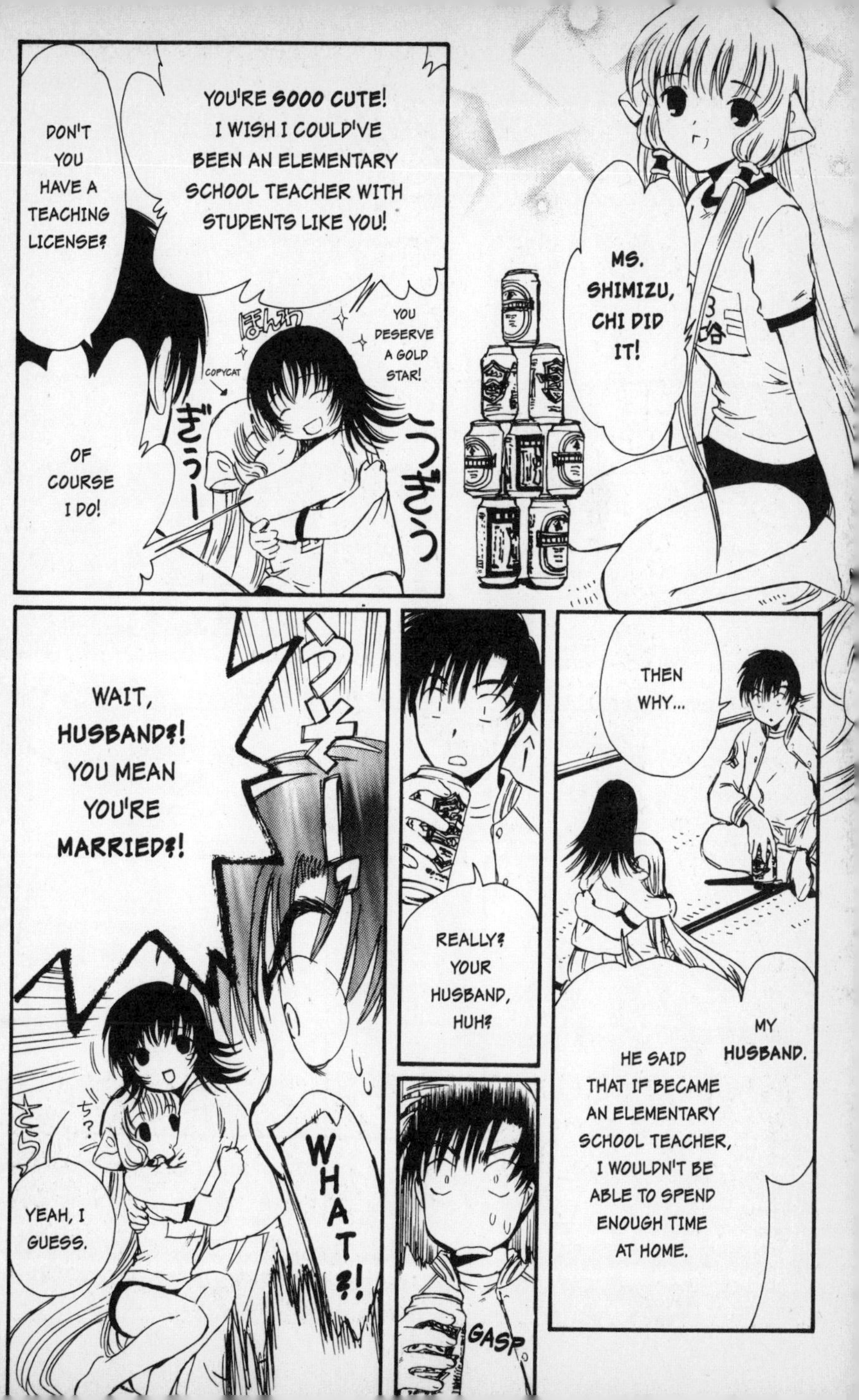
MS. SHIMIZU, CHI DID IT!
YOU'RE SOOO CUTE! I WISH I COULD'VE BEEN AN ELEMENTARY SCHOOL TEACHER WITH STUDENTS LIKE YOU!
YOU DESERVE A GOLD STAR!
ほんわ
DON'T YOU HAVE A TEACHING LICENSE?
COPYCAT
ぎゅー
うぎゅう
OF COURSE I DO!
THEN WHY...
MY HUSBAND.
HE SAID THAT IF BECAME AN ELEMENTARY SCHOOL TEACHER, I WOULDN'T BE ABLE TO SPEND ENOUGH TIME AT HOME.
REALLY? YOUR HUSBAND, HUH?
GASP
うそ！
WAIT, HUSBAND?! YOU MEAN YOU'RE MARRIED?!
WHAT?!
ち？
YEAH, I GUESS.
さら

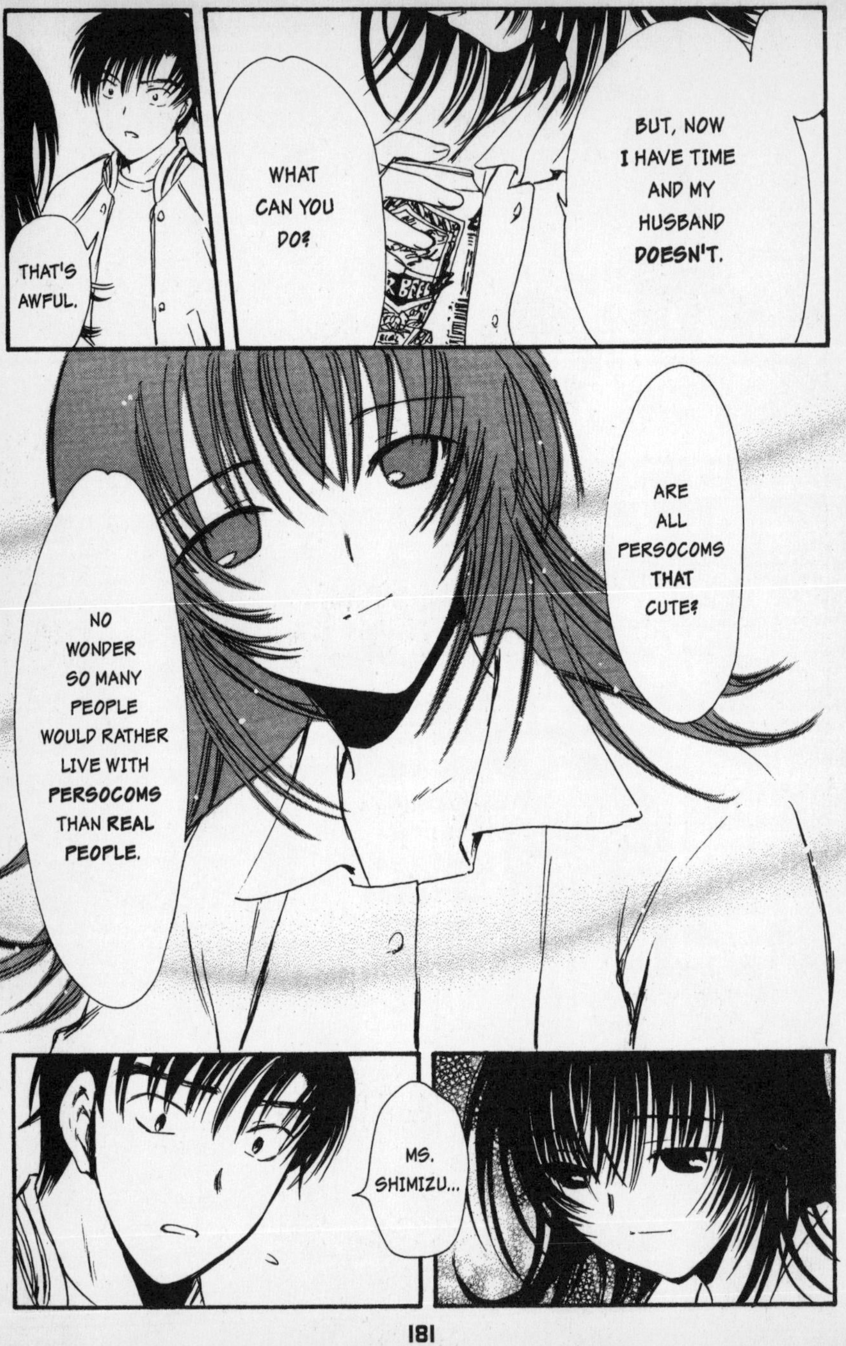
BUT, NOW I HAVE TIME AND MY HUSBAND DOESN'T.
WHAT CAN YOU DO?
THAT'S AWFUL.
ARE ALL PERSOCOMS THAT CUTE?
NO WONDER SO MANY PEOPLE WOULD RATHER LIVE WITH PERSOCOMS THAN REAL PEOPLE.
MS. SHIMIZU...

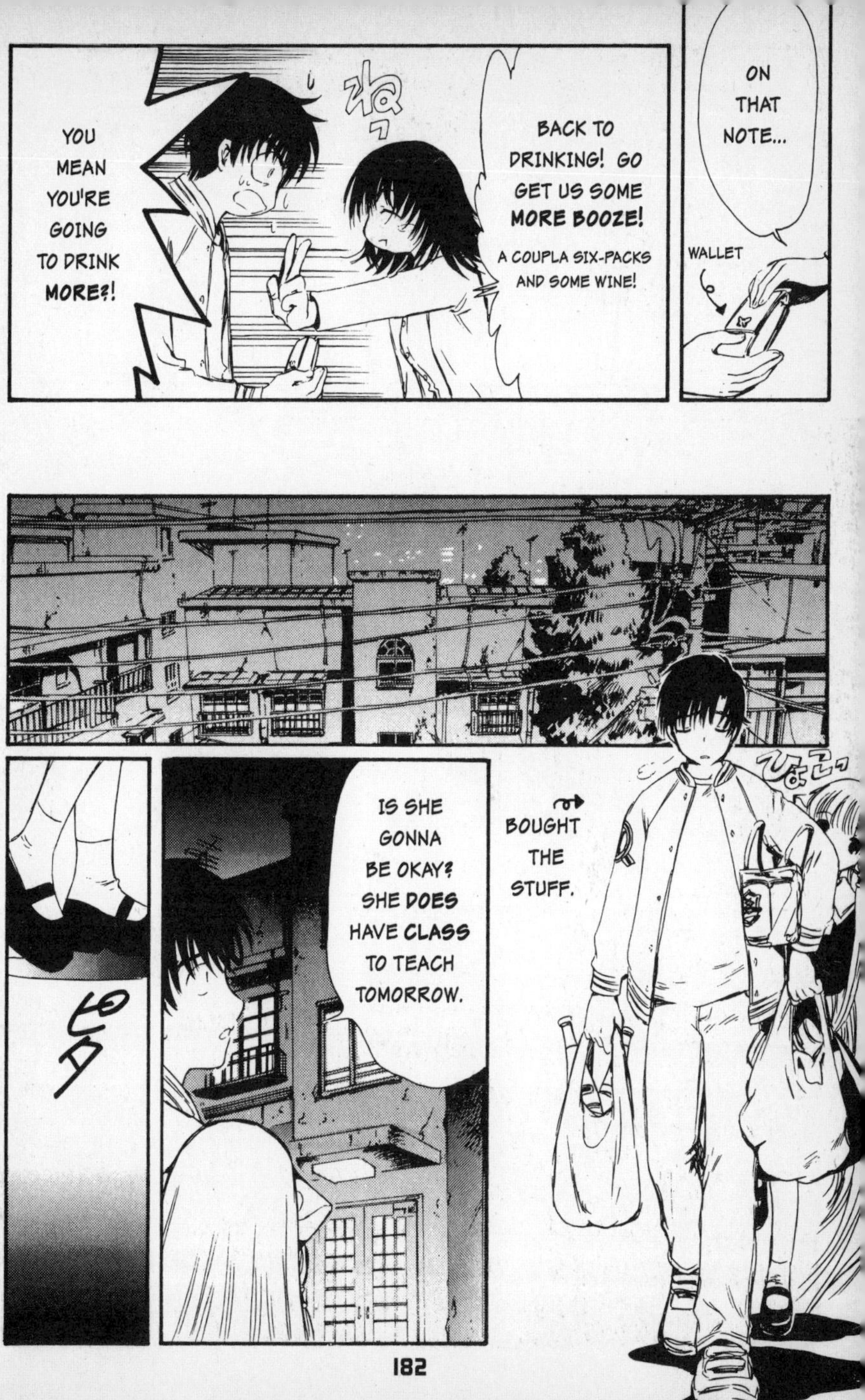
ON THAT NOTE...
WALLET
BACK TO DRINKING! GO GET US SOME MORE BOOZE!
A COUPLA SIX-PACKS AND SOME WINE!
YOU MEAN YOU'RE GOING TO DRINK MORE?!
BOUGHT THE STUFF.
IS SHE GONNA BE OKAY? SHE DOES HAVE CLASS TO TEACH TOMORROW.

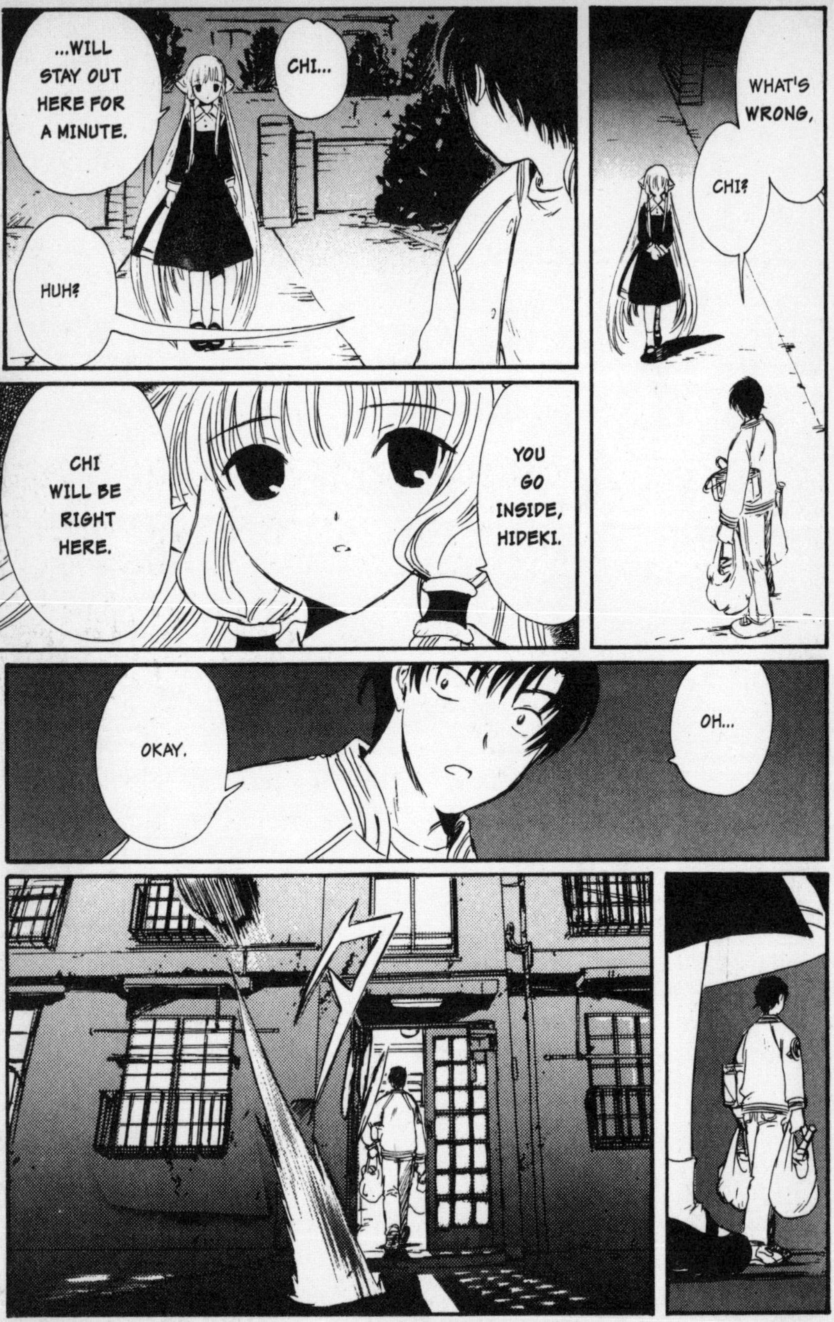
WHAT'S WRONG,
CHI?
CHI...
...WILL STAY OUT HERE FOR A MINUTE.
HUH?
YOU GO INSIDE, HIDEKI.
CHI WILL BE RIGHT HERE.
OH...
OKAY.

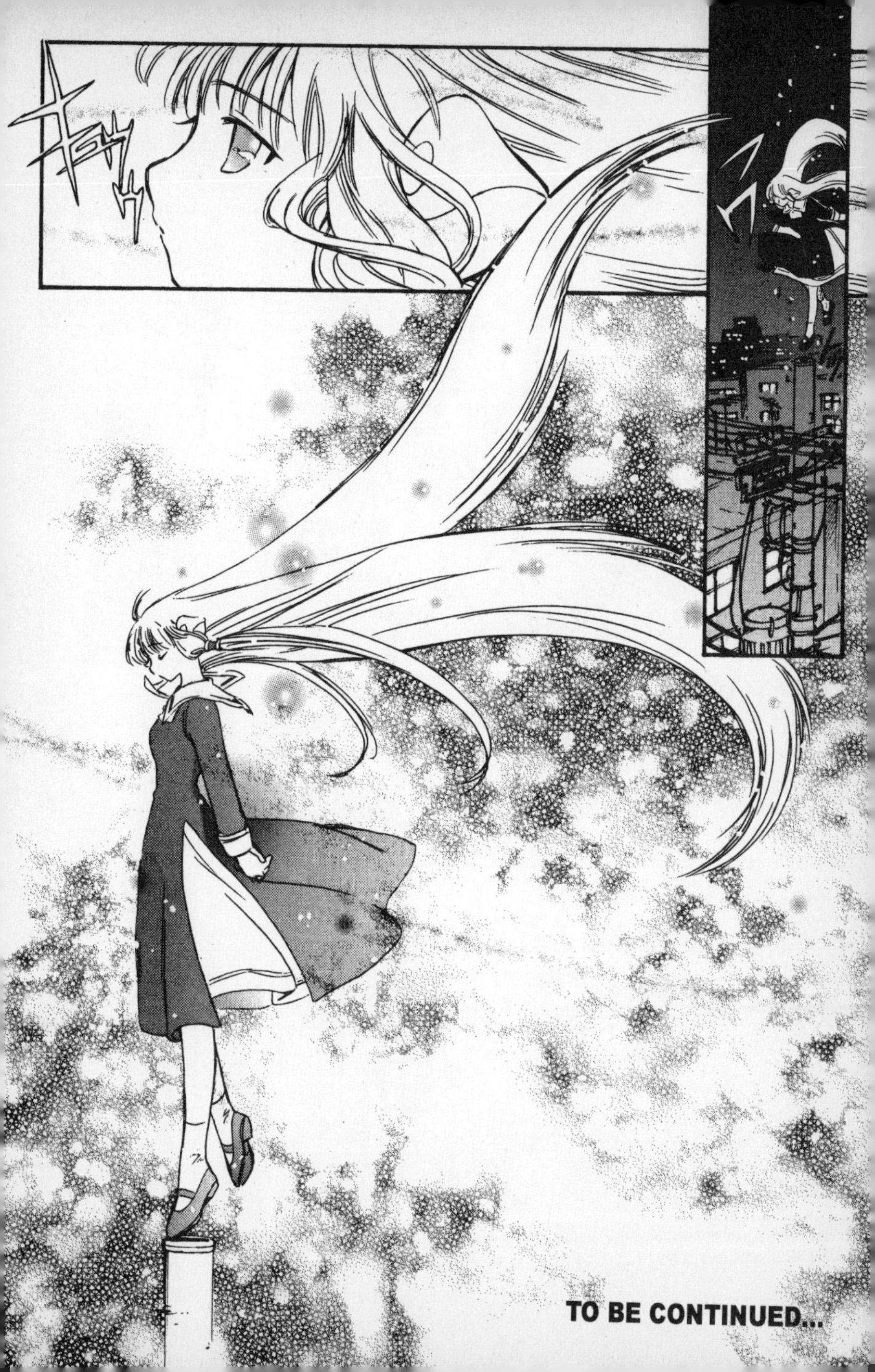
TO BE CONTINUED...

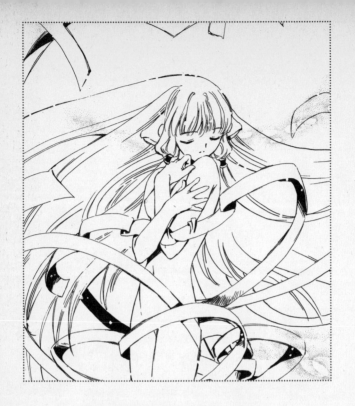

COMING UP IN VOLUME 2

A lot of guys fall in love with their persocoms, but can a persocom fall in love with its owner?

As Hideki searches for the truth about Chi's past, Chi continues to learn at an alarming rate. When Chi discovers that Hideki is broke, she looks for a job to help him make ends meet. But there are a lot of shady businessmen out there who would love to take advantage of a beautiful and innocent persocom like Chi...

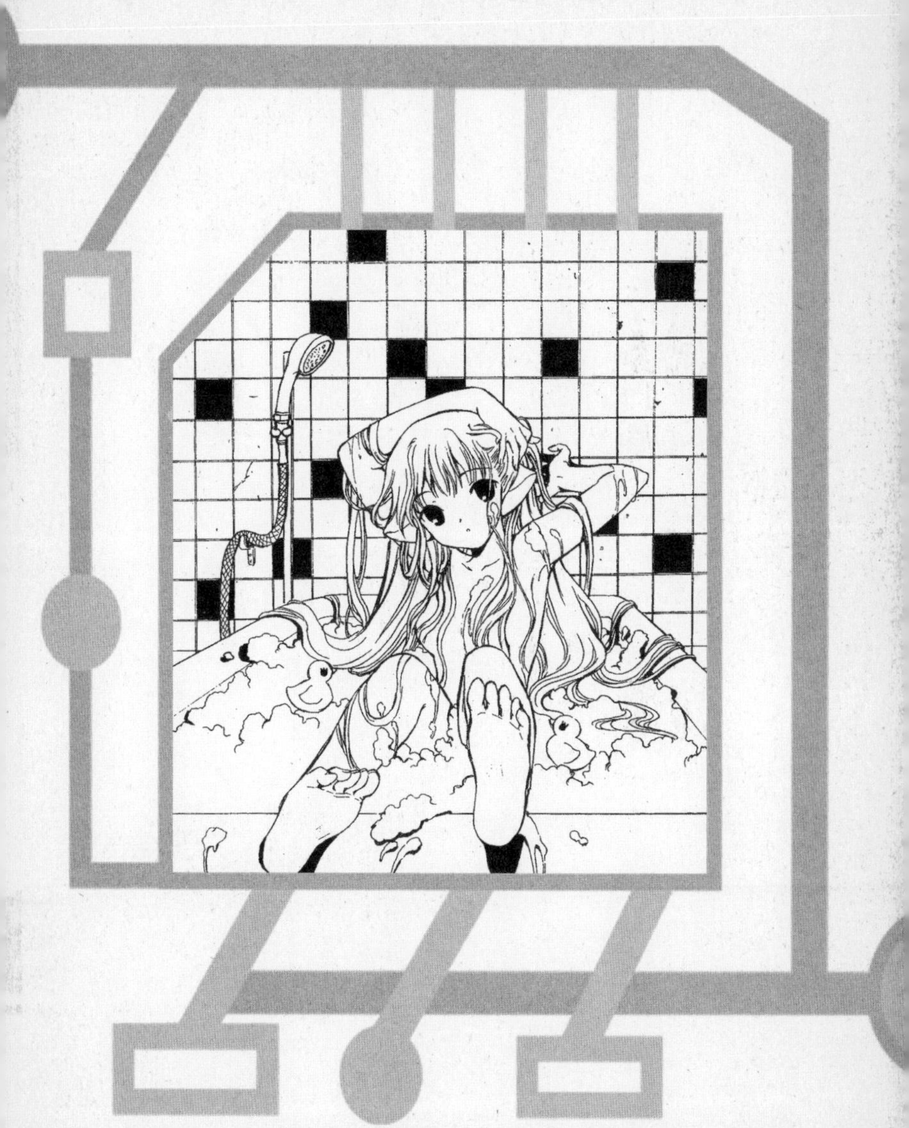

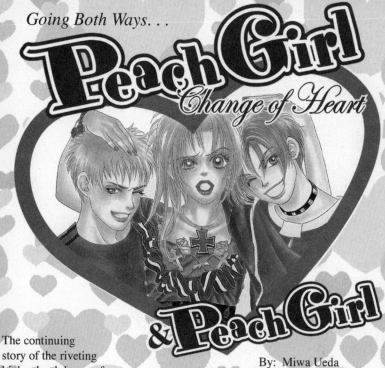

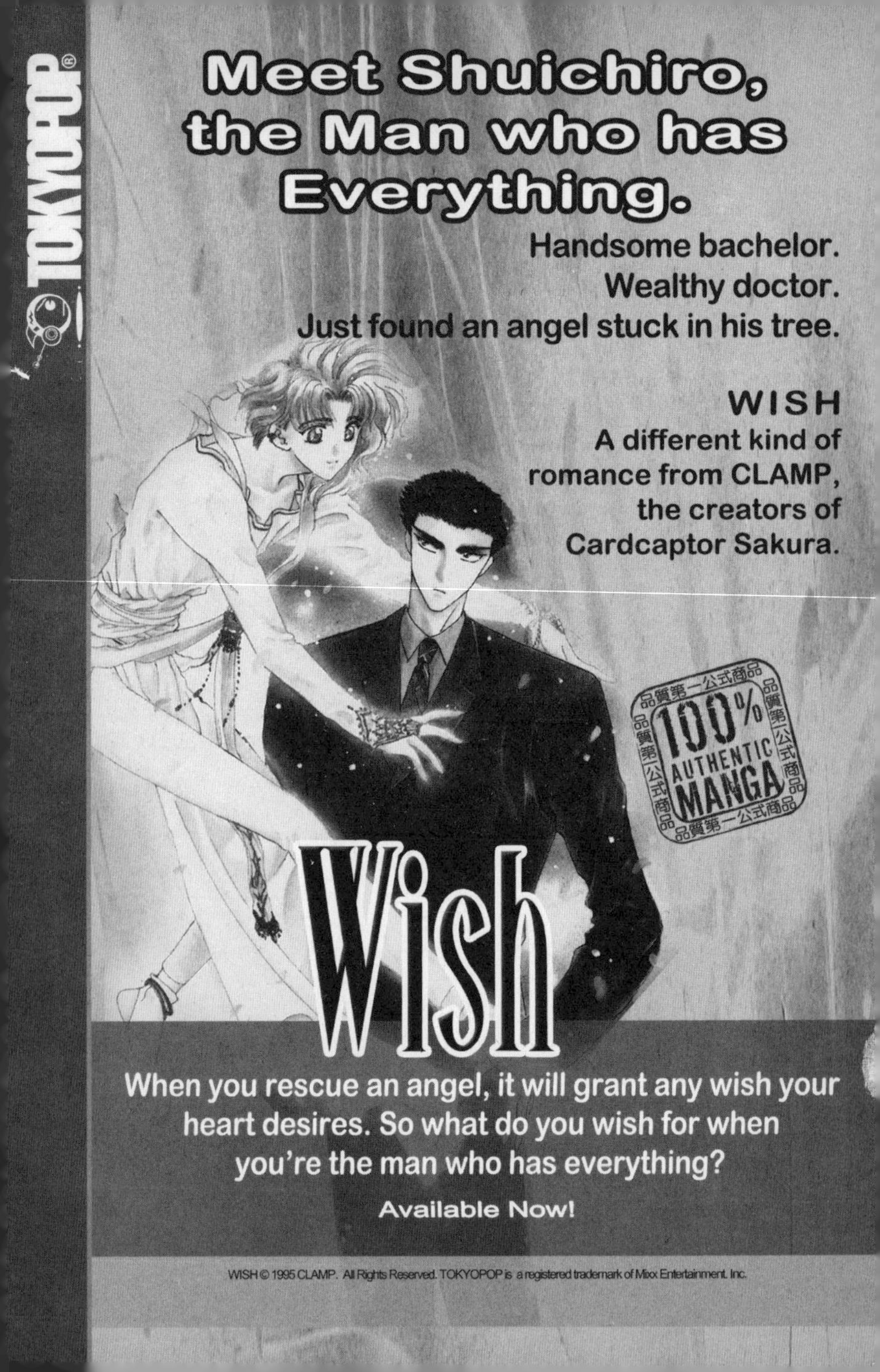
TOKYOPOP®
Meet Shuichiro, the Man who has Everything.
Handsome bachelor.
Wealthy doctor.
Just found an angel stuck in his tree.
WISH
A different kind of romance from CLAMP, the creators of Cardcaptor Sakura.
品質第一公式商品
100% AUTHENTIC MANGA
Wish
When you rescue an angel, it will grant any wish your heart desires. So what do you wish for when you're the man who has everything?
Available Now!
WISH © 1995 CLAMP. All Rights Reserved. TOKYOPOP is a registered trademark of Mixx Entertainment, Inc.

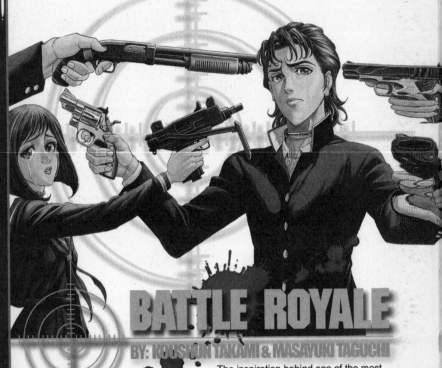

When the curriculum is survival
It's every student for themselves !

TOKYOPOP

BATTLE ROYALE
BY: KOUSHUN TAKAMI & MASAYUKI TAGUCHI

The inspiration behind one of the most controversial films ever released... Lord of the Flies meets Survivor.

*"Outrage, joy, sadness;
the novel Battle Royale
encapsulates all these emotions
and so many more into
a coherent package that is
overwhelmingly powerful"*
– AnimeFringe

VOL. 1 IN YOUR FAVORITE
BOOK & COMIC STORES NOW!

STOP!

This is the back of the book.
You wouldn't want to spoil a great ending!

This book is printed "manga-style," in the authentic Japanese right-to-left format. Since none of the artwork has been flipped or altered, readers get to experience the story just as the creator intended. You've been asking for it, so TOKYOPOP® delivered: authentic, hot-off-the-press, and far more fun!

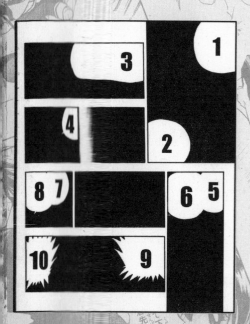

DIRECTIONS

If this is your first time reading manga-style, here's a quick guide to help you understand how it works.

It's easy... just start in the top right panel and follow the numbers. Have fun, and look for more 100% authentic manga from TOKYOPOP®!

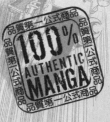

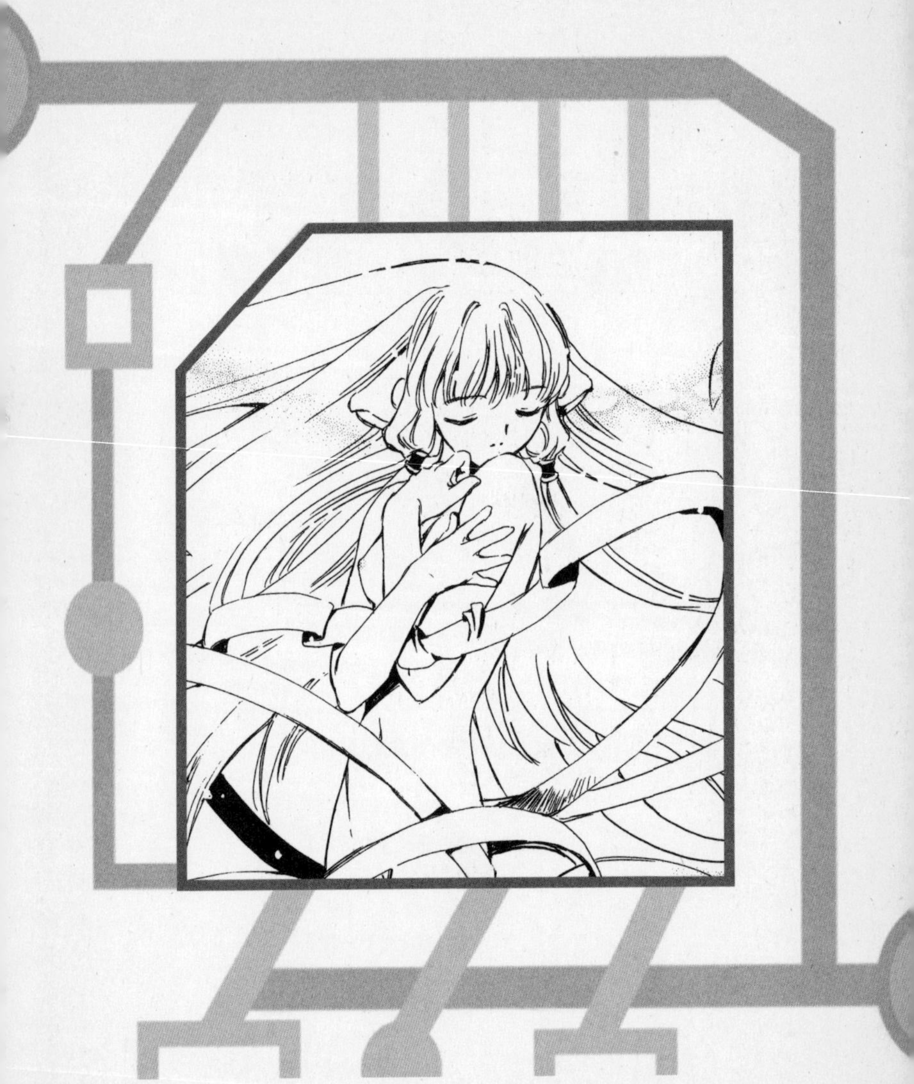